Civic Parties in Divided Societies

Democracy, Diversity, and Citizen Engagement Series

Series Editors: Alain-G. Gagnon and Yasmeen Abu-Laban

Vibrant movements both new and old, inspired by Indigeneity, national self-determination, anti-racism, migrant precarity, and their intersections with other forms of identity, raise profound questions about social justice. Such movements also provoke backlash. These developments beg the interrogation of institutional mechanisms for inclusion as they relate to democracy, citizenship, public policy, and rights across different state forms, including settler colonial and federal states. Centring the heterogeneity of mobilizations and claims-making by citizens, non-citizens, nations, and groups in the twenty-first century, the Democracy, Diversity, and Citizen Engagement Series invites consideration of how people and interests are represented. In light of how nations and people are often divided by state frontiers, the series, with the support of the Interdisciplinary Research Centre on Diversity and Democracy, also showcases work that identifies how interests and representation might be enhanced at local, national, or global levels.

1 *The Parliaments of Autonomous Nations*
Edited by Guy Laforest and André Lecours

2 *A Liberal Theory of Collective Rights*
Michel Seymour

3 *The National Question and Electoral Politics in Quebec and Scotland*
Éric Bélanger, Richard Nadeau, Ailsa Henderson, and Eve Hepburn

4 *Trust, Distrust, and Mistrust in Multinational Democracies*
Comparative Perspectives
Edited by Dimitrios Karmis and François Rocher

5 *Constitutional Politics in Multinational Democracies*
Edited by André Lecours, Nikola Brassard-Dion, and Guy Laforest

6 *Fiscal Federalism in Multinational States*
Autonomy, Equality, and Diversity
Edited by François Boucher and Alain Noël

7 *The Symbolic State*
Minority Recognition, Majority Backlash, and Secession in Multinational Countries
Karlo Basta

8 *Taking Pluralism Seriously*
Complex Societies under Scrutiny
Félix Mathieu

9 *A Written Constitution for Quebec?*
Edited by Richard Albert and Léonid Sirota

10 *Civic Freedom in an Age of Diversity*
The Public Philosophy of James Tully
Edited by Dimitrios Karmis and Jocelyn Maclure

11 *Contemporary Federalist Thought in Quebec*
Historical Perspectives
Edited by Antoine Brousseau Desaulniers and Stéphane Savard

12 *Territories of Inequality*
How Federalism and Redistribution Interact
Edited by Olivier Jacques and Alain Noël

13 *Civic Parties in Divided Societies*
Northern Ireland and Bosnia-Herzegovina
Cera Murtagh

Cera Murtagh

Civic Parties in Divided Societies

Northern Ireland and Bosnia-Herzegovina

McGill-Queen's University Press
Montreal & Kingston | London | Chicago

ISBN 978-0-2280-2601-3 (paper)
ISBN 978-0-2280-2602-0 (ePDF)
ISBN 978-0-2280-2603-7 (ePUB)

Legal deposit third quarter 2025
Bibliothèque et Archives nationales du Québec

Printed in Canada on acid-free paper that is 100% ancient-forest-free, containing 100% sustainable, recycled fibre, and processed chlorine-free.

McGill-Queen's University Press in Montreal is on land which long served as a site of meeting and exchange amongst Indigenous Peoples, including the Haudenosaunee and Anishinabeg nations. In Kingston it is situated on the territory of the Haudenosaunee and Anishinaabek. We acknowledge and thank the diverse Indigenous Peoples whose footsteps have marked these territories on which peoples of the world now gather.

Library and Archives Canada Cataloguing in Publication

Title: Civic parties in divided societies : Northern Ireland and Bosnia-Herzegovina / Cera Murtagh.
Names: Murtagh, Cera, author.
Series: Democracy, diversity, and citizen engagement series ; 13.
Description: Series statement: Democracy, diversity, and citizen engagement series ; 13 | Includes bibliographical references and index.
Identifiers: Canadiana (print) 20250179202 | Canadiana (ebook) 20250179253 | ISBN 9780228026013 (paper) | ISBN 9780228026037 (ePUB) | ISBN 9780228026020 (ePDF)
Subjects: LCSH: Civil society—Northern Ireland—Case studies. | LCSH: Civil society—Bosnia and Herzegovina—Case studies. | LCSH: Political parties—Northern Ireland—Case studies. | LCSH: Political parties—Bosnia and Herzegovina—Case studies. | LCSH: Political culture—Northern Ireland—Case studies. | LCSH: Political culture—Bosnia and Herzegovina—Case studies. | LCSH: Conflict management—Northern Ireland—Case studies. | LCSH: Conflict management—Bosnia and Herzegovina—Case studies. | LCGFT: Case studies.
Classification: LCC JN1572.A91 M87 2025 | DDC 306.209416—dc23

This book was designed and typeset by Garet Markvoort, zijn digital, in 9.5/13.5 Radiata with Intervogue. Copyediting by Shelagh Plunkett.

McGill-Queen's University Press
Suite 1720, 1010 Sherbrooke St West, Montreal, QC, H3A 2R7

Authorized safety representative in the EU: Mare Nostrum Group BV, Mauritskade 21D, 1091 GC Amsterdam, the Netherlands, gpsr@mare-nostrum.co.uk

For my parents, Charlie and Eleanor

Contents

Tables and Figures ix

Acknowledgements xi

Introduction: The Struggle Over Civic Politics in Divided Societies 3

1 Civic Solidarity in Divided Societies 17

2 Northern Ireland, Beyond the Binary 43

3 Northern Ireland: Civic Parties, Ethnic Rules 67

4 The Unwritten Rules in Northern Ireland 85

5 Navigating the System in Northern Ireland 109

6 The Plight of Civic Parties in Bosnia and Herzegovina 138

7 Navigating the System in Bosnia and Herzegovina 177

8 Civic Parties in Northern Ireland, Bosnia, and Beyond 193

Conclusion 211

Notes 219

References 241

Index 269

Tables and Figures

Tables

1.1 Civic party definition and indicators 28

2.1 Political parties in Northern Ireland 49

2.2 Alliance Party electoral performance, 1973–97 50

2.3 Party vote share Northern Ireland Assembly elections, 1998–2022 61

2.4 Alliance Party electoral performance, 1998–2024 64

2.5 Civic party indicators: Northern Ireland 65

6.1 Political parties in Bosnia and Herzegovina 149

6.2 Election results by mandate to the House of Representatives of BiH, 1996–2022 150

6.3 SDP election results to the House of Representatives of BiH, 1996–2022 150

6.4 Civic party indicators, BiH 152

Figures

2.1 Map of Northern Ireland. Source: https://d-maps.com/carte.php?num_car=15984&lang=en. 45

2.2 Party vote share Northern Ireland Assembly elections, 1998–2022. Source: www.ark.ac.uk/elections/. 62

2.3 Trends in party vote share Northern Ireland Assembly elections, 1998–2022. Source: www.ark.ac.uk/elections/. 63

3.1 Marriage equality protest, Belfast, May 2019. Source: Brian Lawless/ PA Wire URN:42957083 (Press Association via AP Images). 77

4.1 Map of council areas in Northern Ireland. Source: https://d-maps.com/carte.php?num_car=27490&lang=en. 86

4.2 Poster of leaflet distributed in North Down during 2019 general election. Source: Mal McCann, *The Irish News.* 97

4.3 Leaflet distributed to homes in Belfast in November 2012 following the flag vote in Belfast City Council (front and back). Source: CAIN, cain.ulster.ac.uk. 100

4.4 Flag protest in Belfast, January 2013. Source: Press Eye Ltd / Shutterstock. 101

6.1 Map of Bosnia and Herzegovina. Source: https://d-maps.com/carte.php?num_car=5660&lang=en. 139

6.2 Political map of post-Dayton Bosnia and Herzegovina. Source: https://d-maps.com/carte.php?num_car=5656&lang=en. 141

6.3 Election results by mandate to the House of Representatives of BiH, 1996–2022. Source: http://www.izbori.ba/. 153

6.4 Trends in election results by mandate to the House of Representatives of BiH, 1996–2022. Source: http://www.izbori.ba/. 154

6.5 Protest in Sarajevo, February 2014. Source: author's image. 172

6.6 Plenum meeting in Sarajevo, February 2014. Source: author's image. 173

Acknowledgements

I could not have written this book or carried out the research on which it is based without the help, support, and encouragement contributed by so many people, to whom I am extremely grateful.

Above all, I would like to sincerely thank the many individuals who gave so generously and selflessly of their time to participate in this research. Their knowledge and insight taught me a great deal and enriched this work immeasurably. I literally could not have done it without them and I owe them a huge thanks.

The work represented here spans three projects: my combined masters/doctoral project at the University of Edinburgh 2012–17, which was supported by an Economic and Social Research Council (ESRC) 1+3 PhD Studentship; my postdoctoral research at Queen's University Belfast 2017–18, which was part of the ESRC project Exclusion Amid Inclusion: Power-Sharing and Non-Dominant Minorities; and my research at Villanova University 2018–24, which was supported by a number of grants and fellowships. I would like to gratefully acknowledge the generous support of the Villanova College of Liberal Arts and Sciences Faculty Research and Development Grant, the University Summer Grant, the Subvention of Publication Program, and the Idol Family Fellowship. The financial support provided by these sources allowed me, among other things, to undertake fieldwork in Northern Ireland and Bosnia and Herzegovina, as well as affording me time and space to develop the book.

I would like to thank my editor Emily Andrew and all of the team at McGill-Queen's for their invaluable support and dedication to this project. Their expertise and professionalism have made me feel in good hands throughout this process and their guidance at every stage has been much appreciated.

A number of colleagues and friends read earlier drafts of parts of this book and offered valuable feedback that enhanced the final work, for which I am most grateful, particularly Siobhan Byrne, Allison McCulloch, John Nagle, Anes Makul, and Damir Kapidžić.

I was fortunate to benefit from the guidance and mentorship of a number of people over the course of this research. I am immensely grateful to my PhD supervisors at the University of Edinburgh, Wilfried Swenden, Liliana Riga, and Eve Hepburn, as well as the principal and co-investigators on my post-doctorate research project at Queen's University Belfast, Timofey Agarin and Allison McCulloch. I am also very thankful to a number of people who offered informal mentorship and advice during my doctoral and postdoctoral journeys, not least Charlie Jeffrey, Nicola McEwen, Dejan Stjepanović, Meryl Kenny, and James Kennedy at Edinburgh and John Garry, Dominic Bryan, and John Coakley at Queen's.

A special word of thanks to Fiona Mackay, who, as my master's dissertation supervisor at the University of Edinburgh many years ago, nurtured my interest in feminist politics and was pivotal to my embarking on this field of research. She has remained over the years an incredible mentor and friend.

My initial interest in this topic was sparked by an experience working with Maureen Murray and Bronagh Hinds, co-directors of Northern Ireland Women's Initiative / DemocraShe in New York in summer 2003. I am very grateful to both for this opportunity.

This research involved extensive fieldwork across Northern Ireland and Bosnia. I was greatly assisted in this by the following people: Anes Makul, Damir Kapidžić, Asim Mujkić, Dino Abazović, Zora Hesova, Nidžara Ahmetašević, Brigid Loughran, Adrian Guelke, Catherine O'Rourke, Bill Rolston, Heleen Touquet, Florian Bieber, Igor Štiks and Siniša Malešević. I am very thankful, too, to the Transitional Justice Institute at the University of Ulster and to the Faculty of Political Science at the University of Sarajevo for institutional support during periods of fieldwork. I would also like to thank Selma Gondžetović, Inga Kotlo, Elma Mahmutović-Hodžić, Sandra Pandurević Dobrijević, and Kristina Varcaković for their translation and interpretation assistance in Bosnia. Thanks too to Timofey Agarin, Allison McCulloch, and Runa Neely for allowing me to use a number of interviews that we conducted jointly.

The bulk of this book was written, very happily, in Galway where I held a Visiting Fellowship at the University of Galway's Moore Institute and School of Political Science and Sociology in 2021–22. Niall O'Dochartagh provided key support and mentorship on book writing, while Niamh Reilly, Daniel Carey, and Iwona O'Donoghue offered invaluable practical support, and Vesna Malešević and Siniša Malešević were great colleagues and friends. I am hugely grateful for the warmth, care, and generosity of my late uncle Brian Tonge and my cousin Fionnuala Tonge during my stay in Galway. They gave me not only a roof over my head but a welcoming place to come home to after long days spent writing, not to mention great practical and moral support.

A number of people offered valuable advice on navigating the unfamiliar terrain of publishing, including Karlo Basta, David S. Meyer, Lee Smithey, Peter Agree, Rachel Kindler, and Brendan O'Leary.

I would like to thank the artist Emic for his permission to use an image of his mural at the Spectrum Centre, Shankill Road, Belfast for the cover of this book, and Cathal Woods, Seosamh Mac Coille, and all the team at Extramural Activity for their permission to use the photograph. Thanks too to Mal McCann at *The Irish News* for his permission to use his photograph and to Martin Melaugh at CAIN for his help in sourcing images.

At Villanova I have so many friends and colleagues to thank for their support, advice, and encouragement to write this book, not least Camille Burge-Hicks, Crystal Lucky, Joseph Lennon, Marcus Kreuzer, Matt Kerbel, Kevin Minbiole, Terri Boyer, Lisa Dolling, Mary Mullen, Heidi Grundetjern, Olukunle Owolabi, Jennifer Dixon, Samer Abboud, Jonathan O'Neill, Deborah Seligsohn, and Megan Quigley. Thanks to Danielle Redden, Kiersten Ludy, Fathe Allen, Jessica Schwartz, and Ingrid Lis for their practical support as well.

Last but by no means least I would like to thank my friends and family for their support, encouragement, and belief in me throughout this process. My mother Eleanor Murtagh was there at every stage to provide academic and moral support. My father Charlie Murtagh was a huge source of practical help and wise advice. Mads Murtagh was always there as a sounding board and problem solver. Judith Tubman and Nicola McDonnell provided great encouragement, while my nieces and nephews Fiadhnait McDonnell, Charlie McDonnell, Cliodhna Tubman, Eoin Tubman, and Cillian Tubman gave me much needed light relief and laughter during periods of writing.

My friends did so much in different ways to support me through this process. A particular thanks to Matt Baker, Orla Carley, Louise Casserly, Caoimhe Collins, Laura Corcoran, Megan Curran, Claire Dolan, Nicole Doonan, Jenni Douglas, Orla Doyle, Leah Eades, Helen Feeney, Marilyn

Finnan, Lauren Hays, Padhraig Higgins, Jennifer Joyce, Nino Kemoklidze, Lauren Kovach, Camilła Lee, Robert Liñeira, Euan Lloyd, Ella Lowbridge, Nicole Matchette, Meaghan McDonald, John McFarlane, Laura McKelvey King, Ryan McQuigg, Liz Morrison, Alene Montgomery, Sarah-Jane O'Hanlon, Anna Pultar, Jenna Raderstrong, Eva Sweeney, Neetha Tangirala, Bernard Tonge, Eoin Tonge, Jorge Valdizan, Carrie Waterman, and Aleksandra Zdeb.

Civic Parties in Divided Societies

Introduction

The Struggle Over Civic Politics in Divided Societies

The events around the 12th of July every year tell us something about the dynamics of politics in Northern Ireland at a given time. The annual celebrations that mark the victory of the Protestant King William III over the Catholic King James II in the Battle of the Boyne in 1690 rarely pass without controversy and often serve as a flashpoint for sectarian violence. Bonfires set alight on the eve of the 12th are sometimes adorned with effigies, including symbols of Catholicism or Irish nationalism. In recent years, however, alongside Irish tricolours and images of Irish nationalist political leaders is a curious addition that does not fit the sectarian (Protestant/Catholic, Unionist/Nationalist, Loyalist/Republican, orange/green) frame: effigies of leaders of Alliance, a civic party, aligned to neither nationalism nor unionism. The targeting of a civic party in ethnonational violence is part of a trend in Northern Ireland politics over the last fifteen years. The phenomenon surfaced notably with the protests of 2012–13 that followed a Belfast City Council decision to cease flying the British Union flag outside City Hall every day of the year. In the loyalist protests that followed, the focus of attack was not nationalist parties but the civic Alliance. More recently, in the wake of the 2016 Brexit vote, the party found itself at the centre of loyalist 'anti-protocol' protests. Far from an irrelevant sideshow to the binary politics of nationalism versus unionism, Alliance has somehow found itself centre stage.

The increasing targeting of Alliance is indicative of a deeper shift taking place in Northern Ireland politics: the rise of civic politics as a force. The flag protest signalled the beginnings of that shift. In the years that followed, that trend would become more pronounced, solidifying in the general election of 2019 when Alliance – which had averaged a single digit percentage vote share since its founding in 1970 and long been dismissed as a marginal party – commanded 17 per cent of the vote, a

9 per cent increase, leaving it in third place in vote share behind the main nationalist and unionist parties, Sinn Féin and the Democratic Unionist Party (DUP) (Tonge 2020, 461). In the same year, issues beyond the ethnonational divide climbed up the political agenda as long battles for the legalization of same-sex marriage and abortion culminated in legislation from Westminster, while socio-economic issues such as healthcare and functional governance dominated the 2019 election campaign (Whitten 2020). In 2020, 42 per cent of people identified as neither nationalist nor unionist, up from 30 per cent in 1999, exceeding those identifying with either of the two main blocs (ARK 2020; ARK 1999). In 2022, civic parties collectively won 20 per cent of the seats in the Northern Ireland Assembly, affirming this as no temporary blip but part of a longer-term realignment. Northern Ireland politics is no longer a rigidly binary landscape but one shaped by three blocs: unionist, nationalist, and civic. That three-way dynamic is now key to understanding post-settlement Northern Ireland politics and, more importantly, its transition.

This shift and the struggles that surround it raise a question of relevance well beyond Northern Ireland: how do societies move on from conflict? How do they begin to 'normalize' and what does that new normal look like? 'Post-conflict' is a term rightly contested by many of the people living in societies after the official 'end' of armed conflict, at odds with their experience of continued violence (Cohn 2013, 21–2). Nevertheless, one indicator of progress towards that desired state is surely civic politics: a term I use in this book for the mobilization of political parties and social movements in so-called deeply divided societies explicitly on identities, affinities, and issues other than ethnonational. A core feature of a deeply divided society is segmentation of politics along ethnic or ethnonational lines. Indeed, 'ethnic' or ethnonational parties – those that explicitly appeal to voters on the basis of ethnic or ethnonational identity and do so with some level of exclusivity – are seen as central to the rise and fall of conflict (Horowitz 1985, 291, 298, 305; Reilly 2006, 811; Zuber 2012, 927). By this logic, the ascent of civic politics stands as a marker of transition away from conflict, towards post-conflict 'normalization'. In theory, politics should emerge and grow organically the further a society moves from its warring past.

Yet, how do these parties emerge and develop in a system that has been designed explicitly to accommodate ethnonational parties? This is the reality of many societies emerging from conflict where peace deals have been brokered through a critical compromise: power-sharing between warring parties. Power-sharing has been implemented as part of peace agreements in conflicts around the globe, from Northern Ireland to Burundi, Bosnia and Herzegovina to Iraq, Kosovo to Sudan, North Macedonia to Lebanon, rising steadily up the international peacebuilding agenda after the Cold War (McCulloch 2021, 2). Designed to serve both *peace* and *democratic governance* after conflict (Noel 2005, xi), power-sharing works by recognizing the main groups to the conflict and including them in government, effectively apportioning each a share of power in return for the cessation of violence. The effectiveness of the model, particularly its consociational variant, has been wildly debated, in scholarship and practice, but one indisputable by-product is its elevation of ethnonational actors and issues and corresponding marginalization of civic actors and issues. This begs the question of how such societies can begin to move away from ethnonational politics, defined by the conflict, and towards a more integrated, civic politics attentive to broader issues?

Writing in 1985, Donald Horowitz observed that 'In a severely divided society, a multi-ethnic party or coalition is a fragile institution' (1985, 396). Yet, despite the patent impediments and pessimistic predictions of theory, civic politics do exist in societies after conflict, including in the institutional context of consociational power-sharing. In systems as ethnonationally divided as Lebanon, civic movements and political groupings have emerged and are beginning to break through the ethnonational infrastructure (Nagle and Fakhoury 2022; Nagle 2018; Deets and Skulte-Ouaiss 2021). Against the odds, these groupings form and sustain, alongside their ethnonational counterparts. Indeed, in some places these parties have even grown to constitute a distinct political force of their own, effecting new political cleavages and even realignment of the party system. In post-settlement Northern Ireland, the struggle for dominance we now witness is not only between the ethnonational blocs of nationalism and unionism but also *between ethnonational and civic politics*. In Bosnia and Herzegovina, thirty years on from the war, civic parties now hold two out of three seats in the state presidency. Defying the traditional theories of party competition in ethnonationally divided societies, ethnonational parties compete not only with other ethnonational parties in their bloc but, increasingly, with civic parties too (Zuber 2012).

This progression is far from linear, however. It is not a tale of smooth transition from ethnonational to civic politics as society moves further from conflict. Ethnonational parties, ethnonational mobilization, and ethnonational voting are alive and well in such societies and continue to prevail, despite the growth of civic alternatives. In this ethnicized environment civic parties and movements find themselves deeply contested. Advances are fragile, contingent, and prone to regression and reversal, especially in polarizing moments that raise ethnonational insecurity. Yet, however delicate, civic politics have gained footholds in many power-sharing places after conflict, navigating barriers and seizing opportunities. Politics in these places can no longer be categorized simply as 'ethnic' or 'ethnonational' in nature but increasingly resemble a hybrid of civic-ethnic mobilization and, moreover, a *contestation* between these two paradigms.

This presents a paradox: how do civic parties survive in a divided society where the institutions have been explicitly designed to accommodate ethnonational groups? This gets to the heart of a question that continues to plague conflict resolution: how do societies move on from conflict, not just to the cessation of violence, but towards a fuller 'civic' democracy – not least when institutions have been put in place to manage the conflict by recognizing (some argue 'freezing') ethnonational identity? (Aitken 2007).

Through the cases of Northern Ireland and Bosnia and Herzegovina, in dialogue with others, this book addresses this puzzle. In so doing, it shines a light on the phenomenon of *civic politics* in divided societies – political mobilization that explicitly eschews ethnonationalism as a basis for organizing and mobilizes people from across society on other identities, allegiances, and issues. Though obscured by the binary lens of mainstream approaches, civic politics is ever-present in divided places and fundamental to progress towards broader social justice and human rights – from gender to LGBTQ+ to migrant rights. The book focuses in on the institutional embodiment of civic politics, *civic parties*: those that seek to mobilize voters on some basis other than ethnonational identity. It explores the survival of civic politics, against the odds, and its potential to offer a route out of ethnonational division.

Probing the largely unexplored and unexplained phenomenon of civic parties in ethnonationally divided places, the book addresses several questions:

- How have civic parties survived, and even grown, in the context of deep division and political institutions explicitly designed to accommodate ethnonational actors?

- What barriers and openings have they faced in the process and how have they navigated these structures?
- More broadly, what role can civic parties play in a society's transition from conflict? Do they hold the potential for transformation from within the institutions?

This book ultimately seeks to shed light on the dynamics of politics in divided societies as they transition onwards from conflict, particularly under power-sharing conditions. Politics in places like Northern Ireland and Bosnia, some thirty years on from a peace agreement, however divided they may still seem, do not tell a simple story of ethnonational polarization. Civic politics coexists, intersects, and competes with ethnonational politics, adding a new and critical dimension. While this form of politics is severely constrained and complicated by the consociational political structures in place, it also finds openings. Understanding this dynamic of politics and its interaction with the institutions is key to understanding the post-war transitions of these societies. What's more, understanding how this politics can vary across contexts, and why, demonstrates how institutions matter and bears lessons for how institutional design can impede and support the development of civic politics in future within these two cases and beyond.

Beyond strictly 'post-conflict' places, over the last decade political movements representing civic resistance have been grappling with the rise of ethnonational identity politics in 'established democracies' in the global north, like in the United States, Canada, the United Kingdom, France, Poland, and Australia and those in the global south, like in Brazil and India (see Tarrow and Meyer 2018; Reilly 2018). The plight of civic mobilizations in divided societies bears resonance with these movements and offers potential lessons for their strategies in resisting the politics of ethnonationalism.

A Note on Terminology

At this juncture some key terms and concepts should be unpacked and problematized. The terms *ethnic* and *ethnonational* appear repeatedly throughout this book. *Ethnic* is a term widely used in the literature on conflict management as an umbrella concept to cover a broad range of 'attributes of common origin' – such as race, colour, language, religion, caste, and nationality (Horowitz 1985, 42, 50). 'Ethnicity is based on a myth of collective ancestry, which usually carries with it traits believed to be innate', Horowitz writes. It is connected to blood or birth but not absolutely; critical is the notion of 'ascription' – that these traits are 'given', rather than chosen (1985, 52–4). For Chandra, membership of an ethnic group is contingent on *descent*-based attributes, including those acquired genetically and through cultural and historical inheritance (Chandra 2006, 297, 400). When the primary basis of political mobilization in a place is descent-based ('ethnic') identity – such as religion, language, or nationality – this is referred to in the literature as 'ethnic politics'. Ethnicity pervades every aspect of politics: parties organize on an ethnic basis, the party system becomes structured along ethnic lines with virtually separate ethnic 'subsystems' emerging for each of the main ethnic groups, with little or no competition between these subsystems, while competition within each subsystem becomes prone to polarization as ethnic parties outbid one another and move further to the extremes (Horowitz 1985; Bardi and Mair 2008, 155). I take a constructivist approach that views ethnicity not as a given fact but as a relational and situational force (albeit a potent one) that can be mobilized politically at moments in time (Brubaker 2002, 167–8, 186; Malešević 2011, 67–8).

Ethnonationalism fuses ethnicity with *nationalism*. Nationalism can be understood as a political sentiment or movement that promotes the *nation* – the socially constructed and powerful idea of a people connected to a particular territory that share a vision of a common past and a common future – and its right to self-government (including statehood) (Enloe 2014, 94; Gellner 1983).[1] Ethnonationalism advocates for the unity and political autonomy of a nation that is bound together based on 'ethnic' identity (Guelke 2012a, 32). This book deals with deeply divided societies and, more specifically, those deeply divided along ethnonational lines. By this I mean places where a particular division (in this case ethnonational) permeates politics and many, if not all, aspects of public and social life over a sustained period of time and constitutes a source of political conflict and potential violence (Choudhry 2008, 4–5; Guelke 2012a, 30). Ethnonational politics is treated here as a subset of ethnic politics, bearing many of the same basic principles, as outlined above. In this way, while this book deals primarily with ethnonationally divided societies and ethnonational parties, at times the term 'ethnic' ('ethnicity', 'ethnic group', 'ethnic party', etc.) is used in the broader, generic sense in line with its 'umbrella' usage in the literature.

Though the literature often presents ethnically divided societies in starkly binary terms, implying a neatly segmented image, the reality of politics in these places tends to be much more complex. This leads us to the even more tricky concepts of *civic politics* and *civic parties*. In a search for a term to relate an alternative form of politics to the dominant ethnonational in deeply ethnonationally divided societies, none fits easily. The term 'civic' is imperfect and comes with baggage. In the field of nationalism, a distinction between 'civic nationalism' – associated with citizenship, choice, and broad inclusion – and 'ethnic nationalism' – associated with narrower ethnic identity, ascription, and exclusion – has been the subject of long debate. Among valid critiques of this distinction are the falseness of this dichotomy (implying nationalism is strictly either/or), the normative assumptions with which it is laden (implying civic = good, ethnic = bad), and its masking of majoritarian (often ethnocentric) thinking that sees minority nationalisms (such as Basque or Quebecois) as 'ethnic' and therefore illegitimate, while viewing majority nationalisms (such as Spanish or Canadian) as 'civic' and therefore legitimate (see Brubaker 2004, chapter 6). Acknowledging these problematic associations, the term civic is used here to convey politics in deeply ethnonationally divided societies that explicitly eschews the dominant ethnonational basis of mobilization and mobilizes on identities, affinities, and issues other than ethnonational. It is not meant to imply the binary opposite of ethnic nor an inherently superior form of politics. With these caveats and qualifications, 'civic politics' and 'civic parties' are used as functional terms that have currency in theory and practice in ethnonationally divided societies and that convey a substantive distinction between two forms of political mobilization in these contexts. This book examines forms of civic politics that can emerge in these societies and the complex ways in which they interact with the dominant ethnonational politics.

It is also worth reflecting here on my own normative position surrounding ethnonationalism. Nationalism is a phenomenon with which my research is fundamentally concerned, specifically the ways it intersects with other forms of identity and affinity, such as gender and class. I see nationalism as a multiform phenomenon, a fact of political life, and one to which I myself am connected in many ways. I do not subscribe to the notion that nationalism is inherently 'bad' or inevitably leads to division and conflict. I recognize the legitimacy of nationalist movements, including ethnonationalist, not least considering past injustices against ethnonational minorities, such as the Catholic/nationalist minority in

Northern Ireland. My own experiences as a scholar, as well as someone born and raised south of the border in Ireland during the late stages of the Troubles, and someone who has lived in both Northern Ireland and Scotland, has given me a particular appreciation of the need in nationally diverse and divided societies to accommodate different national and ethnonational identities in the political system. Yet, I do not believe that this should trump the accommodation of one's other intersecting identities. The post-settlement realities in Northern Ireland and Bosnia are such that the systems in place institutionally privilege ethnonationalism. That has consequences for representation of other intersecting identities and issues of broader social justice. It is with the tensions that can arise between such political arrangements and intersectional representation that this book is concerned.

Research Design

This book represents the culmination of some twelve years' research on civic parties in divided societies with a primary focus on Northern Ireland and Bosnia and Herzegovina. Nested within a broader theoretical and empirical analysis is a focused comparison of a specific element of politics (civic parties and politics) in these two case studies (Pennings et al. 2006, 21). The rationale for comparing Northern Ireland and Bosnia may not be immediately obvious. Northern Ireland is a region in northwest Europe in transition from a violent conflict known as the Troubles that endured for some thirty years from the late 1960s to the late 1990s, and left more than 3,700 people dead and 47,000 injured, and left deep and lasting legacies for politics and society (CAIN 2007). The conflict bears many facets but has been widely characterized as ethnonational in nature (McGarry and O'Leary 1995), centring on two communities defined by descent-based traits and their contestation of the statehood of Northern Ireland, which was created following the partition of Ireland in 1921 and remained under British rule after the secession of the Irish Free State. Politics continue to be shaped by a deep ethnonational divide between two segments, broadly categorized as Catholic/Irish/Nationalist/Republican and Protestant/British/Unionist/Loyalist, and the party system was historically structured into two ethnonational blocs, nationalist and unionist. The Belfast/Good Friday Agreement[2] signed in 1998 was a comprehensive peace agreement that recognized this binary ethnonational divide and implemented a system of consociational power-sharing between the two blocs. Over the last fifteen years, however, a third civic bloc has emerged as a distinct force, complicating this binary and opening up a new dimension in Northern Ireland politics. Bosnia and Herzegovina is a state in southeast Europe some thirty years removed from a brutal war that lasted three and half years, from 1992–95, claimed the lives of more than 100,000 people and left more than 2 million people displaced. The war was waged on ethnonational terms comprising three main factions defined by descent-based attributes and with divergent visions for the future of Bosnia following the collapse of Yugoslavia: Bosnian Serbs, Bosniaks (Bosnian Muslims), and Bosnian Croats. Thirty years on from the war, politics and society remain starkly divided along ethnonational lines. The Dayton Peace Agreement which finally brought the war to a close in 1995 put in place a deeply ethnicized system of consociational power-sharing that recognized Serbs, Bosniaks, and Croats as 'constituent peoples' and which remains in place to this day. The party system is structured into three dominant ethnonational blocs. Yet, amidst deep contestation, a distinct fourth civic bloc exists and has maintained since the war.

These places feature fundamental contextual differences, not least in their geographic locations, the nature of their statehood (Bosnia being an independent state and Northern Ireland a substate entity of the UK), the nature of their respective conflicts (including their duration and intensity), their economies (Northern Ireland's being relatively more developed and industrialized), and their experience of democracy (Bosnia transitioning from one-party socialist rule to multiparty elections only in 1990). Yet, for the purpose of this study they bear critical similarities. Both are societies transitioning from conflicts which were officially drawn to a close in the mid to late 1990s. Both are considered deeply ethnonationally divided societies. That divide shapes politics in both places where most parties organize on an ethnonational basis. In both places, ethnonational parties dominate, measured by the aggregate vote won by these parties in elections (Chandra 2011, 158). Yet, both cases feature civic parties that struggle to break through this ethnonationally dominated system. What's more, both Northern Ireland and Bosnia feature the *consociational power-sharing model*, implemented in both places as part of peace agreements negotiated to end their respective conflicts. And importantly, they feature *different forms* of consociational power-sharing. Northern Ireland represents a case of 'liberal' power-sharing, more flexible and open to identities other than ethnic emerging over time and gaining representation, while Bosnia represents a case of 'corporate' power-sharing in which ethnicity is rigidly inscribed in the institutions (McGarry and O'Leary 2007; McCulloch 2014b, 18–19) and civic parties are granted only very limited recognition in those. Indeed, Northern Ireland and Bosnia are archetypal cases of these two different forms of power-sharing.[3] This variation provides an opportunity to probe whether civic parties face different openings and constraints under different forms of power-sharing and if they adopt different types of strategies under those varying conditions. As such, the comparison offers potential lessons about the institutional conditions that can foster and impede civic politics.

While the same methods were replicated in both cases (Yin 1994, 42, 45; King et al. 1994, 45), Northern Ireland is foregrounded in the analysis. As a place where, twenty-seven years on from peace settlement, civic parties have begun to break ethnonational dominance even amidst the inimical conditions of consociational power-sharing, it forms a critical case where the dynamics of the struggle between civic and ethnonational politics can be viewed in stark relief. The book draws these cases together in a comparative analysis before placing them in a broader dialogue with other cases of transitional power-sharing societies, including Lebanon, Burundi, and North Macedonia.

The book draws on extensive fieldwork in both cases between 2012 and 2023, using elite interviews as a primary method, supplemented by document analysis and a small number of focus groups, to explore the research questions from a variety of perspectives. Interviews examined the perspectives of civic parties and ethnonational parties (via elected representatives, party officials, and organizers), relevant members of civil society (including representatives of NGOs and community organizations), activists, members of the international community (including diplomats and members of international organizations based in-country), and independent observers and analysts (including journalists and academics). I conducted 116 interviews in total: fifty-nine in Northern Ireland (twenty-seven with representatives of civic parties; twelve with representatives of ethnonational parties; twenty with others); and fifty-seven in BiH (twenty-four with representatives of civic parties; eleven with representatives of ethnonational parties; twenty-two with others). Interview questions explored the first-hand experiences of party representatives in the power-sharing system and other actors, such as activists, operating in the broader political framework, probing how they navigated that system, the strategies they devised, and the discourses they used to describe all of this.

Focus groups probed the perceptions of voters pertaining to politics generally and civic and ethnonational parties specifically. The purpose of focus groups was not to offer a representative account of voters' behaviours or views but to glean insight into how they come to form these views, in interaction with others, and how they collectively make sense of the issue of concern (Bryman 2008, 476). In this sense, they were used as a supplementary rather than a primary method (Bartle 2003, 234). I conducted eight focus groups with thirty-eight individuals in total. I conducted five in Northern Ireland, with groups ranging from two to five members with a total of eighteen taking part. Participants were drawn from civil society organizations engaged in cross-community activity, including two women's organizations in Belfast, one student association in Belfast, and two community associations, in Fermanagh and Derry respectively.[4] In BiH I conducted three focus groups, ranging from four to nine members, with twenty participants in total taking part. One group was conducted with postgraduate university students in the state capital Sarajevo; one was conducted with language school associates in Sarajevo; and one with undergraduate university students in Republika Srpska capital Banja Luka.[5]

Documents were analyzed to examine the positions of civic parties at the organizational or official level. These included election manifestos and significant party publications, as well as politicians' speeches (particularly parliamentary and conference) and key media interviews.[6] I derived data from these three sources in an interpretive way and (particularly in interviews and focus groups) primarily to uncover insights on the research question from different positions, rather than to provide verification or confirmation (Mason 2002, 76; Gidley 2012, 271).

I made numerous visits to both Bosnia and Northern Ireland, over an eleven-year period, totalling some two-years of fieldwork.[7] The timing of my fieldwork included critical political moments, not least, in Northern Ireland: the flag protest of 2012–13; the power-sharing crisis of 2017–20; protests over abortion, marriage equality, and Irish language rights during the same period; and the Brexit 'protocol' protests in 2021, and, in Bosnia, the 'Bosnian Uprising' protests and plenum movement of 2014. This afforded me many opportunities for ethnographic observations that have informed and enriched my analysis, including observations of protest events, election campaigns, and political meetings and debates but also those gleaned from interviews, including interview settings (such as party offices and headquarters) and social interactions.

Structure of this Book

Chapter 1 introduces the concept of *civic solidarity* in divided societies and considers how it can survive within a system of *consociational power-sharing*. It contrasts conventional conflict resolution approaches that filter everything through an ethnic lens with the intersectional approach adopted in this book. The chapter presents the institutional embodiment of civic solidarity, the *civic party*. It juxtaposes civic politics with the reality of consociational power-sharing and anticipates the ways in which power-sharing's institutions impede and enable civic parties and the strategies they might adopt in response.

Chapter 2 turns the focus to Northern Ireland. It examines the context for the rise of civic politics, charting Northern Ireland's journey from political violence towards its current 'post-conflict' state. It outlines the contours of the 1998 Good Friday Agreement, then traces the state's tumultuous experience with power-sharing post-1998, paying particular attention to the crises that have erupted since 2016 following Britain's decision to leave the European Union. In bringing civic solidarity to light in Northern Ireland the chapter introduces the main civic parties analyzed in the case: Alliance, the Green Party, People Before Profit, and the Women's Coalition.

So, how do Northern Ireland's civic parties experience power-sharing in practice? Chapter 3 explores the implications of the institutions designed to protect ethnonational communities for civic parties and their politics. As the chapter addresses each rule, it goes beyond the direct and obvious impacts to uncover the deeper implications and how they play out in practice. It gives voice to the civic representatives, presenting their first-hand accounts of not just the observable effects of the rules but how they feel about them.

Yet, the rules on paper are only part of the story. Chapter 4 addresses how civic parties interact with the informal institutions of Northern Ireland politics: its socially shared conventions, practices, norms, and ideas. It probes the informal constraints, including the dominant discourse of ethnonationalism and the phenomenon of ethnonational clientelism which bolster ethnonational parties. In this way, the chapter shines a light on the dynamics of politics in Northern Ireland and other ethnically polarized places that are difficult to quantify and poorly theorized, yet intensely powerful. It also demonstrates the ways in which these informal practices, norms, and ideas are intertwined with, and mutually reinforced by, the formal institutions.

But even amidst these interwoven barriers, civic parties have sustained in post-agreement Northern Ireland and now pose a challenge to the ethnonational political order. Chapter 5 unpicks this puzzle by probing civic party *agency*. It shows how civic parties have strategically negotiated the system, creatively navigating the barriers and seizing key openings that have emerged.

Are these experiences unique to civic parties in Northern Ireland or do they speak to those in other divided societies? Chapter 6 turns to the case of Bosnia and Herzegovina, setting out its deeply ethnicized political structures and the barriers, both formal and informal, that they present to civic parties. How have civic parties in Bosnia endured in spite of this environment? Chapter 7 addresses this question assessing the strategic dilemmas Bosnia's ethnic framework evokes for civic parties, the creative strategies they have used to navigate it and the consequences of those moves for these parties and the civic agenda.

Chapter 8 draws the experiences of civic parties in Northern Ireland and Bosnia together in a comparative analysis, considering the similarities and differences between the cases and what they tell us about the conditions that support and constrain civic parties in divided societies. It places this focused comparison in the context of other divided societies to make a number of broader observations about civic parties' opportunity structure in consociational power-sharing contexts, the strategies they use to negotiate those structures, and their potential to effect change.

The book concludes by reflecting on the wider implications of these insights, theoretically and empirically, for Northern Ireland, Bosnia, and other divided societies and looks ahead to what current global political trends may mean for the future of civic politics in divided societies.

Chapter One

Civic Solidarity in Divided Societies

Politics in so-called 'divided societies' tend to be defined by one central fissure. Yet, even in the most deeply divided societies, the politics of ethnonational division is never the only game in town. Political collectives form based on other identities, allegiances, and issues that cut across the ethnonational divide and even actively reject it. This form of politics, *civic* solidarity, does not supplant the ethnonational divide, but it does intersect and complicate it. And where formal politics is subsumed by ethnonationalism and issues of broader intersectional rights and equality such as gender, race, sexuality, ability, and social justice are pushed down – or even *off* – the agenda, this type of mobilization matters. It is nothing new; in places marked by political violence, from India to Kosovo, it has always existed. But it has been obscured from view by the all-encompassing frame of ethnonationalism. Neither is it confined to civil society; it can and does break into institutional politics in the form of *civic political parties.*

Nowhere is this clearer at present than in Northern Ireland where civic solidarity has moved to the foreground of politics. Civic parties have broken through, sustained and now present a realistic challenge to the ethnonational status quo. What makes this particularly surprising is that Northern Ireland's institutions are explicitly designed to manage the conflict via *consociational power-sharing* between the main ethnonational groups – effectively created to accommodate ethnonational parties. Northern Ireland is not unique in this paradox. Civic parties have emerged and sustained under the hostile conditions of power-sharing in states including Bosnia and Herzegovina, Burundi, and Lebanon. So, how can civic solidarity survive – and even thrive – in the context of ethnonational power-sharing that grants it so little institutional space? Are there ways in which civic solidarity might be reconciled with ethnonational power-sharing? Indeed, over time, might civic parties even represent a route *out* of power-sharing?

This chapter sets out a framework to answer these questions. It brings civic solidarity in divided societies into view, before juxtaposing it with consociational power-sharing and exploring the tensions between the two. First though, let us turn to a basic but fundamental question: of what do we speak when we speak of a 'divided society'?

An Intersectional Lens on 'Divided Societies'

The very term 'deeply divided society' tells a story of its own. It implies that certain places can be categorized as uniquely divided, set apart from others that are largely homogenous and consensual. They feature one central division so deeply entrenched that it structures society and politics, to a dysfunctional (often violent) degree. This classification takes a *singular lens*: society is divided along X lines (ethnic, national, racial, linguistic, etc.), and that divide permeates and defines all aspects of social and political life; other identities, issues, and divisions exist, but they are subordinate. It produces a *binary* picture. This diagnosis has direct implications for the solutions put in place, or even the options considered. Yet, there are other ways to think about such societies.[1] They can be understood through an *intersectional lens*. In this view the salient political division is real and part of people's lived experience, but it exists amidst other divisions and identity categories that intersect and cannot be separated from one another. Any political solution must seek to accommodate these intersecting divisions and solidarities.

In the conflict resolution literature, deeply divided societies are portrayed as those where a particular division permeates many, if not all, aspects of public life over a sustained period of time and constitutes a source of political conflict and potential violence (Guelke 2012a, 30; Lijphart 1984, 22). 'Ethnic' traits – *descent*-based attributes (Chandra 2006, 297) such as race, language, or religion – are considered most prone to division, and fused with nationalism they produce a particularly sharp divide (Guelke 2012a, 32). Ethnonationalism saturates every aspect of politics: the main parties and movements are defined by it and form distinct blocs; competition between blocs takes on a zero-sum logic; every policy issue, from healthcare to transportation, is ethnically framed (a phenomenon Horowitz terms 'ethnic seepage') (Horowitz 1985, 347, 357–8; Chandra 2011, 155; Rabushka and Shepsle 1972).

These understandings of conflict inform the political solutions prescribed to resolve it. A binary approach has characterized this field: *integration* versus *accommodation*. Integrationist approaches seek to overcome divisions in society through integration at the level of civil society, and integrative institutions at the political level. This includes bottom-up, civil society initiatives, policies like shared housing and education, participatory approaches to democracy and a universalist approach to citizenship. Individual rights are prized over group rights, with identity viewed as fluid and multiple (Aitken 2010, 233; Howard 2012, 159; Wilson 2010a, 13). Integrationists, according to McGarry, O'Leary, and Simeon, respect differences in the private sphere but oppose their institutional recognition in the public sphere (2008, 42). They can be categorized into three types: republicans (or civic nationalists), liberals, and socialists (2008, 46).

Accommodationist solutions, on the other hand, recognize the ethnonational divide in society and seek to accommodate its different groups in the political system and public policy (McGarry et al 2008). In this realist view, ethnonational identity may well be constructed but it is nonetheless durable and must be accounted for in the political system (McGarry et al 2008, 37; Kymlicka 1995, 185). Under the accommodationist heading, McGarry, O'Leary, and Simeon group four approaches: centripetalism, multiculturalism, consociation, and territorial pluralism. Centripetalism, largely defined by the work of Donald Horowitz, advocates incentivizing cooperation between ethnic groups and thereby moderation, primarily through electoral engineering. This can lead to power-sharing entailing a voluntary coalition government of the moderate middle (Horowitz 1991; 2001; 2002b; 2014). Multiculturalism advocates the protection of multiple communities in both the public and private realm (McGarry et al 2008, 40). Associated with the work of Will Kymlicka among others, it presents a liberal theory of minority rights. In 'polyethnic' and 'multinational' states – that is, most democracies – group-differentiated rights are needed to supplement individual human rights, including guarantees of representation (Kymlicka 1995, 5; 2004, 65; 2010, 100). Territorial pluralism involves accommodating concentrated ethnic or national communities territorially in the state by creating autonomous sub-state units, as in pluralist federalism based on nationality, ethnicity, language, or religion (McGarry et al 2008, 45; Swenden 2012). Consociation, goes further, designed not just to manage diversity in society but to address deep division and conflict. It does so by accommodating the main groups in society in the political system via executive power-sharing and granting each one extensive protections, including minority vetoes, as well as a range of multiculturalist mechanisms of group autonomy and proportionality (McGarry et al 2008, 41). It departs from centripetal power-sharing in featuring a broadly inclusive executive, with no requirement for elites to moderate to enter (Horowitz 2002). In practice, these four accommodationist approaches are closely intertwined and overlap heavily (Choudhry 2008, 26; Swenden 2013).[2]

The binary lens of accommodation/integration contrasts with an *intersectional lens.* Intersectionality sees individuals as holding multiple identities that cannot be separated from one another but intersect in critical ways that shape one's experience of the world. 'As an analytical tool, intersectionality views categories of race, class, gender, sexuality, nation, ability, ethnicity, and age – among others – as *interrelated and mutually shaping one another*', Collins and Bilge write (2020, 2; my italics). One's experiences of race, nation, ethnicity, gender, and class – and *struggles* within those systems of power – must be contextualized by one another (Anthias and Yuval-Davis 1983, 62). They are interdependent with one another and with political economy (Bakan and Abu-Laban 2017, 223). This approach arose from the failure of the singular lens of conventional theory and policy to account for people's lived experiences – specifically Black and Chicana women in the US in the 1960s and 70s whose particular needs were not addressed by either the feminist movement or the civil rights and anti-racist movements (Collins and Bilge 2020, 3, 74). The erasure of the experience of those multiply marginalized in this way was famously captured by Kimberlé Crenshaw (1989; 1991). When one is positioned at the intersection of two or more systems of power, like race and gender, these experiences are not just layered on top of one another but compound each other and generate particular forms of discrimination and oppression (Crenshaw, 1989; Anthias and Yuval-Davis 1983; Collins and Bilge, 2020, 2). Intersectionality has since advanced, both locally and globally, including through United Nations human rights discourse (Bakan and Abu-Laban 2017).

When this intersectional lens is trained on 'divided societies' it generates a very different view to the conventional account. No longer can we see society solely through the prism of one identity category. Even if less visible in the dominant discourse of ethnonationalism, other identity categories, such as gender, class, race, and sexual orientation, always intersect with the ethnonational in ways that shape people's lives and often compound their marginalization. For example, although conventional conflict resolution approaches treat forms of violence other than ethnonational as peripheral, studies show that gender-based violence systematically *increases* after the cessation of military violence (McLeod 2011, 599). An intersectional perspective then means seeing 'divided societies' as made up not of binary, oppositional categories (e.g. race, ethnicity, nation, gender, class) but of *relational, interconnected* categories (Collins 1998, 921; Collins and Bilge 2020, 33, 225). With this frame, we cannot craft institutions that elevate one identity category above all others and do not allow for expression of other intersecting identities.

In this book I take an intersectional approach to identity, division, and conflict. I use the terms 'divided' and 'deeply divided' society in a qualified way to mean a place whose political structures and discourse are shaped by one overriding identity divide but which, in reality, features multiple intersecting divisions and solidarities. I am not denying the existence nor the power of ethnonational identity nor that it can form the basis of deep division that demands unique solutions, as the conflict resolution literature asserts. I take seriously the dangers of failing to recognize distinct political communities institutionally for both peace and democracy (Gagnon 2021, 107). I am, however, seeking to augment those approaches with an intersectional perspective. Ethnonationalism is never the only source of division in society. And viewing these places through a singular lens and crafting institutional solutions on that basis serves to reinforce the divide and obstruct broader inclusion.

Through an intersectional lens a different form of politics and political solidarity come into view. It is to this phenomenon that we now turn.

Civic Solidarity in Divided Societies

The singular ethnonational frame pushes other forms of politics out of view (Nagle 2016a). Yet, even at the height of conflict in Northern Ireland, Palestine and Israel, Bosnia and Herzegovina, and beyond, alternative politics have existed and held agency: politics I refer to as *civic solidarity*. Civic solidarity – or *civic politics* – is a form of political mobilization in the context of an ethnonationally divided society that mobilizes on issues and identity categories beyond ethnonationalism, be they class, gender, sexuality, environment, or another. Civic solidarity does not deny ethnic or ethnonational identity, but it mobilizes politically on other identity categories and issues, which may well intersect with ethnicity. The term 'civic' is used here as an imperfect term, as outlined in the Introduction, not to erase ethnonational identity nor imply its binary opposite but to refer to alternative, intersecting issues and identities on which groups *choose* to organize.

The politics of civic solidarity in divided societies has been captured in various ways. Its tenets are clearly embodied in *transversal politics*. Transversalism is a model of *coalition politics* that allows for collective action amidst division without violating one's individual identities and attachments, including those associated with the dominant divide. It was first conceived in 1993 by Italian feminists working with women from Israeli and Palestinian communities, theorized by Nira Yuval-Davis (1997). It has also been applied in the work of Black feminists in the US in the 1990s (Collins 1998), bearing much in common with intersectionality. Yet, the principles of transversal politics can be applied beyond feminist mobilizations. Indeed, scholars have argued that transversalism is not an intrinsically feminist practice (Roulston 1999; Byrne 2014, 112), and it has been observed in coalitions including the Black Lives Matter movement (Collins 2017). Transversal politics involves the practices of 'rooting' and 'shifting'. Members of a coalition remain centred or 'rooted' in their own experience, identity, background, and positioning in society but can at the same time 'shift' to empathize and connect with those from different positionings (Yuval-Dais 1997, 130). Coalitions unite on *values* and *goals*, not identity, the boundaries set not in terms of 'who we are' but 'what we want to achieve' (Yuval-Davis 1997, 126; Yuval-Davis 2006a, 281; Roulston 2000, 41). They come together at a particular time to address a particular need (Mulholland and Patel 1999). Such mobilization could be witnessed in the cross-communal Women of Liberia Mass Action for Peace during the Second Civil War in Liberia in 2003 (Tripp 2015) and the 'Belfast Mothers' protest in 1971 that drew together women from across the Protestant–Catholic divide in Northern Ireland to oppose the British Government's removal of free school milk (acenturyofwomen.com). It could be seen in Black feminist movements in the US to tackle gender-based violence (Collins, 1998) and in the multi-racial Black Lives Matter movement that has fought police violence against Black people, including women and LGBTQ+ people (Collins 2017) and institutional racism more broadly.[3] Transversal politics rejects both *universalism* – that denies group attachments and homogenizes identity – and narrow *identity politics* – that cages identity and denies solidarity across those attachments (Yuval-Davis 1997, 119; 2006, 281).[4] Transversalism resonates here with broader multiculturalism debates in the 1990s outlined above about the need to balance unity and diversity in diverse societies, such as Canada, the US, and the UK (See Kymlicka 1995; Gagnon 2000; Abu-Laban, Gagnon and Tremblay 2023).

Collins and Bilge similarly observe 'solidarity politics' and 'coalition-building' in diverse places through an intersectional lens (2020, 51). They observe it in grassroots organizations like the Asian Immigrant Women Advocates (AIWA), a community organization in Oakland and San Jose, California that brought together a diverse coalition of limited English-speaking, low-paid immigrant workers to tackle 'interlocking forms of oppression'. The group avoided political organizing structured along ethnic lines, such as Chinese, Korean, or Vietnamese, and rather understood these identities as 'instruments to be used strategically in complex and flexible ways' (2020, 51). Such coalitions understand the dangers of single issue (and identity) politics and allow their members to hold other identities, beyond the one on which they organize. They are 'conscious coalitions' that leave room for individual identity amidst group solidarity (Collins and Bilge 2020, 183).

Emma Dabiri likewise advocates for *coalition politics* based on shared interest as a route to move beyond racial division and injustice. When people are motivated by genuine shared interest – such as reducing police violence against everyone in poor neighbourhoods – rather than some superficial notion of altruism or allyship with the 'other group', mobilizations are deeper, stronger, and more effective. Indeed, cross-ethnic mobilizations are more destabilizing to the divided status quo than single-identity mobilization. She notes the case of apartheid South Africa in the late 1970s and early 1980s where the regime was 'much more reactionary against, and punitive towards, racially mixed organizations such as the ANC, while maintaining more tolerance towards groups who encouraged separatist lines' (Dabiri 2021, 17–19).

David Hollinger's theory of 'postethnicity' also envisions a form of civic solidarity (Hollinger 2005). Set out as a prescription for the ethnically and racially diverse United States, postethnicity rejects universalism, and its veiled ethnocentrism, but also rejects the narrow identity politics inherent in a system that categorizes people into ethno-racial categories for the purposes of combating discrimination (Hollinger 2005, 8). Hollinger accepts the importance of the ethnic community but sees that affinity as one among several other affinities that one can *choose* to mobilize within. 'A postethnic perspective', he writes, 'favors voluntary over involuntary affiliations, balances an appreciation for communities of descent with a determination to make room for new communities, and promotes solidarities of wide scope that incorporate people with different ethnic and racial backgrounds.' (2005, 3). It does not deny ethnic affinity but does deny its assumed supremacy over other identities.[5]

Civic solidarity lies at the heart of Ashuthosh Varshney's landmark study of inter-ethnic relations in India. Varshney demonstrates how the bonds forged between Hindu and Muslim communities through civic engagement at the local level can act as a bulwark against ethnic polarization occurring on the national level – particularly 'associational' forms such as common membership of political parties (Varshney 2002). He shows, for example, how the inter-group trust developed by an NGO in Utar Pradesh that mobilized women from Muslim and Hindu communities on the issue of ration cards, helped ward off violence when ethnic tensions escalated in 1990 (2002). 'Civic', 'non-ethnic', and 'non-sectarian' social movements – mobilizing on issues from social justice to public services to preservation of public spaces to LGBTQ+ rights – have also marked their presence in other divided places including Northern Ireland, Lebanon, and Bosnia (Nagle 2013, 81, 90; Milan 2020; Milan 2022; Murtagh 2016; Touquet 2011).

Yet, while these accounts relate the power of civic solidarity, missing is the *institutional* piece of the picture. They generally portray civic politics as a phenomenon that exists at the level of civil society – in the form of social movements and grassroots organizations – separate to institutional politics, which, dominated as it is by ethnonationalism, lies beyond its reach. Scholars of civic social movements in Bosnia and Lebanon, for example, underline the perils of traversing the boundary between grassroots and institutional politics where they risk being torn apart by the currents of ethnonationalism. Indeed, for some, the purpose of these movements is not to directly impact institutional politics – say, by mobilizing electoral support or feeding into political parties – but to change the quality of people's everyday life and shift public consciousness (Nagle, 2013: 81;90; Milan 2020; Mujkić 2014; Murtagh, 2016). It is true that civic mobilizations operate most commonly at the level of grassroots politics, often born out of urgent need, be it peace, violence prevention, preservation of public spaces, or basic human welfare. Yuval-Davis outlines the challenge these movements face in making the leap to formal politics where 'hierarchical structures of decision-making' allow little space for the dialogic politics of transversalism (Yuval-Davis 1997, 88).

While recognizing these challenges, I argue that civic mobilizations in deeply divided societies can and do make the transition to institutional politics, in the shape of *civic political parties*. Civic parties can be transient – existing for as long as a particular issue remains urgent, or until they succumb to the forces of ethnonational polarization – but they can also endure and become institutionalized. More than this, these parties have the potential to have a critical effect on their political environment. This book renders civic solidarity visible and brings to light its institutional embodiment in the civic party. It seeks to explain civic parties' endurance, even amidst inimical political institutions, and explore their potential. First though, we must unpack just what constitutes a civic party.

Civic Parties

I define *civic parties* as those in an ethnonationally divided society that explicitly seek to appeal to voters from across society, on some basis other than ethnicity or ethnonationalism. Here they contrast with so-called 'ethnic parties' or 'ethnonational parties' that appeal to and seek to represent voters primarily on the basis of ethnicity or ethnonationalism, to the exclusion of one or more groups. Borrowing from Chandra (2011), I use party *appeal* to voters as the chief criterion for defining a party as 'civic' or 'ethnonational'.

The question of what defines a civic party is by no means straightforward. Should we define it by its appeal to voters? Its support (the identity of its voters)? Its leadership? Even on what defines an 'ethnic party' – a core concept in this field – there is no consensus (Elischer 2013, 6).[6] In his classic conceptualization of ethnic party systems, Horowitz identifies three party types – ethnic, multi-ethnic, and non-ethnic – and distinguishes them according to one criterion: *electoral support* (1985, 292, 298–9). Ethnic parties are those that obtain their support overwhelmingly from one ethnic group (Horowitz 1985, 291, 298). Multi-ethnic parties must include and draw support from all major ethnic groups in society. These groups participate on a pluralistic, group basis, such as the Punjab Congress in India in the 1950s and '60s which brought together Sikh and Hindu communities, even against a backdrop of inter-group conflict (Horowitz 1985, 299, 427–8). Non-ethnic parties, meanwhile, mobilize on an altogether alternative basis to the ethnic dimension, attempting to introduce new cleavages and turn politics in a non-ethnic direction (Horowitz 1985, 300). According to Horowitz, parties can be multi-ethnic or non-ethnic at the national level but ethnic at the local level, as in the case of the Congress Party in India (Horowitz 1985, 301).

Others use *party appeal* – and the *particularity/universality* of that appeal – to define a party as ethnic or otherwise. For Kanchan Chandra, an ethnic party is one that explicitly appeals to voters as a champion of the *particular interests* of one ethnic group, or set of groups, to the *exclusion of others* and makes this appeal central to its mobilization strategy (2011, 155).[7] The core criterion is *appeal* to voters and the core distinction is *particularity* versus *universality*. Here she departs from Horowitz, for whom the 'test of an ethnic party is simply the distribution of support' (Horowitz 1985, 291–2). A multi-ethnic party, for Chandra, also appeals to voters on the basis of ethnicity but champions the interests of *all ethnic groups* on an equal basis, to the exclusion of none. A non-ethnic party forms a residual category: it does not advance the interest of any ethnic group, or, where it does, those demands are not central to its platform (Chandra 2011, 155). What sets an ethnic party apart from others is its move to *exclude* one or more other ethnic groups (Chandra 2011). An ethnic party is still an ethnic party even if it claims to represent more than one ethnic group (e.g. attempting to unify disparate groups under a broad category, such as 'Hispanic' in the United States). A multi-ethnic party is a multi-ethnic party as long as it does not exclude any ethnic groups (Chandra 2011, 157). By this definition, Chandra classifies as multi-ethnic the National Front in Malaysia which mobilized in 1995 to include parties from all salient ethnic categories, including Malays, Indians, and Chinese, and the African National Congress (ANC) in South Africa in 1994, as it did not exclude any salient ethnic category in its appeal to voters (Chandra 2004, 5). By contrast, the Bahujan Samaj Party (BJP) in India can be defined in the period 1984–98 as an ethnic party in that, despite attempting to represent more than 400 castes that make up India's 'Scheduled Castes', it excluded the Hindu upper castes (Chandra, 2004, 15–17). Chandra later identifies eight indicators for ethnic parties: party name, party platform (appeal), issues advocated, implicit campaign message, the groups that support the party, the make-up of its vote, the composition of its leadership, and the electoral arenas in which it competes (2011, 157). She advocates using multiple indicators rather than relying on a single one but identifies platform/appeal and party name as primary indicators (Chandra 2011, 162).

Informed by Chandra's approach, I use *party appeal* as the core criterion to classify parties in an ethnonational party system as 'ethnonational' or 'civic': that is, the platform or message it presents to voters. An ethnonational party then is one that explicitly appeals to the interests of one (or more) ethnonational groups in society, to the exclusion of one or more others, and which defines itself in these terms. A civic party is one that appeals to voters from across society (either as citizens or as members of an ethnonational group) without excluding any on the basis of ethnonational group membership, on some basis other than ethnonational identity, and which defines itself explicitly in these terms. In line with Chandra's approach, (2011), while an ethnonational party may appeal to more than one ethnonational group, it always excludes at least one group in that appeal, either implicitly or explicitly. A civic party, by contrast, may sometimes appeal to voters on the basis of ethnic identity but does so in a pluralistic way to multiple groups and does not exclude any group on the basis of such identity. A civic party can be understood as one in an ethnonational party system that does not exclude voters, implicitly or explicitly, based on ethnonational identity and that explicitly appeals to them on some basis other than ethnonationalism. Civic parties will approach ethnonational identity in different ways, as I expand on below. To operationalize a civic party, I borrow from Chandra's criteria for defining an ethnic party, identifying explicit appeal as the primary, essential indicator. This can be supplemented by five other non-essential indicators: party name, positioning on critical issues (that are divisive for ethnonational groups, such as the constitutional future of the state), electoral support, party leadership, and arenas of electoral contestation (see table 1.1 below). As Chandra notes, classifications are time specific, and a party's appeal to voters may change over time (2004, 3–4) from civic towards ethnonational and vice versa; for example, ethnonational parties may begin to reach out beyond their core ethnic base to all other groups (Murtagh and McCulloch 2021).

How have civic parties been characterized in the literature? They have appeared in various guises, including 'multiethnic', 'nonethnic' (Horowitz 1985, 298–9; Chandra 2004; 2011), 'post-ethnic' (Touquet 2011), 'non-nationalist' (Hulsey and Keil 2019; Pickering 2009; Sasso 2015), 'non-sectarian' (Nagle and Fakhoury 2022), 'cross-segmental' (Agarin and Jarrett 2021), 'non-ethnic counter-bidder' (Coakley 2008, 769-70), 'liberal' (Mitchell 2002) and 'cross-community' (Evans and Tonge 2001). A common feature running through these accounts is *vulnerability*. In his classic work, Horowitz underlines the severe challenges to multiethnic parties' emergence and survival, noting, 'There is abundant evidence on all fronts that durable multiethnic parties and coalitions are rare exceptions where ethnic divisions are sharp' (1985, 437). The ethnic party

Table 1.1 | **Civic party definition and indicators**

Definition	*Indicator*	*Description*	*Essential*	*Distinction: ethnonational / civic*
A party in an ethnonationally divided society that explicitly appeals to voters from across society on some basis other than ethnicity or ethnonationalism, without excluding any voters on the basis of ethnonational group membership	Explicit appeal	Explicit platform or messaging to voters	Yes	Particularistic / universal
	Party name	Indication of ethnonational/ civic orientation in name	No	Party name indicates particular ethnic/ethnonational group(s) / party name does not indicate particular ethnic/ethnonational group(s) and may indicate universal appeal
	Positioning on critical issues	Position on issues of critical importance to ethnonational groups, e.g. statehood, constitutional questions, etc.	No	Position aligns with ethnonational group(s) interest / neutral position
	Electoral support	Ethnonational distribution of party vote in elections	No	Vote concentrated within particular ethnonational group(s) / support roughly distributed across ethnonational groups (indicated by polling data or territorial spread in election results)
	Party leadership	Identity of individuals in leadership positions within party	No	Particular ethnonational group(s) represented in leadership / all main ethnonational groups represented in leadership over time or no reference to ethnonational groups in leadership policy
	Arenas of electoral contestation	Electoral areas/regions/ districts contested by party in elections	No	Only electoral areas with significant particular ethnonational group(s) population contested / all electoral areas contested

system renders little space for these parties or their form of politics. Once parties start to organize on an ethnic dimension, all the incentives nudge parties in this direction, towards ethnic extremism and away from inter-ethnic moderation (Horowitz 1985, 318, 322–3, 340, 342). This centrifugal process leaves any parties organizing on alternate bases, such as class, crowded out and vulnerable to flanking (1985, 338). Multi-ethnic parties are also beset by the difficulty of reconciling different ethnic groups' zero-sum claims within one party and the 'taint' associated with working with members of rival ethnic groups (1985, 427). Facing the choice of 'adapt or die', splits and gradual evolution into ethnically based parties are common fates (1985, 427, 309).

Civic parties have attracted the attention of external actors and outside interventions to support peace and democracy, particularly in African and Asian states but also in Bosnia (Kapadžić 2018, 55). Benjamin Reilly identifies strategies to support civic parties in conflict-prone places, including institutional engineering, such as requiring multi-ethnic party lists for elections and vote pooling electoral systems that encourage cross-ethnic voting and moderation amongst parties, targeting resources and support at civic parties through international donor agencies and NGOs like the US-based National Democratic Institute (NDI) or reforms to the electoral process to incentivize moderation by international bodies such as the Organization for Security and Cooperation in Europe (OSCE) (2006, 819–20, 822–3). Indeed, Elischer underlines the extensive international intervention and aid leveraged via parties to support democracy in Africa (2013, 4). Ethnic party bans became a particularly popular tool in the repertoire of institutional incentives in Africa after the wave of democratization in the 1990s, yet, research suggests their effectiveness has been limited and context-dependent (Bogaards et al. 2013; Bogaards 2013; Moroff 2013).

Civic parties have garnered limited explicit attention in the literature then, and where they have, the emphasis has mostly been on their fragility and dependence on external support. However, the inexorable pull of ethnic mobilization and the exceptionalism of any parties other than ethnic in divided societies has been questioned in more recent scholarship. In his study of political parties in Africa, Sebastian Elischer finds that these parties are much less ethnically defined than assumed in the literature (2013, 24, 30). Party types vary significantly within and across states. In states like Namibia, for example, ethnic and nonethnic parties have coexisted over long periods of time – something that Horowitz deemed exceptional (Elischer 2013, 7, 19). What's more, Zuber finds that ethnic party systems are often 'imperfectly segmented': ethnic parties compete within their own ethnic bloc but also with parties from other blocs and with nonethnic parties (2012, 928). All of this serves to question the argument that all politics in divided societies is 'ethnic' and that civic parties are exceedingly rare, transient, and unsustainable.

Civic parties have broken through in divided societies and played important roles. Parties like the Democratic Party in South Africa (Mitchell 2002) and the Northern Ireland Women's Coalition (Murtagh 2008) have made distinct contributions to peace settlements. Others have assumed pivotal positions in power-sharing institutions like the Alliance Party of Northern Ireland which has periodically occupied the contested justice ministry since 2010 (Mitchell 2015; 2018). Some have even led power-sharing governments, like the SDP in Bosnia and CNDD-FDD in Burundi (Keil and Perry 2015, 85; Vandeginste 2017). Now, in Northern Ireland they have grown to a level where they are threatening the ethnonational status quo and questioning the future of power-sharing on that basis. This is not to say it is easy for civic parties to make it in deeply divided systems – particularly those constructed on the basis of ethnonationalism – but these parties exist and can play significant roles alongside ethnonational parties.

So how can this mode of politics survive and navigate a system predicated on ethnic representation? Before we broach that question, let us take a closer look at the consociational power-sharing system and how it operates.

Consociational Power-Sharing

For the last thirty years, consociational power-sharing has prevailed in international peacebuilding as a model for managing division and conflict in divided societies. First theorized by Arend Lijphart in 1969, 'consociational democracy' recognizes the distinct groups or 'segments' in a divided society and includes each one in government where they share power via their elite representatives (1969). Lying towards the accommodationist end of the spectrum of approaches outlined above, it centres on elite cooperation (Sisk 2002, 34). Lijphart developed the concept with reference to the Western European cases of Belgium, Netherlands, Switzerland, and Austria. His starting point was that in divided societies, 'normal' Westminster style majoritarian democracy will not produce alterations in government and opposition but, rather, permanently include majorities and exclude minorities – thus fuelling the conflict (Lijphart 1969, 30; 1977, 26–9). 'What these societies need is a democratic regime that emphasizes *consensus* instead of opposition, that *includes* rather than excludes and that tries to maximize the size of the ruling majority instead of being satisfied with bare majority consensus democracy' (Lijphart 1984, 23; italics added).

Consociation comprises four basic conditions: a *grand coalition* government comprising all significant groups; a *mutual veto* to protect groups' vital interests; *proportionality* of group representation in public office and resource allocation; and *segmental autonomy* for groups in certain areas, which may be territorial, as in decentralized and multi-national federal states (see Gagnon 2021), or non-territorial, as in culture or education (Lijphart 1977, 25; 35; 43). Lijphart more recently refined this conceptualization to elevate two of these as 'primary conditions': the participation of all significant groups in political decision-making, especially in the executive ('grand coalition' or executive power-sharing), and group autonomy, especially in the areas of education and culture (Lijphart 1995, 859; 2002, 39).[8]

Consociational theory has been further developed in the intervening years by a number of scholars, most notably 'revisionist consociationalists' John McGarry and Brendan O'Leary. McGarry and O'Leary have put forward a number of modifications to Lijphart's model, including: accounting for the role of external actors in consociational settlements; the complexity of settlements and need to include provisions beyond the core institutions, such as agreement on prisoner release and police reform; and, significantly, recognition of the fact that grand coalition is not an essential condition of consociation (2006a: 47, 58–9, 61).[9] McGarry and O'Leary have long advocated consociation as a solution to the Northern Ireland conflict (1990; 2006a; 2006b; 2009; O'Leary 2018; 2019) and, together with others, have explored the application of power-sharing to other conflict zones, including Iraq, Sudan, and Cyprus (McGarry and O'Leary 2007; O'Leary 2012; McGarry 2017; 2021; McGarry and Loizides 2015).

While earlier work on consociational power-sharing mainly *described* democratic systems that emerged organically in segmented places, since the 1990s power-sharing is most often *prescribed* by international actors to end conflicts. Power-sharing is increasingly wielded as a tool of external intervention, implemented as part of comprehensive peace agreements in places including Northern Ireland, Bosnia and Herzegovina, Kosovo, North Macedonia, Lebanon, Burundi, and Iraq and raised as a potential solution to recent and ongoing conflicts, like those in Syria, Cyprus, Catalonia, and even Ukraine and Israel and Palestine (McCulloch 2021,

2; McGarry 2019; McCulloch and McEvoy 2020; Mako 2023; Kaufman 2015; Salamey and Katoul Rahbani 2023: 33; McGarry 2021; McGarry and Loizides 2015; Anderson 2021; Wade 2022; Yehuda 2023; O'Leary 2017). Power-sharing then bears the twin aims of peace and democracy: used as an incentive to warring parties to lay down arms in exchange for political power and, after settlement, as a way to moderate conflict between those groups and keep them invested in stable democracy (see Noel 2005; Jarstad and Nilsson 2008; Hartzell and Hoddie 2003). International actors even play key roles in the continued functioning of power-sharing after settlement in places like Kosovo and Bosnia (Bell 2015; McEvoy 2015; McCulloch and McEvoy 2018a; McCulloch and McEvoy 2018b; Keil 2013; Hulsey and Keil 2020; Walsh and Doyle 2018).

As the practice of consociation has evolved, so too has the theory. A key refinement, spearheaded by McGarry and O'Leary, is the distinction between *corporate* and *liberal* consociation: whether the groups that will share power are pre-determined in the constitution, as in corporate, or decided through the electoral process, as in liberal (McGarry and O'Leary 2007). Systems towards the corporate end of the spectrum – such as Bosnia and Herzegovina, Belgium, Burundi, South Tyrol, and Lebanon – feature institutions like separate electoral rolls for different groups and seats reserved for group representatives prior to elections (McCulloch, 2014a: 505; Nagle 2011, 166–7). Those towards the liberal (or 'hybrid') end – such as Iraq, Malaysia, North Macedonia, Kenya, and Northern Ireland – leave the question of who will share power in the hands of voters, to a greater extent. They include rules like low thresholds for representatives to be eligible for cabinet (government) positions and selecting cabinet members based on election performance (rather than reserved seats) in proportional sequential coalitions, indirect veto rights and human rights provisions for groups and individuals (McCulloch 2014a, 503; McCulloch 2014b, 19; Wolff 2010; McGarry and Loizides 2015). In further theoretical refinements, Bogaards applies a new institutionalist lens to consociationalism to demonstrate the power of not only formal but informal consociational institutions. Through the case of Lebanon, he demonstrates that even the most important corporate features – such as allocating the positions of president, prime minister, and Speaker of parliament to the three designated sects of Maronite Christian, Sunni Muslim, and Shia Muslim respectively – can be informal rather than codified or constitutionalized (Bogaards 2019, 32, 36).

Yet, consociation remains deeply controversial, in theory and practice. For a start, detractors claim it is exceedingly difficult to adopt (Keil and McCulloch 2021; Horowitz 2014). In those cases where it is adopted, critics claim it effectively institutionalizes the divisions it seeks to overcome (Howard 2012, 162). For centripetalists like Horowitz it is deficient in the incentive principle, lacking rewards for ethnonational elites to cooperate or to reach out to voters beyond their own ethnic constituency (Horowitz 2002b). Institutional safeguards for ethnic groups make it highly dysfunctional and prone to deadlock (McCulloch 2021, 6). Far from biodegrading over time (Lijphart 1977, 228), consociation entails incentives for ethnic elites to perpetuate the system, creating 'lock-in' from which there is no clear exit route (Keil and McCulloch 2021; Nagle 2020, 138; Bogaards 2019, 37; Fakhoury 2019). And critically, consociation is slammed as being exclusionary and deterministic. It enforces a singular (ethnic) lens, that makes it blind to other identities, allegiances, and solidarities, and precludes other forms of politics from taking hold (Mujkić 2008; Nagle, 2016; Stojanović 2018). Power-sharing entails an 'exclusion amid inclusion' dilemma: while including the main groups to the conflict it effectively excludes 'others' outside that mold, such as smaller ethnic minorities, groups that organize on a cross-ethnic basis like women and LGBTQ+ people, and those who simply do not identify with any of the main groups (Agarin et al 2018). A model based on elite cooperation, it inhibits mobilizations from below and stands insulated from civil society demands (Fakhoury 2019, 19). Consociation is presented as essentially conservative, in its assumption that such divisions will remain a fixed feature of society (Dixon 2011), and rigid, in its lack of capacity to accommodate shifts in identity and demographics over time (Aitken 2010, 233).

Consociationalists respond with robust realism. For McGarry and O'Leary, power-sharing falls short of the standards of classic liberal democracy, yes, but in the context of violent conflict it is often the only just, workable solution (2006b, 276; 2007, 671). Referring to Bosnia's deeply dysfunctional power-sharing system, implemented as part of the 1995 Dayton Peace Accord, McGarry argues, '20 years after Dayton, most people [in BiH] would accept it again, warts and all' (2017). What's more, McGarry and O'Leary maintain that the more flexible and inclusive liberal consociation answers a number of the critics' concerns (McGarry and O'Leary 2009). Pragmatically, Bell concedes that in most of the places it has been implemented, power-sharing is the 'only game in town', so must be engaged by feminists and other critics to make it more inclusive (Bell 2015).

But how do the principles of civic solidarity and consociational power sharing sit together? Decidedly uneasily. The most obvious clash is over *identity*. Theories of civic solidarity see identity through a constructivist and intersectional lens. It is never a given thing; always fluid, contextual, and relational; always in process, never finished (Hall 1990 in Cockburn 1998, 212). What's more, identity is *performed*: something one does rather than something one has (Collins and Bilge 2020, 167). Identity is therefore inherently *coalitional*, continually forming solidarities with others. It can even be *strategic*, with one choosing to mobilize a particular politically salient identity category at a particular moment in time for their best advantage (Collins and Bilge 2020, 163, 186). One's multiple identities are interconnected and 'co-forming' according to Collins and Bilge: they cannot be separated out or ranked (2020, 168).[10] Consociational theory treats identity as a more solid category. While McGarry and O'Leary acknowledge that identity is socially constructed, they regard it as nevertheless durable. In places like Northern Ireland those identities have defined politics for hundreds of years; they cannot be wished away (2006b, 271; 2009, 70). Identity is recognized as the basis for designing political institutions. Ascriptive identities and affiliations – particularly ethnonational – are deemed to run deeper politically than those chosen such as socialism or environmentalism. Other identities, like gender, are acknowledged but deemed lower order to ethnonational identity, in political salience (McGarry and O'Leary 2009). Under power sharing, identity is treated in a binary, either/or, way. This precludes accommodating multiple and intersecting identities in the political system (Byrne and McCulloch 2017). 'Consociationalism scholars do not pay attention to non-ethnicized resistance or advocacy because it is politics in excess of the theory – a theory laser-focused on an ethnonational story of conflict', as Byrne puts it (2020, 65).[11]

Another misfit concerns their *concepts of politics*. Civic solidarity, while it can and does make the transition to institutional politics, is situated within the realm of contentious politics. It originates as a *bottom-up* phenomenon, from activism over issues that draw people together to address a particular need. Consociation is an overwhelmingly *top-down* enterprise, centring on the cooperation of political elites who are supposed to represent relatively homogenous groups. Consociational theory grants little agency to bottom-up political activism outside of the formal structures of institutions, such as social movements. A core criticism of consociation is that it is elite-dominated and requires a 'passive and deferential role for all nonelite groups' (Lijphart 1977, 49), that it remains insulated from civil society and the integrating force it could exert (Wilford 2010,

149; Wilson 2010, 18; Nagle 2011, 173; Byrne and McCulloch 2017). Viewing 'other' identities like gender and class as important at the personal or social level but not at the political level, consociation betrays a narrower, more masculinized definition of politics that centres the institutional. Theories of civic solidarity take a broader, feminist view of politics as also pertaining to informal, non-institutionalized contexts (Mulholland and Patel 1999).

Finally, the apparent *priorities* of civic solidarity and consociation diverge. While civic solidarity tends to emerge out of quests for *justice* (such as gender equality and anti-violence), consociation arises out of an over-riding concern for *peace* and stability. Scholars admit that conflict resolution strategies can entail a trade-off between the two, and power-sharing weighs more heavily on the side of peace (albeit negative peace) (Bell 2015; Stojanović 2018). Civic coalitions, on the other hand, generally prioritize justice and equality – which may entail radical transformation and rupture that destabilizes the post-conflict order (Mackay and Murtagh 2019). Indeed, in places like Lebanon and Bosnia, the discourse of 'stability' and 'security' has been used to maintain power-sharing and resist reforms, in spite of its dysfunctions and injustices (Nagle 2020, 140; Bieber 2018).[12] This state is highly impervious to bottom-up movements for social justice.

Given these tensions, how might we expect civic parties to mobilize in power-sharing systems?

How Do Civic Parties Navigate Power-Sharing Systems?

In probing how civic parties are impacted by power-sharing and, in turn, navigate that system, this book pursues an institutional analysis. Institutions – broadly conceived – are critical to understanding political behaviour and outcomes. I conceive of institutions in line with Hall and Taylor's description, as 'the formal and informal procedures, routines, norms and conventions embedded in the organizational structure of the polity of political economy' (1996, 938). This includes then not only *formal institutions*, such as official rules, regulations, and procedures, but also *informal institutions*, such as conventions, practices, norms, values, and ideas – 'socially shared rules, usually unwritten, that are created, communicated and enforced outside of officially sanctioned channels' (Helmke and Levitsky 2004, 727). Here I borrow from feminist institutionalism[13] to see informal rules as 'hidden and embedded in the everyday practices …

disguised as standard and taken-for-granted practices and norms' (Chappell 2014, 576), more elusive to analysis but no less determining (Mackay et al 2010, 580). I treat formal and informal institutions as two ends of the same spectrum and see the interplay between them as critical to explaining political outcomes (Mackay et al 2010, 576).

Institutional Barriers

On the face of it then, consociation creates an inhospitable environment for civic solidarity. The *formal institutions* of consociational power-sharing – grand coalition government, proportional representation of groups, group autonomy in specific areas, and group veto – present direct and obvious barriers to civic parties. For a start, they appear blind to civic parties' existence. Each is predicated on the representation, inclusion, and empowerment of the main ethnic groups, with no recognition for groups mobilizing on other bases or across multiple ethnic identities. Grand coalition entails automatic or assisted entry into government for the main ethnic groups primarily. Likewise, proportional representation grants access to power and public goods to members of those groups, giving them a clear competitive advantage over others. Group autonomy assigns ethnic groups relative independence over certain policy areas like culture and education, with no such power handed to civic coalitions. This can clearly marginalize civic parties from power and relevance in that realm. At a deeper level, it could even frustrate civic agendas in spheres like education and culture. The group veto empowers ethnonational groups and grants them protection in the legislative process, effectively by allowing them to block policy agendas that they oppose on those grounds. This veto clearly leaves civic parties at a competitive disadvantage – lacking any such protection – and may well be used to block civic agendas that may be perceived and presented as threatening ethnic interests. Each of these institutional structures has direct effects but also indirect: shaping public understandings of politics and conditioning voter behaviour. Combined, they have the potential to leave civic parties marginalized and excluded from power and their agendas potentially contested or even co-opted.

At the *informal institutional level*, the 'unwritten rules' of consociational systems could be expected to reinforce these formal barriers. Here we are dealing with the social and cognitive features of institutions, not least shared understandings and frames, ideas, and discourse (Hall and Taylor 1996, 947; Mackay et al 2010, 575). This includes the dominant political discourse in operation, as well as informal systems like patronage, political attitudes, and shared logics of political representation. Consociation enforces a dominant, singular *discourse* of ethnonationalism. I understand discourse as sanctioned knowledge in a given context, formed through political interaction; 'what is "in the true" and, hence, what it is possible to speak of' (Bacchi and Rönnblom 2014, 174). The dominant discourse in a given political context, helps explain why certain ideas succeed and others fail (Schmidt 2008, 305). It shapes the way ideas are interpreted and heard, what ideas and issues are admissible for the political agenda and what issues are not, what issues gain traction and how issues must be framed in order to gain traction. In the dominant discourse of power-sharing, the understanding of society as divided along singular lines is accepted and all politics is thus filtered through this ethnonational lens. This renders other forms of identity and affiliation invisible and provides no language, no frame of reference, for civic solidarity. This manifests notably in political debate – the speech of political representatives in the institutions and beyond and in the media – in the way in which politics is filtered, interpreted, and represented to the public. In this singular ethnic frame, civic political actors can find themselves *marginalized* and ignored. At other times, they can find themselves *contested*, as civic solidarity is perceived as a threat to the ethnonational status quo: portrayed as irrelevant, as weak and even traitorous to ethnonational solidarity. In a discourse that does not always see civic solidarity, civic coalitions can also find themselves vulnerable to *co-optation* by ethnonational forces.

Beyond discourse, consociational power-sharing, by granting ethnonational parties considerable autonomy in the institutions and over 'their groups', arguably facilitates the informal practice of ethnonational *patronage and clientelism* – already deeply problematic in ethnically divided societies. Chandra describes a 'patronage-democracy' as one in which the state monopolizes access to jobs and services and in which elected officials have discretion in the implementation of laws allocating the jobs and services at the disposal of the state – and to do so on an individualized basis (2004, 6). In a landmark study into ethnic parties in India, she establishes a firm link between ethnic mobilization and patronage (Chandra 2004, 14–15). Ethnonational patronage and clientelism poses clear disadvantages and dilemmas for civic parties and groups that operate outside these networks. Public attitudes towards politics and, moreover, the relationship between civil society (or politics at the grassroots level) and the political realm (politics at the formal level) are critical conditions for civic politics; when that link is complex, ethnicized, or disconnected, as we see in many divided societies, civic parties struggle to take hold. The practice of ethnic proportionality also ingrains a 'logic of ethnic representation' in the minds of voters whereby in Bosnia, Bosniaks should be represented by Bosniaks, Croats by Croats, in Lebanon, Sunnis should be represented by Sunnis, and so on (see also Deets and Skulte-Ouaiss 2021).

Openings and Agency

Yet, while taking institutions seriously I acknowledge that outcomes for civic parties are shaped by both structure and *agency* – their actions and choices, including using institutions as a strategic resource (Chappell 2014, 575; Mackay 2014, 591). As well as being constrained by power-sharing institutions, then, civic parties also hold the capacity to strategically navigate those institutions: to resist, adapt to, and even find critical openings within them. Certain strategic choices stand out as being potentially pivotal – and tricky – for civic parties. Particularly determining is how they *position themselves* relative to the divide, how they *engage with power-sharing*, the *issue space* they occupy, their *policies* on ethnonationally contentious issues, and their *electoral strategies*.

A critical decision for civic parties – and key point of variation between them – is how they position themselves with respect to the ethnonational divide in society. I previously classified civic parties along a spectrum from *accommodationist* to *integrationist* (Murtagh 2020). Here I add a third category of *intersectional* parties that operate beyond that binary spectrum.

Accommodationist parties are those that recognize the ethnonational divide and seek to accommodate different groups within their organization. They tend to accept the need for consociational power-sharing and seek to adapt to its ethnonational structures, perhaps even mirroring them in their own internal organization through internal ethnic quotas for party positions, candidate lists, etc. Accommodationist parties may present themselves as 'multi-ethnic', resembling a pluralistic alliance of separate ethnic groups, or 'cross-ethnic', making an explicit virtue of their attempt to reach across the ethnic or ethnonational divide as part of a peace and reconciliation agenda. They tend to take a 'cross-community' approach and advance policies that celebrate diversity and multiculturalism and recognize the distinct segments that make up society, including separate but equal schooling. When it comes to electoral mobilization, they tend to adopt a differentiated strategy that takes ethnonational representation and ethno-territorial spread into account in terms of voters, seats, and districts targeted and candidates selected. Parties that embody accommodationist traits include the early Alliance Party of Northern Ireland (following its formation in 1970), the Social Democratic Party (SDP) in Bosnia, the People's Democratic Party (PDP) in Nigeria (Kendhammer 2010, 51) and the Congress Party in India (Bogaards 2014, 46).

Integrationist parties, on the other hand, seek to move beyond the ethnonational divide towards a more integrated society. They appeal to voters on an individual basis with little or no reference to ethnic group identity, rather positioning themselves as 'normal' parties with broad policy agendas. They tend to oppose, or at least take greater issue with, consociational power-sharing, its accommodationist principles standing in contradiction to their own. Integrationist parties may present themselves as 'non-ethnic', campaigning on alternative issues and cleavages, such as class, environment or socially 'progressive' issues, and attempting to transcend the ethnic cleavage and move towards a more issue-based politics. They tend to take a 'one community' approach with emphasis on human rights and equality and oppose policies that recognize communal differences, such as segregated housing and education. They eschew policies such as ethnic quotas, either for elected office and public administration or internally within their own parties. In terms of electoral mobilization, they strive to take a more standardized, uniform approach that does not take ethnonational representation or ethno-territorial spread specifically into account. Examples of integrationist parties include the contemporary Alliance Party of Northern Ireland, the African National Congress (ANC) in South Africa (Bogaards 2014, 82), and the historic Communist Party in Cyprus (Coakley 2009a, 469).

Intersectional parties, meanwhile, go beyond this either/or binary between integration and accommodation, appealing to voters on an individual basis while acknowledging and allowing for ethnic group identity, among other group identities. They see ethnic identity as intersecting with the primary issue/allegiance on which their party mobilizes – be that gender, social justice, environmentalism, or another cause – without making ethnicity central to their orientation. Intersectional parties may present themselves as 'post-ethnic', recognizing the distinct ethnic identities in society but viewing those as fluid and overlapping, with solidarity possible on common civic interests (Touquet 2011). Intersectional parties take a more flexible and strategic approach to the identity divide than either accommodationist or integrationist parties. They tend to pragmatically accept the power-sharing system and seek to navigate it to their best advantage, which may entail, for example, members designating as a particular ethnic group in order to assume positions reserved for that group. They celebrate the internal diversity of their parties and while taking a strong stance on the issues that are core to their organization (e.g. human rights, climate change). They tend to eschew fixed collective positions on contentious policy issues such as constitutional change, not necessarily avoiding them, but preferring to deal with them through internal dialogue and deliberation. Their electoral mobilization tends to reflect this pragmatism and strategic use of identity where opportunities arise. Examples of intersectional parties include the Green Party Northern Ireland and Naša Stranka in Bosnia.

These positionings are ideal types, not fixed categories nor mutually exclusive. In reality, parties do not always fit neatly into one grouping. They exist on a spectrum on which they may move over time, often strategically, in response to institutional incentives. Indeed, parties can display more than one positioning at the same time, sometimes reflecting different strands within the party, that lie in tension with one another (Murtagh 2020). Critically, parties can *strategically adapt their positioning* to their power-sharing environment. A party operating in a rigid corporate power-sharing system that entails ethnic quotas for elected office might adopt an accommodationist positioning, seeking to represent the separate ethnic groups within its party organization so that it can avail of those positions – as the SDP has effected in Bosnia, taking up roles reserved for Bosniaks, Croats, and Serbs (chapter 7). Civic parties might use identity strategically and creatively in this way (explicitly or implicitly), presenting themselves as more accommodationist, integrationist, or intersectional depending on the institutional opportunities that present themselves.

Secondly, civic parties can choose to *engage with the power-sharing institutions* in different ways. The question of how to engage with power-sharing can represent a core dilemma for civic parties, whose principles often run contrary to a system predicated on ethnic representation. In the case of civic movements in Lebanon, Nagle demonstrates three different strategies adopted for engaging in its highly ethnicized power-sharing system: 'hegemonic compliance' where the movement replicates consociational structures, even imposing internal ethnic quotas; 'constructive engagement' where it pragmatically uses the system to achieve reform;

and 'active resistance' where it actively challenges the system (Nagle 2018). Civic parties then may participate fully in the power-sharing institutions, even taking up positions in government reserved for 'others' or indeed different ethnic groups. On the other hand, they might, on principle, decline to participate in a system that contradicts their civic ethos or even campaign for its abolition.

Third, in a system structured around a binary ethnonational divide, civic parties must stake out their own distinct *issue space* or niche and choose how to frame it. They must advance an alternative cleavage – be it socio-economic or relating to functionality, accountability, and good governance or social liberalism/conservativism. Occupying this ground, and being seen and heard doing so, is a tricky feat for civic parties. It requires careful navigation to avoid entanglement in ethnonational debates. It also calls for nimble adaptation to seize ground that opens up from societal shifts, like economic crises or so-called 'culture wars' relating to issues like sexuality, gender, and migration.

Fourth, when it comes to *policy*, civic parties face difficult choices in polarized environments where many policy issues are ethnically charged and contentious, not least those concerning cultural expression and constitutional change. Parties may have to choose whether to engage on such issues and take a position (perhaps seeking to occupy a distinct civic niche), allow for a diversity of positions among members, or avoid them entirely. They run the risk of ethnonational contestation on the one hand and marginalization on the other.

Finally, competing in *elections* requires civic parties to make difficult choices. This may include which districts to contest, whether to seek geographic (and ethnonational) spread across the state or consolidate their vote in particular cities or regions, whether to seek ethnonational balance among candidates put forward, etc. These choices can pit electoral growth against the party's civic principles.

Civic parties in power-sharing systems then do have choices, albeit constrained. Those choices are conditioned by their institutional environment and the particular mix of sanctions and incentives it presents. In a system based on ethnonational representation, the options are often double-edged, potentially producing short-term advantages but deeper tensions. Of real interest is how these parties *adapt* to this environment and endure.

By seeing how civic parties have effected this up close in two divided settings, this book seeks to illuminate the broader phenomenon. This bears lessons not just about the impact of particular institutions on civic parties but the strategies civic parties and movements can adopt to prevail in the face of deep division and ethnicized structures. How do the experiences of civic parties in Northern Ireland compare to those in Bosnia and Herzegovina? If we follow the logic of consociational scholars like McGarry and O'Leary (2007) and McCulloch (2014), it would be reasonable to expect civic parties to find more space in more liberal power-sharing systems than more corporate systems where ethnic representation is more strictly inscribed. Northern Ireland, a largely liberal system that officially recognizes other parties (other than nationalist and unioninist) and grants them a role in the institutions, should offer more openings to civic parties than more rigid and ethnicized corporate systems, like Bosnia where seats are reserved for Bosniaks, Croats, and Serbs and others are granted only minimal recognition at the national level. We might also expect to see different strategies adopted in the face of these more ethnicized institutions, with different consequences. If this proves the case, it bears implications for how institutions are designed after conflict and the type of politics they can spawn. These are propositions we probe in the chapters that follow.

Conclusion

This chapter has not sought to introduce a new form of politics emerging in divided societies nor advocate for its possibility. It has shone a light on a politics that already exists but is often rendered invisible: *civic solidarity*. This form of politics remains robust in severely divided places, even in the context of power-sharing institutions that inscribe ethnonational representation. Here we have exposed the agency and resilience of civic solidarity and its viability within power-sharing institutions through civic parties. In so doing, we have pointed the way to a new way of thinking about democracy in divided societies: one where transformation becomes possible from within the institutions. But, having anticipated the political opportunity structure civic parties face in power-sharing systems, and the range of strategic choices they hold to navigate it, how do civic parties fare in a power-sharing system in reality? Let us turn our focus to Northern Ireland to see how the principles translate into practice.

Chapter Two

Northern Ireland, Beyond the Binary

The Northern Ireland elections of 2022 made headlines around the world. For the first time in the contested state's one-hundred-year history, a nationalist party (that champions Irish reunification) had prevailed over its unionist rival (that seeks to maintain the union with Britain). Sinn Féin had emerged on top, with twenty-seven out of ninety seats, to the Democratic Unionist Party (DUP)'s twenty-five, thus entitling it, for the first time, to the post of first minister in Northern Ireland's power-sharing government and effecting an historic feat in a statelet designed to ensure a unionist majority. To add to the rupture, in the wake of the election the DUP refused to enter government and serve as deputy first minister (co-equal to first minister in power, if not in symbolism), ostensibly in protest over the ongoing constitutional crisis around Brexit, leaving the region to continue without a functioning government. The story was one of ethnonational division and constitutional crisis.

Yet, there was another story to be read, one that would make less impact in the international press and did not fit the binary narrative of Northern Ireland politics. A party that was neither nationalist nor unionist emerged in third place in that election. Building on strong performances in three 2019 elections, The Alliance Party of Northern Ireland (APNI) had overtaken moderate nationalist and unionist parties to win 13.5 per cent of the vote and increase its seat share in the power-sharing Assembly from eight to seventeen. Collectively, civic parties had garnered 17 per cent of the vote and 20 per cent of the seats and were now emerging as a distinct bloc alongside unionism and nationalism, threatening to finally break the ethnonational bipolar party system. This story could arguably be equally determining for Northern Ireland's future.

How did we arrive at a point where civic solidarity appears to be rivalling ethnonational polarization? This chapter sets out the context for the rise of civic politics, amidst ethnonational polarization, in Northern Ireland. It introduces the case of Northern Ireland and charts the path of civic politics in the divided polity over the last fifty years, with a particular focus on the post-settlement (post-1998) period. The chapter exposes the consistent presence of civic solidarity amidst ethnonational polarization since the outbreak of the conflict and explores the ways in which it has maintained ground through the peace process and post-Good Friday Agreement power-sharing era – and the crises along the way – before significantly expanding in the last ten years. In the process, it presents the main parties in this field since the agreement – most notably APNI, as well as the Green Party Northern Ireland and People Before Profit, plus the historical Northern Ireland Women's Coalition (1996–2006).

A Stable Presence from Conflict Towards Peace

In light of their recent electoral rise, civic parties in Northern Ireland have begun to attract attention in media and scholarship. Alliance is now considered a 'main party' alongside the four main ethnonational parties which have dominated this space since the 1970s: in order of current size, on the nationalist side Sinn Fein and the Social Democratic and Labour Party (SDLP) and on the unionist side, Democratic Unionist Party (DUP) and Ulster Unionist Party (UUP) (see table 2.1). Yet, civic politics is not a new phenomenon in Northern Ireland, a statelet that was brought into being in 1921 from the partition of Ireland. Throughout Northern Ireland's contested history, political groups have come together across the ethnonational divide and endured – even making the transition to institutional politics as political parties. To be sure, the violent conflict known as the Troubles which emerged in the late 1960s, did not render fertile ground for civic politics. This violence erupted out of a failed and thwarted movement for civil rights after some fifty years of unionist majority rule from the Stormont government in Belfast, discrimination and exclusion of the Catholic minority. As the conflict escalated, the British government reacted by deploying army troops to the region in 1969, a move initially welcomed by many in the Catholic population, but which would later sow hostility between the state and the minority community (Cochrane 1999, 25; Tonge 2005, 14). Spiraling conflict in the shape of sectarian killings, rioting, and forced evictions elicited a violent and disproportionate response by the local security forces, including

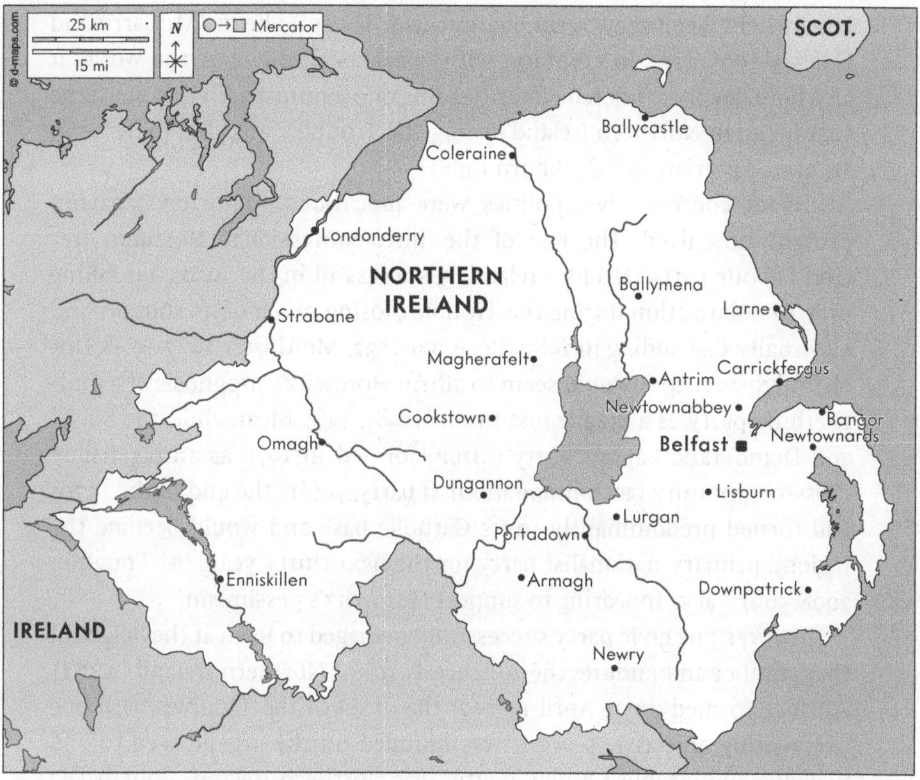

Figure 2.1 | Map of Northern Ireland.

the introduction of internment for suspected members of paramilitary organizations, primarily the Provisional IRA, in 1971 (Cochrane 1999, 25). Meanwhile, recruitment to republican and loyalist paramilitaries increased apace. Amidst the unionist government's wrong-headed response to the crisis, the British government assumed responsibility for security and ultimately for governance as the Stormont Parliament was prorogued and direct rule imposed in 1972 (Tonge 1998, 47). The Troubles would continue for some thirty years, claiming the lives of approximately 3,720 people, leaving 47,541 people injured, and scarring the lives of many more, and the very fabric of society, in countless ways (CAIN 2007). The conflict that unfolded had many dimensions but, centring on the border and the contested nature of the British state in Northern Ireland, to which those in the Protestant/Unionist/Loyalist community were largely loyal and the Catholic/Nationalist/Republican community largely held illegitimate, 'ethnonationalism' lay at its heart (McGarry and O'Leary 1995, 170). In common with conflicts throughout the world, it also bore deeply gendered effects, leading one feminist activist to observe that living in Northern Ireland during the Troubles was akin to living in an 'armed patriarchy' (Cockburn 1998).

In that context, civic politics were precarious. Many civic parties proved short-lived. The fate of the 'inter-confessional' Northern Ireland Labour Party (NILP) – relatively successful in the 1950s but falling prey to polarization during the Troubles, losing much of its support and eventually disbanding in 1987 (Rose 1971, 232; McAllister 1977, 19; Ó Dochartaigh 2021, 4) – would seem to affirm Horowitz's prognosis of a multi-ethnic party as a 'fragile institution' (1985, 396). Meanwhile, the Social and Democratic Labour Party (SDLP) formed in 1970 as an ostensibly cross-community (accommodationist) party, yet by the end of the 1970s had turned predominantly to its Catholic base and would become the region's primary nationalist party for the next thirty years (McLoughlin 2008, 569) – also appearing to support Horowitz's pessimism.

However, one civic party successfully managed to form at the height of that conflict and endure: the Alliance Party of Northern Ireland (APNI). Alliance formed on 21 April 1970, at the onset of the Troubles with one overarching objective: *peace*. It was founded on the urgent need to end violence and establish a new politics for Northern Ireland – one based on *alliance* between Protestants and Catholics. In response to the struggle over civil rights and subsequent outbreak of violence, the New Ulster Movement formed in 1969 as a political pressure group. The group quickly became a springboard for a new party advocating *non-sectarianism*, *anti-violence*, and *democratic reform* (Eggins 2015, 19). Led by a Catholic, Oliver Napier, and a Protestant, Bob Cooper, inter-religious partnership was core to its offering (APNI 1970a; 1970b). The source of Northern Ireland's problems, in Alliance's view, was not partition of the island but the division between Protestants and Catholics within Northern Ireland. Its solution could be found in a 'dual compromise' where Catholics would not face discrimination and Protestants would not be coerced into a united Ireland (Cushnahan 1979). A recruitment poster in 1972 displayed an image of two children sheltering from violence under the caption: 'Think of their Tomorrows. Join Alliance Today'.

As the conflict raged and the search for resolution intensified, Alliance was called upon to play that peacebuilding role. It took part in a short-lived power-sharing experiment, following the 1973 Sunningdale Agreement (Dixon 2001, 143), taking up two ministerial positions in the executive alongside 'moderate' unionist and nationalist parties the Ulster Unionist Party (UUP) and the SDLP. That initiative collapsed after five months, however, in the face of intense opposition from hardline unionist forces outside the process, including an Ulster Worker's Council strike (McEvoy 2015, 49). The party nevertheless continued to contest elections through the 1970s and '80s, averaging a vote share of 8.5 per cent, and to put forward proposals for a political settlement. According to the civic party types outlined in chapter 1, the early Alliance Party then positioned itself (in its name and its appeal), as explicitly *accommodationist.* As we explore in chapter 5, however, in later years the party shifted progressively towards a more integrationist positioning, championing policies such as integrated education and shared housing, while in recent years it has also exhibited an intersectional stance.

A significant step towards peace came in 1985 with the signing of the Anglo-Irish Agreement by the British and Irish governments, which granted the Republic of Ireland a consultative role in the governance of Northern Ireland and an advocacy role on behalf of Catholics in the region (Mitchell 2015, 172). The subsequent 'peace process' which emerged into public awareness in the early 1990s brought both barriers and openings for civic parties. Alliance became less central to peace efforts as the conflict moved on, however, and peace attempts increasingly shifted to focus on: a) partnership between the British and Irish governments (intergovernmentalism), and b) accommodation of nationalism and unionism, extremes and all – with lesser need for a mediating 'middle ground' (Leonard 1999). Secret talks between then leaders of the main nationalist party the SDLP, John Hume and its more 'extreme' republican counterpart aligned with the Provisional IRA, Sinn Féin, Gerry Adams, brought the latter publicly into the process and paved the way for paramilitary ceasefires in 1994 (Tonge 1998, 141).

The announcement of multi-party peace talks two years later, to be chaired by US Senator George Mitchell,[1] provided the impetus for another civic party to enter the scene: the Northern Ireland Women's Coalition (NIWC). Elections to the 110-member Forum for Political Dialogue and Multi-Party Peace Talks were held with the low-threshold system of d'Hondt party list 'plus top-up' to allow ten parties to take part. With the talks only open to parties, driven by the need to include the voices of women and civil society in the process, the new party formed on the eve of the 1996 elections, for the sole purpose of influencing the peace agreement. Women formed the backbone of civil society and community life throughout the Troubles, found themselves severely excluded from formal politics with only three women MPs elected to Westminster in Northern Ireland prior to 1998 (Gilmartin 2019, 91). Thus, this alliance of women of both national affiliations and none, with its roots in the women's movement, effectively seized the opportunity presented by this critical juncture of constitutional change to enter formal politics (Dobrowolsky 2003, 117). The NIWC's appeal to voters was very clearly civic. The diverse grouping united around three core principles – inclusion, human rights, and equality – with a determination to bring these values to bear on the negotiations and the agreement itself (Fearon 1999; Fearon and McWilliams 2000, 121). The NIWC's philosophy embodied the principles of *transversalism* (Murtagh 2008), as explored in chapter 1. While respecting the distinct national identities that exist in Northern Ireland, it maintained that solidarity on other matters was possible. It resisted taking a stance on the constitutional future of Northern Ireland and rather than identifying as neither nationalist nor unionist, the party positioned itself as nationalist, unionist, *and* other (NIWC 1998; Fearon and McWilliams 2000, 124). In this way, the civic party positioned itself in accommodationist but also intersectional terms.

Civic parties left their mark on the settlement that would emerge from those talks in numerous ways. The NIWC wielded an influence far beyond its two seats, securing provisions for a civic forum, a deliberative body representing civil society that would sit alongside the Northern Ireland Assembly (which was established in 2000 but suspended with the Assembly in 2002 and never reinstated), victims' rights, women's rights, integrated education, and mixed housing (Fearon 1999; Kilmurray and McWilliams 2011). The party also played a key mediating and facilitating role, meeting with both Sinn Féin and the loyalist Ulster Democratic Party (UDP) when those parties were excluded from the talks (Kilmurray and McWilliams 2011). Alliance, which secured seven seats, was influential in securing the electoral system adopted for the new power-sharing Assembly (PR-STV) and, crucially, the recognition of 'others' in the power-sharing institutions, alongside unionists and nationalists (Leonard 1999). It also played a 'policing' role in the negotiations, monitoring enforcement of the 'Mitchell principles' – ground rules for the talks – and

Table 2.1 | Political parties in Northern Ireland

	Party name (translated)	*Formed*	*Positioning*	*Constitutional position*
UUP	Ulster Unionist Party	1905	Moderate unionist; centre right	Maintain union with Great Britain
DUP	Democratic Unionist Party	1971	Hard-line unionist; conservative	Maintain union with Great Britain
SDLP	Social Democratic and Labour Party	1970	Moderate nationalist; social democratic	United Ireland with the consent of the people of Northern Ireland
Sinn Féin	'We Ourselves'	1970 (current form) 1905 (original form)	Hard-line nationalist / republican; democratic socialist	United Ireland
APNI	Alliance Party of Northern Ireland	1970	Civic; nationally non-aligned; liberal	No change to the constitutional status of Northern Ireland until a majority of people consent to such a change
GPNI	Green Party Northern Ireland	1985	Civic; environmental and social justice	Does not campaign for constitutional change to the status of Northern Ireland
PBP	People Before Profit Alliance	2005	Civic; democratic socialist	United Ireland

Table 2.2 | Alliance Party electoral performance 1973–97

Year	*Election*	*% vote*
1973	Council	13.7
1973	Assembly	9.2
1974	Westminster (February)	3.2
1974	Westminster (October)	6.3
1975	Convention	9.8
1977	Council	14.4
1979	Westminster	11.9
1979	European	6.8
1981	Council	8.9
1982	Assembly	9.3
1983	Westminster	8.0
1984	European	5.0
1985	Council	7.1
1987	Westminster	10.0
1989	Council	6.9
1989	European	5.2
1992	Westminster	8.7
1993	Council	7.6
1994	European	4.1
1996	Forum	6.5
1997	Westminster	4.7
1997	Council	4.7

Source: http://www.ark.ac.uk/elections/.

censuring other parties for contravening those rules (Farry and Neeson 1999, 1233; Mitchell 2002, 127).

Yet, civic parties were also marginalized in some ways during the negotiations. Leonard observes, the inclusion of the 'extremes' undermined the argument that Alliance was a pivotal core to discussions and shifted the debate towards solutions based on accommodation and away from those based on integration, which the party championed (Leonard 1999). The centrepiece of the ultimate agreement was of course, conscociational power-sharing, a system designed to ultimately accommodate unionism and nationalism with little thought for civic actors. Both NIWC and Alliance wholeheartedly endorsed the agreement and, despite some misgivings on the part of the latter about power-sharing, supported the system as a means towards peace.

Peace Agreement

After some two years of often tumultuous talks, on Good Friday 10 April 1998, those negotiations finally culminated in the signing of the Belfast ('Good Friday') Agreement by the two governments and eight of the major parties. The agreement marked the beginning of a new era for Northern Ireland: power-sharing between nationalists and unionists. It set out the democratic institutions within Northern Ireland, devolved from Westminster, as well as its relations with the United Kingdom and the Republic of Ireland. Broad inclusion (encompassing the 'extremes' on each side) and British–Irish intergovernmental cooperation were the defining features and most notable departures from the power-sharing experiment of 1973 (McLoughlin 2012, 177). At the heart of the agreement was a recognition of two competing ethnonational groups with divergent aspirations and mutual security concerns and an attempt to address their fears and accommodate their goals within a new political configuration (Mitchell 2015, 26). It put in place a Northern Ireland Assembly and Executive based on the principles of consociational power-sharing whereby unionist and nationalist communities would be recognized and each guaranteed proportional representation in legislature and government as well as veto powers.

The agreement extended well beyond internal power-sharing arrangements, to comprise a complex package of mechanisms, including elements of self-government, federalism, and confederalism as well as external dimensions (McGarry and O'Leary 2006a; McGarry and O'Leary 2009; McEvoy 2015, 64; Wolff 2009, 120; O'Leary 2019). It contained three strands: Strand One dealing with matters internal to Northern Ireland (the establishment of a power-sharing assembly and executive); Strand Two with Northern Ireland's relations with the Irish Republic and the establishment of the North–South Ministerial Council (NSMC) and North–South Implementation Bodies; and Strand Three covering relations with the British government and the establishment of 'East–West' institutions the British–Irish Council and the British–Irish Intergovernmental Conference. The agreement also comprised extensive human rights and equality provisions, including the establishment of an Equality Commission and a Human Rights Commission and a commitment to incorporate the European Convention of Human Rights (ECHR) into Northern Ireland law. The critical issues of policing reform and decommissioning of weapons were delegated to independent commissions (see Walsh 2017).

The issue of sovereignty and statehood, fundamental to the conflict, was navigated by enshrining the principle of *consent*. The agreement committed that Northern Ireland would remain within the United Kingdom until a majority of the people in Northern Ireland wished otherwise (McGarry and O'Leary 2006a, 56).[2] Meanwhile, Articles 2 and 3 of the Republic of Ireland's Constitution were amended, following a referendum, to remove the state's territorial claim to Northern Ireland. The settlement also adopted a creative, pluralistic approach to identity, giving the people of Northern Ireland the right to identify as British or Irish or both and allowing for dual citizenship (Mitchell 2015, 31). The agreement was ratified in simultaneous referenda in Northern Ireland and the Irish Republic, supported by 71 per cent of voters in the former and 94 per cent in the latter (ARK 1998b)

The Power-Sharing Institutions

The barriers to civic parties in the political system established by the GFA are both real and obvious. The power-sharing institutions – primarily the Northern Ireland Executive and Assembly – are explicitly designed to accommodate nationalism and unionism. Firmly rooted in the principles of consociation, sketched out in chapter 1, they feature, to varying degrees: executive power-sharing between groups in an inclusive coalition; proportional representation of parties in the legislature and executive; mutual vetoes for both groups; and relative autonomy for each group in certain policy areas (Horowitz 2002a, 194; Lijphart 1977, 25–44; O'Leary 2019). On entering the Assembly representatives must designate as 'Nationalist', 'Unionist', or 'Other' to facilitate these group protections (Standing Orders of NI Assembly 2024). To make up the broadly inclusive Northern Ireland Executive, made up of eight departmental ministers, parties that wish to participate are allocated seats proportionally using d'Hondt, a formula based on party strengths in the Assembly. Leading that executive, the first and deputy first ministers – co-equal positions, despite the misleading titles – are nominated through a separate process, by the largest and second largest parties, respectively, in the largest and second largest designations (Nationalist, Unionist, or Other) (McEvoy 2015) and one may not hold office without the other (Northern Ireland Act 1998). In the case that the largest party is not from the largest designation, however, that party can still nominate a first minister, and the largest party from the largest designation is entitled to nominate the deputy first minister (Northern Ireland Act 1998). The electoral system, Single Transferrable Vote (STV), facilitates proportional representation of ethnonational groups in the Assembly through 'their' respective parties, while the preferential aspect facilitates the possibility of cross-ethnic transfers (voters awarding lower order preferences to parties outside their core ethnic bloc) (Reilly 2001, 131). As for mutual veto, Assembly rules ensure concurrent majorities among nationalists and unionists via so-called 'cross-community votes' on certain high stakes decisions and on those relating to the communal divide – in which the votes of Others do not count towards the concurrent majority. These votes can be triggered by a 'Petition of Concern' signed by thirty members (McEvoy 2013, 254). The 2006 St Andrew's Agreement also introduced a veto into the Executive, where if a decision cannot be achieved by consensus, any three members, out of ten, can require the subsequent vote to be taken on a cross-community basis.[3] By way of group autonomy, each community enjoys some policy independence, most notably in culture and particularly education, with separate, proportionally funded primary and secondary school systems (Fontana 2017; Coakley 2009b, 124).

Northern Ireland's consociation is generally classed as 'liberal' (flexible and largely civic in nature) as opposed to 'corporate' (rigid and ethnic in nature) in that it is designed to accommodate any group that emerges as salient through elections, rather than pre-defined quotas of specified groups, as seen in Bosnia and Herzegovina and Lebanon (McGarry and O'Leary 2009, 36; McCulloch 2014a, 503). Nevertheless, it does bear some corporate elements: ethnonational groups are named (in the requirement to designate as Nationalist, Unionist, or Other) and privileged in the cross-community voting procedures (McCulloch 2014a, 506).

Power-Sharing in Practice

The practice of power-sharing has been decidedly rocky. The institutions have been out of operation about 40 per cent of the time since established in 1998, acutely prone to disputes between the main power-sharing parties – initially the more moderate unionists and nationalists the UUP and SDLP from 1998–2003, followed by the more hardline Democratic Unionist party (DUP) and Sinn Féin from 2003–present (McClements 2022b). The system has been collapsed on six occasions, with one period of non-functioning lasting five years, 2002–07, following disputes over disarmament and security issues, and another three years

2017–20, following a corruption scandal plus a series of rows relating to ethnonational identity, transitional justice, and broader equality. The institutions collapsed once again in February 2022 when the DUP withdrew in protest over the Brexit protocol and were not reestablished until February 2024. Indeed, five cross-party, British government brokered, agreements have come in the wake of the Good Friday Agreement, generally aimed at resolving such crises.[4] Most notable have been the 2006 St Andrew's Agreement and the 2020 New Decade New Approach, both of which re-established power-sharing between DUP and Sinn Féin and introduced various tweaks to the system along the way. So, how have civic politics fared in this journey?

The years that followed the Good Friday Agreement were tumultuous, for Northern Ireland politics generally and civic politics specifically. The 108-member Assembly was elected in 1998 and the power-sharing Executive formed with the four main parties – on the unionist side, the UUP and DUP and on the nationalist, the SDLP and Sinn Féin – with the UUP and SDLP (the 'moderates' and largest parties of each bloc) awarded the co-premier positions of first minister and deputy first minister respectively. Alliance and NIWC garnered just over 8 per cent of the votes and eight seats in the 108-member Assembly. Some significant progress was made during this period in terms of peace and security. Weapons were officially decommissioned in 2005 and the new Police Service of Northern Ireland, to replace the contested Royal Ulster Constabulary, came into force in 2001. But this came against the backdrop of political instability and continual crisis. The institutions were suspended on four occasions between 2000 and 2007, primarily over disputes between the main power-sharing partners, UUP and SDLP, over progress on weapons decommissioning (McEvoy 2015, 78). The longest suspension lasted five years from 2002–07. This was a challenging period for civic parties. The continual crises saw them at times in danger of becoming 'collateral damage'. In 2001 three members of Alliance strategically 're-designated' from Other to Unionist while NIWC's two members redesignated, one to Unionist and one to Nationalist, in a bid to ensure sufficient unionist support under Assembly rules to reinstall then First Minister David Trimble and save the institutions from collapse (Mitchell 2015, 178). Against this backdrop, the 'centre ground' contracted: in the 2003 elections the NIWC lost the two seats it gained in 1998, while Alliance's vote share shrank from 6.5 per cent to 3.7 per cent. The traditional 'extremes' of each bloc,

DUP and Sinn Féin also replaced the more moderate UUP and SDLP as the largest parties.

In November 2006 the St Andrews Agreement (SAA) signed by the main political parties and the British and Irish governments, finally restored the Assembly and Executive the following year. In a trade-off between the two largest parties, the deal saw Sinn Féin agree to accept the legitimacy of the Police Service of Northern Ireland (PSNI), and DUP agree to share power with Sinn Féin. The SAA also introduced a number of reforms to the operation of power-sharing, including to the election of first and deputy first ministers (McEvoy 2015, 94).[5] However, focusing on the two largest parties it also represented something of a narrowing from the broad inclusion of the GFA and its emphasis on broader human rights and equality agendas, including gender equality (Rouse 2016).

After Assembly elections in March 2007, power-sharing resumed in May with the unlikely partners of Sinn Féin and the DUP at the helm. Civic parties' fortunes were revived somewhat: they collectively garnered 7 per cent of the vote and Alliance was joined by the Green Party Northern Ireland in the Assembly (see table 2.3). Mobilizing on a platform of environmental and social justice, the party had grown out of the Northern Ireland Ecology Party launched in 1983, before changing its name in 1985 and becoming a region of the Green Party of Ireland in 2006. In line with the civic party classification set out in chapter 1, the Greens could be categorized as an intersectional party, mobilizing on an alternative axis to the ethnonational one.

This second phase of power-sharing saw some significant progress towards peace and political stability, not least the transfer of justice powers to the Northern Ireland Executive through the Hillsborough Agreement of 2010. Given the historically contentious nature of policing and justice between nationalists and unionists in Northern Ireland, Alliance was awarded the Justice ministry through a special 'cross-community' vote outside of the normal d'Hondt procedures. Yet, this was also a period of volatility and crisis. The terrain of the conflict began to perceptibly shift from issues of physical peace and security (weapons, policing, etc.) to security with respect to culture and identity. Symbolic issues like Orange Order parading, flags, and emblems rose to the fore in a society still marked by deep segregation and sectarianism, not least in education and housing, with the number of 'peace walls' at the interface of Protestant and Catholic neighbourhoods increasing after 1998 (around ninety-seven in total as of 2017) (Belfast Interfaces Project 2017; García Alcaraz 2024) and only around 7 per cent of children taught in integrated schools (Department of Education, NI). This all took shape against a backdrop of recession and economic austerity, imposed by a UK Conservative-led government after 2010. This was also a period in which gender rights and LGBTQ+ rights rose up the political agenda, not least abortion and marriage equality. Developments in the rest of the UK and the Republic of Ireland exposed the lagging progress on these rights in Northern Ireland and by 2015 it was the only part of the UK where same-sex marriage remained illegal.

The institutions, still led by DUP and Sinn Féin, came close to collapse on a number of occasions. The year 2012 witnessed the most serious challenge to the peace process in a decade as violent loyalist protests erupted over a decision to discontinue the flying of the Union Flag over Belfast City Council every day of the year (Nolan 2013). What's more, in an ironic twist, Alliance found itself the central target of this violence, having proposed the compromise option of flying the flag on designated days, and holding the balance of power in the council. The rise of contentious cultural and symbolic issues (including flags, parading, and dealing with the past) led to another round of talks in 2014 and the signing of the Stormont House Agreement by the British and Irish governments and most of the parties in the Executive. This included a number of reforms to the power-sharing institutions, most notably provisions for an official opposition at Stormont for those parties that declined to take the seats to which they are entitled in the Executive.[6]

Just a few months later, however, the institutions were plunged into further crisis over allegations of continued links between Sinn Féin and the IRA. Another series of negotiations culminated in the signing of A Fresh Start in 2015, which delivered a financial package for the region in return for a pledge by the parties to implement controversial UK government welfare reforms, amongst other measures.[7] Meanwhile, the power-sharing veto in the Assembly known as the Petition of Concern became increasingly controversial and a sticking point between power-sharing partners. The veto had been triggered on occasion on issues not overtly relating to community protection. Most notably, nationalist parties used the veto to block the implementation of UK welfare reforms in Northern Ireland in 2015, while the DUP wielded it the same year to block the legalization of same sex marriage (McDonald 2015a; 2015b). In the 2016 Assembly election, the DUP and Sinn Féin again prevailed, while the other parties entitled to seats in the Executive (UUP, SDLP and Alliance) opted to remain in opposition. An Independent Unionist member replaced Alliance in the role of Justice minister.

Interestingly, during this turbulent second phase of power-sharing post-2007, amidst polarization and continued societal segregation, societal attitudes suggested a widening of civic space. In a 2015 survey, 40 per cent of people identified as neither unionist nor nationalist (with 33 per cent identifying as unionist and 25 per cent as nationalist) (ARK 2015), an increase from 30 per cent in 1999 (ARK 1999). Meanwhile, in the 2011 census, 29 per cent of people identified as Northern Irish first and 21 per cent as Northern Irish only, compared with 40 per cent as British only and 25 per cent as Irish only (NISRA 2011).

The civic bloc in politics also managed to grow in size, power, relevance, and pluralism. The Alliance was awarded the Justice Ministry in 2010 and a second seat in the Executive after the 2011 election through regular d'Hondt procedures. The party's share of the vote in the Assembly rose from 5 per cent in 2007 to 7 per cent in 2016. Beyond the Assembly, Alliance pulled off the dramatic feat of breaking through into Westminster in 2010 with then Deputy Leader Naomi Long winning its first seat in the UK Parliament, unseating then DUP leader Peter Robinson in East Belfast, a former DUP stronghold. In 2016 the highly effective and electorally successful Naomi Long succeeded David Ford as Alliance leader, further adding to the party's appeal. As noted, Alliance was joined in the Assembly in 2007 by the Green Party, which won one seat in 2007, held it in 2011, and increased to two seats in 2016. Meanwhile, in 2013 the short-lived NI21 Party, which split from UUP, also opted to designate as Other. In 2016 the People Before Profit (PBP) Alliance, a leftist civic party operating across the island, broke through to win a seat. Like the Greens, PBP could be categorized as an intersectional civic party, seeking to mobilize voters on another dimension to the ethnonational one (in this case, class or socialist ideology). The combined vote share of civic parties increased from 8 per cent in 1998 to 12 per cent in 2016.

Expansion Amid Crisis

Despite the continual crises that erupted post-2007, power-sharing nevertheless rumbled on and held together for ten years. That relative stability came to an end in 2017, when the institutions collapsed and remained so for three years. This marked a new phase of political crisis for Northern

Ireland: one of a different order to that seen in the previous ten years, now somewhat existential. The UK's vote to leave the European Union (EU) in June 2016 marked a critical juncture that fundamentally changed the parameters of Northern Ireland politics. Narrowly passed in the UK as a whole, by 52 per cent, the referendum was not supported by a majority in Northern Ireland where 56 per cent voted to remain. Supported by only one main party, DUP, the Brexit campaign had gone largely under the radar, and now the result came as a rude awakening. As the UK government moved towards a 'hard Brexit' (quitting the Single Market and Customs Union) under new Conservative Prime Minister Theresa May, the impossibility of Northern Ireland remaining fully aligned with the UK in terms of customs and trade while also maintaining a seamless land border with the Irish Republic became apparent. And so, the spectre was raised of a 'hard border' between Northern Ireland and the Irish Republic (soon to become the land frontier between the UK and EU), that had been consigned to history during the peace process.

Brexit thus fundamentally undermined the principles of the Good Friday Agreement that was based not just on power-sharing within Northern Ireland but on confederal linkages both east–west and north–south. The move pitted Strands Two and Three of the agreement against one other, imposing an either/or choice that contradicted the very spirit of the settlement (Murphy and Hayward 2018). Brexit effectively pulled the rug from under the deal, which was underlain by common British Irish EU membership and the common interests that arose from that (Guelke 2019). As Brendan O'Leary puts it, 'in 1998 all Northern Irish futures had presupposed a European roof', (2018, 229). The new reality posed potentially grave implications for Northern Ireland's peace and security, economy and politics – none of which had evidently caught the attention of those driving the vote at Westminster.

If the 'border question' had been parked by Good Friday Agreement's principle of consent, it was now very much back in play (Guelke 2019). Immediately, the prospect of Irish unification arose as a potential route back to EU membership for Northern Ireland and a solution to the border dilemma, and, for the first time in generations, started to garner serious consideration not just by Sinn Féin but with new civic nationalist groups that began to emerge, calling for the Irish government to respond to these demands. On the other side, the accelerating debate provoked existential fears among unionists and a retrenchment of the position of unionist parties, most notably DUP, which has resisted any form of special status of Northern Ireland that would see it diverge from the rest of the UK. The party first obstructed a deal between the UK and EU and later, when such a deal had been reached in the shape of the Northern Ireland Protocol, suspended the operation of power-sharing in Belfast, walking out in protest in February 2022. In this way, Brexit pitted nationalists and unionists against one another, compromised the British government's position as neutral arbiter, severely damaged British–Irish relations and, overall, posed a serious threat to the peace process (see Guelke 2017; Guelke 2019; Hayward 2018; Hayward and Murphy 2018; O'Leary 2018; O'Leary 2019; O'Leary 2022; Keating 2022; Walsh 2024).

Against this backdrop, a more homegrown crisis was brewing at Stormont. After just eight months, the new DUP–Sinn Féin power-sharing Executive collapsed when the nationalist party withdrew its support over a number of disputes with its unionist partner. Chief among these was a scandal over a botched renewable heating initiative scheme in which the DUP leader was embroiled, but others were the party's failure to agree to Irish language legislation (promised in the SAA), its use of the veto to block same-sex marriage, and the failure to agree on proposals to deal with Troubles legacies. Ten years of uninterrupted power-sharing abruptly came to a close. A three-year crisis ensued in which several rounds of talks between the parties and the British and Irish governments and an election in March 2017 failed to bring a resolution. Tensions were exacerbated in June 2017 when, after a snap UK general election, the DUP entered into a 'confidence and supply' arrangement with Theresa May's Conservative government at Westminster, raising serious questions about the UK government's neutrality vis-à-vis Northern Ireland and the DUP's influence over ongoing UK–EU negotiations (Walsh 2024, 8–9).

The fallout of 2017 bore many continuities and was in some ways a culmination of tensions fermenting for several years, surrounding identity, dealing with the past and broader human rights, particularly those relating to gender and sexuality. Yet, there was a difference this time. The calculations of the main parties had clearly shifted and it appeared that neither Sinn Féin nor the DUP had their sights focused on Stormont. Amidst the political vacuum, movements for Irish language rights and broader human rights persisted. Pressure to decriminalize abortion increased as the Republic of Ireland voted by referendum in 2018 to remove a constitutional ban on abortion. In October 2019, legislation was brought forward from Westminster to legalize same-sex marriage and abortion, bypassing Stormont.

The logjam was finally broken in January 2020 when, after another UK general election in December 2019 called by new Prime Minister Boris Johnson, in which DUP and Sinn Féin performed poorly, the secretary of state for Northern Ireland threatened fresh Assembly elections if a deal was not done.[8] Minds were focused and the New Decade New Approach Agreement (NDNA) was signed which reinstated power-sharing, this time with the five parties back in government, including the Alliance again in the Justice Ministry. The agreement included a number of reforms to power-sharing, not least to veto rules and executive power-sharing, as discussed in chapter 3.[9]

Under the severe strain of the twin crises of the COVID-19 pandemic and the ongoing row over Brexit, the new power-sharing government held for a time. Nevertheless, after two years, the DUP brought it down once again. The protocol on Ireland/Northern Ireland agreed between the UK and EU in December 2020 as part of the EU–UK Trade and Co-operation Agreement (TCA), to avoid a hard border on the island of Ireland effectively placed a customs border in the Irish Sea, at ports between Northern Ireland and Great Britain. Viewed by unionist parties and loyalist groups as undermining the Union, the protocol has been a source of deep discontent and protest.[10] In February 2022 DUP First Minister Paul Givan resigned from his post, bringing the Executive down with him (as, under the rules, neither the first minister nor deputy minister can hold office without the other). Assembly elections held in May 2022 – in which Sinn Féin emerged with the most seats and therefore won the right to nominate first minister for the first time, leaving DUP in second place – failed to resolve the impasse (ARK 2022c). The crisis deteriorated as the UK government itself later refused to fully implement the protocol on the basis of its alleged disruption of trade between Northern Ireland and the mainland, and brought forward a bill at Westminster to override parts of the agreement. Yet, under the new leadership of Prime Minister Rishi Sunak, a new deal between the UK and the European Commission, was reached in February 2023, the Windsor Framework. Designed specifically to address the DUP's concerns and get them back into government to restore power-sharing, the agreement amended the protocol by effectively creating a system of green lanes and red lanes, whereby goods travelling from Great Britain set to remain in Northern Ireland would require fewer checks and minimal paperwork. The Windsor Framework initially failed to entice the DUP back into power-sharing and the institutions remained defunct. In the vacuum at Stormont, again, Westminster stepped

Table 2.3 | Party vote share Northern Ireland Assembly elections, 1998–2022

	1998		*2003*		*2007*		*2011*		*2016*		*2017*		*2022*	
	%	*Seat*	*%*	*Seat*	*%*	*Seat*	*%*	*Seat*	*%*	*Seat*	*%*	*Seat*	*%*	*Seat*
DUP	18.1	20	25.6	30	30.1	36	30.0	38	29.2	38	28.1	28	21.3	25
Sinn Féin	17.6	18	23.5	24	26.2	28	26.9	29	24.0	28	27.9	27	29	27
UUP	21.3	28	22.7	27	14.9	18	13.2	16	12.6	16	12.9	10	11.2	9
SDLP	22.0	24	17.0	18	15.2	16	14.2	14	12.0	12	11.9	12	9.1	8
APNI	6.5	6	3.7	6	5.2	7	7.7	8	7.0	8	9.1	8	13.5	17
NIWC	1.6	2	0.8	0	—	—	—	—	—	—	—	—	—	—
GPNI	0.1	0	0.4	0	1.7	1	0.9	1	2.7	2	2.3	2	1.9	0
PBP	—	—	—	—	0.1	0	0.8	0	2.0	2	1.8	1	1.1	1

Source: www.ark.ac.uk/elections/.

in to resolve the dispute over the Irish language. The Identity and Language (Northern Ireland) Act 2022 of the UK Parliament provided official recognition of the Irish language in Northern Ireland and officially recognized Ulster Scots as a minority language. In February 2024, after months of talks, the DUP finally agreed a deal with the UK government to re-enter power-sharing. The Executive was restored, this time with Sinn Féin's Michelle O'Neill taking up the post of first minister and DUP's Emma Little-Pengelly in the role of deputy first minister. The parties were joined in the Executive by the UUP and Alliance, with the latter again taking up the Justice Ministry plus another ministry granted through the regular d'Hondt procedures. SDLP this time opted to form an official opposition. The UK general elections held in July 2024 further established the rise of Sinn Féin and decline of DUP, which, coming off the back of successful 2023 local elections, placed it as the largest party in Northern Ireland at all three governmental levels: Westminster, Stormont, and local (*BBC News* 2023; 2024) (see table 2.3 and figures 2.1 and 2.2).[11]

Where do civic parties stand amidst this polarization and dysfunction? One might assume that the combination of constitutional change and institutional crisis would spell disaster for non-aligned players. But the civic bloc was not wiped out, not even contracted. On the contrary, it grew significantly in size and influence. Throughout the power-sharing crisis, Alliance maintained a position that was both highly critical of the

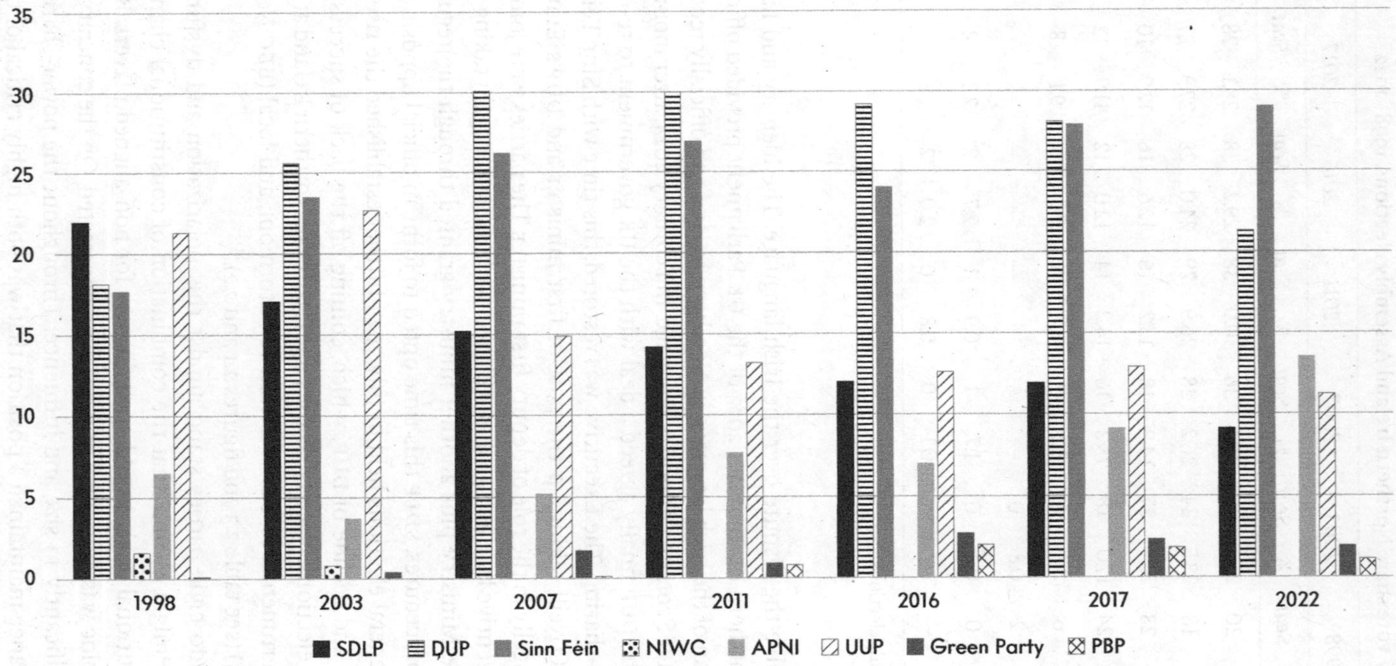

Figure 2.2 | Party vote share Northern Ireland Assembly elections, 1998–2022.

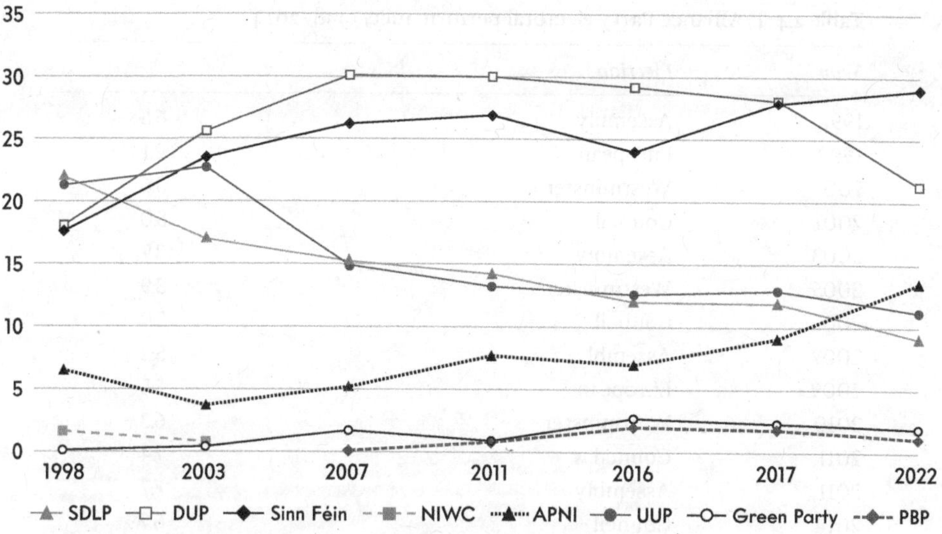

Figure 2.3 | Trends in party vote share (%) Northern Ireland Assembly elections, 1998–2022.

power-sharing parties for their failure to resolve the impasse and return functioning governance to the region, and constructive in offering potential solutions, including on the Irish Language Act. The 2017 Assembly election, held at the peak of the nationalist/unionist row, saw the three main parties in the civic bloc – Alliance, Greens and PBP – increase their vote share by 1.5 per cent, to 13.2 per cent. Amidst a reduction in the number of seats in the Assembly from 108 to 90 in that election,[12] they managed to hold eleven out of twelve seats, thereby increasing their seat share from 11 per cent to 12 per cent (see table 2.3).

Although Brexit threatened to be highly damaging for civic parties, those parties in fact moved to play an active and vocal role in the debate, most notably Alliance. The party was unreservedly pro-Remain and subsequently pragmatic in supporting the implementation of the protocol as mitigating the worst aspects of Brexit for Northern Ireland. Alliance, the Green Party, and PBP's position in that debate placed them on the same side as the main nationalist parties – opening them up to contestation by unionist parties. Yet, amidst the polarization, they maintained that consistent position. In 2019, held at a dismal time in Northern Ireland politics, some two years into the Stormont stalemate and three years into the Brexit debacle, Alliance scored three record electoral performances. The

Table 2.4 | Alliance Party electoral performance, 1998–2024

Year	*Election*	%
1998	Assembly	6.5
1999	European	2.1
2001	Westminster	3.6
2001	Council	5.0
2003	Assembly	3.7
2005	Westminster	3.9
2005	Council	5.0
2007	Assembly	5.2
2009	European	5.5
2010	Westminster	6.3
2011	Council	7.4
2011	Assembly	7.7
2014	Council	6.7
2014	European	7.1
2015	Westminster	8.6
2016	Assembly	7.0
2017	Assembly	9.1
2017	Westminster	7.9
2019	Council	11.5
2019	European	18.5
2019	Westminster	16.8
2022	Assembly	13.5
2023	Council	13.3
2024	Westminster	15.0

Source: http://www.ark.ac.uk/elections/.

party increased its vote share by 5 per cent in the local elections, 11 per cent in the European elections, and 9 per cent in the UK general election. It saw a 65 per cent increase in its local government seats (Tonge 2020), recorded its best ever European result, and won a historic 17 per cent of the vote in the Westminster election, coming in third in vote share behind the DUP and Sinn Fein (see table 2.4). Scholars such as Coakley and Whitten predicted at the time that this shift was no 'flash in the pan' but part of a slow, longer-term realignment of the party system (Coakley 2021, 20; Whitten 2020, 313). The results of the 2022 Assembly election would seem to support that view. As noted, Alliance increased its vote share in that poll by 4.4 per cent to 13.5 per cent and increased its number of seats by

Table 2.5 | Civic party indicators: Northern Ireland

Party	*Name significance*	*Appeal**	*Critical issue / position*	*Party vote / support*	*Leadership*	*Arena of contestation*
APNI	Civic: signals accommodation (coalition)	Civic: integrationist	Irish unity: neutral / no fixed position	Broadly cross-community with predominant representation in east	No official policy, but ethnonational balance historically observed in practice	Contested all constituencies in 2022 Assembly election
GPNI	Civic: signals issue-based politics (environment)	Civic: intersectional / programmatic / issue-based (environmental)	Irish unity: not prioritized	Broadly cross-community with predominant representation in east	No official policy	Contested all constituencies in 2022 Assembly election
PBP	Civic: signals ideology (socialism)	Civic: intersectional / programmatic (socialist)	Irish unity: pro-unity	Predominant representation in cities (Belfast [West] and Derry/ Londonderry)	No official policy	Contested 12/18 constituencies in 2022 Assembly election (including North, South, East, and West Belfast)
NIWC	Civic: signals accommodation (coalition)	Civic: intersectional / accommodationist / integrationist	Irish unity: neutral / pluralistic / no fixed position	Predominant representation in east	Policy of dual leadership, one from each ethnonational community	Contested 7/18 constituencies in 2003 Assembly election

Source: https://www.ark.ac.uk/elections/.

*Essential indicator

nine to seventeen. Collectively, the civic bloc secured 17 per cent of the vote and 20 per cent of the seats – albeit now dominated by Alliance, with PBP holding its one seat but the Green Party losing both of its seats. The poll cemented the place of Alliance as third party and of the civic bloc as a distinct entity alongside nationalism and unionism. Alliance boosted its representation further in the 2023 local elections, increasing its vote share by 1.8 per cent but its seat share in local councils by 26 per cent. In the 2024 UK general election, the party held steady. It maintained one seat at Westminster with only a minor reduction in its vote, emerging fourth in seat share and third in vote share (BBC *News* 2024).

Conclusion

Although obscured by the focus on nationalism and unionism, civic politics have held a stable presence in Northern Ireland from the very start of the Troubles. Civic movements have effected the critical transition from grassroots to institutional politics in the form of political parties. The region's transition from conflict towards peace and, ultimately, power-sharing has presented these parties with numerous challenges, at times threatening to squeeze them out of existence, not least in the early years of power-sharing. But that transition has also offered them some openings. Amidst contractions, the overall space available to civic parties has expanded since the GFA, and they have effectively navigated that shifting space. Despite the inhospitable nature of the power-sharing system, they have maintained a presence amidst the various crises that have erupted. Indeed, against the backdrop of the most serious constitutional crisis since the agreement, following the 2016 Brexit vote, they have ironically grown and now constitute a distinct third bloc in Northern Ireland politics. This suggests creative agency and adaptation. So how have civic parties and movements experienced post-agreement politics in practice and how have they effected expansion amidst such seemingly adverse conditions? It is to these questions that we turn in the next three chapters. We start with the power-sharing institutions.

Chapter Three

Northern Ireland: Civic Parties, Ethnic Rules

On 11 February 2020, the top political news story from Northern Ireland was not accompanied by the usual image of the imposing Stormont Assembly, or a tense exchange between the unionist and nationalist co-premiers but of Robyn Peoples and Sharni Edwards enjoying a champagne toast on their wedding day in Carrickfergus, Co. Antrim (*The Guardian* 2020). Peoples and Edwards made history by becoming the first same-sex couple to get married in Northern Ireland after an eight-year legal and political battle for legalization of marriage equality. The change in the law, which came into effect in January 2020, brought Northern Ireland into line with the rest of the UK and the Republic of Ireland where the reform had been introduced in 2013–14 and 2015 respectively (McCormick and Stewart 2020, 557). Yet, when it finally arrived, the change came not from the seat of power in Belfast but from London. After its passage was obstructed in the Northern Ireland Assembly by the use of a power-sharing veto in November 2015, marriage equality was eventually legislated for at Westminster in October 2019 during a three-year hiatus at Stormont. The marriage equality saga paints a telling picture about civic politics and power-sharing, in Northern Ireland and beyond. Bringing the power-sharing institutions into direct collision with broader human rights, it threw into stark relief the challenges of progressing civic politics in a system predicated on ethnonational representation. Its singular ethnonational lens leaves other intersecting identities, including gender and sexual identity, on the outside, required to fight for inclusion, and facing contestation along the way.

We know from chapter 1 that civic solidarity has an inimical relationship with power-sharing institutions in theory. Its singular ethnic lens contradicts the multi-lens of intersectionality. But what does that relationship look like in practice? How do civic parties experience power-sharing institutions day-to-day and what risks and opportunities do they encounter in that framework? Let us examine this up-close in the case of Northern Ireland.

'Others' in a Binary System

The last chapter set out the workings of Northern Ireland's power-sharing institutions. A number of these institutions impose a binary either/or ethnic representation logic and defy the reality of intersectionality. In this way they marginalize civic actors and deny them a meaningful role that is equal to their nationalist and unionist counterparts. None is more blatant than the so-called 'designation' rule whereby members of the Legislative Assembly (MLAs) must designate as Nationalist, Unionist, or Other on entering the legislature and related voting procedures in which the votes of nationalist and unionist designations carry more weight. In line with the mutual veto principle, these concurrent majority voting rules ensure cross-community consent on 'key decisions' (McEvoy 2013, 254). Such votes – including financial votes, the election of the Speaker and changes to the Standing Orders (Wilford 2010, 139) – require either 'parallel consent' – an overall majority including a majority of Unionists and Nationalists – or 'weighted majority' – the support of 60 per cent of members including at least 40 per cent of both blocs. In these decisions, ultimately, the votes of Others do not count. The rule can also be triggered following a 'Petition of Concern' signed by at least thirty out of ninety (previously 108) members (Standing Orders of NI Assembly, 2024). Horowitz describes how the rule makes it more rewarding to be a member of one of the two ethnonational communities (2001, 90) and 'violates' the interests of unaffiliated legislators 'in pursuing politics ... on terms of equality with other political actors' (Horowitz 2002a, 195). For Wilford it creates 'two orders of Assembly members' in key decisions: 'those whose votes always "count" and those whose votes never do so' (2010, 139). Scholars argue that the rule may undermine civic parties and occasionally incentivize people to switch to Nationalist and Unionist designations (Coakley 2021, 14). 'In effect unionist or nationalist votes and parties are more important within the Northern Ireland Assembly, a fact that may not be lost upon voters,' according to Evans and Tonge (2001, 115). The rule departs from the principle of self-determined or 'liberal' consociation (Lijphart 1977; McCulloch 2014a). What's more, it clearly obstructs intersectional expression.

How do civic parties deal with this tension? Alliance is deeply critical of power-sharing in general. Yet it has also been pragmatic about a system that appears the only game in town. From the 1980s it advocated a liberal form of power-sharing that fosters cooperation between parties across the divide, accommodates more flexible notions of identity, and facilitates integration of society. Though the Good Friday Agreement fell short of these ideals, the party still supported it, while condemning the more rigid, corporate aspects of the system (Farry and Neeson 1999). It has maintained this critical stance since, reserving particular censure for designation and cross-community voting rules, campaigning for these to be replaced with provisions for a simple weighted majority vote, with no need for designation (APNI 2003; 2007; 2011; 2013; 2015; 2016; 2017; 2022). Similarly, the Green Party has campaigned to end community designation and replace it with a rule requiring a two-thirds weighted majority requirement on certain votes (GPNI 2011; 2016; 2017; 2022). A number of scholars have echoed these calls for reform (O'Flynn 2003; Wilford 2010). Indeed, such a proposal was considered by a 2013 Assembly and Executive Committee established to review D'Hondt, Community Designation and Provisions for Opposition (Northern Ireland Assembly 2013). It was not recommended, however, and neither did the committee return to the proposal after it was reinstated in January 2020.

But ideals aside, how do civic parties experience these rules and what impact do they have on their politics? Civic representatives depict designation as morally wrong, unfair, and an affront to their principles. One Alliance representative referred to designation as 'direct discrimination', stating, 'It's structurally embedded within the system that you are a unionist or a nationalist and if you're neither you count for less'.[1] Another Alliance MLA expressed a deep sense of injustice at the rules: 'there was an academic paper this week which described [designation] as "irking some people" ... That my vote doesn't count in the same way as others, it doesn't "irk" me, it quite simply is wrong. And the people who voted for me expect and need me to have the same value vote as everybody else in this institution.'[2]

Civic representatives referred to the 'disempowering' impact of designation and even found the label offensive and dismissive of intersectional collectives. 'So, who are we? What are we? We are nothing. Others mean nothing', as one exasperated Alliance MLA put it.[3] A Green MLA expressed similar frustration: 'What does "Other" mean? ... It's completely dismissive of who you are and what your politics are, and the message that you want to put forward.'[4] The effect also puts civic parties in a bind, making it tricky to raise the issue in the public arena, for risk of highlighting this impairment to voters: 'Well, it's not something we trumpet ... "In these votes our vote doesn't count" ... We do want to point out the ludicrous nature of the system whereby if you are, by definition, cross-community, your vote doesn't count in a cross-community vote. So yeah, we do highlight it at times, but it's disempowering.'[5]

That disempowering effect is also felt in real terms. One Alliance MLA observed that every time a budget decision is taken in the Assembly, her vote and the votes of her colleagues do not count on an equal basis – a situation that leaves an increasing portion of the electorate with unequal representation.

> It's sickening, it's absolutely sickening. One of the most key [powers] that this place [Northern Ireland Assembly] has is how we spend the money on the public, and we don't count [in budgetary votes], and that's just unfair. And what it does mean then is you have a minister who'll bring forward policies on housing, on schools, on health, and basically a third of the population doesn't have a say on that.
>
> And while we might be small numbers in the Assembly, and people [say], 'Well it doesn't really matter, it's only eleven "Others" out of ninety [MLAs]', wait till the next election – what if that becomes 25 per cent or 30 per cent of the vote in this place?[6]

In the event, Others claimed eighteen out of ninety seats in the 2022 Assembly election (20 per cent). The secondary status of Others also prevents civic parties from holding the balance of power in key votes in the Assembly and thus playing a more significant role, as they do in some local councils across Northern Ireland.[7]

These rules and their implications came into sharp focus in 2001 when members of Alliance and the NIWC temporarily re-designated from Other to Unionist and Nationalist to save power-sharing from collapse, as outlined in chapter 2. Following the return of the Assembly after a suspension over a weapons-decommissioning row, a cross-community vote (parallel consent) was needed to re-elect the first and deputy first ministers – and hence keep the Executive in place. It was not certain that Unionist votes would be sufficient to secure that side of the vote, however (McEvoy 2013, 254). In order to reinstall the premiers and preserve power-sharing, the civic Northern Ireland Women's Coalition (NIWC) negotiated a change to the Assembly rules to allow one of its two MLAs to re-designate from Other: one to Unionist and one to Nationalist (Mitchell 2015, 178). This still proved insufficient to secure the Unionist vote however, and pressure mounted on the Alliance to follow suit. Following much soul searching within the party – given its long-standing opposition to designation – three of its six MLAs agreed to re-designate to Unionist for seven days, in return for a commitment from the British government to launch a review of the voting procedures (Mitchell 2015, 179). The decision to re-designate was a source of division within the party with two of its MLAs refusing to do so and a majority of party members opposing the move (Evans and Tonge 2003). Then Party Leader David Ford presented the move as an act of self-sacrifice for the greater good of preserving the GFA (Ford 2001). Yet, Alliance received little reward for this 'contortion', as Tonge observes, given the subsequent collapse of the institutions anyway and squeezing of civic parties at the 2003 elections (2005, 100).

Ford recounts the conflict the party's decision invoked in him, which made him feel 'physically sick'. 'Because I'd spent my time in politics trying to get away from that kind of nonsense, and yet the only way we could actually move things on … was by swallowing everything I believed in.'[8]

Reflecting on the affair twenty years on, another Alliance MLA comments that 'those twenty-two minutes … have hung over the party for a long time.'[9] The re-designation affair demonstrates the awkward and invidious position in which civic parties can find themselves in post-agreement politics, having to compromise their principles for the sake of political stability. It also speaks to their difficulty in acting on their own intersectional terms in an environment that requires ethnonational mediation and accommodation.

On the question of whether the rules impact directly on civic parties' electoral performance, no cross-community representative made this claim explicitly, and some cast doubt upon it.[10] Those asked if this issue was ever raised by voters, or if they appeared aware of it, responded in the negative.[11] Civic representatives stressed the symbolic impact of these rules first and foremost – the inequality they represented, the fact that they imposed on them an identity that they did not themselves recognize and somehow denied them a sense of legitimacy as civic actors within the system.[12] One Alliance MLA argued that the rule sends out 'a very dangerous message to society that we are perpetually divided'.[13] Another believed that nationalist and unionist parties were well aware of these impacts of the rule and were actively retaining it to preserve their power at the expense of Other parties. She recounted how the above-mentioned Assembly and Executive Review Committee – on which she served from 2020–22 – pushed the issue of designation down the agenda in favour of issues like supporting an official opposition, opting not to take oral evidence on the matter. 'And what makes it very sickening is the fact that other parties *know* this ... and they're actively going against rectifying it.'[14]

Yet, civic party representatives also demonstrated creative agency in the face of these rules. Parties have used the ceremony of signing in to the Assembly as an opportunity to demonstrate their opposition to designation. For example, Green Party MLAs have previously signed in as 'Feminist' and 'European' while Alliance representatives have registered as 'Cross-Community' and 'United Community Other', People Before Profit as 'Socialist', and the NIWC as 'Inclusive Other'[15] – symbolic acts of resistance, although their votes still officially counted as Other. Indeed, for NIWC leader Monica McWilliams the designation requirement evoked no great tension: '[NIWC] signed in as "Inclusive Other" and that was a position we lived very comfortably under.' She even viewed the capacity to re-designate in 2001 as a strength, allowing the Women's Coalition to creatively navigate the institutions and demonstrate its cross-community principles – encompassing nationalist, unionist, and other identities.[16]

In the scholarly world, some have defended designation as a necessary protection against dominance of one community over the other and questioned the extent of its discrimination of civic parties. Schwartz accepts that the rule entails a degree of unfairness but argues that even in cross-community votes, Others' votes still count towards the 'super majority' and are just less decisive than those of Nationalists and Unionists (Schwartz 2011, 351). McGarry and O'Leary acknowledge that the rule 'may create a minor incentive for people to vote nationalist or unionist, as their votes would count more' (2009, 34) but, overall, deny that civic parties are held back by power-sharing rules (2009, 67). In their submission to the 2013 review, McCrudden, McGarry, O'Leary, and Schwartz argued that under the liberal consociational arrangements in place in Northern Ireland, the rules do not prevent parties that designate as Other from holding the offices of first or deputy first minister nor do these rules negatively impact their electoral prospects. Indeed, civic parties' overall support increased between 1998 and 2013 (McCrudden et al. 2013, 235; see also McCrudden and O'Leary 2013, 484).

The Ethnic Veto

Another power-sharing institution that places civic parties in an awkward position is the Petition of Concern (PoC), an effective veto for unionist and nationalist voting blocs whereby thirty MLA signatures triggers a cross-community vote in the Assembly. While intended to serve as a mechanism for the protection of minority rights, given the lack of strict definition in legislation of what can constitute such a concern – a 'permissive' application (McCulloch 2018, 736) – the veto has been used on a number of occasions by nationalist and unionist parties to block ordinary legislation to which they are opposed on other grounds. In the 2011–16 term, 116 PoCs were tabled (Haughey 2019, 707) and 12 per cent of their topics during that time have been deemed 'non-ethnic equality issues', most notably when used by Sinn Féin, SDLP, and the Green Party to prevent UK government welfare reforms being implemented and, most controversially, by the DUP to oppose same-sex marriage (see case study 3.1 below) (McCulloch 2018, 748). The case has been made that these are legitimately issues of special concern to nationalism and unionism, given the historic socio-economic inequality between the two communities, and the strong links between unionism and Presbyterian churches which are ideologically opposed to marriage other than between a man and a woman[17] (McCulloch 2018, 750). Yet, the fact remains that welfare and LGBTQ+ rights are issues that impact the population as a whole, irrespective of one's ethnonational identity or religion. More blatantly, the DUP came under heavy criticism from rival parties in November 2020 when it used the veto to block a proposal to extend COVID-19 lockdown restrictions (Clarke and McClements 2020). But rights and wrongs aside, how exactly has the veto impacted civic politics in Northern Ireland?

On a practical level, the rule has been blamed for blocking progress on broader inclusion, equality and human rights, such as equal marriage. Furthermore, civic representatives suggest that the veto has frustrated their agenda and limited their agency. For example, on a Sinn Féin motion on marriage equality in 2013, in a compromise move, the Alliance put down an amendment which would have exempted religious institutions from the reform. However, that amendment had no hope of passing or even serious consideration following the DUP's use of the veto.[18] More broadly, the veto can have an insidious effect, stymying political debate on contentious issues, as one Alliance MLA explained:

> There's no incentive in the Assembly's structure for people to cooperate. People are handed a veto so that they can stop things they don't like.
>
> We've never had the conversation with the DUP about what protections you would need for churches before you would be able to live with [same-sex marriage] ... Because they can just say 'No' and then the conversation stops and there's no incentive to move it on.
>
> So, the conversation doesn't happen internally in the party, doesn't happen externally, doesn't happen with their stakeholders, or their voters. It just doesn't happen. And I think that that is our biggest loss.[19]

The prohibitive effect of the veto has also been observed with respect to abortion. Abortion was eventually legalized, bringing it into line with the rest of the UK, in 2019 through legislation at Westminster during the three-year hiatus at Stormont. During a prior Stormont debate in 2016 to ease the region's previously highly restrictive laws then Alliance Justice Minister David Ford put down an amendment to legalize abortion in cases of fatal fetal abnormality. The amendments were, however, ultimately rejected. An Alliance colleague attributed the lack of debate between parties and ultimate rejection of the proposal, to those parties' awareness of the veto.[20] Indeed, the PoC was also used on the other side of the abortion debate – by Sinn Féin, the Green Party, and Alliance – in 2013 and in 2015 to block a DUP amendment that would have further tightened Northern Ireland's highly restrictive laws, making any woman who terminated a pregnancy in a hospital or clinic outside of the National Health Service subject to a prison sentence (*BBC News* 2015). People Before Profit representative Eamonn McCann observed after the vote, 'Any move towards either liberalization or further restriction will be stymied by a petition of concern from one side or the other. Stormont cannot handle the abortion issue. It was never designed to. The same goes for equal marriage.' (McCann 2015).

These moves illustrate the veto's effect of shutting down debate that could otherwise lead to consensus building. When the site of legislation for these issues switched to Westminster during the 2017–20 collapse of

Stormont, though the shift opened up the opportunity for success for the movements in question, it also closed down any possibility for debate at Stormont (McCormick and Stewart 2020). Veto disputes played out in the media around issues like equal marriage or welfare reform also ethnicize these matters, detracting from an informed debate that might lead to progress on the rights-based issue at hand.[21]

Symbolically, the PoC is also perceived as a further inequality for Other parties, who can sign the petition (and have done so on issues like welfare reform) but whose votes do not count equally in the subsequent cross-community vote (McCulloch 2018). One Alliance representative said, 'We find it hugely frustrating that on issues which are core to us around human rights, equality and, particularly, integration in a shared society ... our votes count for less. It's a perversion of democracy really that we count for less on the issues that matter most to our voters'.[22]

Given the debacle over marriage equality, which fed into the 2017–20 political crisis, reform of the PoC was one of the key elements of the New Decade New Approach Agreement (NDNA) that restored power-sharing in January 2020. The changes were designed to restrict its use, increase accountability to the public and require debate before the veto could be triggered. Parties agreed that its use 'should be reduced, and returned to its intended purpose' committing to tabling or supporting PoCs 'only in the most exceptional circumstances and as a last resort'. Most notably, the petition can no longer be triggered by a single party. Additional hurdles include a fourteen-day 'cooling off' period after the petition is triggered, a written justification, and restrictions that it cannot be invoked before the second stage of a bill or on issues of misconduct.[23] Following the reforms, the PoC was sought for the first time in March 2022 by the DUP to block an Alliance Party bill to promote integrated education. Its bid failed when the UUP refused to sign the petition and the legislation passed. This indicates the positive impact of the reforms on this occasion, while also demonstrating that the veto remains an option that can be threatened and used by parties.

Case Study 3.1: Marriage Equality

Few issues have been as politicized in Northern Ireland in recent years as marriage equality. The 2015 vote to legislate for equal marriage in the region was the fifth legislative attempt at Stormont, the first tabled in 2012 by the civic Green Party. On each occasion the DUP – a deeply socially conservative party with particularly strong stances on LGBTQ+ people – used the PoC to block the proposal (Hayes and Nagle 2016, 26). With the first four attempts failing to garner simple majority support among MLAs, the veto was irrelevant. By November 2015, however, opinion had shifted and a narrow majority of MLAs voted for the motion put forward by Sinn Féin, the Green Party, and the SDLP, by fifty-three to fifty-two votes (McCulloch 2018). Despite this majority, after the cross-community vote was triggered, the required support among nationalists and unionists was absent and the legislation fell. Its triggering amounted to a 'misuse' or 'abuse' of the rule in the eyes of civic party representatives.[24]

What followed was a legal and political 'saga' that unexpectedly brought LGBTQ+ rights to the fore of Northern Ireland politics and sparked renewed controversy about the PoC (McCormick and Stewart 2020). Marriage equality became another dividing line between power-sharing partners DUP and Sinn Féin, the unionist party vehemently opposing it, the nationalist championing it and conflating it with its broader agenda for equal rights (for the Catholic/nationalist/republican community) and 'parity of esteem' (McCulloch 2018, 750; Nagle 2016b, 868). Indeed, a 'shameful disrespect' towards the LGBTQ+ community, as well as women and ethnic minorities, on the part of the DUP was one of the five charges against the party levelled by then Sinn Féin Deputy First Minister Martin McGuinness in his resignation letter which essentially collapsed the power-sharing Executive in January 2017 (McGuinness 2017).

The extended power vacuum that followed was creatively utilized by activists, who, in the absence of Stormont, turned their focus to Westminster. After much lobbying, in March 2018, in a highly unusual move post-devolution, legislative efforts were taken up in the UK the House of Lords by Conservative Peer Lord Hayward and in the House of Commons by Labour MP Conor McGinn, the latter reflecting that, 'the Assembly being in cold storage should not mean that Northern Ireland remains a cold house for LGBT rights' (McCormack and Stewart 2020, 563). Pressure mounted further following the paramilitary killing of journalist and LGBTQ+ rights activist Lyra McKee in Derry in April 2019 during the political

Figure 3.1 | Marriage equality protest in Belfast city centre, May 2019.

deadlock and a subsequent call by her partner for the UK government to legislate for equal marriage. Moves at Westminster finally culminated in the passage of an amendment to the Northern Ireland (Executive Formation) Bill in July 2019 (passed to avoid the triggering of an election) which required the secretary of state to make regulations for marriage equality in Northern Ireland (as well as duties to decriminalize abortion and some other measures) unless an Executive was formed by 21 October 2019. After a failed attempt by DUP, UUP, and TUV members to revive the Assembly on that day, regulations were ultimately introduced by the secretary of state in January 2020 (McCormack and Stewart 2020, 564).

The marriage equality affair tells us a number of things about civic politics under power-sharing. First, it demonstrates how the institutions can be used to not only *marginalize* civic agendas pertaining to equality and human rights but actually frustrate and even block those agendas. In this case, a consociational device designed to protect ethnonational interests was wielded at the expense of those of LGBTQ+ people, pitting one kind of minority rights against another and effectively subordinating the latter. Activists interviewed expressed frustration at the prohibitive effect of the veto and other power-sharing mechanisms, which have left LGBTQ+ rights in Northern Ireland significantly lagging the rest of the UK and Ireland, and not only with respect to marriage: 'When it comes to how you actually effect change through those political processes and the legislative bodies, we just have hurdles which exist here that do not exist in other jurisdictions. And that's largely down to the way that the Assembly is constructed ... that system is actually not created to govern. It's certainly not created to affect change. It's created to slow everything down.'[25]

A number of activists spoke of their frustration prior to 2019 at winning the battle for marriage equality, first in terms of the public support (evidenced through public opinion polling) and then political support (among a majority of MLAs), yet that right still being denied to LGBTQ+ people in Northern Ireland because of the political institutions in place.[26] They spoke of the 'blockage' at Stormont for human rights and equality and held little faith in the power-sharing system's capacity to ever deliver for those rights, even if reformed. One activist referred to Stormont as a 'failed entity' when it comes to human rights,[27] while another reflected that, despite Stormont being defunct for eighteen-months at the time, he did 'not miss it'.[28] While the legalization was a major win for the movement, the fact that it had to bypass Stormont was a regret, for one leading activist, and spoke volumes about the flaws of the system.[29]

Second, it shows how veto rules can close down 'civic' space and constrain civic parties' agency. The stymying effect of the PoC on debate, discussed above, was clearly witnessed on marriage equality, where the Alliance attempt at compromise, with an amendment to exempt religious institutions, received no oxygen. This not only curtailed the debate but deprived the civic party the opportunity to play a meaningful role.

Third, the rule allowed the civic agenda to be ethnicized and left it at risk of being co-opted by certain ethnonational interests and contested by others (Nagle 2016b, 868). The entanglement of the issue in 'orange versus green' politics, and particularly in the protracted row between DUP and Sinn Féin during Stormont's 2017–20 collapse, created a tricky situation for LGBTQ+ activists. While fighting for marriage equality and welcoming the forthright support of Sinn Féin, the LGBTQ+ movement had to tread carefully to avoid perceived 'capture' by nationalist interests.[30] Indeed, the charge was levelled by a UUP member that the movement was being 'used' by the nationalist party (McCulloch 2018, 750). Likewise, while the movement campaigned for reform of the PoC in light of the affair, some activists did not want marriage equality to be held up as a 'red-line' by Sinn Féin for going back into power-sharing during cross-party negotiations in 2018.[31] They related being wary of such politicization of LGBTQ+ rights and the consequences if the issue was to be later dropped in favour of other priorities – something that almost transpired in a leaked draft deal in February 2018 that Sinn Féin was prepared to sign up to that included a commitment to Irish language legislation but not marriage equality.[32]

This case study once again shows how civic parties and movements in power-sharing systems can find themselves and their politics marginalized, contested, and co-opted. In a system devised with a singular ethnic lens, intersectional identities and positionings can get lost in the shuffle or, worse, caught in the crossfire.

Disunited Government

How do the rules for forming and operating government in Northern Ireland impact civic politics? The Northern Ireland Executive is designed to be a broadly inclusive coalition. Through the liberal D'Hondt system parties (of any designation; Nationalist, Unionist, or Other) are entitled to seats if they command sufficient voter support as demonstrated through Assembly elections. On this basis, the Alliance gained a ministry in 2011 which it held until 2016, the Department of Employment and Learning (in addition to the contested Justice Ministry that it had taken up outside of regular d'Hondt procedures in 2010). The 2014 Stormont House Agreement also provided for an official opposition of those parties entitled to ministerial positions but that choose not to take them – an option taken by the moderate unionist and nationalist parties UUP and SDLP, and civic Alliance, after the 2016 election until Stormont's collapse in 2017, and by the SDLP in 2024.[33] The Executive is therefore open to Other designated parties on an equal basis to their Nationalist and Unionist counterparts and has allowed Alliance to participate.

Nevertheless, the inclusive 'grand coalition' style design of the Executive has also been criticized for requiring little by way of cooperation from parties before they take their positions – leading to a disunited, dysfunctional government. Critics charge D'Hondt with leading to 'chopped up government' (Wilford 2009), creating party fiefdoms in the Executive, where power is 'shared out' rather than shared between parties (Nagle 2011, 167–8). This lack of joined up government leads to a lack of policy cohesion that can hold back progress on policies relating to broader equality and social justice. In this sense the Alliance advocates for d'Hondt's replacement with a voluntary coalition by parties that can command a weighted majority in the Assembly (Murphy and Evershed 2022, 99). In an attempt to address the problem, the Stormont House Agreement introduced a requirement that, after an election, the parties intending to take up ministries agree on a draft Programme of Government, which is passed to the Assembly for approval once the Executive is formed.[34] Yet, representatives from sectors campaigning on these issues still lament the difficulty in achieving progress in the context of a fractious government, before and after this change.[35] One representative of an LGBTQ+ advocacy organization reports that legislative change to advance LGBTQ+ rights has been entirely contingent on which party holds the ministry in question. The organization had very limited contact with the Department of Health for nine years while it was controlled by the DUP but achieved quite rapid change once Sinn Féin took over the department, including reversing the lifetime ban on gay men donating blood in 2016 (Connolly 2016).[36] Another leading figure in the sector expressed the frustration of trying to work with an Executive in which the minister with responsibility for LGBTQ+ issues refuses to meet with your organization.[37] Indeed, in an indictment of the system's capacity to deliver for broader equality and human rights, a number of figures in the gender and LGBTQ+ sectors remarked that greater progress was achieved on these rights during the period of direct rule from Westminster 2002–07 and Stormont's collapse 2017–20.[38] One abortion rights activist reported a 'big push' for legalization in 2008, prior to the transfer of justice powers to Northern Ireland and another during the 2017–20 hiatus.[39] And ultimately, abortion and marriage equality were legalized during the latter period, from Westminster.

'Co-Equal' Premiership

The rules for the election of premiers in the Executive likewise present openings and barriers for civic politics. The Executive is led by the co-equal first minister and deputy first minister. Since the 2006 St Andrews Agreement (SAA) these positions have been nominated by the largest parties the largest and second largest Assembly designations respectively (prior to which they were elected in a cross-community Assembly vote) (McEvoy 2015). Prior to the 2022 election the first minister position had been filled by a unionist, nominated by the largest party within that bloc (UUP from 1998–2002 and DUP from 2007–22) and the deputy first minister position had been filled by a nationalist, nominated by the largest party from that bloc (SDLP 1998–2002 and Sinn Féin 2007–22). These rules leave the positions, in theory, open to a party from the Other designation should Other become the largest or second largest bloc. However, if the Alliance were to advance to become the second largest party in a future election, it would still not be entitled to one of the positions until a point when Others had become the second largest designation.

The rules for the election of the co-premiers have, however, also been claimed to contribute to a logic of ethnonational representation and, in this way, marginalize civic politics and parties. Despite being equal in power, because the titles suggest a hierarchy, significant emphasis is placed at elections on which party will emerge as largest and take the 'top spot' of first minister. The contest has become particularly intense in recent years given the electoral decline of unionism, and the DUP in particular (after the 2017 election unionists made up the largest number of MLAs in Stormont but for the first time no longer commanded a majority), stoking fears of nationalism overtaking unionism for the first time and Sinn Féin gaining the right to nominate the first minister. The question of which party would take the first minister role became particularly contentious in the 2022 election and dominated the campaign, as polls predicted a Sinn Féin win and the DUP cast doubt on whether they would serve as deputy first minister in this event. Indeed, fears of such a scenario arguably precipitated the DUP's withdrawal from the Executive in February 2022, officially in protest over the Brexit protocol but widely perceived as a bid to heighten unionist insecurities and mobilize voters ahead of the polls in May. In the event, Sinn Féin did surpass DUP for the first time in the 2022 polls to entitle it to the position of first minister. Up until February 2024 the DUP continued to refuse to form government and take up the position of deputy first minister, ostensibly on the grounds of its opposition to the Brexit protocol.

In any case, the type of competition generated by the contest for first minister feeds into the 'ethnic tribune' appeal of the two largest nationalist and unionist parties, whereby voters in a power-sharing context opt for the strongest advocate for their group (Mitchell et al 2009), and sidelines the role of non-ethnic players.[40] Human rights and LGBTQ+ activists spoke of how such rules helped push wider equality issues off the agenda and make every election instead about who will emerge as the largest ethnonational bloc and party.

'I think the design of our Assembly and Executive drives people towards the green-orange voting blocs, and then drives them towards who's identified as the dominant party within [those blocs]. So, that dynamic brushes aside the detail of social issues. It's one big steamroller driving how people vote and driving who gets into positions of power.'[41]

To remedy this effect O'Leary advocates changing the titles of the co-premiers to 'joint first ministers', to reflect the reality of their parity of power and soften any future DUP losses (2018, 235).

As well as the rules for election of first minister and deputy first minister, the rule that one cannot hold office without the other, brings with it the threat of institutional collapse, and have been blamed for contributing to dysfunction and instability (Haughey 2019, 707). The 2020 New Decade New Approach Agreement addressed this issue by introducing a reform to allow for more time after a first or deputy first minister resigns before an election needs to be called – extended from seven days to up to six months (Haughey 2020, 2). Therefore, when the DUP first minister resigned in February 2022 the other ministers in the Executive remained in position as caretakers and the Assembly continued to function before being dissolved for the regular elections in May 2022. Nevertheless, while a marked practical improvement on the previous arrangement, the DUP's withdrawal from the most senior position in government was still highly significant, in real and symbolic terms, and triggered a political crisis. This environment of continual crisis clearly frustrates the civic agenda as no policy can be progressed when the institutions are not functioning. What's more it can heighten ethnonational insecurity and push voters to vote tactically from a place of fear rather than positive choice – a dynamic that never favours civic parties.[42]

Elite Dominance

The power-sharing institutions have also been characterized as elite-centric and insulated from civil society. That obstructs civic politics and progress towards broader human rights and equality issues such as LGBTQ+, disabilities, racial equality, and reproductive rights, critics claim.[43] While it could be argued that every government is elite-centric, a particular gap has been observed in Northern Ireland between politics at the institutional level and at the grassroots. As in other conflict societies, institutional politics in Northern Ireland prior to the agreement resembled 'war by other means', highly polarized, hostile, confrontational, and inhospitable to groups and individuals not engaged or aligned in that conflict. The sphere of informal, grassroots politics meanwhile has been traditionally more 'civic' in nature and often the only avenue to progress broader 'bread and butter' issues as opposed to more state-centric and security-related issues that dominated 'high politics' (Gilmartin 2019, 92). The two spheres are sometimes characterized as 'parallel universes' in Northern Ireland.

This dynamic is deeply gendered: women have been historically excluded from institutional politics (only three women MPs in Northern Ireland were elected to Westminster prior to the GFA) but highly active in grassroots politics, on issues like healthcare, childcare, and peace in their communities (Gilmartin 2019, 93). This gap has narrowed significantly since the agreement, where women's descriptive representation in the Assembly has risen from 13 per cent to 36 per cent in 2022. But its effects are still keenly felt in substantive terms, with issues like reproductive rights and women's health pushed down the agenda in favour of those relating to ethnonational interests (Pierson and Thomson 2018). The fact that abortion rights were only extended to Northern Ireland in 2019 via legislation passed at Westminster during a hiatus at Stormont speaks to this point. Indeed, for a further three years, abortion services remained virtually non-existent as the Department of Health at Stormont failed to commission those services. In October 2022 the UK secretary of state moved to directly intervene to do so (Oppenheim 2022). Advocates for greater representation of civil society in the institutions also point to the gap between public opinion and electoral politics, where more people identify as 'neither nationalist nor unionist' than with either of the two traditions, yet nationalist and unionist parties occupy 80 per cent of the seats in Stormont (ARK 2022b; ARK 2022c). Others highlight the discrepancy between public will and political outcomes, with legislation to introduce marriage equality vetoed at Stormont in 2015 despite a majority of Catholics and of Protestants supporting the policy (Haughey 2019, 707; Cromie 2015).

The Civic Forum – a body made up of civil society representatives to operate alongside the Assembly – secured under the GFA by the Women's Coalition, was conceived as a corrective to this elite dominance and means of giving direct voice to the more civic-oriented grassroots politics in the system. The body collapsed with the institutions in 2002, however, and was never reinstated (Mackay and Murtagh 2019). Some advocates have called for its re-establishment as a much-needed bridge between civil society and electoral politics[44] (Pierson and Thomson 2018). The 2020 NDNA does provides for an annual citizens' Assembly. But with limited scope and power compared to the civic forum and no funds dedicated as of 2022, it has not satisfied these demands.[45]

Conclusion

Northern Ireland's institutions were not conceived with intersectionality in mind. They were not designed to accommodate actors, issues, and identities beyond unionism and nationalism. These facts are underlined by the experiences of civic parties and civil society groups, in the system. In line with the expectations set out in chapter 1, in-depth analysis here shows that rules designed to protect unionism and nationalism in the power-sharing institutions marginalize and compromise civic politics. Community designation and veto procedures disempower and 'other' civic parties. Executive power-sharing creates a fractious environment inimical to advancing broader civic agendas, while premier election rules bolster nationalist and unionist parties. What's more, the elite-centric system allows limited input from civil society to counteract these binary forces. Yet, as also anticipated, the institutions do provide small openings and cracks for civic politics to seize. Although they are granted lesser power, Others are at least given official recognition and have the capacity to take part in the Executive and even take up premier roles, should they command mass levels of support. We also see civic parties creatively navigating the designation rule on occasion and using it to express their resistance to binary politics. And, as we interrogate in chapter 5, they have managed to seize space and significantly expand that space over the last twenty-five years.

Yet, these formal institutions are only part of the story of civic politics in Northern Ireland. How do civic actors deal with the equally powerful informal conventions, understandings and practices of politics? It is to this question we now turn.

Chapter Four

The Unwritten Rules in Northern Ireland

On 3 December 2012 violence erupted on the streets of Belfast in what was deemed one of the most serious threats to the peace process since the 1998 Good Friday Agreement. Loyalist protesters charged Belfast City Hall as riots ensued across the city and, in the days that followed, politicians had their offices and homes physically attacked and threatened (Nolan et al 2014). At issue was the removal of the (British) Union Flag from flying over Belfast City Hall every day of the year in favour of a policy of flying it on designated days only. The central target of this attack was not a nationalist or unionist party, as the narrative of Northern Ireland politics goes, but the non-aligned civic party, Alliance. In a unionist–nationalist stalemate in Belfast City Council between flying the flag every day or not at all, the party put forward the compromise 'designated days' policy that reflected its 'shared future' agenda and, holding the casting vote, its members were pivotal to its passage. In the days, weeks, and months that followed the vote, the Alliance found itself targeted in intimidating, violent, and potentially life-threatening ways in a campaign facilitated by the main unionist parties DUP and UUP. Far from an irrelevant side-show to the binary politics of nationalism versus unionism, the Alliance was now centre stage – albeit for reasons it neither anticipated nor desired. This was a struggle not between rival ethnonationalisms but rather between that ethnonationalist status quo and a new form of politics that challenged its dominance: civic solidarity.

The flag affair illustrates the treacherous environment that civic movements and parties must navigate in Northern Ireland's political game and, moreover, the *unwritten rules* of that game. Beyond the formal institutions explored in chapter 3, the informal institutions – conventions, practices, norms, values, and ideas of the system – obstruct civic politics

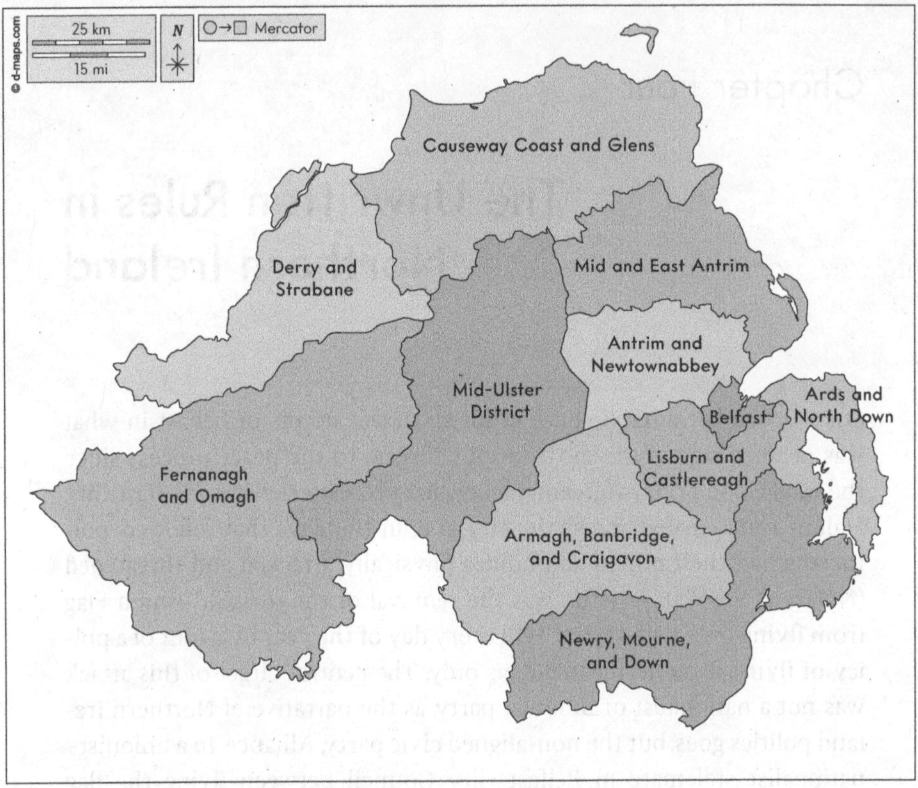

Figure 4.1 | Map of local council areas in Northern Ireland.

in profound ways. These socially shared understandings are more difficult to pinpoint than official procedures but no less potent. What's more, they intimately intertwine with those formal structures. In this chapter we examine the informal barriers civic parties face in Northern Ireland, in the shape of institutional recognition of the binary, ethnonational discourse, ethnonational patronage, and shared logics of ethnonational political representation. How have these informal barriers interplayed with the formal institutions to constrain and complicate civic politics? And how have civic parties negotiated this minefield?

Legitimacy in a Binary System

The principle of binary ethnonationalism runs through Northern Ireland politics. It lies at the heart of the Good Friday Agreement, which committed to '*parity of esteem* and of just and equal treatment for the identity, ethos, and aspirations of *both communities*'.[1] The agreement provided for the establishment an Equality Commission (1998), among other specific measures as outlined in chapter 2. Yet, less formally, the principle created a presumption – in line with the 'group autonomy' condition of power-sharing – of autonomy for unionism and nationalism in certain spheres, most notably *education* and *culture*. That binary principle has permeated politics and with clear consequences for those that do not fit neatly into either category. The challenge for civic movements in progressing civic and intersectional policies that do not align with this principle – such as integrated education, shared housing, public space and symbols – is real. In this context, civic actors lack allies and ideological space in pursuing their policy goals. What's more, set against the official recognition of the ethnonational binary, the legitimacy of civic policies is contested and portrayed as an attack on community rights and culture.

Culture is particularly treacherous terrain for civic parties in divided societies. Deeply contested and emotive, it is inextricably bound with ethnonational identity. A presumption towards autonomy in the cultural realm legitimizes this contest and leaves those advocating for a more shared culture in a tricky position. Since the agreement, the contestation of culture has become particularly pronounced; as conflict between nationalist and unionist parties over peace and security issues have receded, those over identity-related issues such as flags, symbols, emblems, parading, and language have escalated in what some have termed the new 'culture war' (Mitchell and Miller 2017, 236; Bryan and Gillespie 2021, 113). The flag protest in 2012–13 in which the Alliance was violently targeted for its role in the decision to cease flying the Union flag at Belfast City Hall every day, is a clear demonstration of how the civic party's policies place it in the crossfire of these 'culture wars'. The Alliance policy of promoting shared public space was depicted by unionist parties as posing a threat to ethnonational identity and cultural rights and the party bore the brunt of the resulting anger (see case study 4.1 below).

Another major dispute in the realm of culture has surrounded the Irish language. As outlined in chapter 2, the impasse between the DUP and Sinn Féin on delivery of Irish language legislation was core to the political crisis of 2017–20. In line with institutional recognition of cultural autonomy under power-sharing, the Good Friday Agreement included support for the Irish language while the St Andrew's Agreement promised an Irish Language Act, which was not delivered (and was ultimately passed by Westminster in 2022). The Irish language issue proved a tricky one for civic parties to navigate. For the most part they found themselves *marginalized* from this debate which centred on the row between the main unionist and nationalist parties. However, civic parties also found their position *contested* at times. While both the Alliance and Greens supported an Irish Language Act, the politicization of the issue made it tricky for them to navigate. They each reported being depicted by the DUP as 'treasonous' to unionism for supporting the act or even 'Sinn Féin lovers' – accusations they shrugged off.[2] These claims resonate with a broader 'traitor' discourse used by unionist politicians vis-à-vis the Irish language, including towards those promoting the language within the Protestant/Unionist/Loyalist (PUL) community.[3] Yet, civic parties also reported having their ideas *co-opted* in the negotiations. One Alliance representative reflected on the fact that a leaked draft agreement between the DUP and Sinn Féin in 2018 to break the deadlock was directly in line with compromise proposals put to the parties by the Alliance – for a three-stranded approach incorporating legislation for Irish (associated primarily with Catholic, nationalist culture), Ulster Scots (associated primarily with Protestant, unionist culture), and other languages, identities, and cultures (an approach later reflected in the 2020 New Decade New Approach Agreement (NDNA) and the 2022 legislation). Yet, the party received no credit for this contribution.[4]

Culture is a particularly treacherous field for civic parties, as they seek a shared culture in an environment where it is treated as indivisible and zero-sum (see Bryan 2015; Bryan and Gillespie 2021). Education is similarly tricky. Seen as pivotal to the preservation and reproduction of ethnonational identity and community, educational autonomy is closely guarded by ethnonational parties in divided societies. It is scarcely surprising then that Alliance's integrated education policies are heavily resisted and contested, particularly now by unionist parties, as the community faces demographic decline. Catholics outnumbered Protestants for the first time in the 2021 Northern Ireland Census, 46 per cent to 44 per cent (NISRA, 2022b).[5]

The current system of primary and secondary schooling, which is organized and publicly funded on a religious basis (Fontana 2017), is a right stoutly defended by nationalist and unionist parties. Only 70 of Northern Ireland's 1,000 schools are integrated, as opposed to denominational Catholic or Protestant, teaching roughly 7 per cent of its pupils, a proportion that has only minimally increased since the signing of the Good

Friday Agreement (Department of Education, NI). The Alliance Party has long advocated a move away from this segregated schooling system towards an integrated public education system (APNI 1998; 2003; 2007; 2011; 2013; 2016; 2017). The 2017 Assembly election manifesto presents a nine-point plan to deliver integrated education, including a commitment to an Integrated Education Bill to ensure every child has the right to attend an integrated school, legislation it brought forward in 2021 that was finally passed in March 2022 (APNI 2017a; Meredith 2021). Yet, making headway with this agenda is a challenge given the lack of support among the main ethnonational parties, particularly in the context of a DUP–Sinn Féin led Executive. One Alliance MLA expressed the difficulty of pushing for new integrated schools and 'transformation' of denominational schools in his constituency, where he is the only representative to support the policy and believes his constituency colleagues would actively campaign against any such moves.[6] Likewise, at the national level the party faces a dearth of partners at Stormont with whom to fight for this issue, aside from the Greens and People Before Profit in recent years, which between them held three seats in the 2017–22 term.[7]

What's more, civic parties face misrepresentation and contestation of this policy in the dominant ethnonational discourse. In 2013 the Alliance published a flagship strategy for a 'shared future' for Northern Ireland entitled 'For Everyone', which set out ambitious integrationist policies for education, as well as the economy, children and young people, public space, culture, and dealing with the past. On education, it pledged to create more opportunities for shared and integrated education as steps towards a 'single overarching education system in Northern Ireland', advancing specific targets such as a minimum of 20 per cent of children being educated in integrated schools and 40 per cent in mixed schools by 2020 (APNI 2013). Following the report's publication, however, one Alliance MLA recounts a report in the nationalist-aligned newspaper *The Irish News* under the headline, 'End Catholic Education' (Manley 2013) – a characterization he described as 'grossly unfair and inaccurate'.[8] In fact, the strategy acknowledged the current system of communal education and accepted that, 'for the foreseeable future, there will remain a number of different education sectors' and that a single, overarching, shared education system can encompass these different sectors with cross-sectoral collaboration between schools (APNI 2013).

Nevertheless, in a significant feat, the Alliance finally passed the Integrated Education Bill in March 2022. The legislation, albeit heavily amended, provided for a number of measures to support expansion, including setting minimum targets for the number of children being education in integrated schools (Bain 2022). Its passage told two tales: about the contestation of civic policies but also the shifting ground of Northern Ireland politics. The bill was opposed by unionist parties who claimed it discriminated against the religious sectors. The DUP's attempt to trigger a Petition of Concern to block it failed, however, when the UUP declined to sign up to the veto, although still voting against the bill. The legislation was ultimately passed by civic and nationalist parties, reflecting a shift from a bipolar party system towards a three-bloc (nationalism, unionism, civic) system with unionism in recession (Emerson 2022).

The institutional legitimacy granted to binarity and group autonomy, particularly in the realms of education and culture, can serve to marginalize civic parties, deprive them of space to pursue their distinct civic agenda, contest their legitimacy, and even coopt their policies. These are themes to which we return below.

Political Discourse

Ethnonationalism forms the dominant discourse of Northern Ireland politics, saturating political debate. Power-sharing legitimizes and reinforces this discourse, with all politics filtered through an ethnonational lens. In this context other issues and agendas are easily pushed to one side, obscured, or even delegitimized. As Drapeau-Bisson argues, the dominant 'orange versus green' frame of Northern Ireland's power-sharing system filters the issues that are admissible on the political agenda, narrowing the space available for other issues, including abortion rights, and pushing them into the extra-institutional space of mobilization (2020, 94). The institutional recognition of nationalism and unionism is replicated in media narratives. In this context, civic parties lack ideational space in the political debate to pursue their distinct brand of politics. They face *marginalization, contestation,* and *co-optation.*

Marginalization

The discursive hegemony of ethnonationalism sees issues of ethnonational identity dominate and, at times, drown out civic issues of concern to all citizens. This culture consigns the civic agenda to the periphery of politics and creates an environment that is inimical to the advancement of issues which are not specific to either community, such as those pertaining to social justice, environment, gender, or human rights. Indeed, a tendency for MLAs to focus disproportionately on symbolic and divisive issues, such as flags and parades, and a corresponding lack of progress on 'bread and butter issues' in the Assembly has been highlighted in the annual Peace Monitoring Report (Nolan 2013, 145). Civic party representatives complain of difficulties within this environment in getting their voices heard and advancing policies that relate to wider society rather than communal interests.[9] One senior Alliance MLA explains the challenge this side-lining of the civic agenda can pose for the party, not least in terms of the media coverage it receives: 'A lot of public policy and the media narrative around Northern Ireland is weighted against us. So, often in elections you have "battle within unionism" [narrative], "battle within nationalism", and … "how do we cover the Alliance Party, their narratives?"'[10]

Likewise, a Green MLA argues that the binary narrative of Northern Ireland politics and its culture of ethnic representation is embedded in the institutions and then reproduced in the media. 'If you're not a Nationalist or a Unionist you're seen as irrelevant – oh you might get thirty seconds on the radio just to tick the box … And it produces a culture, doesn't it? And that's how culture and understanding is replicated, reproduced, and kept alive.'[11]

On the civil society level, one citizens' rights campaigner and commentator complains of the platforming of extreme voices that are not representative of wider public opinion, citing the example of a well-known loyalist activist after a violent protest against the Brexit protocol in October 2021. Meanwhile the growing number of voices that represent non-nationalist and non-unionist identities are sidelined:

> Take the Loyalist Communities Council – an umbrella origination that includes illegal, criminal gangs. They've made threat after threat after threat to political representatives … and they continue to be platformed in the media. All they have to do is put their hands up at a meeting and they're in the papers.
>
> Whereas those who advocate for a more nuanced position or those who represent the growing cohort of people that don't identify as nationalist or unionist, their views are not represented, they're not platformed in the media anywhere near as much, if at all, in many instances. And I think the media does have a role to play in how it represents Northern Ireland.[12]

Indeed, Alliance Leader Naomi Long recently criticized state broadcaster the BBC for giving an 'open mic' to anti-protocol voices, well out of proportion to their number in society, while SDLP MLA Matthew O'Toole questioned the 'level of prominence consistently given to a small section of hardline voices' on a popular radio show on BBC Radio Ulster (Simpson 2022). This chimes with Whiting and Bauchowitz's argument that media portrayals may play a role in creating the perception of polarization of civil society in Northern Ireland in spite of the reality of general convergence since the agreement (2022).

NGOs representing non-sectarian agendas also feel this filtering of issues through an orange and green lens. The then president of the cross-community students association NUS-USI, for example, reported the need, when lobbying political parties, to couch demands in terms of their impact on 'Catholic students' or 'Protestant students'.[13] This sense of marginalization appears to reinforce the 'othering' civic parties feel in the institutions, as a result of rules like designation, cross-community voting, the veto and policy autonomy for nationalism and unionism.

Contestation

Civic parties in Northern Ireland stand outside the dominant ethnonational binary and face few competitors in their own civic bloc. Yet, this does not mean that they do not face competition from their ethnonational counterparts. The political landscape in Northern Ireland has undergone considerable change in the last fifteen years and no longer resembles a purely 'bipolar' system made up of two separate party blocs, nationalism and unionism, with little to no competition between them, but increasingly a tripartite system of nationalist, unionist, and civic blocs. In this new landscape civic parties compete with unionist and nationalist parties for some of the same sections of the vote (O'Leary 2018). This aligns with Zuber's argument that in ethnically divided societies, electorally different ethnic blocs or 'markets' are 'imperfectly segmented', so that ethnic parties do not only face competition from other ethnic parties within their own bloc but also potentially from certain ethnic parties from other blocs and from non-ethnic or civic parties (Zuber 2012, 928). As the largest civic party, Alliance occupies the unique position of facing competition from all three sides: unionist, nationalist, and civic. Indeed, it competes intensely with ethnonational parties in certain areas, most notably with the DUP in constituencies like the Protestant-majority, traditionally unionist stronghold of East Belfast. In this contest, civic parties encounter a number of competitive discourses from ethnonational parties, including that of being *weak, irrelevant, suspicious*, and *traitorous*.

In a polarized environment, adopting a position of cooperation and compromise can lead civic parties to be caricatured as *weak*.[14] Alliance Deputy Leader Naomi Long explained: 'The other caricature that you need to overcome is that to be liberal is somehow to be woolly and weak ... I would say that a lot of the people that I know in Alliance are actually people with very strong opinions, people with a very strong drive.'[15]

Another trope the party encounters from its ethnonational opponents and, indeed, indirectly from the media, is *irrelevance*. One Alliance MLA argued that this was a deliberate strategy of these parties to dismiss cross-community parties and cross-community politics more generally, in an attempt to play down their significance:

> I think at the time [the 2010 UK general election] the party was given the recognition that [winning the East Belfast seat] was a huge achievement. But as time has gone on, I think the communications strategies of other political parties have tried to dampen the significance of that.
>
> You still have East Belfast, for example, rather lazily by the media referred to as a 'unionist constituency'. In May 2010 it voted for an explicitly cross-community MP. So why not refer to it as a 'cross-community constituency' then? And so, the scale of the challenge to get that message across is significant, whenever you have a media that is willing to lazily adopt some of those labels at times.[16]

This 'irrelevance' discourse was evident in an interview with one DUP representative who dismissed the notion that his party faced any competition from the Alliance.[17]

A third discursive strategy used by Alliance's ethnonational counterparts to compete with them is *suspicion* of its civic, cross-community stance and insinuation that the party is in fact aligned to one ethnonational community or the other. A number of civic representatives described the reluctance of their ethnonational rivals to accept their non-aligned stance and their tendency to try to characterize the party as 'really' nationalist or 'really' unionist.[18] Naomi Long outlines this tactic: 'Our opponents will try, based on individual decisions, to characterize us as unionist or nationalist, depending on their own views. There's a tendency for people to try to characterize us in that way because it's a comfortable place. People always want to put you in a box in Northern Ireland and when you defy that and you refuse to be boxed off, I think people find that quite challenging because they keep wanting to know what you are *really*, as though what you are really can't be what I am, which is an open, liberal, tolerant person."[19]

Likewise, one Alliance councillor in Belfast City Council, where the party held the balance of power between nationalist and unionist parties during the 2012–13 flag dispute describes the perils of that position: 'If we hold the balance of power, we're essentially the king makers, but that's a blessing and a curse all rolled into one. It is, because you watch the tweets going out from one council meeting; one minute we're part of a pan-nationalist front, the next we're a closet unionist party ... We're just voting on the issues.'[20]

In light of these attempts to 'expose' cross-community parties as truly unionist or nationalist, one Green Party MLA said he was conscious of his voting record in the Assembly. If seen by his ethnonational opponents to have voted more often with one bloc than the other, he anticipated that this would 'come back at him' at election time:

> By the nature of our politics we tend to be more left of centre, which means when it comes to voting we probably vote more with SDLP and Sinn Féin. That's not exclusively the case and certainly we don't follow their whip, but I can certainly see my unionist colleagues in [my constituency] thinking ... again it's that thing, 'I must put him into a box; what is he? He's voting with them ones again.'
>
> It's something I'm mindful of and it's certainly something I'm fully expecting to come back at me at the next election. I fully expect some of my unionist colleagues-stroke-opponents to bring some of that stuff out.[21]

An Alliance MLA relates the same difficulty for the party in cross-party negotiations (such as during the 2017–20 hiatus) and also in the Executive, where it held a sole ministry (Justice) in the 2020–22 mandate. She describes how Alliance's Justice Minister Naomi Long was regularly accused by her Executive partners of 'letting their side down' when her decisions happened to side with unionist parties or nationalist parties. 'It's a difficult line to walk ... when you're not satisfying everybody, and the polar opposites want you to take their side but at the same time kick you when you're with their opponents.'[22]

Indeed, ethnonational party representatives interviewed demonstrated this tendency, portraying Alliance alternatively as a 'soft unionist' party or nationalist sympathizers. One Sinn Féin MLA argued that, by accepting the constitutional status quo, Alliance is de facto unionist: 'I mean most people, most nationalists, would look upon the Alliance Party as a soft unionist party. Their position is not for a united Ireland, their position is that they're happy within the, inverted commas, "United Kingdom" and British jurisdiction and all of that.'[23] Meanwhile, a UUP MLA expressed distrust at the party's constitutionally non-aligned stance: 'How cross-community they are is quite hard to know ... The problem is with them, you don't know whether they're unionist or nationalist. Do they want to be in the United Kingdom or do they want to be in an all-Ireland state? Because to me that's the constitutional issue, that's the main issue that needs answered here in Northern Ireland. It would leave me very unsure of where they are, unsure of why you would vote for them.'[24]

Going beyond suspicion, civic parties also experience the accusation that they have somehow acted *traitorously*, betraying one community by cooperating with the 'other side'. This 'traitor' trope has a long lineage in Northern Ireland political discourse, particularly in the unionist tradition where a perceived failure to support and defend the Union can incur the 'Lundy' slur (see McKay 2021). These hostile discourses are most prevalent at moments of instability and polarization, when ethnonational insecurity is intensified. Members of Alliance interviewed cited polarizing events such as the republican prisoners' hunger strikes of 1981, when the Alliance lost much of its electoral representation in the Catholic areas of West Belfast, and the Anglo-Irish Agreement of 1985, which gave the Irish government a consultative role in the administration of Northern Ireland, and which Alliance supported in the face of unionist opposition, as some of the most challenging times for the party, points where support for the two ethnonational blocs was reinforced and its cross-community position marginalized.[25] Long expressed the party's difficulty during such periods: 'In some ways, the more reinforced the blocs are, the more challenging it is to be able to make headway because I think fear is the driver in those elections. It's no longer about people voting for what they want. It's about voting against what they're afraid of. And ... it's very, very difficult to reach into that and give people a more optimistic perspective.'[26]

For the Alliance, the discourses of suspicion and treachery have become more prevalent in recent years as the party has grown in strength and come to represent a greater threat to its nationalist and unionist rivals.[27] They manifested violently in the flag protest in 2012, explored below. Yet, that violence was the culmination of the build-up of unionist and loyalist attacks and intimidation over a decade as the party's electoral fortunes rose and represented an increasing threat to unionism, according to party leadership at the time (McCaffery 2012). In 2002 the Alliance encountered such attacks after the party supported a Sinn Féin candidate, Alex Maskey, for lord mayor of Belfast, the first republican politician to hold the position. Although the election was inevitable after Sinn Féin became the largest party in the council, one senior unionist dubbed an Alliance representative a 'Provo' (a reference to the Provisional IRA) for backing Maskey. Party members also experienced private intimidation from loyalists in the aftermath of the vote, including harassment and threatening phone calls (McCaffery 2012), and one MLA described how his home was subsequently attacked by local loyalists.[28] Alliance members claimed the party was subject to a number of large-scale leafletting campaigns in working-class Protestant areas in the decade leading up to the flag protest, misrepresenting the party's policies on other sensitive issues, and that these moves intensified following the party's dramatic Westminster win in East Belfast in 2010 (McCaffery 2012).

And the Alliance found itself once again deeply – sometimes violently – contested following the Brexit vote of 2016. As a stridently pro-EU party, it campaigned to remain in the referendum and, in the wake of the Leave vote, for special treatment for Northern Ireland in the UK–EU deal to mitigate the worst impacts of a hard Brexit on the region – pragmatically supporting Theresa May's controversial 'backstop' and then Boris Johnson's protocol. These policy decisions, which inadvertently placed Alliance and other civic parties on the same side as nationalist parties and, indeed, the Irish government, have seen the party come under intense contestation from their unionist party rivals as well as loyalist groups, who have accused it of endangering the Union and even betraying unionists. Criticisms have ranged from insinuations to accusations to online abuse, intimidation, and even threats of physical attack. Despite Alliance's attempts to present the issue as a cross-community 'non-ethnic' one, unionist parties have routinely depicted it as aligning with nationalists and the Irish government. The DUP, in particular, has used the discursive tactic of lumping Alliance in with nationalist parties and the Irish government in their criticisms, in a bid to discredit the party (Murphy and Evershed 2022, 106). Similarly, prominent unionist opponent of the

Figure 4.2 | Poster distributed in North Down during 2019 UK general election.

protocol Kate Hoey, a former Labour MP and now peer, uses the Alliance's stance to place it on the side of nationalism (Quoted in Young 2021):

> Now I can understand the republican party and I can understand the nationalist SDLP for wanting to make the Protocol the issue that helps to further their political aims.
>
> What I cannot understand is why the Alliance Party, the party that was meant to be even handed, why the Alliance Party want to rigorously, rigorously implement the Protocol.

And I would say that they have shown ... when it comes to the crunch, when it comes to the crunch the Alliance Party will always support those who want to destroy the union.

Election campaigns are key moments for this traitor trope to be deployed against the Alliance. During the 2019 general election campaign Alliance Party candidate for North Down Stephen Farry was accused of being 'part of a pan-nationalist front' and the party depicted as serving as 'useful idiots' for Sinn Féin (Kane 2019). Furthermore, an election leaflet distributed in the constituency read: 'The Unholy Alliance: If you vote for them the IRA win' (see figure 4.2). One Alliance MLA reported a torrent of online trolling over Brexit since 2016 as well as having her constituency office graffitied about the issue and bins set alight. Alliance is particularly vulnerable to these attacks, compared to nationalist parties, she notes, given their vocal stance on Brexit and the fact that, unlike their nationalist counterparts, they are present in traditionally unionist areas, such as Newtownards, Co. Antrim where her office is based.[29] This makes the party as 'easy target' of sorts. The MLA observed that nationalist parties were generally slow to respond publicly to such attacks on the Alliance and suggested that, by portraying unionism in a negative light, these incidents can be politically useful for Sinn Féin.[30]

Case Study 4.1: Flag Protest 2012–13

The contestation of civic politics in Northern Ireland played out dramatically in the political dispute that engulfed the Alliance Party over the issue of flag flying at Belfast City Council in 2012–13. Culture is deeply contested in the Northern Ireland conflict. Contestation over cultural symbols dates back to the eighteenth century and has continued through the peace process and into the power-sharing period, manifesting around issues such as Orange Order parading, the naming of buildings, streets, towns, and parks, the wearing of sports shirts, and, of course, the flying of flags (Nolan et al 2014, 18; Bryan 2015). In December 2012, Belfast City Council (BCC) confronted the question of how and when the Union Flag should be displayed at Belfast City Hall – an issue that placed the agendas of 'shared space' and 'cultural autonomy' into tension. After a long review of flag flying at BCC, initiated by nationalist parties in 2011 and including an Equality Impact Assessment, the council voted on a motion that the flag would cease to be flown every day and instead fly only on eighteen designated days of the year. This motion was put forward by the Alliance, which held the balance of power on the council with six councillors compared to twenty-four nationalist and twenty-one unionist members, as a compromise option between the unionist position that the flag should fly every day and the nationalist preference for its permanent removal. In the wake of the council vote on 3 December 2012, in which the Alliance held the casting vote, protesters stormed the courtyard and violent street protests ensued and spread to a number of other locations in Northern Ireland. Alliance members were singled out in this violence. Over the following days an arson attempt was made on one of its party offices, while another was ransacked. One female councillor was forced to leave her home after receiving death threats, while the home of two other councillors (a married couple) was attacked and that of another sixty-year-old female councillor was broken into by four masked men. Then Alliance MP Naomi Long received a credible threat on her life and was advised by police not to leave her home or enter her constituency office in East Belfast. A petrol bomb was subsequently thrown into a police car protecting her office, forcing a female police officer to flee (Nolan et al 2014, 42–3). Street protests continued for some four months after the vote, including at Alliance offices, albeit mostly non-violent.

These attacks did not emerge organically from the grassroots but were precipitated by an organized political campaign. This notably included the distribution of 40,000 inflammatory leaflets in predominantly Protestant areas of the city which featured the Alliance's signature yellow colour and singled out the party as responsible for the policy, depicting it as nationalist sympathizing and revealing the contact details of party members (BBC *News* 2012) (see figure 4.3). The leaflets did not feature any other party's branding but it has been claimed that they were produced and distributed by the DUP and UUP in a joint effort (Nolan et al 2014, 37). The campaign was notably concentrated in East Belfast, traditionally a DUP stronghold and where the party had faced increasing competition from Alliance in recent years, including the significant blow

Figure 4.3 | Leaflet distributed to homes in Belfast in November 2012 following the vote on flying the Union flag in Belfast City Council.

of losing the Westminster seat previously held by then DUP leader Peter Robinson, to the Alliance's Naomi Long in 2010. Indeed, the leaflet tellingly named Long as the individual to lobby, supplying her phone number and email, despite the fact that she was not a member of Belfast City Council (Nolan et al 2014, 37). While the attacks on Long's office were condemned by the leaders of the DUP and UUP, a UUP MLA and DUP MLA attended a protest outside her office the following day (Nolan et al 2014, 47). Figure 4.4 shows a protest following the decision by Belfast City Council, including a banner that reads: 'Defend Our Flag: Smash the Alliance Party'.

Ethnonationalist narratives play a powerful role in post-agreement politics. The principle of 'parity of esteem' lay at the heart of the agreement. While nationalism has interpreted this principle as equality (or redress of past inequalities), within working class Protestant/Unionist/Loyalist (PUL) communities it has often been felt as an erosion of that community's position in society and a loss of its cultural heritage and identity (Nolan 2013, 17; Halliday and Ferguson 2016, 537). In this zero-sum logic, 'democratically secured removal of British symbols' can be easily perceived as a loss to the Catholic community's gain (Parr 2017, 43). A common feeling among members of Alliance interviewed was that this narrative of loss had been exploited by unionist parties in the flag dispute and deployed against the Alliance. The Alliance's actions were depicted as *weak* and *traitorous* – 'selling out' unionists.[31] Then MP Naomi Long, who was heavily targeted in the dispute, described how unionist opponents tried to portray her as 'the common enemy' and

Figure 4.4 | Flag protest targeting the Alliance Party making its way from Belfast city centre en route to East Belfast, January 2013.

a 'Sinn Féiner in sheep's clothing' in order to unite the community against Alliance and for their parties:

> There's a narrative that has been fed into loyalist communities now for a long time by unionist representatives, which is part of a strategy of 'You need us because we're fighting your corner, because you're losing out; you're losing out and you need stronger unionism'.
>
> So, the narrative in unionism ... dating right back, has always been that once you've compromised you're weak and you've lost something and what you need is for somebody stronger to come in who'll never do that again.[32]

Likewise, another Alliance MLA described ethnonational parties' attempts to 're-sectarianize politics in Northern Ireland in order to quell cross-community politics', as illustrated by the flag dispute: 'I think there's an explicit strategy from some of the other political parties to create and manufacture identity-based issues in order to heighten people's fears that compromise is somehow a win-lose situation as opposed to a win-win situation. And I think we have a challenge to communicate that everyone can benefit out of compromise, everyone can benefit out of building a shared future. Some of the parties are manipulating those issues [flags, emblems, dealing with the past, parading] and using those to try and inflame people's fears against cross-community politics.'[33]

Interviews with unionist politicians were revealing of these narratives. While condemning violence perpetrated in the wake of the flag protest, they expressed little sympathy for Alliance, portraying its actions as naïve and speculating that they would be punished by unionist voters at the ballot box for this 'betrayal'.[34] An exchange with one UUP member illustrates this attitude:

> UUP MLA: There is no excuse for any violence that was turned on [Alliance] or indeed any other party or individuals. So, I believe they weren't treated well in that sense. But politically they do have to stand up and explain why they took the vote in the way they did. I don't believe they've done that very successfully. Because they do get quite a lot of unionist voters ...

> because they're seen by some unionists maybe as being a very soft side of unionism.
>
> Author: Do you think that the flag dispute will make those voters see them differently?
>
> UUP MLA: I think it will, yeah. I think it will.[35]
>
> Yet, despite unionist parties' predictions that punishment never transpired. As I explore further in the next chapter, the Alliance vote held up in the subsequent elections in 2014. In the local elections its vote dropped by only 0.7 per cent nationally and it lost one seat on Belfast City Council but retained the position of fulcrum between nationalism and unionism (Nolan et al 2014, 129). Meanwhile, in the 2014 European elections the party received its best result to date in the contest, rising 16 per cent to take 7.2 per cent of the vote (see table 2.4).

Co-optation

As well as marginalizing and contesting civic issues, the dominant ethnonationalist discourse can leave issues monopolized as the domain of nationalism or unionism. Given the historical power dynamics of the conflict, nationalism has in some ways laid discursive claim to the so-called 'equality agenda' in Northern Ireland politics. Minority rights, enshrined in the Good Friday Agreement, has become a site of contestation between nationalist and unionist parties post-agreement, presented by the former as a means to redress past inequalities between the two communities and the latter as a nationalist attempt to erode unionist culture and position in society (Nagle 2016b, 862). This contestation has spilled over into issues of broader equality and human rights, such as gender and LGBTQ+, in a demonstration of 'ethnic seepage' (Horowitz 1985; Nagle 2016b, 863). Socially liberal/conservative debates have risen in salience in the last ten years, with issues like same-sex marriage and abortion playing a prominent role in elections, including for Westminster, despite these matters being devolved to Stormont (Tonge and Evans 2015, 128). In another contentious example, the DUP tabled a bill in 2014 seeking to introduce a 'conscience clause' into equality legislation whereby individuals and businesses could be exempt on the grounds of religious belief – a response to a row over a Christian-owned bakery's refusal to make a wedding cake for a same-sex couple (Hayes and Nagle 2016, 27).

The politicization of broader equality issues has brought some progress, such as Westminster legislating for marriage equality and abortion in 2019. Yet, it has also brought some unwelcome consequences for the communities affected and civic politics more broadly. The debate surrounding same-sex marriage, for example, became muddied by the nationalist/unionist cleavage, with Sinn Féin championing the policy and DUP opposing it (Tonge and Evans 2015, 130; Thomson 2016, 496). This played out visibly with the DUP's use of the veto to block nationalist party motions to legalize equal marriage and Sinn Féin highlighting that move as one of its reasons for withdrawing from the power-sharing partnership in 2017, as discussed in the last chapter. In this sense, Nagle observes that nationalist parties in Northern Ireland have, to some extent, co-opted the LGBTQ+ rights agenda (Nagle 2016b, 868). This is part of a broader phenomenon observed in divided societies referred to as 'homonationalism', where ethnonationalist groups 'seek to co-opt the language of LGBT rights as a means to advance their own political platforms as liberal and progressive in distinction to their ethnonational rivals, who are framed as conservative and reactionary' (Nagle 2016b, 868). Founder member of NIWC and gender activist Bronagh Hinds has argued that marriage equality, abortion, and other progressive policies, like gender quotas, are held back in Northern Ireland by such perceived nationalist party ownership – potentially alienating unionist voters and frustrating broad cross-societal consensus around these issues.[36] Likewise, Thomson underlines the danger for these broader rights agendas being politicized along sectarian lines (2016, 496–7). Equality and human rights activists also expressed the challenge of navigating these issues in Northern Ireland, where the perception of being aligned with nationalist parties is both dangerous and difficult to escape.[37]

As well as civic issues being co-opted to ethnonationalism, civic party policies are also susceptible to co-optation by other parties and even the British and Irish governments. Progressive and compromise positions put forward by these parties are often eventually taken up by other parties but without the credit necessarily being attributed. This was felt in the case of the Irish Language Act, as discussed above, where Alliance members noted that their proposals to the negotiations were absorbed in the 2018 draft party agreement, without any recognition of that contribution.[38] Similarly, though later associated primarily with Sinn Féin, the first legislative moves towards marriage equality at Stormont were initiated by the Green Party and the first motion brought forward by the Greens in partnership with Sinn Féin (Spedding 2012). This dynamic can be read as an erasure of civic party agency, reflecting their marginalization within the dominant ethnonational discourse. The dynamic could also be interpreted in a more positive light, however. O'Leary notes that the emergence of 'the others', such as Alliance, but also the more short-lived NIWC and NI21, has prompted some of the main parties to update their platforms (O'Leary 2018, 236). In this sense, civic parties are exerting their influence on Northern Ireland politics, albeit sometimes under the radar.

Logic of Ethnic Representation

The dominant discourse of ethnonationalism also leads to a normalization and legitimization of ethnonational representation. In this culture politicians explicitly or implicitly claim to represent 'their' community, advocate for its perceived interests and make exclusive appeals for its support. This schema of ethnonational representation appears prominent in the minds of voters, as well as the political classes. A survey carried out following the 2011 Assembly election found that voters attributed responsibility for the lives of Protestants primarily to the DUP and that for the lives of Catholics mostly to Sinn Féin (Garry 2013). This embedded culture was cited by one DUP MLA interviewed as an obstacle to his reaching out to Catholic voters. Given the culture of ethnonational representation and the 'zero-sum' discourse that characterizes Northern Ireland politics, he believed his work in Catholic areas would be perceived by his Protestant supporters, not as additional to, but at the expense of work undertaken in their areas: 'So, if we were perceived in our own community to be pursuing Catholic votes, nationalist votes, the inevitable consequence of that would be … some people would say, "You're doing that instead of [pursuing] unionist votes."'[39]

The framing of political representation as ethnonational clearly runs deep in the political culture of Northern Ireland making alternative forms of representation – cross-ethnic, non-ethnic or civic – a challenge to advance. This framing is reflected and reinforced by the institutional rules unpacked in the last chapter. Not least of these is the requirement for Members of the Assembly to designate as Nationalist, Unionist, or

Other and privileging of the two ethnonational designations in legislative decision-making. Likewise, the election of the first and deputy first ministers by the largest parties in the largest and second largest Assembly designations reinforces the idea that these two positions will be occupied by a nationalist and unionist, while their titles, which imply a hierarchy, drives ethnonational competition.

Ethnonational Clientelism

Another effect of the parity principle manifests materially: through the allocation of public funds. The structure of the power-sharing Executive outlined in chapter 2, in which government departments run by rival parties enjoy relative autonomy and insulation from one another, has been blamed for contributing to a lack of transparency and accountability in politics and, worse still, corruption and cronyism. This effect was writ large during the Renewable Heat Initiative scandal in 2016 which mired then DUP First Minister Arlene Foster, who had been minister for the Department of Enterprise, Trade, and Investment which administered the scheme. Flaws in the scheme, which was designed to encourage business to switch from fossil fuels to renewable energy, saw it go vastly over budget, which could have cost the public purse an estimated £700m over twenty years. The scandal triggered the collapse of the power-sharing Executive in January 2017 and led to the establishment of an inquiry that reported in 2020 (*BBC News* 2020).

These structures have also led to a degree of patronage and clientelism in Northern Ireland politics, in which departments – and hence the parties that control them – have significant discretion over the community initiatives and organizations to which public funds are allocated. Northern Ireland politics is by no means unique in featuring clientelism, and other factors undoubtedly contribute to this practice, not least its small size (similar to the Irish Republic). Nevertheless, the power-sharing structures add an extra layer in facilitating clientelist practices. The Executive set-up, dominated as it is by ethnonational parties, clearly privileges those organizations aligned with nationalist or unionist communities. What's more, it arguably reinforces the dominance of these organizations in society and, in turn, gives nationalist and unionist parties a competitive advantage over their civic rivals. Clientelism claims were invoked during the controversy that erupted over the awarding of £1.7m through the Social Investment Fund (SIF), a fund to tackle social deprivation administered by the Executive Office (the department of the first and deputy first ministers), to an organization called Charter NI which was headed by an alleged commander of the loyalist paramilitary group the Ulster Defense Association (UDA). It later transpired that the DUP Speaker of the Assembly held close ties with the organization, including attending board meetings and lobbying funders on its behalf (Morris 2017). These revelations gave rise to claims that the DUP had used SIF to help it attract electoral support from hardline loyalist communities (Morris, 2017). A subsequent audit into the fund found a significant lack of transparency and due process in the way it was administered by the Executive Office (McCormack 2018). Indeed, the fact that funds for community relations are administered directly by the Executive Office department and not by an arms-length independent body has been highlighted as problematic by leaders in the voluntary sector.[40]

This clientelist dynamic, can clearly leave civic parties marginalized and at a competitive disadvantage to their ethnonational rivals.[41] On the level of civil society, it can bolster community organizations aligned with nationalism or unionism at the expense of other issues, groups and sectors. Representatives of some non-aligned community organizations, such as those representing racial and ethnic minorities, the environment and LGBTQ+ communities, felt the marginalizing effect of this informal framework.[42] Less directly, ethnonational clientelism – whereby, for example, community organizations in nationalist majority areas are reliant on the patronage of Sinn Féin MLAs and ministers while those in unionist majority areas are reliant on that of the DUP – further entrenches the culture of ethnonational representation discussed above. The adverse impact of ethnonational clientelism on civic parties and movements is not unique to Northern Ireland and has been observed in other consociational settings, not least Bosnia (Milan 2020) and Lebanon (Nagle 2018; Deets and Skulte-Ouaiss 2021), as we explore in chapter 6 (see Cammett et al 2022, for nuanced analysis of the interplay between ethnonational politics and clientelism).

Conclusion

Civic parties face real and direct barriers in Northern Ireland's power-sharing institutions, as chapter 3 made clear. Yet, these formal barriers reflect and reinforce deep informal barriers, embedded in the institutional culture, political discourse, clientelist practices, and ethnic frames for political representation. In a system whose legitimacy is derived from ethnonational representation, the legitimacy of civic politics faces challenges. With the principle of binarity sanctioned in the peace agreement, policies based on sharing and intersectionality, especially in culture and education, encounter a legitimacy problem. Furthermore, in that dominant discourse, civic parties struggle to be heard and to advance their agendas and to do so on their own terms. The civic agenda faces marginalization, contestation, and co-optation, pitfalls that must be navigated with care. Beyond the direct, institutional structures, then, the informal, cultural, and ideational space of Northern Ireland politics is just as tricky for civic actors to navigate. What's more, the formal and informal institutions interplay in intricate ways to obstruct civic parties and their politics.

Yet, while this contestation represents real risks to civic parties that can impede their progress, ironically it also underlies their increasing recognition by ethnonational actors as a *threat*. The 2012–13 flag protest was a moment in Northern Ireland's post-conflict politics that signalled a shift slowly taking place: the rise of civic politics as a force. In the intervening years that trend has become more pronounced, solidifying in 2019–22 when the Alliance moved to third place in elections behind the main nationalist and unionist parties Sinn Féin and DUP. Issues beyond the ethnonational divide have risen up the agenda as long battles for the legalization of same sex marriage and abortion culminated in legislation from Westminster in 2019. Meanwhile socio-economic issues such as healthcare and inflation, dominated most recent election cycles. In 2020, 42 per cent of people identified as neither nationalist nor unionist, more than those identifying with either of the two main blocs (ARK 2020). In many ways, the flag protest demonstrated that the battle lines in Northern Ireland politics were being redrawn. This was no longer a rigidly binary landscape but one shaped by three blocs: unionist, nationalist, and civic.

The fact that civic politics have endured and grown against this backdrop tells a powerful story. But just how have civic parties and movements effected that feat? It is to their agency that we now turn.

Chapter Five

Navigating the System in Northern Ireland

On 24 June 2016, Northern Ireland awoke to an utterly changed political reality. The UK had voted to leave the European Union (EU), a political and economic union of then twenty-eight states of which it had been a member, in common with the Republic of Ireland, for forty-three years. To the surprise of many, across and beyond the state, the referendum was narrowly carried by 51.9 per cent. Northern Ireland had rejected the proposal, voting by 56 per cent to remain within the EU but with the vote taken on a statewide basis that did not matter. Northern Ireland was set to leave the bloc and become the site of the new and only land frontier between the UK and EU. Overnight the parameters of post-Good Friday Agreement politics had transformed. If that agreement temporarily 'settled' the question of the border in Irish politics, the Brexit vote blew it wide open. Amidst uncertainty over the implications for Northern Ireland's economy, political stability, and peace, Sinn Féin immediately called for a referendum on Irish unification as the only way to avoid the return of a catastrophic 'hard border' on the island. The DUP, the only main party to support Leave, affirmed its unequivocal position that Northern Ireland must remain fully aligned with the UK in the divorce to come. The 'constitutional question' was now back on the agenda, in a big way.

These circumstances – constitutional crisis, ethnonational insecurity, and polarization – would appear a perfect storm for civic parties. Horowitz, who deemed multi-ethnic parties 'a fragile institution' (1985, 396), would surely predict their obliteration in the fallout. Yet, ironically, these parties have grown substantially over that period, in size, number, and relevance. Three are now represented in the Northern Ireland Assembly, making up 17 per cent of the vote share and 20 per cent of seats in the

2022 election, compared to 8 per cent and 7 per cent respectively in 1998. The largest, Alliance, came third in seat and vote share in those elections, overtaking the main moderate unionist and nationalist parties – after commanding an average vote share of just 7 per cent between 1974 and 2019 (Tonge 2020, 462). Alliance also now occupies the high-profile Justice Ministry in the power-sharing government. More remarkable is that civic parties have reached these heights not only amidst political crisis but in spite of the marginalizing effects of the power-sharing system explored in the last two chapters.

This seeming paradox speaks to the fact that civic actors are not just passive victims of political structures or of events. They have agency and can respond creatively to their circumstances, finding openings and exploiting them, even in the most unlikely conditions. So, how have civic parties adapted to not only survive but expand in this environment? This chapter examines the strategies civic parties use to navigate post-agreement power-sharing: to negotiate barriers but also seize openings. For, as well as erecting obstacles to civic parties, Northern Ireland's power-sharing system has, somewhat unexpectedly, afforded them opportunities. Yet, the story is not straightforward. These openings can place civic parties in a position that compromises their ability to pursue their own distinct politics and, on occasion, push them back into the limiting role of mediator.

The chapter starts by examining how civic parties have positioned themselves with regard to the ethnonational divide and adapted those positionings over time. It then explores the ways in which they have engaged with the power-sharing institutions. It goes on to show how civic parties have claimed discursive space in a changing political landscape and approached elections before probing how they have navigated divisive questions about Northern Ireland's constitutional future.

Party Positioning

In a divided society, fundamental to how a party defines itself is where it stands on the ethnonational question. In chapter 1 I categorized civic parties into three broad categories based on their goals vis-à-vis the divide in society: *accommodationist, integrationist,* and *intersectional.* Accommodationist parties essentially seek to accommodate the divide in society, by explicitly recognizing the different ethnic groups and representing them internally and externally on a pluralistic basis. Integrationist parties ultimately aspire to a more integrated society and therefore eschew ethnic representation, seeking to appeal to voters on an exclusively non-ethnic basis. Intersectional parties, meanwhile, recognize and respect ethnic group identity and, while not making it central to their offering, acknowledge the need to accommodate it alongside voters' other intersecting (and equally important) identities and affinities such as race, gender, class, and environment. When it comes to positioning on this accommodationist/integrationist/intersectional spectrum, civic parties in Northern Ireland show not just variation but *adaptation* and *evolution* over time in the transition from conflict towards relative peace and power-sharing.

The most interesting journey can be observed in Northern Ireland's largest and longest-standing civic party, Alliance. At its formation in 1970, Alliance positioned itself clearly as an *accommodationist* party. The goal of partnership between Catholics and Protestants was explicit in its appeal, its leadership (led by a Catholic and a Protestant), and even its name (APNI 1970b; Cushnahan 1979). In its first two years the party attracted representatives from both unionist and nationalist affiliations, including four Stormont MPs and one Westminster MP (Eggins 2015, 35). The early party also positioned itself as *moderate*: a voice of reason between the 'extremists' and necessary bridge between nationalism and unionism (APNI 1972b; Leonard 1999). It presented itself in distinctly pragmatic terms as a vehicle to a more functional politics in Northern Ireland (APNI 1972b). A 'self-defined balancing role' defined its early years, shown in a 1973 election candidate survey (McAllister and Wilson 1978, 220, 223). This bridging role was one it was called upon to play at various points in its history – not least in the short-lived Sunningdale power-sharing agreement in 1973–74 and the 1996–98 all-party negotiations that led up to the GFA. Indeed, in 1992 the party even redesigned its logo with the 'A' deliberately made to look like a bridge (Eggins 2015, 233).

Yet, alongside accommodation, *integration* has always run deep in the party's ethos. Leonard describes two principal strands in the Alliance: 'bridge builders', that sought to create conditions for peace by mediating between nationalism and unionism, and 'civic liberals', that sought to put forward a non-ethnic integrationist agenda. These accommodationist and integrationist elements have co-existed uneasily at times (Leonard 1999). Integration lies at the heart of Alliance policies including integrated education, mixed housing, and shared public space. The party also views itself as strongly liberal, championing individual rights, civil liberties, and freedom of expression by contrast to exclusivist group rights and prescriptive identities. In expressing what the party stands for, Alliance members consistently highlight these twin principles of integration and liberalism.[1] Alliance representatives commonly defined themselves in contrast to all other parties in the system, as something of a lone voice of reason in the midst of ethnonationalist politicking.[2] This 'exceptionalism' discourse marks a continuation from its early period (APNI 1970a; 1970b).

In defining Alliance, members in interviews, unlike in early party statements, did not refer to the religious or ethnonational make-up of its members or representatives. Rather, they talked about the party's ethos and goals. This thinking is reflected in Alliance's internal party structures, as well as its position on governing arrangements. The party eschews internal quotas for positions within the party leadership based on ethnonational or religious identity, as an approach that would run contrary to its principles. Indeed, members took pride in the fact that they did not know the religious or national affiliation of their party colleagues, nor members. As one senior representative articulated: 'I've no idea, we never ask them. We don't ask people what religion they are; we don't ask people what view they take on the border – that's their own choice, the party's not defined around those issues'.[3] Another recounted that after the death of a close party colleague, she and other members had to enquire in which of the town's two churches (Catholic or Protestant) the funeral would be held.[4] When it comes to leadership, however, ethnonational balance has been observed, if not officially: the party has been led by three Catholics and three Protestants to date. Furthermore, the deputy leader has generally been chosen from the other religion to the leader (Eggins 2016, 214).

Modern Alliance then presents itself as a civic party in its own right, not a conduit between nationalists and unionists. Indeed, members distanced themselves from the 'mediator' or 'bridge-builder' position – a role one senior member consigned to the party's past:

> That was our historic assumption, that we were the honest broker; that we never had any views of our own, we were just there for the process and as and when there was a blockage, we would either produce an idea or sacrifice ourselves in some convoluted way to make things move along.
>
> At times the party was put in that situation, and it always acted in what we viewed as being the best interests of Northern Ireland as a whole, even if that at times maybe cut across what would have been the more narrow interests of the party. Today, with the

situation a bit more bedded down, we're called on to play that role less often.[5]

Other members rejected the accommodationist role as a misrepresentation. Far from being a party of the 'moderate middle' that exists to forge compromise between two extremes, they argued, Alliance is a party with its own distinct agenda[6] (see also Neeson and Farry 1999, 1224). That agenda is 'radical change', according to Long: 'But I'm not sure, because of the way we're parodied on occasion, that people actually get the message. They just assume that we don't have an agenda other than to find a compromise between the two extremes. We actually have our own political agenda which is about removing the two extremes as the main political force in politics and finding a different alignment in politics.'[7] Then Leader David Ford likewise maintained that the party represented, not a compromise between two tribal positions but 'an alternative to tribal politics altogether'.[8]

Yet, more recent statements by Alliance members also suggest a growing *intersectional* understanding of its position. The party embodies a liberal, cosmopolitan view of identity that aligns with intersectionality. Whilst respecting that people in Northern Ireland hold different religious, ethnic, and national identities and aspirations, it maintains that identity is not fixed but fluid, multiple, and complex (APNI 2013, 14). The late former Alliance MLA Anna Lo – a Chinese-born politician, then the only ethnic-minority member of the Northern Ireland Assembly – expressed this in personal terms:

> For generations we've been voting for our community … and I think we need to be moving away from that, to let people see that we need to be voting on what the parties will do for you – on jobs, on employment, on education, on health – rather than keeping your identity.
>
> Is [identity] that important, really? What is an identity anyway? Orange identity or green identity. We all have multiple identities. As far as I'm concerned, I'm a mother, I'm a woman, I'm a politician, I'm against sexism. There are so many identities, I don't want to be defined as just one identity.[9]

Alliance members highlighted the increasing emergence of shared and civic identities in Northern Ireland, pointing to recent public opinion data showing an increasing proportion of people identifying as neither unionist nor nationalist (42 per cent in a 2020 survey, as shown) and as Northern Irish (20 per cent in the 2021 census) (NISRA 2022c). One Alliance MLA argues, '[Alliance is] passionate about a fluid, diverse identity … people should be given the opportunity to decide for themselves rather than being labelled.'[10]

Over time then, the Alliance's positioning has evolved in line with the political situation, as the focus has moved from the cessation of violence to establishing a more positive peace and 'normalization', with a progressive shift in emphasis from accommodation to integration and, more recently, intersectionality.

The Northern Ireland Women's Coalition (NIWC) demonstrates interesting parallels and contrasts with Alliance. Formed in 1996, for the express purpose of influencing the peace negotiations, it is hardly surprising that the NIWC positioned itself as largely *accommodationist.* It presented itself as a party comprising nationalists, unionists and others; British and Irish identities and both.[11] The party's leadership and representation in the all-party talks and the first Assembly reflected that accommodationist stance, with one representative from a Catholic, nationalist background and one from a Protestant, unionist background. So too did its approach to governance. The NIWC accepted the necessity of the consociational power-sharing system as a transitional framework and had no problem with the Other designation, according to former leader and MLA Monica McWilliams. Indeed, McWilliams draws a line between the NIWC and the Alliance in this respect:

> [W]e had always said that, unlike the Alliance, that we were nationalist, unionist and other. And we had no difficulty having that description. Whereas Alliance describes themselves as the party of the centre, we said 'no, we're truly cross-community, the people in our party are nationalists and unionists and others who wish to bring those identities into a coalition where we can work out from that what we want to do in order to reach an agreement.'[12]

By contrast to Alliance, the NIWC supported affirmative action externally to ensure equal representation, including gender and religious quotas – most notably for the new police service of Northern Ireland, established following the 1999 Patten Report which recommended a 50–50 recruitment policy for Catholics and Protestants (Tonge 2005, 99).

Yet, NIWC also exhibited a distinctly *intersectional* positioning. While respecting the different national identities in society, it maintained that solidarity on other issues was possible, in line with 'transversal' politics, as explored in chapter 1 (Fearon 1999). Far from requiring members to abandon their national identities and sidestep issues relating to the conflict, women were encouraged to 'bring their baggage into the room' when engaging internally within the party and externally in the peace talks and beyond[13] (Fearon and McWilliams 2000, 128; Meyer McAleese, 2009). Civil rights activist and former Mid Ulster MP Bernadette McAliskey, observes a tension in NIWC between positioning itself as a feminist party in its own right or as a party of peacemaking – lamenting the fact that it ultimately followed the latter path and disbanded in 2006 (featured in O'Neill 2017). Her observation speaks to the coexistence of accommodationist and intersectional strands within the party.

The Green Party Northern Ireland, founded on one core agenda, aligns most closely with the *intersectional* positioning. It does not situate itself on the integration–accommodation spectrum, rejecting the premise of that distinction and actively resisting such labels. The Green Party is an all-island party but does not prioritize reunification (Garry et al 2022). Representatives distinguish the Greens from Alliance in the sense that it is 'naturally cross-community' by virtue of being an *issue-based party*, rather than one focused on reconciliation.[14] Then Green Party leader and MLA Steven Agnew argued that the party differs from the Alliance in the sense that it is not defined by anti-sectarianism but rather by its policies – social justice and combatting climate change. Opposing sectarianism is something that the party takes for granted, rather than its 'raison d'être':

> Maybe one of the reasons why I wasn't attracted to the Alliance Party is that by being a cross-community/anti-sectarian party, it's what you're against almost more than what you're for. You know, you even describe it as a 'cross-community party'; in any other country it would be called a 'party'…
>
> We're defined by our policies, we're defined by what we're for, we're defined by our policies on social, environmental justice, decision making at the lowest effective level and direct democracy, non-violent direct action, and these types of things.[15]

The Greens' intersectional positioning is also reflected in its approach to governance, where it has called for reform of the power-sharing system but has not made it central to its agenda. It does pursue integrationist policies, such as integrated education, but this is framed within its broader platform for social justice, rather than one singularly committed to tackling division in Northern Ireland. In this sense the party's civic stance appears taken-for-granted, rather than something it highlights.

The newest civic party People Before Profit (PBP) also positions itself in intersectional terms. PBP explicitly rejects the politics of sectarianism and seeks to represent a new form of politics defined by its socialist agenda. In its Assembly election manifestoes it defines itself as a 'radical alternative to the failed policies of the Stormont establishment and their communal headcount politics' (2022) and 'the anti-establishment alternative' (2017). PBP self-consciously seeks to present itself as embodying the new Northern Ireland. While foregrounding its re-distributive socio-economic policies, it supports integrationist and reconciliatory policies, such as integrated education, an end to paramilitarism, and support for victims (2022; 2017). PBP also promotes socially progressive, inclusive policies, championing LGBTQ+ rights and migrant rights. The party's non-aligned credentials have been questioned, however. Its representation is strongest in Catholic/Nationalist/Republican majority areas such as West Belfast and Derry/Londonderry. It is vocal on Irish language rights and sections of its most recent manifestos even appear in Irish. It is part of an all-Ireland party and favours a referendum on Irish unity and 'ending partition' to create a 'radical, reunified Ireland based on progressive socialist politics' (PBP, 2022) – a position that leads Garry, O'Leary, and Pow to classify it as a 'nationalist' party (Garry et al 2022).

Over time then, a subtle shift can be observed among Northern Ireland's civic parties from an accommodationist position, necessitated by conditions of conflict and peacebuilding, towards a more integrationist stance, as society moved towards a more positive form of peace, and ultimately towards a more intersectional approach which allows for a diversity of ethnonational affinities, yet is not defined by them. This has come as society has 'normalized' and other identities, issues, and cleavages – primarily social and economic – have risen in salience. Alliance, Greens, and PBP are relatively self-aware in this positioning, which they see as more sustainable and resonating more strongly with voters. Yet, the transition from accommodationist to integrationist, on to intersectional, is neither straightforward nor complete, particularly for Alliance. While the integrationist and intersectional stances may be more appealing to voters and members of the contemporary party, the legacy of its accommodationist role can come back into play, especially at critical moments when the need for mediation between nationalist and unionist parties arises. Positioning is evidently a key strategic choice for civic parties, and one that can elicit tensions.

Engaging in the Power-Sharing System

In chapters 3 and 4 we saw the barriers that the power-sharing system presents to civic parties in Northern Ireland. Yet, as the only game in town, how do they engage with that system and what role do they play within it? This is a dilemma that faces every civic party and movement operating in a consociational power-sharing system, the principles of which run directly contrary to its own. The main civic parties in Northern Ireland align most closely with the 'constructive engagement' strategy, described by Nagle and outlined in chapter 1 (2018). The Alliance and the Greens advocate reform of the consociational system to move towards more flexible, integrative power-sharing. Yet, these parties have consistently participated in the Assembly and, in the case of the Alliance, even the Executive (since 2010). Maintaining a critical stance at the same time as being part of the institutions can be a fine line to tread.

Alliance has taken a principled but pragmatic approach towards power-sharing. The party took part in the short-lived Sunningdale power-sharing executive of moderate parties in 1974. From the 1980s it promoted a flexible, voluntary form of power-sharing that favoured a coalition of moderate parties (Eggins 2015, 89). It actively participated in the peace negotiations of the 1990s, performing something of a 'watchdog' role (Leonard 1999; Farry and Neeson 1999, 1233). Yet, the GFA delivered a much more rigid and binary model of power-sharing than the party favoured, that centred on nationalism and unionism, including the 'extremes'. Though this was far less conducive to Alliance's fortunes, it still supported that agreement.

Post-agreement, Alliance has maintained its critical stance towards power-sharing, proposing reforms in every manifesto and pushing for change from within the Assembly. First and foremost, it calls for an end to the designation and associated veto rules, which it refers to as 'institutional sectarianism' and their replacement with a designation-free weighted majority system of voting (APNI 2022a). This would be a qualified majority (perhaps two-thirds) to which designation would be irrelevant (APNI 2022b). Alliance wants to see voting in the Executive – where there is provision for 'cross-community votes', effective community vetoes – taken on the same principle. When it comes to the formation of the Executive, it calls for voluntary coalition decided through negotiation between the parties that would be subject to a vote in the Assembly (APNI 2022). The Executive would operate on the basis of collective responsibility, while the provisions in the Assembly for an effective opposition to form would be strengthened (APNI 2022). Furthermore, Alliance wants to see the positions of first minister and deputy first minister renamed 'joint first ministers' to 'end what has become a contrived yet polarizing contest over which party has a claim to the "higher" office, when in effect the posts are equal in standing in all respects' (APNI 2022). The party has pushed for overhauls through the Assembly and Executive Review Committee, on which it had one member in the 2017–22 mandate. The 2022 Assembly result, that saw Alliance more than double its seat share and rise to third place, granted these calls a hearing in the media, even internationally (Murtagh 2022; Young 2022). The Green Party has also called for removing community designation in the Assembly. Similarly, it has pushed for greater cooperation and cohesion within the Executive, advocating a new legal duty that would require government departments and bodies to work together on cross-departmental issues (GPNI 2022).

When it comes to the Assembly's designation system, civic parties deeply resent having to designate as Other, as shown. Nevertheless, if they wish to take their seats, they have little choice but to live with it. Yet, as well as campaigning for reform, they have demonstrated creative resistance to the system. Members have signed in to the Assembly as 'Inclusive Other', 'United Community Other', 'Feminist', 'European', 'Cross-Community', and 'Socialist'.

Notwithstanding the institutional barriers civic parties protest, the power-sharing system has also presented them with undeniable opportunities: some structural, some ad hoc. Alliance has long been critical of the d'Hondt procedures, whereby parties are automatically awarded seats in the Executive (on a sequential basis), based on their strength in terms of Assembly seats – and urged a more consensual approach to executive formation that would require prior agreement of the parties (more in line with the centripetalist approach to power-sharing, as outlined in chapter 1). In practice, however, the system for forming government after elections has largely benefited Alliance. Structurally, d'Hondt has afforded Alliance the opportunity to participate in the Executive. The party was awarded its first Executive ministry through the procedures in 2011, one it retained until 2016. Beyond the rules established in the agreement, Alliance has also benefited from ad hoc arrangements – most notably the extraordinary appointment of the Justice Ministry. The contested Justice brief, which neither nationalist nor unionist parties trusted the other to hold, was only devolved to Stormont from Westminster following the 2010 Hillsborough Agreement. Due to the contested nature of justice and policing in the context of the Northern Ireland conflict, the position was awarded outside of the normal d'Hondt procedures, through a cross-community vote, won by Alliance's then leader David Ford in 2010, again after the 2011 election and by leader Naomi Long after the resumption of power-sharing in 2020 and again in 2024.[16]

Far from disadvantaging civic parties then, some scholars have pointed to the ways in which Northern Ireland's relatively liberal consociational structures – that do not pre-determine what groups will be in government but allow this to be determined by the outcome of elections – can actually privilege civic actors (see Mitchell 2018). McGarry and O'Leary present Northern Ireland's form of power-sharing executive – open to any party, regardless of designation – as favourable to smaller actors (2006, 274). Together with McCrudden and Schwartz they also point to the fact that there is no restriction to non-aligned parties taking on the roles of first and deputy first minister, should they grow to that level (McCrudden et al. 2013, 235). According to the rules of the GFA, as modified at St Andrews, the party with the most seats in the Assembly is eligible to nominate the first minister, regardless of designation – leaving this possibility open to Alliance in future (Garry et al, 2022). However, under those rules, the Alliance could conceivably come second in an election and still not be entitled to the position of deputy first minister if Other was not the second largest designation (Murphy 2023, 100).

From 2011–16 Alliance enjoyed two ministerial seats – one as a result of the regular power-sharing procedures plus an additional one due to the transitional nature of the power-sharing institutions. This was more than either of the second largest unionist or nationalist parties, UUP and SDLP, at the time – a fact underlined by representatives of unionist and nationalist parties interviewed.[17] Likewise, after the 2022 Assembly election Garry et al calculated that the Alliance was entitled to two out of ten portfolios in the Executive (with four for Sinn Féin, three for DUP and one for UUP). With that proportion (20 per cent) above both Alliance's first-preference vote share (13.5 per cent) and its seat-share (19 per cent), 'it can hardly complain that the system works against the party in this respect' (2022). The scholars advocate changing the rules so that the first and deputy first ministers are allocated by d'Hondt, in common with other portfolios and the titles equalized. However, they also argue that the Justice minister role should be filled in the same way, leaving it open to nationalist and unionist parties and no longer the preserve of Alliance, Others, or independents (Garry et al 2022). These changes would remove undue impediments to Alliance but also some advantages.

A number of Alliance members attested to the benefits of being in government, in boosting the party's profile, influence in the political system, and perceived relevance amongst voters.[18] Representatives attributed the party's nomination for the role of Justice minister to the perception amongst other parties of Alliance being trustworthy and 'in a position of reasonable integrity and reasonable balance'.[19] Other representatives felt the party's execution of the role had contributed to a reputation it already held of being a credible 'honest broker in politics in Northern Ireland'[20] and capable of commanding 'the respect of the entire community'.[21] One MLA said, 'the more we're exposed to the public and the more the public is exposed to us, the more they get to understand our message. And that has come about through [Executive] ministers'.[22]

The ability to participate in government has clearly expanded the Alliance's power and relevance over the last fifteen years and contributed to its electoral rise. Agarin and Jarrett find that the Alliance's participation in government has made it more electable. While participating fully in government, the party has embraced a critical and scrutinizing role towards the Executive of which it is part, not least during the COVID-19 pandemic (2022). As well as the Justice ministry, Alliance's non-aligned position helped its former leader John Alderdice secure the role of Speaker in the first Assembly 1998–2003 (Agarin and Jarrett 2022).

Yet, participating in a power-sharing system about which it holds strong objections has brought tensions for Alliance. Whilst the party eschews the 'middle-man' label, in some ways its place in the Executive has reinforced this intermediary image, not least in the contested Justice ministry. The decision to enter the power-sharing government to take on this role in 2010 prompted debate within the party.[23] After the 2016 elections former Alliance leader Seamus Close publicly warned the party against taking up the post once again to avoid being seen as 'patsys' of the main unionist and nationalist parties (Young 2016). The damage inflicted by the re-designation affair in 2001, when some Alliance members temporarily redesignated from Other to Unionist in a bid to save Stormont from collapse, was clearly still fresh in the minds of some members.

Beyond the Assembly and Executive, the party has been called on to play a mediation role in the many multi-party negotiations over the years – including leading up to the 2020 New Decade New Approach (NDNA) deal. The 'watchdog' role was invoked in interviews when party members referred to its place in these talks and in the power-sharing institutions.[24] While willingly stepping into this role at times and benefiting from the profile afforded, members of the contemporary party expressed discomfort with it. The re-designation affair was referenced in grave terms as a low point for the party.[25] One MLA expressed resentment at being placed in the mediator position, which proves thankless and pulls the party away from its own policy goals: 'Whenever the [NDNA] negotiations were going on ... there tended to be a bit of "ask Alliance what they think" or get us to drop the little pearls of wisdom into the other parties ... So, it felt a bit like we were the inbetweeners. And then it felt quite strange whenever we turned around and went, "OK, we have asks as well."'[26] This 'peace-making' dynamic is replicated within the Executive, the member observes, creating a tricky environment for Justice Minister Naomi Long to navigate. Long is expected to perform the role of conduit between nationalism and unionism when needed, but, also, targeted by her power-sharing partners if she aligns with one side over the other in decisions.[27]

Civic parties operating within the power-sharing system then walk a fine line between constructive engagement and principled objection to that system. The system in Northern Ireland has offered them some openings – not least in the Executive – that they have embraced. Yet, those opportunities can prove double-edged, threatening to compromise their values, policies and autonomy and drag them back to a role they are trying to consign to the past.

Claiming Issue Space

For some thirty years the discursive space occupied by civic parties in Northern Ireland was a small and precarious one. Yet, since the GFA the space in the political sphere for identities and issues other than ethnonational has expanded and civic parties – most notably Alliance – have effectively claimed it. These shifts have been driven by internal and external forces. As Northern Ireland has moved further from armed conflict, new social cleavages have emerged. The increase in physical security since the agreement has increased public demand for a shared society, opening up space for civic politics. Inward migration has further fuelled drives towards diversity and inclusion. In the economic transformations of the last fifteen-to-twenty years, a distinct socio-economic cleavage has emerged. Meanwhile, a fault-line has also deepened around liberal/conservative social values, driven by both global trends and domestic issues such as marriage equality and abortion.

Notwithstanding political polarization and continued segregation, there has been a marked shift in the direction of social integration and diversity. As already seen, there has been a sustained decline in identification with the traditional labels of nationalism and unionism. The largest proportion of respondents in an annual survey continue to identify as 'neither unionist nor nationalist', reaching a peak in 2018 at 50 per cent before dipping in subsequent years (37 per cent in 2023), (ARK 2018; ARK 2023b). Meanwhile, since 2012, around a quarter of people have identified with the Northern Irish label, roughly equally among Protestants and Catholics (Coakley 2021, 10; McNicholl 2018; 2019). Todd examines 'everyday identity change', which involves 'individual reflexive distantiation from key social and symbolic divisions' across both parts of Ireland. Though not always sustained nor necessarily translating into voting behaviour, she finds this change to be meaningful and pervasive, particularly in the North (2018, 7, 31–3).

While Brexit has seen a reawakening of the constitutional debate and some flux with regard to constitutional preferences, data indicate a relative contentment with Northern Ireland's constitutional status quo, as a devolved part of the UK with institutional links to the Republic of Ireland. A plurality of respondents in the 2022 survey (49 per cent) believed that the long-term policy should be for Northern Ireland to remain part of the UK – albeit with a fall of 6 per cent in the proportion satisfied with the status quo since 2020 (Hayward et al 2022). Northern Irish society has also become more diverse – not least racially, ethnically, linguistically, and religiously – over the last twenty years. According to the 2021 census, the number of people living in Northern Ireland who were born outside the UK and Ireland grew from 27,226 (1.6 per cent) in 2001 to 81,500 (4.5 per cent) in 2011 to 124,300 (6.5 per cent) in 2021 (NISRA 2022a). Public opinion data paint a picture of a society preoccupied with quality of life that wants to live in a more integrated, functional, and 'normal' Northern Ireland. In the 2023 survey, 67 per cent of people would prefer a mixed religion school for their children, compared to 23 per cent who prefer one of their own religion only, for example (ARK 2023a). Recent surveys also show support for stable, devolved power-sharing and cooperation between parties of nationalist and unionist blocs (ARK 2021a).[28] Furthermore, they indicate support for reforming the power-sharing institutions in a way that would favour civic parties and politics (Hayward et al 2022).[29]

These changes have clearly rendered fertile ground for civic parties, not least Alliance. Of those who identified as 'neither nationalist nor unionist' in the 2020 survey, 38 per cent claimed to support Alliance Party, with 11 per cent (the second largest proportion) supporting the Greens, and another 11 per cent the SDLP (McManus 2022). Indeed, the Alliance appears to be drawing support from across both communal backgrounds and none. Of those who identified as Alliance supporters in the 2020 survey, 32 per cent were Protestant, 20 per cent were Catholic, and 46 per cent selected 'No religion'. When those who opted for 'No religion' were asked what one they were brought up in, 52 per cent said Protestant, 35 per cent Catholic, and 12 per cent said they were from a non-religious background (McManus 2022). In a 2023 survey, in contrast to the main nationalist and unionist parties, roughly equal proportions of Catholic and Protestant respondents declared support for Alliance (17 per cent and 16 per cent respectively) and the Greens (2 per cent and 1 per cent) (ARK 2023c).

The Alliance has been deft at capitalizing on these shifts. The party embraces the rise of new, emerging, and more fluid identities, such as 'neither/nor' and Northern Irish, as shown above. Representatives regularly take the opportunity to highlight the prevalence of these identities in their statements.[30] The 2017 Assembly election manifesto states, 'we have seen a gradual movement away from rigid and reinforcing approaches to identity where "Protestant=Unionist=British' and 'Catholic=Nationalist=Irish", to a situation where more and more people, especially young people will see themselves as both a little bit British and a little bit Irish, increasingly identify as Northern Irish, and also reference themselves as European.' (APNI 2017a).

What's more, Alliance has convincingly staked ownership to the 'shared future' agenda. Since the agreement the party has made policies such as integrated education, shared housing, shared space, the removal of so-called 'peace walls', as well as fighting for a more integrated 'normal' political system as discussed above, central to its platform (APNI 2013;

2016; 2017; 2022). In key party statements, the shared future cause is identified as the party's 'USP' (unique selling point) (APNI 2015, 3; APNI 2016, 3). Likewise, one Alliance MLA interviewed said, 'Within [Northern Ireland politics] there are essentially three coherent positions. You have the unionist position which the DUP own, you have the nationalist position which Sinn Féin own, and you have the shared future, alternative position which we own.'[31] Alliance's bid to occupy this civic niche and own the 'shared future' issue space has been highly successful – even to the detriment of other civic parties like the Greens which lost both its seats in the 2022 Assembly election. Garry, O'Leary, and Pow observe that Alliance has become the 'tribune' of Others (Garry et al 2022).

Another development that has expanded the discursive space for civic politics is the rise of the socially liberal/conservative cleavage. In line with global and regional trends of secularization, the power of the traditional churches over how people live their lives and form opinions, particularly younger generations, has declined significantly over the last thirty years in Northern Ireland (Coakley 2021, 3; Todd 2018, 54, 61). While 9 per cent of people in 1998 identified as having 'no religion', by 2022 that proportion had risen to 28 per cent (ARK 1998a; ARK 2022a). With this decline has come a growing liberalization in social attitudes, particularly relating to gender and sexuality. This trend has made its way into politics with issues around gender and LGBTQ+ rights rising in salience, most notably marriage equality and reproductive rights. As elsewhere, this social liberalism has been met with equal resistance and backlash on the conservative side, most notably from the DUP. The politicization of such issues reflects broader global trends of socio-cultural polarization – and to an (ironic) degree – even a 'normalization' of Northern Ireland politics.

Equal marriage and abortion each became the subject of major political disputes from 2017–20, as discussed in chapter 3. Movements for their legalization were driven in part by developments, not just in the rest of the UK, but the Irish Republic where they were finally legalized after referenda in 2015 and 2018. These movements are among the most vibrant in contemporary Northern Ireland. Indeed, the Gay Pride March is now among the largest of all parades in Belfast, rivalling the annual 12th of July parade. Despite attempts to sectarianize marriage equality and abortion debates, these movements have seen mobilization and solidarity across the communal divide. The human rights campaigns have gone above and beyond ethnonational allegiance, underlined by their appeals to Westminster to intervene, on the one hand, and solidarity between abortion rights activists north and south of the Irish border, on the other, with the social media hashtag 'The North is Next' emerging after the 2018 referendum in the Republic.[32] Whiting and Bauchowitz note that 'moral issues' like same-sex marriage and abortion cut across the sectarian divide with attitudes to these issues determined by age rather than religion, thus forming a 'nonethnic cleavage' (2022). Similarly, O'Leary observes that the rise of social liberalism in Northern Ireland in recent years has borne cross-cutting elements, supported by both civic and nationalist parties (2018). Ó Dochartaigh, meanwhile, sees an alternative majority forming in Northern Ireland, that is socially liberal, as well as pro-EU, and disposed to stronger links with the Republic of Ireland (2021, 19).

The emergence of this new 'socially liberal/conservative' cleavage has created clear discursive space, into which civic parties have stepped. Alliance, the Greens, and PBP have each been vocal advocates of marriage equality and abortion and made them central to their platforms. While the Greens and PBP at times took more radical stances, Alliance positioned itself on occasion as a moderate voice seeking to find compromise amidst the polarization. This stance could be witnessed in its legislative attempts to exempt religious organizations from having to administer same-sex marriages, discussed in chapter 3. Unlike communal identity issues like flags and parades, these are issues on which where their distinct voice can be more easily heard, with lesser risk of ethnonational contestation.

As well as socio-cultural developments, economic shifts have also seen a pronounced socio-economic cleavage emerge in Northern Ireland politics. From the 2008 global financial crash to the austerity policies that followed from the UK government in the 2010s to the resulting diminution of public services such as welfare and healthcare, up to the inflation/cost-of-living crisis of the 2020s, basic standards of living have progressively moved front and centre in Northern Ireland politics. Socio-economic forces have formed the backdrop to every political development in this period, including the disaffection evident in the flag protest and the protocol protests (Halliday and Ferguson 2016, 527). The first direct manifestation came with the row over implementation of the UK Government's Welfare Reforms 2012–15, which brought power-sharing close to collapse. In recent years this cleavage has become more pronounced. The dominant issues in the 2019 general election – aside from

Brexit – were quality of life related, most notably healthcare (Whitten 2020). Meanwhile, all parties in the 2022 election prioritized the cost of living amidst rising inflation.

Civic parties have clearly seized the openings that this period of economic uncertainty has rendered for them. It is no coincidence that People Before Profit gained legislative representation for the first time in the Irish Republic in 2011, followed by Northern Ireland in 2016. The Green Party, which champions social justice, also increased its representation from one seat to two in 2016 – a rise to which the increasing salience of environmental concerns in the context of climate change undoubtedly contributed. Meanwhile, for Alliance, which holds a more moderate economic position, its reputation as a sensible party that focuses on 'bread and butter' issues and advocates 'regional development' came into focus (Agarin and Jarrett 2022). More recently, the backdrop of dysfunction at Stormont amidst the public service crisis in the 2019 general election (Whitten 2020, 319) and the cost-of-living crisis in the 2022 Assembly election, gave Alliance, a strong platform to position itself as a rational and responsible player seeking to restore stability and make the institutions work for the people (see also Todd 2018, 46).

These structural shifts have undoubtedly been advantageous for civic parties. Yet, we must also acknowledge civic parties' agency in bringing these issues to the fore and raising their political salience. Moreover, their advocacy and policy work over many years positioned them to promptly step into that space and capitalize on these shifts when they arrived. The expansion of the civic space in Northern Ireland politics in the last decade has of course been driven by another crisis, related to the economic one: the UK leaving the European Union. It is to this development that we now turn.

Negotiating Constitutional Change

How does a civic party deal with an ethnonationally charged constitutional crisis? Horowitz (1985), who deemed multi-ethnic parties particularly vulnerable at moments of heightened tension, would hardly hold out much hope for them in this situation. Yet, one civic party – Alliance – has thrived in the wake of Brexit and remains so far unscathed in the ensuing debate about Northern Ireland's constitutional future. How has the party effected this and how might it and other civic parties survive in the event of a 'border poll'?

Case Study 5.1: Navigating Brexit

As in all contested states, the question of borders permeates politics in Northern Ireland. The existential question at the heart of the conflict – of whether Northern Ireland should remain in the UK or reunify with the Republic of Ireland – had somewhat receded to the background with the GFA. By enshrining the principle of 'consent' – required from the people of Northern Ireland (via referendum) for any change to its status in future – the peace agreement managed to quell the constitutional question, for a time. When Britain voted to leave the European Union, however, that question was kicked promptly back into play. Brexit has served to push the main parties further apart than ever since the 1998 agreement. Indeed, it formed the overriding backdrop to the power-sharing disputes and crises that marked the years from 2017–20 and 2022–24.

How have civic parties responded to this crisis? Given the ethnonational character of this issue and the polarizing – often toxic – nature of the debate, we might expect them to avoid it as much as possible. Yet on the contrary, civic parties, most notably Alliance, have leaned into that debate. As a strongly pro-EU party that holds Europeanness central to its identity, Alliance campaigned for Remain.[33] In the wake of the vote, it maintained an unapologetically Remain stance, initially calling for a second referendum on democratic grounds (Murphy and Evershed 2022, 106). As time went on the party accepted the result and shifted tack to pragmatism: seeking to mitigate the adverse impacts on Northern Ireland and pushing for the softest possible Brexit (Murphy 2023, 97). It actively engaged in the search for solutions to the UK government's dilemma of avoiding a hard border on the island while maintaining the integrity of the United Kingdom and Northern Ireland's place within it. To this end, in 2017 it produced a policy paper framed in common sense, evidence-based, and solutions-focused terms. The paper put forward detailed proposals for 'special status' for Northern Ireland to mitigate the impact of Brexit on the region – including remaining in the EU Customs Union and Single Market (APNI 2017b). Stressing hard-headed benefits for Northern Ireland over identity, the paper discusses the protection of North–South as well as East–West economic links. It references Northern Ireland's ability to determine its own constitutional future (in line with the consent principle) and even acknowledges the prospect of Irish unification following a border poll (2017).

As negotiations ensued, Alliance accepted the Northern Ireland Protocol, signed by the UK and EU in 2020, which guaranteed that there would be no physical infrastructure placed on the land border with the Irish Republic, effectively by shifting customs checks and controls to the ports at the Irish Sea that separates Northern Ireland and mainland UK. In its 2022 election manifesto the party refers to itself as 'Protocol pragmatists', calling for the implementation of the imperfect agreement as the least worst option available. The party has consistently rejected unionist party claims that the protocol undermined the United Kingdom and Northern Ireland's place within it (Murphy 2023, 97). Alliance has also been very clear about its willingness to work with not just the UK government but the Irish government as well, with which it found much common cause on the issue (2022). Indeed, it has participated in several all-Ireland initiatives on Brexit that unionist parties DUP and UUP boycotted (Ó Dochartaigh 2021, 13). Leader Naomi Long took part in the Irish government's All-Island Civic Dialogue on Brexit in 2016 and delivered a speech to the All-Island Brexit Forum in 2018 while the party contributed to the Irish Parliament's Joint Committee on the Implementation of the Good Friday Agreement (Murphy and Evershed 2022, 102). Its 2022 manifesto highlights the party's active engagement and achievements on Brexit, including its proposal for 'grace periods' on implementation of the protocol and 'green channels' for goods entering Northern Ireland from the UK and set to remain there – versions of which were later adopted (2022). In terms of democracy, it also stresses the need for Northern Ireland's to be represented in EU–UK decision-making bodies (APNI 2022). In this sense Alliance has positioned itself in the Brexit debate as something of a voice of reason and neutral arbiter: seeking to inform the debate and broker solutions for the best outcome for Northern Ireland.

Brexit has also inevitably proven a tricky issue for the party, however. As shown in chapter 4, its strident Remain stance and inadvertent alignment with nationalist parties on the issue has opened it up to contestation and backlash from unionist and loyalist quarters, including accusations of being part of a 'pan nationalist front' and 'useful idiots' for Sinn Féin (Kane 2019). So, how has the party navigated such attacks? Its actions demonstrate both steadfastness and mindfulness of the risks. The party has endeavored to decouple the issue of Brexit from the constitutional debate – and, as much as possible, take the (ethnonational) politics out of the issue (Murphy and Evershed 2022, 104–6). Rather, it has sought to frame the issue and its actions in pragmatic, common sense terms: doing what is best for all Northern Ireland citizens. When it comes to alliances and associations, it has acted intentionally. The party has cooperated unapologetically with the Irish government, as shown. In spite of unionist accusations, on a number of occasions it has formed a united front in joint statements with other pro-Remain (chiefly nationalist parties), including a joint delegation with Sinn Féin, SDLP and the Greens to EU Chief Negotiator Michel Barnier. Ó Dochartaigh observes, 'Rather than seeking a middle ground between unionist and nationalist positions on Brexit, the Alliance had aligned with non-unionist parties against the unionist position' (2021, 13).

Yet, the party has also shown caution concerning alliances that might compromise its civic image. In the 2019 UK general election, Alliance chose not to enter a pro-Remain electoral pact (whereby these parties stood aside for one another in certain seats), with Sinn Féin, SDLP, and the Greens (Murphy and Evershed 2022, 109). This decision was clearly informed by a desire to avoid the taint of alignment with nationalism. As the only party to run candidates in every constituency, it criticized its opponents for 'divisive and sectarian' electoral pacts (Madden 2019; Whitten 2020, 318). The strategy thus chimes with its longstanding self-image of standing apart from other parties and 'owning' the civic space in Northern Ireland politics.

Considering its performance in subsequent elections, this approach has so far proven effective. Far from being punished at the ballot box for its forthright stance, Alliance has advanced significantly since 2016. As outlined in chapter 2, amidst a reduction in the size of the Assembly from 108 to 90 seats in the 2017 Assembly election the party held its eight seats and even grew by 2 per cent. In 2019, against the backdrop of a collapsed Northern Ireland Assembly and vexed EU–UK negotiations, Alliance secured three dramatic electoral victories. In the local elections, it increased its seats by 65 per cent on the previous election. In the European elections it broke through to secure representation for the first time ever, winning one of Northern Ireland's three seats. In the snap UK general election in December 2019 – dubbed the 'Brexit election' – the party won a Westminster seat for only the second time in its history, doubling its vote share and emerging as the third largest party in the region. That place was cemented in 2022 when the party's vote increased by 4.5 per cent, winning 13.5 per cent of the vote and seventeen seats, up from eight in the previous election.

While the party's performance in the post-2016 period builds on steady growth, its dramatic expansion does indicate a Brexit dividend (Tonge 2020; Ó Dochartaigh 2021; Murphy and Evershed 2022). Somewhat ironically, the development has given the party a platform, increased its relevance and, in many ways, allowed it to showcase what it does best: advance common-sense solutions free from identity politics. In a 2023 poll, Alliance, together with SDLP, were named the most trusted of the five Northern Ireland parties in managing Northern Ireland's interest with respect to the protocol (Phinnemore et al 2023). Murphy also notes the opportunity Brexit has afforded Alliance to further carve out its distinct civic identity and distinguish itself from unionism (2022, 102). After the flag protest, one might say Brexit has gone one step further in distancing itself from the image of a 'soft unionist' party. Indeed, Alliance representatives attest to the opportunity Brexit has afforded the party. Speaking at a public event, one MLA pointed to the trust Alliance commands among voters on all matters Brexit,[34] while another observed that the development has pushed voters who previously supported DUP and UUP towards Alliance.[35] A leading activist for civic politics in Northern Ireland, furthermore, sees Brexit as exerting a unifying and mobilizing effect on civic-minded voters, including young people.[36]

The last ten years have witnessed major constitutional ructions on the islands of Britain and Ireland. Even prior to 2016, the 2014 Scottish independence referendum (ultimately rejected but still supported by 45 per cent of the electorate) initiated a 'constitutional debate' about the future of devolution in the UK and sovereignty across 'these islands'. The UK's decision to leave the European Union in 2016 marked a game changer in that debate. For Northern Ireland, it fundamentally challenged the principles of the GFA (not least consent) and upended any notion of the constitutional question being put to bed by the agreement. As Sinn Féin's calls for a border poll have redoubled, a number of civic initiatives for Irish unity have also sprung into being, not least Ireland's Future which has organized a number of large events and fora. Following pressure from civil society and their Sinn Féin rivals, the Irish government (Fianna Fáil–Fine Gael coalition) has engaged in the debate and made some preparatory moves, including establishing the Shared Island Unit in the Department of the Taoiseach (prime minister) in 2021, albeit to promote reconciliation, economic development and positive north–south relations, rather than push for Irish unity (2021). A number of research projects have been launched to investigate attitudes and feasibility and potential future constitutional constellations.[37] Unsurprisingly, unionist parties have so far largely refused to engage in these debates and initiatives.

So how has Alliance navigated the reinvigorated constitutional debate post-Brexit? Alliance's constitutional position has evolved in subtle but important ways over the years from 'soft' unionism in its early years to a non-aligned position characterized by avoidance post-GFA, to a more neutral position characterized by diversity and openness post-Brexit. For much of the party's history, its focus on making Northern Ireland work, rather than engaging in constitutional politics, was interpreted as support for the constitutional status quo and unionism by default (Leonard 1999; Mitchell 2015). Early party statements even set out a constitutional position based on support for Northern Ireland remaining part of the United Kingdom but with devolved government (APNI 1970a; 1970b). In 1998 the party moved towards a more neutral stance on Northern Ireland's constitutional future by embracing the GFA's 'consent principle'. Yet, its image as a 'soft unionist' party persisted. Leonard depicted the Alliance's constitutional position as ambiguous and inadequate in a context where separate national identities and constitutional aspirations are a fact of political life (Leonard 1999, 67). In its apparent belief that 'effective history dates from the foundation of Northern Ireland in 1920', the party failed to address nationalist grievances, he argued, and it was hardly surprising that it was widely viewed as a moderate unionist party (1999, 26). Analyzing an Alliance membership survey in 2001, Evans and Tonge described Alliance's 'innate unionism' as 'incidental', but still compromising its goal of reaching across the communal divide (2001, 106). They portrayed its constitutional stance as one of avoidance, with a 'don't mention the constitutional question' feel to some of its literature (2001, 109).

Fast forward some two decades and while the Alliance's official constitutional position remains largely the same – based on the consent of the people – that position now has different implications. Following the GFA, the party had remained quiet on the question of Irish unity or any constitutional change. Such questions tended to be brushed off by party representatives, who maintained that Northern Ireland itself must, first and foremost, unite and become integrated and functional. Post-Brexit, however, such questions are not so easily dismissed. The 'status quo' of remaining in the UK and the prospect of unifying with the rest of Ireland now meant different things. The former now means life outside the EU with all its implications for Northern Ireland's peace, security and economy (however mitigated), not to mention broader implications for all UK citizens. The latter now holds the promise of a route back into the EU for Northern Ireland, making it a more realistic prospect and reasonable consideration for many who would not previously have considered it (including 'civic unionists'). In this context, shutting the constitutional question down becomes untenable and unsustainable. And so, Alliance has moved gradually from a position of avoidance and silence to one of more diversity of expression within the party and openness to engage in the debate. In the process, the perception of Alliance as a de facto unionist party has begun to shift. Indeed, Ó Dochartaigh points out that when unionism is no longer the majority position in Northern Ireland, the 'consent position' no longer means 'unionism by default' (2021, 11).

The shift is subtle but perceptible. On the one hand it can be witnessed in Alliance's official policies and statements. The party has shown a willingness to engage in the constitutional debate post-Brexit, unlike unionist parties, that have rejected its very premise. It has supported initiatives like the Irish government's Shared Island initiative and did not object to the creation of an All-Island Citizens' Assembly to consider constitutional and other all-island policy issues (Murphy 2023, 102). Leader Naomi Long even engaged in a televised discussion on the topic of Irish unity in March 2021 alongside leaders of nationalist parties and parties in the Irish republic (Murphy and Evershed 2022, 112). This stance was confirmed by then Alliance MP Stephen Farry at the party's 2020 annual conference when he said, 'We don't believe that there is currently the case for a border poll, and nor are we pursuing one, but we do recognize that there is a very fluid situation and multiple active debates are underway' (Farry quoted in Murphy 2023, 101).

This greater openness to engage can be seen in the statements of individual party representatives, and the subsequent reactions within the party. In 2014, then Alliance MLA and European election candidate, the late Anna Lo stoked internal controversy when she said she believed a united Ireland to be 'viable' (Lynch 2014), underlining Alliance's discomfort with the constitutional question. By contrast, in more recent elections, Alliance candidates, such as Patrica O'Lynn and others, have openly referred to their nationalist and Catholic community backgrounds, signaling a greater comfort in the party in dealing with ethnonational identity[38] (RTE News, 2022). This also speaks to a subtle shift from an integrationist to a more intersectional approach, as discussed above: away from wholesale avoidance of ethnonational identity, towards a more open approach that allows for a diversity of ethnonational identity within the party, alongside other types of identity.

This increasing freedom of expression, coupled with an openness to engage, was echoed in interviews with Alliance. Representatives referred to the fact that discussions were ongoing within the party and that this was a debate they were 'up for'. To do otherwise would see them left behind on a matter of fundamental importance and at the centre to political discourse – a danger for unionists parties.[39] Indeed, party leader Naomi Long has urged unionist parties to engage (Manley, 2020). Rather than having no view on the issue, the party hosts a diversity of views, representatives stress. Indeed, Long acknowledges that some supporters who were formerly agnostic on the border have become more engaged with such issues post-Brexit.[40] Recent polling bears this out, with one poll showing that a sizable 27 per cent of Alliance supporters support Irish unity (with 44 per cent favouring remaining in the UK with devolved government) (McManus 2022).

In the event of a border poll, representatives predict that the party would remain neutral or 'agnostic' – but that does not mean passive.[41] One MLA foresees the party playing the role of 'honest broker' in that debate, as it has many times before, asking critical questions and informing the debate. This is the position its members would want it to take, she believes, and indeed, one it has already been playing: 'Where there's a position we're talking about for the Alliance, it's the potential for us to ask those questions. We're going to get kicked by anybody anyway, so we'll just ask those questions: "What will education look like?" "How will we deal with all the civil servants employed by the Northern Ireland civil service?" "Where do their jobs go to?" "How will the government work?"… "If a border poll is brought forward, what's the question going to be?"'[42]

The potential for a referendum on Irish unity in the medium term future no doubt poses risks for Alliance and other non-aligned parties.

In trying to hold a neutral position, the party will inevitably meet resistance and contestation from either side. 'Unfortunately, what it does mean is that unionists are saying "How dare you! Even by thinking about this you're destroying the country"', one Alliance MLA observes, 'whatever factual piece we put forward, unionists will say "They're trying to get rid of Northern Ireland" and nationalists will say, "You're asking difficult questions, you're just trying to be [awkward]."'[43] The tricky line the party must tread on the issue was underlined by the criticism invoked after Alliance leader Naomi Long pulled out of a conference organized by Ireland's Future in June 2024, leaving another Alliance MLA to represent the party. The event took place during the UK general election campaign in which Long was attempting to unseat a DUP MP in the traditional unionist stronghold of East Belfast (Gordon 2024).[44]

Some have predicted that the party would be torn apart by such a referendum. However, evidence of recent years shows a greater willingness to engage and a more intersectional stance which allows for more internal diversity and, potentially, flexibility. What's more, the sizable group of 'other', neither unionist nor nationalist, voters in Northern Ireland are increasingly seen as being pivotal to any referendum on Ireland's future (Hayward 2020; O'Leary 2021; ria.ie 2022). This reality calls for parties to speak to and represent their (many and varied) interests. In their focus groups with 'others' on the island who have been traditionally marginalized from constitutional debates – women, ethnic minorities, and young people – McEvoy, Todd, and Walsh demonstrate the need to engage these groups in the debate and an appetite among these groups to get involved (2022, 164). Alliance is surely ideally placed to step into the role of representing the 'other' position. Without underestimating the challenges a referendum would bring for the party, it is conceivable that Alliance could play an important role in the process and even help foster a more civic debate, focused on policy issues such as economy, healthcare, education and social rights – akin to the debate that led to the 2014 Scottish Independence referendum (Murtagh and Murphy 2025, 67). Whether the party might also facilitate more contentious discussions around shared symbols, such as a new national flag and anthem, in the run-up or aftermath of a referendum, is another question that arises.

The prospect of a border poll raises potential strategic dilemmas: avoid the issue and risk being consigned to irrelevance, engage, and risk backlash from both sides – or, indeed, get stuck once again in an intermediary role. How Alliance walks this line in the event of a referendum on Northern Ireland's future will no doubt be critical to its fate.

Electoral Strategy

Civic parties in divided societies face a difficult balancing act between consolidating their vote where it is and attempting to secure broad cross-ethnic support. Northern Ireland is no different. Whilst parties like Alliance and Greens attract fairly evenly balanced support from voters with Protestant and Catholic backgrounds, as shown, territorially that support has historically lain predominantly in the east (of the River Bann), the more urban, economically developed region where Protestants historically formed the majority. Alliance's support within the east was historically concentrated in more affluent and suburban areas, contributing to the image of a soft unionist, middle-class party.[45] In interviews Alliance representatives acknowledged the challenge of breaking through 'west of the Bann' but also the importance of striving for this as a 'cross-community' party. As a relatively small party, however, many felt this must be balanced against the need to consolidate its existing support.[46] The strategy appeared to be one of mobilizing across the region and working to gain representation outside its traditional strongholds in Belfast, greater Antrim, and Down, while also seeking to capitalize on and deepen its gains in those areas. 'That's why it's vital that we grow equally, that our appeal is what it is: cross-community. But you have to take your advantages where those advantages are', as one put it.[47]

As Alliance's electoral support has increased over the last fifteen years, however, so has its spread. Socio-economically, the party has been making gains outside of suburban areas, most notably in the more urban, working-class constituency of East Belfast, home to party leader Naomi Long. Geographically, it has also been making inroads in the west. While thirteen of Alliance's fourteen seats in the Northern Ireland Assembly following the 2022 elections lay in the east, its vote and electoral presence in the west has increased (ARK 2022c). In the 2023 local government election the party gained representation in all but two of Northern Ireland's eleven District Councils (Derry and Strabane and Mid Ulster) (*BBC News* 2023). At the same time, demographic changes – the fact that Catholics outnumbered Protestants in Northern Ireland for the first time in the 2021 census (46 per cent to 44 per cent) (NISRA 2021) and the rise of those aligned to no religion – stand to make the east-west divide less salient in Northern Ireland politics. Nevertheless, as Alliance seeks to continue to grow as a civic party, balancing that growth against representation across the region is something of which it will have to remain mindful.

Conclusion

Writing in 2004, Brendan O'Leary noted that because the 'others' have not been 'at the heart of the conflict' it is 'not surprising that they are not at the heart of the resulting pacts' (2004, 272). Some twenty years later, Northern Ireland's 'other' parties have moved very much towards 'the heart' of things. In spite of their marginalization in the 1998 power-sharing agreement, to which O'Leary alludes, civic parties have since grown in number, size, and power, well beyond what many would have predicted. More surprising still, the most rapid expansion has come in the midst of a polarizing constitutional crisis post-2016. Against that backdrop, civic parties have grown to make up a distinct third civic bloc, dominated by Alliance, reconfiguring Northern Ireland politics. In this chapter I have sought to explain this apparent paradox by examining civic party agency in navigating a deeply divided polity.

We have seen that civic parties have survived – and even begun to *reshape* – that system by adapting to their environment, skillfully negotiating barriers and seizing opportunities. They have evolved in their positioning with respect to the ethnonational divide, in line with societal attitudes, from a more accommodationist to a more integrationist and, ultimately, an intersectional approach. While opposing divisive elements of the power-sharing system and campaigning for its reform, they have also participated in and benefited from that system. In a shifting discursive landscape, they have moved nimbly to capitalize on identity, demographic, economic, and social trends and secured a distinct civic niche in politics. Perhaps most impressively, civic parties have even managed to surf the wave of constitutional change, presumed fatal for civic actors, ironically benefiting from the Brexit crisis and, so far, staying above the fray on the divisive question of Northern Ireland's future status.

This adaptation has required some twists and turns, however, that have threatened to compromise these parties' civic principles and frustrate them in operating on their own terms. Participating in an ethnic system entails risks. It can leave them vulnerable to attack by ethnonational rivals. At times the only role it permits them is mediator – one they deeply resist.

The approaching constitutional debate bears particular pitfalls for these parties in both senses and how civic parties emerge from it remains to be seen. What is undeniable, however, is that the space for civic politics has grown considerably since 1998 – by virtue of structural forces but also active expansion on their part. This space is also less precarious than in the past, underlined by the fact that the civic position has been attacked more than ever over the last ten years (indicating the threat it represents to ethnonational politics). Yet, civic parties' have become increasingly resilient against this targeting. This reality is illustrated by the cases of the flag dispute and Brexit, in which the Alliance stance was deeply contested and yet the party's electoral fortunes went up in the aftermath. Amidst the barriers they put up, transitional, flexible power-sharing systems can allow space for civic politics to emerge and offer sufficient openings for civic parties to exploit and expand. Civic parties' fortunes in Northern Ireland in recent years raise the question of whether these parties could even be a potential route out of power-sharing over time.

The travails of civic parties in Northern Ireland politics may appear uniquely paradoxical. But the phenomenon of civic parties struggling to seize space in an ethnonationally divided system is not particular to Northern Ireland. From North Macedonia to Lebanon to Burundi, civic parties and movements have echoing stories to tell. The case of Bosnia and Herzegovina offers a particularly apt comparison: a society severely divided along ethnonational lines, transitioning out of a brutal war that was brought to an end by a peace agreement in 1995 – three years before the GFA and, critically, embodying a similar power-sharing logic. It is to Bosnia that we now turn to explore the barriers and openings civic parties there have faced post-war, and how they have navigated them, before bringing the experiences of Northern Ireland and Bosnia together and into dialogue with other divided places.

Chapter Six

The Plight of Civic Parties in Bosnia and Herzegovina

'Gladni smo na tri jezika,' the banner read: 'We are hungry in three languages'. Activists took to the streets in cities and towns across Bosnia in spring 2014 in the largest social uprising seen since the 1992–95 war. They were protesting the conditions of life in the post-war state and, crucially, the deeply dysfunctional political system based on representation of the state's three designated ethnonational groups: Bosniaks, Croats, and Serbs. The movement represents agency and hope. With no other avenue available, citizens took matters into their own hands and gained national and international attention for their demands. Yet, it also represents the dysfunction of the power-sharing system and its blockage to civic politics. And, given that the movement did not result in systemic change at the institutional level, it speaks to the imperviousness of that system to bottom-up civic mobilization.

Civic parties and movements in Bosnia traverse a highly ethnicized space, less than three decades removed from a devastating war. The Dayton Peace Agreement that brought that war to an end in 1995 put in place a system in which representation of the three ethnonational groups to the conflict was deeply embedded. Yet, civic parties occupy a discernible space in that system, comprising about 20 per cent of the vote. So, how do civic parties interface with the ethnicized political sphere? This chapter examines the structural environment civic parties traverse in Bosnia and the barriers they encounter in the written and unwritten rules of politics.

Keeping Multi-Ethnic Bosnia Alive

The consistent presence of civic parties in Bosnia should not obscure the reality of a system overwhelmingly dominated by ethnonational parties and ethnonational politics. That system and its dynamics can be traced

Figure 6.1 | Map of Bosnia and Herzegovina.

back to the war that ravaged Bosnia for more than three-and-a-half years from 1992–95. Fought on 'ethnonational' grounds, the war left more than 100,000 people dead, an estimated 2.2 million displaced,[1] and rendered untold physical and psychological devastation from which the country is still recovering. Amidst the break-up of Yugoslavia, this diverse, multi-ethnic Yugoslav republic of Muslims (later termed Bosniaks), Serbs (Orthodox), Croats (Catholic), and many of mixed and other heritage, succumbed to war in April 1992 as the Serb-led Yugoslav Army – in a purported bid to keep Yugoslavia together and protect the Serb minority after Bosnia declared independence in a referendum boycotted by the majority of Serbs – laid siege on the capital Sarajevo (Malcolm 1996). That siege would last 1,425 days and wreak horror to which the bullet holes on the walls of apartment buildings and craters in the pavements still bear testament. Initially a war waged by the Serb-led Yugoslav army against allied Bosniak and Croat forces in the shape of the Bosnian army, fighting broke out in 1993 between Muslim and Croats in Herzegovina and central Bosnia. The conflict that brought the term 'ethnic cleansing' into the lexicon, saw the use of detention camps, and of sexual violence on a mass scale as a weapon of war (Malcolm 1996, 245). The world watched as the greatest bloodshed Europe had witnessed since the Second World War unfolded, including the massacre of an estimated 8,000 Muslim men and boys by Serb forces in Srebrenica in July 1995, in an act the International Criminal Tribunal for the former Yugoslavia (ICTY) and the International Court of Justice (ICJ) would later deem genocide.

Dayton Peace Agreement

That war was finally drawn to a halt, following a NATO-supported military campaign by Bosniak and Croat forces (having come to a truce a year earlier) against Serbs forces, with the signing of the internationally brokered General Framework Agreement for Peace in Bosnia and Herzegovina or Dayton Peace Agreement (DPA)[2] by the leaders of Bosniak, Serb and Croat forces at a military base in Dayton Ohio in the US on 14 December 1995 (Malcolm 1996, 268). Dayton's purpose was two-fold: to end a war and to establish a multi-ethnic state. It represented an attempted compromise: to appease the Bosniak desire for a unified and multi-ethnic Bosnia, while simultaneously addressing Serb and Croat demands for self-government and fears of Bosniak domination (Belloni 2009, 356; Keil 2013, 136). The constitution of Bosnia and Herzegovina, contained in Annex 4 of the DPA, created a federal (some have argued confederal) state composed of a weak central state and two federal entities – the Serb dominated Republika Srpska (RS; Serb Republic) and the Bosniak–Croat Federation of Bosnia and Herzegovina (FBiH), a 49:51 territorial split that recognized the new territorial segregation resulting from ethnic cleansing (see figure 6.2).[3] The document recognized Bosniaks, Croats and Serbs as the 'constituent peoples' of Bosnia and Herzegovina and detailed rigid provisions for their shared power within the political institutions.

The political system to which Dayton gave birth is rigidly consociational and corporate in form, comprising a loose, complex, and asymmetrical federation. The multi-layered structure is composed of a 'threadbare' central state, two entities with considerable autonomy – one

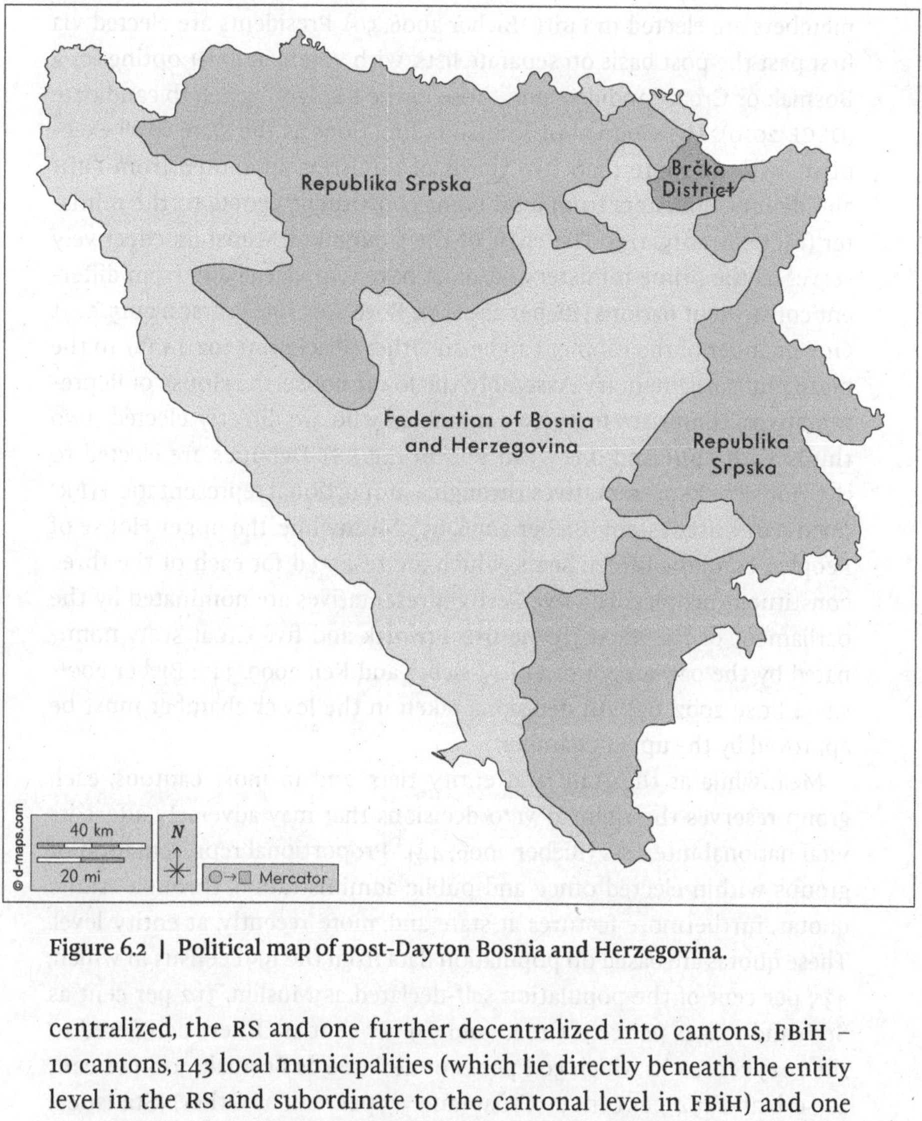

Figure 6.2 | Political map of post-Dayton Bosnia and Herzegovina.

centralized, the RS and one further decentralized into cantons, FBiH – 10 cantons, 143 local municipalities (which lie directly beneath the entity level in the RS and subordinate to the cantonal level in FBiH) and one semi-autonomous district (Brčko) (Bose 2002, 24; 216; Stjepanović 2014, 4; Kapidžić 2020a, 85). The principles of consociational power-sharing are stringently embedded in this system (Bieber and Keil 2009, 345).

Aligning with the 'grand coalition' principle, governments at state and entity levels must include members of all three 'constituent peoples'. A three-member state presidency, made up of one member from each group, rotates its chairmanship every eight months during a four-year term. The Serb member is directly elected in the RS while the Bosniak and Croat members are elected in FBiH (Bieber 2006, 50). Presidents are elected via first past the post basis on separate lists, with voters in FBiH opting for a Bosniak or Croat candidate and those in the RS electing a Serb candidate (OSCE 2010). The Council of Ministers functions as the state-level executive, with no more than two thirds of ministers appointed from FBiH and deputy ministers from a different constituent people to the minister (McEvoy 2015, 113). The chair of the Council of Ministers effectively serves as the prime minister and must have two vice chairs from different constituent nations (Bieber 2006, 52; Bose 2002, 65; Pearson 2015, 223). One member of the cabinet can be an Other (Piacentini 2021, 442). In the bicameral parliamentary Assembly, the lower house, the House of Representatives, comprises forty-two members who are directly elected (two thirds with FBiH and one third within the RS). Deputies are elected to the House of Representatives through a proportional representation (PR) open party list system (Bieber 2006, 95). Meanwhile, the upper House of Peoples, contains fifteen seats, which are reserved for each of the three constituent peoples. The five Serb representatives are nominated by the parliament of the RS with the five Bosniak and five Croat seats nominated by the parliament of FBiH (Bieber and Keil 2009, 347; Bieber 2006, 54–5; Bose 2002, 62). All decisions taken in the lower chamber must be approved by the upper chamber.

Meanwhile at the state and entity tiers, and in most cantons, each group reserves the right to veto decisions that may adversely affect its vital national interests (Bieber 2006, 44).[4] Proportional representation of groups within elected office and public administration, through ethnic quotas, furthermore features at state and, more recently, at entity level. These quotas are based on population data from the 1991 census in which, 43.5 per cent of the population self-declared as Muslim, 31.2 per cent as Serb and 17.4 as per cent Croat (and 7.9 per cent as Other), compared to the 2013 census in which 50.1 per cent declared as Bosniak, 30.8 per cent as Serb and 15.4 per cent as Croat (and 3.7 per cent as Other) (Statistical Agency BiH 2013).[5] Finally, group autonomy is granted at state level by devolving power down to the entities and, in FBiH, to the cantons (Bieber 2006, 44–5). This three-way power-sharing principle now runs through the top three tiers of government in Bosnia: state, entity, and canton (Bieber 2006, 43–4).

Alongside these structures, the constitution also entails extensive human rights guarantees, including the right to safe return for refugees displaced during the war in their pre-war residences,[6] and allowing voters to cast their vote in the municipalities in which they lived before the war, based on the 1991 census, in an attempt to see electoral outcomes reflect pre-war ethnic heterogeneity (Kennedy and Riga 2013, 176).[7] Abazović voices misgivings about the contradictions at the heart of Dayton: 'Declaring a unified state of Bosnia-Herzegovina while recognizing two antagonistic entities, proclaiming democracy while entrenching ethnically based institutional structures and reaffirming individual rights while legitimizing ethnic majoritarianism, from the outset raised serious concerns as to which political concept in Bosnia-Herzegovina would prevail' (2014, 36).

Brokered internationally, Dayton also carved out a central role for international actors in the power-sharing system (Ahmetašević 2024; Bell 2015, 14; Keil 2013, 106). The DPA provided for an internationally appointed high representative to oversee the 'civilian implementation' of the peace settlement. The powers of the Office of High Representative (OHR) have grown substantially since Dayton, initially charged with facilitating, coordinating, and reporting on the activities of the international community in Bosnia and, in 1997, adorned with legislative and executive powers (Ahmetašević 2024; Bieber 2006, 83–4), including the capacity to impose laws and dismiss elected representatives and public officials. Bieber even deems the OHR the most influential institution in Bosnia (2006, 84). International actors have also been embedded in a number of state-level institutions including the Constitutional Court and the Central Bank (Bieber 2006, 59). Merdzanovic describes post-war Bosnia as a case of 'imposed consociation', with international actors critical to the establishment of the regime and continuing to exert influence in its operation (2017, 25–6).[8]

From its inception the 'Dayton system' has been the subject of broad criticism for its dysfunction, inefficiency, discrimination, and institutionalization of division. In the some thirty years that have followed the state has been beset by continual crisis. The extensive protections for ethnic groups within the corporate consociational model have left it vulnerable to deadlock and rendered progress elusive (Belloni 2009, 359–60; 2007, 46). The heavy decentralization of the state has fuelled separatist moves by Serb nationalists in RS, led by Alliance of Independent Social Democrats (SNSD) leader and RS president Milorad Dodik, and calls by Croat nationalist parties for a third Croat entity. For these reasons, among others, Kapidžić assesses 'it is not possible to speak of a liberal or consolidated democracy in BiH' (2020a, 83).

Bosnia's relatively unprecedented international intervention in state-building and democratization has itself also been the subject of criticism (see for example Merdzanovic 2015; Ahmetašević 2024; Chandler 1999). Ahmetašević frames the experiment to create a 'semi-protectorate' in colonial terms (2024, 10–11). She finds a catalog of failures that mirror the broader state-building intervention, not least lack of local legitimacy, failure to centre the Bosnian population, lack of transparency and accountability, and failure to curb the power of ethnonationalist parties (2024). Merdzanovic even charges Bosnia's 'imposed consociationalism' with fostering extremism and dysfunction: as the OHR steps in to pass important legislation and keep governance running, the domestic political elites are 'absolved from the necessity to engage in genuine political debate and can instead concentrate on sustaining their patronage networks, which further strengthens their hold on the state' (2017, 27).

Constitutional reform has been continually on the agenda since Dayton, with a number of internationally facilitated attempts tried and failed, particularly in 2006 and 2008 (Belloni 2009, 360; Merdzanovic 2017, 23, 32). The ethnicized framework has now seen the Bosnian constitution found to be in breach of the European Convention on Human Rights on five occasions, firstly and most notably in the 2009 Sejdić-Finci ruling and subsequently in Zornić, Pilav, Slaku and Pudarić cases.[9] In the initial case, taken by a Roma and a Jewish citizen of BiH, the European Court of Human Rights found the Bosnian Constitution to be in breach of the ECHR in its requirements for candidates seeking election to the state presidency and the House of Peoples to designate as one of the three constituent peoples (McCrudden and O'Leary 2013, 478). By determining that one must be a Serb from the RS or a Croat or Bosniak from FBiH to run for either office, the ECHR ruled that the Bosnian constitution discriminated against Serbs from FBiH and Bosniaks and Croats from the RS, as well as others who do not identify with any of these ethnic identities. The four subsequent rulings have underlined the urgency for reform. Despite significant pressure from the international community and protracted EU-facilitated negotiations however, Bosniak, Croat, and Serb political parties have as yet been unable to agree on changes to the electoral procedures to implement these rulings and liberalize Bosnia's consociational framework.

Bosnia's slow progress on constitutional reform has been blamed for holding the country back in its long journey towards European integration – a seemingly endless process that at this point has wrought as much public fatigue and disillusion as hope (Štiks and Horvat 2014, 83).

Nevertheless, in December 2022 the European Union awarded Bosnia candidate status, six years after its application (Karčić 2022).[10] This move was triggered by a shift in EU enlargement policy towards the Western Balkans following the Russian invasion of Ukraine in a bid to increase European integration in the face of this external threat (Makul and Kalamujić 2024, 31).[11]

Bosnian Party System

It is hardly surprising that ethnonational parties have dominated this system. The first political parties in Bosnia emerged during the early twentieth century along ethnoreligious lines, dominating pre–Second World War politics, before the League of Communists, which formed along the religious–secular cleavage, took power in the Socialist Federal Republic of Yugoslavia (SFRY) (Bieber 2006, 7; Kapidžić 2015, 314). Ethnonational parties resurfaced in Bosnia's first multi-party elections in 1990, which followed the disintegration of the Communist Party. They secured almost three quarters of the vote, while non-nationalist parties emerging out of the former communist establishment – the League of Communists-Social Democratic Party (SK-SDP) and the Union of Reform Forces of Yugoslavia in BiH (SRSJ BiH) – together won 27 out of 130 seats (Kapidžić 2015, 315, 319–20; Bose 2002, 212).[12] Sasso argues that the defeat of the civic option in the early 1990s in Bosnia was closely tied to the decline of Yugoslavia, as widespread dissatisfaction with communist rule helped delegitimize the whole non-nationalist option (2015, 379, 384). Today, the Bosniak and Croat political spheres remain dominated by the war-time parties, Party for Democratic Action (Stranka Demokratske Akcije; SDA) and the Croat Democratic Union of Bosnia and Herzegovina (Hrvatska Demokratska Zajednica Bosne i Hercegovine; HDZ BiH) respectively, while the Serb bloc is led by the Alliance of Independent Social Democrats (Savez Nezavisnih Socijaldemokrata; SNSD), which overtook the Serb Democratic Party (Srpska Demokratska Stranka; SDS) in 2006.

Ethnonational parties' goals have altered little since the war (Stojarova 2010b). Serb nationalist parties persist in seeking greater autonomy for the Serb Republic, as well as closer ties to Serbia, and – at the extreme end – independence. Croat nationalists, likewise, campaign for increased autonomy for the Croat community on a par with Serbs and Bosniaks, through reforms including cantonization of the state or even the creation of a third entity (Żdeb 2016), as well as stronger ties to Croatia. Bosniak parties meanwhile call for the weakening or abolition of the entities and creation of a more unified 'civic' Bosnia with strengthened national institutions (Basta 2016, 945; Stojarova 2010c; Merdzanovic 2017, 33). The constitution and its reform form a central issue dimension in party competition and a source of ethnic outbidding. Having so far failed to achieve their constitutional ambitions, parties instead use these goals to mobilize voters (Sedo 2010). As Basta argues, these are not just three distinct constitutional positions but three *narratives*, connected to group identity and internalized by political elites and populations (2016, 954, 965). As well as the instrumental importance of institutions for political elites, they carry heavy symbolic and emotional weight, further vexing constitutional reform (Basta 2016, 954; 2021).

The political landscape then is one of three 'ethnically bound party subsystems with a high degree of independence', plus a fourth nonethnic subsystem, with very limited competition for voters between them (Kapidžić 2020a, 85; Kapidžić 2017; Hulsey 2015b, 52).[13] This complex party system has remained highly stable. Electoral volatility is low with an average of 5.8 per cent. While voters might switch between parties within 'their' ethnic bloc, they almost never vote outside their bloc, especially those that vote for Serb and Croat parties (an average 1.6 per cent) (Kapidžić 2018, 56; Kapidžić and Komar 2022, 549). Evidently, this closure strictly limits the appeal of non-ethnic parties (Kapidžić and Komar 2022, 549).

Nevertheless, alongside Bosnia's three ethnonational party blocs, parties that seek to operate across and beyond ethnicity have emerged and maintained a fourth 'civic bloc' (see tables 6.1, 6.2, and 6.3 and figures 6.1 and 6.2). While Kapidžić contrasts this 'not so well-defined multiethnic or nonethnic party subsystem' to the three tightly defined Serb, Croat and Bosniak blocs (2020a, 85), the civic bloc has remained relatively stable over time. These parties make up 20 per cent of the vote nationally and 25 per cent in FBiH, approximately (Hulsey and Keil 2019, 409; 2020, 347). Three main parties currently make up this bloc: the Social Democratic Party (Socijaldemokratska Partija Bosne i Hercegovine; SDP), Naša Stranka (Our Party), and Democratic Front (Demokratska Fronta; DF).

The SDP is the oldest and largest of these parties. The party emerged in 1991 as the successor of the League of Communists and presents itself in traditional social democratic terms, promoting social justice and equality (Vrgova 2012, 464). It draws proudly on its Yugoslav socialist legacy and certainly has benefited from this infrastructure (Hulsey and Keil 2019, 410; Sasso 2015, 388). In terms of European party families, members align SDP to social democratic and labour parties. In its program, the SDP casts itself explicitly as a 'multi-ethnic party', appealing to all main ethnic groups in society, to the exclusion of none. This multi-ethnic accommodationist ethos is reflected in its policy of internal ethnic quotas, with a rule that every party council must have at least 20 per cent representation of ethnic minorities, as well as 35 per cent of women and 33 per cent of youth (Touquet 2012b, 213). The party's constitutional agenda is a centralizing one, advocating strengthening state-level institutions, weakening of the ethnic veto for state institutions and a more pluralistic, multi-ethnic democracy (Bieber 2006, 41; Pickering 2009, 72; Basta 2016, 956). The SDP has even proposed the abolition of entities in the past (Touquet 2012b, 213). The current program is more moderate, stating that the party 'accepts the current state system' but believes it is necessary to 'restructure the existing state-administrative system – by achieving a general political consensus of the parliamentary parties of Bosnia and Herzegovina – in order for the state of Bosnia and Herzegovina to become a functional decentralized state' (SDP 2015, 26).

The SDP's self-proclaimed multi-ethnic status is deeply questioned in Bosnia, however. That is due to the nature of the party's support which lies predominantly in FBiH and, at that, in Bosniak-majority areas of central Bosnia and urban centres, with strongholds in Sarajevo and Tuzla. It struggles to make gains in the Serb-dominated RS or Croat majority areas of FBiH (Touquet 2011, 456). A study of municipal elections between 2006 and 2014 found that support for SDP lies predominantly in areas where Bosniak parties do well and that the party competes primarily with Bosniak parties for support (Hulsey 2015). The SDP's support in the RS has remained consistently low, averaging 2–3 per cent in the 2006 and 2010 general elections (Hulsey 2015, 49). Whilst the party has stood candidates in the Serb-majority entity, its support there is thought to lie primarily amongst the Bosniak minority community, with a significant share of the vote from the absentee ballots cast outside the entity. It is also worth noting that the party's constitutional position (for a more centralized, non-ethnic state), is shared by the main Bosniak parties and reflects the majority attitudes of the Bosniak population (Basta 2016, 956). The SDP's success at the national level has fluctuated, from 7 per cent in FBiH in 1996 to a high of 27 per cent in 2000 and 26 per cent in 2010, standing at 13 per cent in the 2022 election (see table 6.3). It has taken part in governing coalitions at the state and FBiH levels, most notably in 2001–02 and 2010–14. In 2022, for the first time, it secured the position of Bosniak member of the presidency, won by Bosniak party SDA in every election up to that point. It has participated in the state-level executive coalition, the Council of Ministers, including after the 2000, 2010, 2018, and 2022 elections. According to the civic party typology outlined in chapter 1 the SDP aligns most closely with the accommodationist type.

Naša Stranka is a smaller and newer civic party that emerged in 2008 out of an NGO campaign by civil society activists and artists to make Bosnian politicians more responsible for citizens' wellbeing (Touquet 2011, 457). The party advances social democratic policies, similar to SDP but with a greater emphasis on liberalism and human rights. It stands for equality for citizens of BiH regardless of ethnicity and, critically, for a more civic, transparent, and effective form of politics for Bosnia (Naša Stranka 2008a). Members tend to liken themselves to green parties in European democracies such as Germany,[14] though the party is also affiliated to the Alliance of Liberals and Democrats for Europe (ALDE) party group.[15] In terms of support, similarly to SDP, the party's representation is confined to FBiH and therein heavily concentrated in the urban centres of Sarajevo and Tuzla. While it fielded candidates in the RS in its first general election in 2010, since then it has contested solely in FBiH. Naša Stranka's electoral base has been growing steadily since its formation, gaining its first foothold at the entity level (in FBiH) in 2014 and then at state level in 2018. It currently holds two seats in the House of Representatives. According to the typology in chapter 1 the Naša Stranka aligns most closely with the intersectional type.

The Democratic Front (DF) is the newest party in the civic bloc, formed in 2013 after its leader, Željko Komšić, split from the SDP. The ideological positioning of DF is most difficult to place. In many ways it differs little from SDP in this regard, as social democratic and self-professed multiethnic and civic party. If anything, it places greater emphasis on its civic credentials and its vision of a 'civil Bosnia'. The party emphasizes equal rights for all citizens, regardless of ethnicity, and advances a vision of a more integrated, functional state. Representatives stress their aspiration for a 'normal' state, in line with Western European democracies, and support for membership of the EU and NATO.[16] The DF remains largely defined, however, by its charismatic leader, Komšić and the brand of civic Bosnia that he represents, rather than any particular policy agenda. Indeed, some have characterized the party as embodying 'civic populism' or even civic (Bosnian) nationalism.[17] Like its counterparts, DF's support lies mainly in Bosniak-majority areas of FBiH. Its electoral success has been very much tied to that of SDP's, securing five seats in the House of

Table 6.1 | Political parties in Bosnia and Herzegovina

	Party name (translated)	*Formed*	*Split from*	*Positioning*	*Constitutional position*
SDA	Party of Democratic Action	1990	—	Bosniak nationalist; conservative	Pro-centralization; strengthened BiH state
SBiH	Party for BiH	1996	SDA	Bosniak nationalist; centre-right	Pro-centralization; strengthened BiH state
SBB BiH	Union for a Better Future of BiH	2009	—	Bosniak nationalist; populist right	Pro-centralization; strengthened BiH state
SDS	Serb Democratic Party	1990	—	Serb nationalist; conservative	Further autonomy / secession for the RS
SNSD	Alliance of Independent Social Democrats	1996	—	Serb nationalist; populist right	Secession for the RS
HDZ BiH	Croatian Democratic Union of BiH	1990	—	Croat nationalist; conservative	Creation of a third Croat entity
HDZ 1990	Croatian Democratic Union 1990	2006	HDZ BiH	Croat nationalist; conservative	Creation of a third Croat entity
SDP BiH	Social Democratic Party of BiH	1991 (1909)	—	Civic; social democratic	Pro-integration; pro-centralization and strengthened BiH state
Naša Stranka	Our Party	2008	—	Civic; liberal	Constitutional reform on civic lines
DF	Democratic Front	2013	SDP BiH (Founder split from SDP)	Civic; social democratic	Pro-integration; pro-centralization and strengthened BiH state

Table 6.2 | **Election results by mandate to the House of Representatives of BiH, 1996–2022**

	1996	*1998*	*2000*	*2002*	*2006*	*2010*	*2014*	*2018*	*2022*
SDA	19	17	8	10	9	7	10	8	8
SDS	9	4	6	5	3	4	5	3	2
SNSD	—	—	1	3	7	8	6	6	6
SBiH	2	0	5	6	8	2	0	0	0
HDZ BiH	8	6	5	5	3	3	4	5	4
SBB	—	—	—	—	—	4	4	2	0
SDP	2	4	9	4	5	8	3	5	5
DF	—	—	—	—	—	—	5	3	3
Naša Stranka	—	—	—	—	—	0	0	2	2

Source: http://www.izbori.ba/.

Table 6.3 | **SDP election results to the House of Representatives of BiH, 1996–2022**

Year	*Election*	*% (FBiH)*	*Seats*
1996[a]	General (BiH HoR)	7.1	2
1998	General (BiH HoR)	14.5	4
2000	General (BiH HoR)	27.3	9
2002	General (BiH HoR)	15.7	4
2006	General (BiH HoR)	15.4	5
2010	General (BiH HoR)	26.1	8
2014	General (BiH HoR)	9.5	3
2018	General (BiH HoR)	14.2	5
2022	General (BiH HoR)	13.4	5

Source: http://www.izbori.ba/; Bieber 2006; Hulsey 2015b.

Note:

a. In 1996 the SDP stood as part of the United List electoral coalition, including other parties: UBSD, HSS, MBO, REPUBLIKANCI.

Representatives its first general election in 2014, at the expense of SDP losses, but shrinking back to three seats in 2018 and 2022 amidst the SDP's recovery. As explored further below, DF is the most difficult of the main civic parties to classify according to the typology developed in chapter 1, exhibiting elements of accommodationist, integrationist and intersectional civic party types.

Beyond the centrality of ethnicity, a number of features distinguish Bosnian party politics – and shape civic parties' experience. Ideology plays a minimal role in party politics. Regardless of parties' formal declarations of belonging to wider European party families, party programs tend to be ethnicized (Džankić 2015, 535). Party positions shift considerably between elections, often in response to the wills and ambitions of party leaders and party programs often diverge significantly from party actions (Sedo 2010). Relatedly, parties are highly centralized and personalized, concentrated around the party leader, with limited internal party democracy (Sedo, 2010; Touquet 2012b, 212; Vrgova 2012, 428) Critically, patronage and clientelistic networks play a determining role, as parties use public resources to distribute material benefits to citizens conditionally, in exchange for political support (Kapidžić 2020a, 94). While elections in Bosnia are generally classed as free and fair by international monitoring bodies such as the OSCE, as Kapidžić demonstrates, 'what happens before and after elections is much more problematic and ultimately undermines the democratic process by creating an uneven playing field' (2020a, 93). Hulsey and Keil argue that ethnonational parties in Bosnia differ primarily in terms of the personal networks of their leaders, rather than in their ideologies (2019, 408). Another pervasive feature is the patriarchal culture within parties and politics. Despite moves to increase women's representation in politics since Dayton, including the adoption of gender quotas of 40 per cent in 2000, women only made up 19 per cent of members in lower house following the 2022 election (IDEA 2023). Beyond descriptive representation, Byrne and McCulloch show that power within parties remains largely in the hands of men (2012). Tied to a deep culture of political distrust in society is the ingrained gendered notion that politics is a dirty business in which women have no place (Helms 2007). These traits speak, in part, to the legacies of recent war and to decades of one-party rule. They remind us that the Bosnian state and its democracy are yet to be fully consolidated (Stojarova 2010c; Keil 2013, 88). That democratization process has been further challenged in the last ten years

Table 6.4 | Civic party indicators, BiH

Party	*Name significance*	*Appeal**	*Critical issue/ position*	*Party vote/ support*	*Leadership*	*Arena of contestation*
SDP	Civic: signals universalist ideology (social democracy)	Civic: accommodationist / programmatic (social democratic)	State centralization/ decentralization: pro-centralization	Predominantly Bosniak, concentrated in FBiH	No official policy	Across both entities
NS	Civic: signals unity/ solidarity	Civic: intersectional	State centralization/ decentralization: pro-centralization	Predominantly Bosniak, concentrated in FBiH and urban centres	No official policy	Predominantly FBiH
DF	Civic: signals universalist ideology (democracy)	Civic: accommodationist, integrationist, and intersectional	State centralization/ decentralization: pro-centralization	Predominantly Bosniak, concentrated in FBiH	No official policy	Predominantly FBiH

Source: https://www.izbori.ba/Default.aspx?CategoryID=48&Lang=3&Mod=0.

*Essential indicator

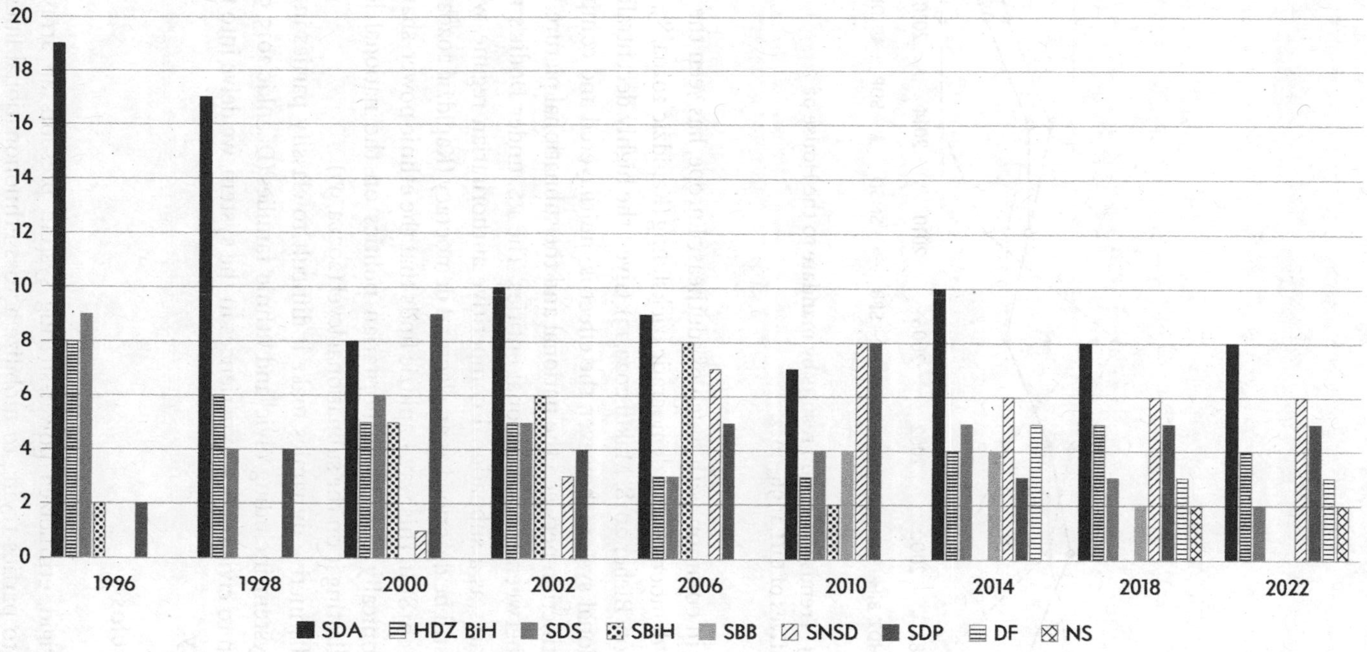

Figure 6.3 | Election results by mandate to the House of Representatives of BiH, 1996–2022.

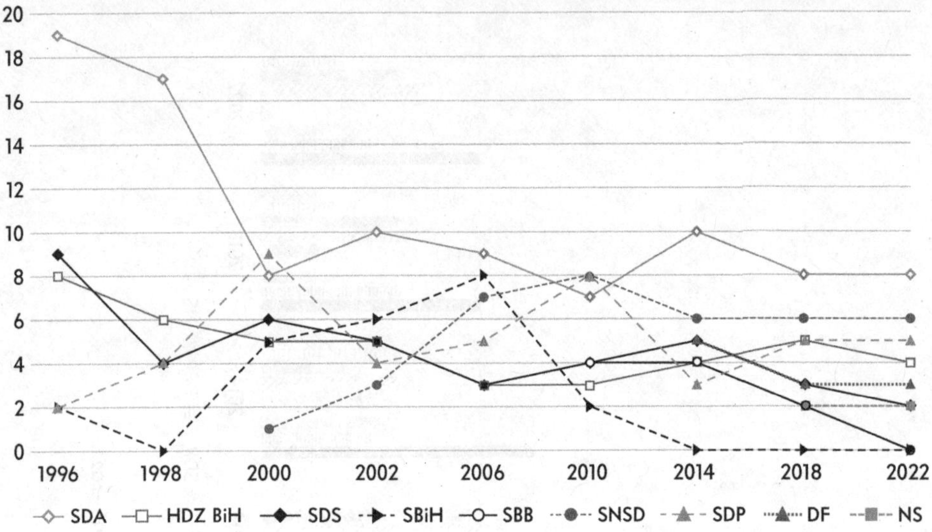

Figure 6.4 | **Trends in election results by mandate to the House of Representatives of BiH, 1996–2022.**

as Bosnia, in common with much of southeast Europe, has seen the rise of illiberal democracy and democratic backsliding (Kapidžić 2020a, 83; Kapidžić 2020b; Bieber 2018; Makul 2022, 13). Given the highly decentralized consociational system, however, the effect is multilayered and complex, with a distinction between the national and the subnational picture, and variation between the subnational entities. The RS, under Dodik's rule, now operates as a subnational competitive authoritarian regime, while FBiH can still be described as an electoral democracy (Kapidžić 2020a, 87, 96; Bieber 2018). In this way, Kapidžić finds that the ethnic power-sharing system ironically curtails authoritarian politics on the national level while facilitating it on the subnational level (2020a, 97).

These distinctive dynamics make it difficult to classify parties in the Bosnian system, including 'civic' and 'ethnic' families (Džankić 2015, 539). As we turn to civic parties' experiences in the system, we delve into that complexity.

Formal rules

Bosnia's rigid, ethnicized power-sharing system presents an array of obstacles to parties trying to mobilize across ethnononational lines or, indeed, with no reference to ethnicity. Here I explore some of the most obvious – ethnic quotas, ethnic decentralization, ethnic vetoes – as well as a more subtle barrier, coalition government.

Ethnic Quotas

Bosnia's consociational system represents a mixture of ethnic and territorial power-sharing (Hulsey and Stjepanović 2017, 48; Keil 2013, 95–6). As well as representation based on territory (e.g. entity, canton), it entails an elaborate system of ethnic representation through reserved seats or 'quotas' for positions in government, legislature, and public administration at various levels (the latter on a more informal basis). Quotas are applied most prominently in the three-member state presidency, the Council of Ministers (central state government) and the upper houses of parliament (the House of Peoples) at state and entity levels. Whilst at entity level, the upper houses in FBiH and the RS contain seats reserved for Others alongside Serbs, Bosniaks, and Croats, state level institutions of the presidency and the upper house of parliament entail no recognition for non-ethnic actors (Hodžić and Stojanović 2011). These electoral rules blatantly exclude those who do not identify with one of the three constituent groups, for whatever reason (including identifying with another minority ethnicity, being of mixed ethnic background or rejecting ethnic labels altogether), and those who do identify with one of the groups but find themselves residing in the 'wrong' entity (e.g. Serbs living in FBiH and Bosniaks and Croats living in RS) (Stojanović 2018). Indeed, as noted, the injustice has seen several cases taken to the European Court of Human Rights in Strasbourg and now five rulings state that the Bosnian Constitution violates the European Convention on Human Rights (ECHR) for only allowing people who identify ethnically to stand for the presidency and the House of Peoples. Following the landmark Sejdić-Finci ruling in 2009, again in 2014 in the case of Zornić v Bosnia and Herzegovina, the court ruled that Bosnia was in violation of the ECHR for not allowing Azra Zornić to stand for election to the House of Peoples or the presidency because she refuses to declare affiliation to one of the three constituent peoples (ECHR 2014). And in 2016 it ruled that the state discriminated against Ilijaz Pilav for barring him from standing for the presidency as a Bosniak living in the RS (ECHR 2016).[18] In spite of much debate and pressure from the international community, reforms to comply with these rulings have yet to be adopted. As it stands then, actors positioning themselves as explicitly non-ethnic are theoretically denied recognition and positions of power in these state institutions. What's more, the rules arguably socialize voters to a system of ethnonational representation in which Bosniak citizens are represented by Bosniak representatives, Serbs by Serbs and Croats by Croats.

Ethno-Territorial Decentralization

The territorial element of power-sharing presents a tricky terrain for civic parties. The division of the territory into largely ethnically homogenous political units and decentralization of power to those units presents a patent obstacle to parties that try to traverse ethnic boundaries. The 'entities' form the electoral units for the two upper tiers of governance – state and entity level – with one third of delegates to the state House of Representatives directly elected in the Serb-dominated RS and two thirds elected in the Bosniak–Croat FBiH. Meanwhile the Serb member of the tripartite state presidency is elected in the RS while the Croat and Bosniak members are elected in FBiH. At cantonal level within the FBiH entity, eight of the ten cantons have either a Bosniak or Croat majority, while the majority of local municipalities are mono-ethnic in make-up. Such decentralization to ethnically homogenous electoral units evidently provides little incentive for parties to organize on a cross-ethnic basis and poses considerable costs for attempts to do so (Mujkić and Hulsey 2010, 154; Touquet 2012a, 236; Bahtić-Kunrath 2011, 916). The use of multi-member list PR electoral system in these constituencies, furthermore, does not require parties to appeal to voters from more than one ethnic group to get elected (Aitken 2007, 260; Belloni 2004, 339). This speaks to the 'paradox' of federalism (Erk and Anderson 2009) and 'ethnic partition' (Jenne 2009) as a means of managing ethnonational conflict: defusing ethnic tensions on the one hand but at the same time structuring politics along ethnonational lines and socializing parties and voters in this way.

'State-wide', 'cross-territorial' parties thus remain an exception in Bosnia. The majority of parties operate within only one entity and those that organize in both entities tend to attract support from only one ethnic group. Civic parties also struggle to escape this trend. The core support of SDP, DF, and Naša Stranka lies in Bosniak majority areas of FBiH, as noted, with scant representation in either the RS or Croat majority areas of FBiH. A number of civic representatives lamented this reality. SDP representatives pointed to the representation the party commanded in the RS, which included three members of the eighty-three-seat RS National

Assembly and the vice president of the entity in 2010–14 (Central Election Commission BiH 2010). Yet, they admitted that these representatives were themselves Bosniak and their support came primarily from members of the Bosniak minority community in the RS, most of whom were 'returnees' (formerly refugees and displaced people).[19] Likewise, some noted that the support the party garners from Croat and Serb voters in BiH tends to come from those living in areas of FBiH where they form the national minority.[20]

Ethnic Vetoes

A feature of Bosnia's power-sharing institutions that has been particularly contentious is the *ethnic veto*. Designed as a safeguard, each group possesses an ultimate block on legislation that affects its national interest. Bieber and Keil note Bosnia's use of 'wide-ranging veto rights with low thresholds and executive and legislative veto players' (2009, 353). Veto players include both executive and legislative actors and the procedure features in the presidency and the parliamentary Assembly at state level and both upper houses at entity level. In the state parliament, a decision in either chamber can be declared to be destructive of a constituent people's 'vital national interest' (VNI) by a majority of delegates within one national bloc present and voting in the House of Peoples. The decision is then referred to a three-member commission convened by the chair of the House of Peoples and made up of a delegate of each bloc. If consensus is not reached within five days the decision is then referred to the Constitutional Court (McEvoy 2015, 111–12). Furthermore, within the three-member presidency, a decision by two members can be declared by the third to adversely affect their group's vital interest. The decision is then referred to the relevant entity parliament and if the president's dissent is supported by two thirds of the vote in the RS National Assembly or the majority of the Bosniak or Croat bloc in the FBiH House of Peoples, that decision is overturned (Bose 2002, 64). Ethnic interests are further safeguarded by the 'entity veto' in the House of Representatives, whereby a decision can be blocked by two-thirds of the representatives from either entity (McEvoy 2015, 112).

Bosnia's veto system has been heavily criticized for creating impasse in the passage of legislation, efficient governance and progress (Bahtić-Kunrath 2011, 899; McEvoy 2013, 263; 2015, 114). Serb delegates constitute Bosnia's chief veto players, exercising the block primarily through entity voting and generally for the purpose of maintaining the constitutional status quo and blocking any movement of powers from the entities to the state (Bahtić-Kunrath 2011, 907). In the 2006–10 legislative period it has been estimated that only 30 per cent of planned legislation was in fact adopted (Bahtić-Kunrath 2011, 899; McCulloch 2014a, 507). The frequent use of the blocking procedures can imbue Bosnian politics with a sense of continual conflict, highlighting this absence of cooperation to the public as the defining feature of politics. Indeed, intransigent use of the veto can be exercised by elites to display their ethnic tribune credentials and reap electoral rewards, as did SNSD in the 2010 elections (Bahtić-Kunrath 2011, 914).

Civic party representatives bitterly condemned Bosnia's veto system, for arresting progress in the country and, in some cases, for its detrimental effects on their party. A number of SDP members blamed the system, and its misuse by ethnic parties, for preventing the party from advancing its agenda in the 2010–14 mandate, stifling decision-making in the Council of Ministers and blocking proposed legislation in areas like economic development, poverty alleviation, and anti-corruption.[21] They also cited the use of the veto to block the SDP's attempts to form government at state and FBiH levels following the 2010 elections, when it emerged as the largest party on both tiers but was blocked by Croat and Serb delegates in nominating a Croat member for prime minister, leaving Bosnia without a central government for over a year.[22]

Some SDP representatives partly blamed the veto procedures for its declining popularity after its 2010–14 term and the general disillusion with the party following a positive 2010 election campaign. With no allies amongst other parties, nor the ethnonational party-controlled media, they felt the SDP received the blame for the governing coalition's lack of cooperation and progress on social and economic matters during this period – in spite of the fact that this failure resulted, in their view, from ethnonational parties' frequent use of the veto.[23] One SDP member of the state parliament suggested the regular use of the veto contributed to an atmosphere of 'panic and fear' in Bosnian politics, which made voters more likely to support ethnonational parties.[24] In this way, the veto procedures arguably contribute to the marginalization of civic politics.

Coalition Government

Access to government under Bosnia's proportional representation power-sharing system, at state, entity and cantonal levels, is only viable through coalition with other parties. Given the dominance of ethnonational parties and dearth of non-ethnonational actors in the system however, this presents considerable impediments and a potential strategic dilemma to civic parties in terms of forging alliances with other parties, either in the form of pre-election pacts, post-election governing coalitions or, indeed, day-to-day cooperation on policy and legislation. Entering government at state and entity level, almost inevitably entails partnership with ethnonational parties.

Civic parties note the dearth of other parties with which they can do business.[25] A senior Naša Stranka's official accepted the necessity of working with ethnonational parties, in order to wield any influence in the system, but noted that the party's members were extremely reluctant to associate with ethnonational actors, presenting a strategic challenge.[26] Members of the DF also raised pre- and post-electoral alliances as a thorny issue which it had to consider ahead of elections, with the prospect of a controversial pact with populist Bosniak party SBB BiH floated in 2014 (Union for a Better Future of BiH).[27]

Yet, even where available, cooperation and alliance among civic parties can be tricky. Fragmentation and lack of alliance within the civic bloc was evident in Bosnia from the first multiparty elections in 1990 (Sasso 2015, 313, 375). Pacts between civic parties in post-Dayton politics have been few and their record limited, with the 2001–02 Alliance for Change coalition of ten parties proving unstable and transient. One member of the Sarajevo canton for Naša Stranka expressed the difficulty of doing business with any other party in cantonal Assembly, including the SDP, as their lack of ideological profile and the fact that they obtain their direction solely from their leadership make them unreliable allies. Naša Stranka had considered forming an electoral bloc with other civic centre-left parties ahead of the 2014 general election, he said, but abandoned the idea for these reasons.[28] The challenge of civic party cooperation was again illustrated by the breakdown of the historic coalition that formed in the Canton of Sarajevo after the 2018 election, bringing together opposition parties, primarily Naša Stranka, SDP and DF, and notably excluding Bosniak party SDA. The coalition led by Naša Stranka's Edin Forto proved short-lived however, falling apart in January 2020 when DF abandoned its pact with NS and SDP, following a shift in alliances connected with the formation of the state-level coalition government, and formed a new coalition with Bosniak parties SDA and SBB (European Commission 2020; Sarajevo Times 2020).

Forming government with ethnonational parties remains an option for civic parties, of course, and one taken at state and FBiH entity level, most notably by SDP 2010–14. This move comes with risks, however, as we explore in chapter 7.

Unwritten Rules

However steep the barriers erected by the constitutional rules, it is the unwritten rules that tend to be front of mind for civic representatives when they describe their experiences. A political discourse imbued with ethnonationalism, a pervasive system of ethnonational clientelism, a dearth of civic alliances and high levels of political disillusion make this a particularly adverse environment for civic politics. And of course, the formal and informal barriers intertwine, inform and reinforce one another in intricate ways.

Political Discourse

The discursive strategies used by ethnonational parties work to at times *marginalize* and at times to *contest* the civic position in Bosnian politics.

In a country some thirty years removed from a devastating war, fear retains strong currency in politics. This 'security dilemma' is routinely stoked by ethnic parties against the ethnic other to bolster their support, with the side effect of *marginalizing* civic parties. Piacentini observes that this fear is strongly connected to the recent memory of war, and the perception of ethnonational parties as a source of protection (2019, 283). In an example of how war trauma can be exploited, one SDP representative suggested that the vandalism of Muslim graves and war memorials around election time is often perpetrated on behalf of Bosniak nationalist parties.[29] Indeed, during the 2022 general election campaign, ethnonational parties used the war in Ukraine to reawaken war fears, particularly in light of RS President Milorad Dodik's visit to Russian President Vladimir Putin (NDI 2022). Civic party representatives lament ethnonational parties' continued ability to manipulate voters' fear of the other ethnic community and the zero-sum threat of loss.[30] Some express frustration at the ease with which these parties could win votes in this fashion, as opposed to having to campaign on social and economic issues and demonstrate achievements.[31]

Members of Naša Stranka were particularly exercised about the competitive discursive strategies deployed by their ethnonational party rivals and the impact it had on their party. One member of the party leadership underlined the challenge for civic parties to get through to voters in this context: 'In RS it is quite impossible to talk about political issues and … not address issues of war … This is how the big parties win, they throw the ball to each other. They pump up the hatreds and tensions between each other and sort of rely on the people to vote out of spite. "Well I know he's a crook, but at least he's my crook"'.[32]

Amidst this discourse of fear, positive, issue-based campaigning becomes a major challenge,[33] as one leading Naša Stranka representative attests: 'They bring this country to the edge of the war before every election … It's the fear. It's the cheapest and most available fuel in politics and if you're going to use it, it's really hard to go against it. It's *really* hard. Especially when you're talking about just normal, reasonable things – like how we're going to organize public transportation.'[34]

The Naša Stranka representative maintains that it is possible to get through to voters with the party's message of hope and a better future for Bosnia based on democratic reform and social democratic policies. However, this requires significant time and resource and progress is prone to reversal:

> [You can] go to Republika Srpska, Banja Luka, and you sit with a guy who is a really radical nationalist … After three hours he's not a nationalist anymore, he's a worried father, he's worried about his job and things like that.
>
> So all you need to do is spend three to four hours with 3.5 million people! Or, you go and you say: 'Long live Serbia!' And they all go 'Long live …' and you can go in five minutes to your next rally.[35]

Findings from focus groups with citizens also reveal an awareness and resentment of these ethnonational discourses.[36]

In this climate, civic messages are often interpreted and heard differently by different ethnic communities (see Basta 2016). Civic parties' policies and positions are regularly *contested* by ethnonational parties: deliberately framed in ethnonational terms, sometimes as a threat of the ethnic group. In competing with civic parties then, ethnonational parties deploy discursive strategies that frame their civic counterparts varyingly as: *weak*, *illegitimate*, *suspect*, and even *traitorous*.

A number of civic representatives interviewed cited attempts by ethnonational parties to paint them as *weak* and ineffectual in the face of the threat from the ethnic other and thus incapable of adequately representing voters' interests.[37] Representatives of both SDP and Naša Stranka complained of being treated as *illegitimate* representatives of the three constituent peoples, when they served in roles reserved for members of these communities under the ethnic quota system.[38] Civic parties also encounter the discursive strategy of *suspicion*. In the prevailing discourse of fear and insecurity, the non-ethnic or multi-ethnic stance is regularly not accepted as credible and these parties are painted as '*really* ethnic'. Given their presence overwhelmingly in Bosniak-majority areas of FBiH and low profile in the RS, the accusation most commonly levelled at civic parties is that they are really Bosniak parties masquerading as multi-ethnic. This discursive strategy was displayed in interviews with representatives of ethnonational parties. A (Croat) HDZ representative of Mostar City Council, typifies this view, maintaining that not a single multi-ethnic party exists in BiH: 'In the leadership they have Croats, they have Serbs ... but by membership and especially by their voters, they are a Bosniak party.'[39] Likewise a (Serb) SNSD representative argued that, with its pro-centralization position, SDP will only ever attract significant votes from the Bosniak community and therefore only ever *be* a Bosniak party.[40]

One SDP representative thus complained that, on the one hand, her party was accused by Serb and Croat parties of *really* being an ethnic (Bosniak) party and, on the other, by Bosniak parties of not being able to truly represent Bosniaks.[41] DF has also experienced skepticism of its multi-ethnic stance, particularly in the RS, where it has to combat the claim that it is a Bosniak party, particularly given that its leader Željko Komšić (an ethnic Croat) fought during the war with the Bosnian army.[42] This suspicion of the civic position was also evident in the controversy over then president of Naša Stranka Dennis Gratz's name – a key marker of ethnic identity. The events erupted when it was revealed during the 2008 municipal elections, in which Gratz stood as a candidate, that he had changed his name from Muhamed Gračić (a traditionally Bosniak name) to Dennis Gratz (Touquet 2011, 465). This affair left the Naša Stranka member accused of trying to hide his true ethnic identity and – particularly by his Bosniak opponents – of being ashamed of that identity.[43]

Civic parties' positions in the perennial debate about constitutional reform is particularly subject to ethnonational framing and contestation. While civic parties' policies vary, they tend to support some level of centralization of power to the state and greater national integration – moves that are read by Serb and Croat parties as part of a majoritarian, Bosniak agenda. One Naša Stranka's representative recalls how promoting the proposals for constitutional reform commissioned by the party in 2012 – which included strengthening the state level and organizing the country into four ethnically neutral entities and two districts – was depicted as a move to abolish the RS (Sarčević 2012).[44] This underlines the 'symbolic baggage' attached to the different institutional options, with reforms potentially perceived very differently within each ethnonational community (Basta 2016, 968; Kapadžić 2018, 56).

Some of the more hostile discourses used by ethnonational parties towards civic parties go beyond insinuation to explicitly portray them as *traitorous*. The 'traitors' ('izdajnici') accusation retains currency in post-war Bosnia (Grandits 2007, 106, 115, 117–18). Civic representatives interviewed reported encountering this 'traitor' allegation, explicitly or implicitly.[45] Some described how their party's stance on certain policy issues, which they deemed to have no relevance to ethnicity, was played by their ethnonational opponents as a betrayal of their community. One SDP representative of the (state-level upper house) House of Peoples BiH, for example, cited the state-wide residency law, which was supported by the SDP but vetoed by Bosniak parties who claimed it would discriminate against Bosniak returnees in the RS. The member said the SDA portrayed the SDP in the media as endangering Bosniaks living in the RS, after which he received 'hundreds of threatening emails saying, "You are betraying the Bosniak people" ... I was really aware that passing this law was part of the reform process BiH needs to go through. But still, it's a very strange feeling.'[46] Another SDP representative pointed to the pressure the party came under from the Bosniak party SDA during the debate that preceded the census carried out in 2013, to support its campaign for people to declare their ethnicity Bosniak, their religion Islam and their language Bosnian, in order to boost these figures in the outcome.[47] Meanwhile, one Naša Stranka representative of Sarajevo canton and Serb delegate to the House of Peoples FBiH reports accusations from his opponents in the cantonal Assembly that he fought with the Serb forces in Sarajevo in the war. While he vehemently rebutted the claim at the time, he argues that such insinuations can linger with voters, as he heard play out in a subsequent party focus group: 'One guy said, "You know, I really like [NS representative] but he was with the Četniks [Serb paramilitary group] during the war". And the other guys says, "Really? Oh, I didn't know that. I really liked him, but now that I hear that ..."'[48]

Civic party representatives tended to interpret such attacks as motivated by self-preservation on the part of the ethnonational parties, who see them as a threat to the dominance of ethnonational politics and, hence, their power.[49] The Naša Stranka representative referenced above who designated as Serb observed that the accusations of his association with the Serb army surface most strongly when he appears to pose a political threat to his rivals, such as following the proposal in 2014 that he be nominated as prime minister of the cantonal government of Sarajevo.[50] Another Naša Stranka representative saw ethnic party animosity as driven by her party's challenging of their nepotistic practices.[51]

Focus groups with citizens suggest that these ethnonational framings also find resonance with voters. Discussions in a group conducted with students in RS – each of whom identified as Serb (or Bosnian Serb) – reveal a strong suspicion of 'multi-ethnic parties'. Some participants claimed that there were no such parties in BiH and that those that did proclaim themselves as such – namely SDP and Naša Stranka – were 'fake', harbouring Bosniak identity and a majoritarian agenda. One participant argued that the SDP had damaged the very concept of 'multi-ethnic' and, even of citizenship, using these terms as bywords, to his mind, for Bosniak. He further claimed the party 'abused' the system by getting a candidate elected as Croat member of the presidency through predominantly Bosniak votes.[52] Another participant said, '[Naša Stranka] are clearly a Muslim, Bosnian, Bosniak party; they're not multi-ethnic. That's just a mask … What SDP and Naša Stranka are doing is just spreading their own identity, *their* Bosnian identity. That's not our Bosnian identity. I have a Bosnian identity: I am Bosnian Serb – I wrote it there [in the participant questionnaire].'[53] This claim echoes Serb and Croat parties' perceptions of calls for a 'civic state' by both Bosniak parties and civic parties, as a thinly veiled majoritarian agenda – 'a ruse for a Bosniak ethno-national state' (Basta 2016, 964).

Ethnonational Clientelism

Fundamental to understanding the relationship between voters and parties in post-war Bosnia, is the practice of patronage. Patronage and clientelism are a form of social organization characterized by 'patron-client' relationships in which 'relatively powerful and rich "patrons" promise to provide relatively powerless and poor "clients" with jobs, protection, infrastructure and other benefits and services in exchange for various forms of loyalty' (UNDP 2009, 74). Patronage runs deep in Bosnia and is intimately connected to ethnonational mobilization. A UNDP study found that Bosnian society is heavily based on informal social and familial networks, whereby personal connections are routinely used – and often necessary – to obtain public goods and services (UNDP 2009, 69). 'Štela' – a local concept connoting a form of nepotism – is as a core currency in Bosnian society (UNDP 2009, 74). This informal system is commonly used for gaining access to employment, public services, particularly better education and healthcare, and obtaining official documents, and can range in scale from small favours to bribery and corruption (Touquet 2011, 141; UNDP 2009, 74). Political participation is associated by citizens primarily with joining a party to gain connections and hence personal benefits (UNDP 2009, 69). Whilst not unique to Bosnia the UNDP report notes that what is unusual in the state is the scale of the phenomenon, appearing to 'pervade entirely' so many institutions (UNDP 2009, 85). Politics is deeply invested in this clientelistic culture where 'political patronage networks are widespread and influence all levels of government' (European Commission 2014, 15).

The most prominent feature of patronage in Bosnia, according to Kapidžić, is the use of public resources, such as employment, to reward individuals and strengthen party structures (2020a, 94). Bosnia hosts a large public sector and political parties, which control significant state resources, act as patrons, providing public goods and services to 'their' loyal clients – voters (Abazović 2007, 196; Grandits 2007, 108; Hulsey and Keil 2020, 346). State-owned enterprises (SOEs) (many entity-owned), such as FBiH and RS electricity companies and railways and BH Telecom Company, make up about 11 per cent of total employment: as such, control of their job opportunities and resources can be a key resource for parties (Parodi and Cegar 2019, 6; Kapidžić 2020a, 94). Some scholars have characterized the main parties' seizure of control of state resources, including through the privatization of previously state-owned assets, as 'state capture' (Džankić 2018).

The types of goods that parties can offer in contemporary Bosnia range from positions on the boards of state companies at the higher level, to public sector jobs, school and university admissions, and agricultural subsidies at the lower levels. These goods are exchanged for party loyalty, membership, and indeed votes at election time, a reciprocal obligation which often extends beyond the individual to their family. The relationship can entail elements of intimidation as well as co-optation, with clients required to 'take care' in order to keep the jobs or other goods granted them (Grandits 2007, 108–9). Kapidžić describes this as 'relational clientelism', based on long-term relationships and more permanent benefits, as opposed to 'electoral clientelism', based on one-off transactions such as vote buying on election day (2020a, 94). Party control in BiH extends, notably, to the media, which remains starkly divided along ethnonational lines and under strong influence from the respective political parties (Abazović 2007, 201; Manning 2004, 64; Freedom House 2013). Elections become contests over different patronage networks as parties vie for control of state resources, including budgets, employment opportunities, and state assets (Hulsey and Keil 2020, 346).

Bosnia's informal system of patronage and clientelism, in which parties can use their political and economic power to both co-opt and intimidate, forms a major obstacle to civic parties. These conditions grant an advantage to the main ethnonational parties, as Kapidžić explains: 'By using illiberal politics and informality as a mechanism to control SOEs, dominant ethnic parties are able to connect voting preferences to economic benefits. The result is a large number of ethnically defined political machines with stable voting patterns where opposition parties are at a significant disadvantage' (2020a, 95). Civic parties depict this system as a major asset to the ethnonational parties in BiH and handicap to those seeking to play a different game. Naša Stranka members were most forthright about its detrimental effect on their progression.[54] Part of the party's raison d'etre is to 'clean up' politics and in its electoral programs it has explicitly criticized 'nepotism' in Bosnian politics (Hulsey and Keil 2019, 410). One member of the leadership explained that, staking its reputation as a new party that does not engage in corruption, Naša Stranka did not take up the positions on boards of publicly owned companies to which it was entitled. This principled stance made the party very 'unsuccessful' in Bosnian politics in the short term, he said, depriving it of power in these spheres and making it less attractive to donors seeking to influence the political process. This, in turn, renders Naša Stranka less able to secure media coverage, which, he claimed, can be bought in Bosnia.[55] Indeed, one senior party official recounted that a number of new members who joined the party after its founding, left when they realized that they were not going to secure any personal gains, such as employment, from their membership.[56] Likewise, a member of the party presidency emphasized the challenge Naša Stranka faced when other parties are 'literally … buying votes'. She cited the example of a Bosniak party which held the agriculture ministry in her canton, allocating agricultural subsidies to those thought likely to vote for the party. In this context, she argued, even with the best agricultural policies, it is difficult for a small party, with neither the power nor the will to engage in clientelistism, to compete.[57] Forming a financial barrier to small, new players, patronage appears a particular impediment to Naša Stranka.

For SDP, ethnonational party patronage has made it difficult to advance in Serb and Croat majority areas, according to members. Representatives identified it as a key barrier to it breaking into these regions where such parties had strong 'infrastructure' and control over state resources.[58] One SDP member of the House of Peoples explained:

> What you have is really domination of these political parties on the local level. For example, you have principals of schools who are appointed if they belong to a political party. And managing boards … It is a strong political infrastructure built in those areas and it's very difficult to eradicate it. They engage local people and they tell them 'we need to keep our status here, we need to keep our influence here, otherwise you will lose your positions, you will be driven out'. So, this is how they basically get their support and why it is difficult to break into that.[59]

An SDP member and former city mayor articulated how this system of 'political rent' makes it very easy for ethnonational parties to maintain power in BiH. Some SDP interviewees claimed that civil servants appointed by other parties had obstructed the SDP's agenda when in office 2010–14 (including tactics like hiding mail from ministers) and stifled its progress.[60]

As well as co-opting voters, party clientelism is used as a tool of intimidation and deterrence in BiH, as one senior member of DF attested. Some influential members of society received blackmail that they may lose their positions if they were to declare support for the new party, he reported.[61]

Citizens who participated in focus groups were keenly aware of the pervasiveness of party patronage in Bosnia and the issue emerged at the foreground of discussions.[62] Participants expressed deep cynicism about political parties and political participation, agreeing that the *only* reason that one would join a party was in order to secure a job or improve one's employment prospects.[63] In explaining why people vote overwhelmingly for ethnonational parties, participants pointed to small material gain and fear of losing benefits, in the context of widespread unemployment and poverty. 'I think the problem is that people are afraid. Because they are always thinking about the small things ... They are giving them cows ... small amounts of money. 100KM [€50] is enough to buy a vote I think."[64] Participants expressed the belief that electoral fraud was widespread,[65] with one reporting that public employees were sometimes required by their local ruling party to take a photograph of their ballot paper.[66]

Nevertheless, civic parties have themselves been accused of utilizing clientelist networks to their own advantage – most notably SDP which was charged with engaging in the system on a scale equal to that of the ethnonational parties, not least during its term in state government 2010–14 (see also Sasso 2015, 388).[67] Two SDP members of state parliament admitted that the SDP also attempts to secure jobs and positions for its supporters in order to compete with the other parties.[68] One claimed, however, that at the same time the party was trying to change legislation to eradicate such practice on the macro level.[69]

The patronage system appears to work hand in hand with ethnic party competition to instill fear in voters that not voting for the dominant ethnonational party in their area will result in a very real loss. Patronage then contributes to ethnonational party dominance in Bosnia, in a path dependent fashion – used as a tool to perpetuate their political power and set high costs for parties that seek to break through and change voter preferences.

Political Distrust and Disconnect

Civic space outside the purview of parties is extremely underdeveloped in Bosnia. Much of it is co-opted by political parties, and, moreover, structured along ethnonational lines. In this context, civic party representatives underline a dearth of allies in civil society, notably, among trade unions and media.[70]

Yet, on a deeper level, civic parties must also contend with deep-rooted distrust among the electorate in the political class and the political system. A 2019 poll showed that citizens of the Western Balkans have less confidence in their national governments than their counterparts in OECD–EU countries and, of those, Bosnian citizens had the very least trust (23 per cent compared to 45 per cent in OECD–EU states) (OECD 2020, 29). Piacentini notes high levels of distrust in the system, disdain for politics and general apathy, particularly among younger people (2019, 283). Whilst this political disillusion and apathy could theoretically translate into an appetite for civic parties, the evidence from focus groups and interviews suggests that this culture rather presents a further challenge.

With little trust in political elites or belief in the capacity for politics to produce change for the good, civic party messages often fall flat. This political disillusion and apathy emerged potently in focus groups. Participants in the student group in the RS referred to political parties as 'business groups' which had no relation to ideology.[71]

Such apathy arose as a source of grievance for civic representatives, for which they blamed their ethnonational counterparts. One SDP parliamentarian bemoaned the absence of trust in all political elites and the fact that voters make no differentiation between the parties in this sense.[72] Naša Stranka representatives furthermore expressed frustration at voters' lack of faith in the political process and its knock-on effect on their party. One lamented the fact that many voters respond positively to the party's policy but nevertheless continue to vote for ethnonational parties: 'They do not realize that they have the key to the changes in their hands.'[73] One member of the party leadership related the challenge of trying to convince voters in this climate that a vote for Naša Stranka was not a waste of time:

> Our biggest enemy is [the] apathy that the nationalist parties have produced. Because they rely on very little amount of votes and usually these votes are bought. So, they don't want people to get optimistic and to have some sort of aspirations. This is what we are trying to sell to people – hope.
>
> But in this country economic stagnation and general [corruption] has made people very cynical. So when you tell them, like Obama, like hope, they laugh. They just observe us as naïve.[74]

Civic disillusion and apathy in the post-war state form a hefty obstacle for civic parties trying to sell the possibility of change. What's more, civil society has also remained markedly under-developed in the post-war context. International peacebuilding efforts have seen a depoliticization and 'NGO-ization' of civil society (Touquet 2015, 403; Abazović 2007, 199; Belloni 2007, 111–12; Ahmetašević 2024, 91). This has stifled bottom-up civic activity at community level, which could feed into the development of civic parties.

That being said, the last ten years have seen a subtle shift taking place in Bosnian civil society, as citizen protest has become more frequent, in line with both regional and global trends. Vibrant movements – most notably the 2014 uprising – have arisen over particular grievances and proceeded to challenge the ethnopolitical division and dysfunction of the

Dayton system, as well as authoritarian tendencies in government (Repovac Nikšić et al 2022, 143). The 2014 plenum movement was preceded by the 'JMBG' protests in 2013 sparked by an inter-ethnic political dispute over the issuing of identification numbers which resulted in the death of a child unable to travel for lifesaving medical treatment (Armakolas and Maksimovic 2013). It was followed by the 'Justice for Dženan' movement in FBiH following the unresolved death of Dženan Memić in Sarajevo in February 2016 and, in similar vein, the 'Justice for David' movement in the RS following the apparent murder of twenty-one-year-old student David Dragicević in 2018 (Repovac Nikšić et al 2022). Indeed, solidarity across entity lines emerged between these two parallel movements (Repovac Nikšić et al 2022, 152).

Despite this significant and positive development for civic politics in Bosnia, it has not automatically translated into a boost for civic *parties.* The toxic and ethnicized nature of politics in the post-war state has led many civic grassroots organizations and movements to eschew engagement with the formal political sphere through avenues such as alliances with political parties (including civic parties), advancement of overtly political issues or, indeed, party formation. This was clearly witnessed in the 2014 uprising which very intentionally resisted any alliance with political parties – *including civic parties* – and even the international community (case study 6.1 below). Similarly, in 2018 the Justice for David movement in RS, did not engage with any political parties, distancing itself from politics –nor did it have any direct impact on electoral outcomes in the RS (Hulsey and Kiel 2020, 359). While the Justice for Dženan movement notably extended further than other contemporary movements into the political realm (Repovac Nikšić et al 2022, 150),[75] social movements' political engagement in Bosnia has remained strictly limited. And national-level movements remain rare. Attempts to unite the Justice for David and Justice for Dženan movements across entities were repressed by the authorities in RS under SNSD leadership, in a similar strategy of containment used to limit the spread of the 2014 plenum movement to RS (Kapidžić 2020a, 90; Mujanović 2017). As a result, these movements each remained largely subnational. Furthermore, they did not lead to any immediate change at the institutional political level. These challenges are explored further in case study 6.1 below.

Ultimately, the prevalence of distrust in politics leads to a disjuncture between grassroots and formal civic politics and a blockage in that critical pipeline between the two spheres.

Case Study 6.1: The 2014 Bosnian Uprising

In February 2014, a non-ethnic protest dramatically broke out in Bosnia. Against a backdrop of political division and civic passivity, the mobilization invoked the possibility of bottom-up transformation. Nevertheless, it chose to refrain from entering the fray of institutional politics. Rather, it adopted an approach that appeared at once political and apolitical; pursuing demands for political accountability, yet resisting invitations to engage with formal political actors, institutions or matters of high politics.

The 2014 mobilization began in Tuzla, a north-eastern industrial city with a strong tradition of multi-ethnicity, worker solidarity, and non-nationalist politics (Armakolas 2011, 230), as a workers' protest in response to the closure of a number of factories following their allegedly corrupt privatizations. On 5 February these localized protests turned into mass demonstrations in which public anger was directed at much wider grievances: widespread poverty, unemployment, corruption, and political inaction. Violence erupted as protesters clashed with police and occupied cantonal government buildings (Busuladžić 2014). The scenes in Tuzla quickly found resonance and by 7 February protests had spread to towns and cities across FBiH, including Sarajevo, Mostar, Zenica, and Bihać. After a dramatic beginning, when public buildings were set alight, including cantonal offices in Tuzla, Sarajevo, Zenica, and Mostar, the movement quickly transformed into a peaceful and, moreover, organized, action (see figures 6.5 and 6.6).

Within days a new body had formed as the institutional arm of the protests, known as the plenum. This civic forum operating on the principles of direct democracy was established in a number of towns and cities, attracting a diverse range of citizens (Husarić 2014, 68). The plenum hosted deliberative debate from which demands were formulated and presented to the relevant political institutions. Demands included government resignations, revision of allegedly corrupt privatizations, cuts to excessive benefits for politicians, the installation of expert governments, and investigation into the events surrounding the initial protests including the treatment of protesters by police.[76]

The action elicited some immediate responses: four cantonal governments resigned and some agreed to end certain privileges for

Figure 6.5 | Protest in Sarajevo city centre, February 2014.

political representatives. In Tuzla canton an expert government was installed, undertaking to work in cooperation with the plenum. The activity dissipated in May 2014, however, following limited response from governments, particularly at the FBiH entity level, and with the onset of devastating floods in BiH and the wider region.

In spite of some expectation, the civic movement did not attempt to enter the sphere of formal politics. Early and definitively, it chose not to form a political party nor form alliances with parties or even to lobby these actors nor form serious pacts with NGOs or international actors (Milan 2020, 94–5). It refrained from entering debate on constitutional reform, keeping the focus strictly on basic social and economic issues. It remained, furthermore, relatively local in scale, making limited attempts to extend horizontally, across entities (to the RS), or vertically, to state level.

The movement's reluctance to engage in formal politics drew some criticism, with one academic commentator lamenting such 'strategic mistakes' (Keil, 2014). One representative of an international democratization NGO dismissed the mobilization as a leftist 'Occupy 2.0', which missed its opportunity to effect real change by failing to form a political party or engage with existing parties to influence their programs.[77] Underlying the plenums' resistance to engage in institutional politics, lay an acute awareness of the structural environment in which they were operating, the restricted openings it afforded to civic political actors and the threats it posed (Murtagh 2016).

In the dominant political discourse, the civic nature of this mobilization was subject to intense contestation and *manipulation*. In the wake of the protests 'ethnonational spin' was spread by all three nationalist blocs in a bid to ethnicize, divide, and delegitimize the movement (Mujkić 2016). Serb and Croat elites thus claimed the action was orchestrated against *their people* and painted the movement as a solely Bosniak affair. The leader of the ruling party in the

Figure 6.6 | Plenum meeting in Dom Mladih Sarajevo, February 2014.

RS, SNSD and president of the entity Milorad Dodik depicted it as an attempt to destroy the RS, casting veterans' protests there as coordinated by Bosniak nationalist forces (Balkanist 2014). Croat nationalist leaders meanwhile presented the movement as a Bosniak effort to majoritize the country and abolish cantons – and hence Croat autonomy.[78] Some Bosniak elites, furthermore, portrayed the action as an external move to fracture the unity of the Bosniak people, while others reportedly attempted to co-opt the movement. Plenum activists reported efforts, most notably by the populist Bosniak party SBB BiH, to infiltrate the plenums for electoral advantage in the October 2014 general elections.[79] Parties' framings of the protests as violence-oriented also clearly played on people's raw memories of war (Milan 2020).

The movement also encountered active *intimidation* by political parties and authorities, activists reported. A number claimed police brutality, as well as attempts to portray protestors as criminals (Hodžić 2014, 53; Ibrišimović 2014, 32). Some Mostar activists alleged that police were deterring protesters from moving into a street on the Croat-majority west side of the city in a bid to give it the appearance of a Bosniak-only action.[80] Given the control parties exert over public resources and extensive clientelistic networks, participants were reportedly threatened with losing their jobs, with family members losing jobs, or with having their businesses exposed to prohibitive fines if they did not quit the activity. Members of the Mostar plenum related that the numbers of Croats and Bosniaks participating in the protests and plenum were about equal at the beginning of the action, yet following intense intimidation from the local Croat ruling party HDZ, Croat participation dropped off over time.[81] One prominent activist in the Mostar plenum noted that, tellingly, no 'cross-ethnic threats' were made by parties: 'SDA did not threaten a single Croat or Serb. They were all threatening their own people.'[82]

Clientelistic intimidation appeared to deter wider participation in the movement – and, critically in some areas, cross-ethnic participation. Many of those actively involved in the action were reported to be either unemployed or self-employed with no dependence on government contracts.[83] Activists furthermore pointed to threats by ethnonational elites to delegitimize protesters, as a means to discourage mobilization. One Sarajevo activist reported being named by a member of a Bosniak party in the Sarajevo canton during a televised Assembly meeting and having her family linked to Serb nationalist party SDS in a bid to discredit her – an implicit warning to other potential activists to stay away from the protests.[84]

The political context in which the movement operated elucidates the reasoning behind its choices. On one level, political engagement did not fit with the principles of a movement born out of rejection of the political establishment. Yet, the level of aversion towards any form of engagement also reflects a strategic response to the political environment. In a self-defensive rationale, interaction with formal politics was very consciously avoided by the leadership in a bid to preserve the civic movement.

Furthermore, short-term political change was not the ultimate goal of this movement. The mobilization's raison d'être lay deeper: in fundamental shift in civic discourse and thinking. In this view, awakening citizens to the possibility of change, and their own power to effect it, could be the first step in a bottom-up process of real reform in Bosnian politics (see Arsenijević 2014, 7; Gordy 2014, 112). Activists believed any attempt to interact with the political structures for short-term ends would inevitably divide and delegitimize the movement as a civic force, placing this goal in peril. The 2014 protest movement thus navigated the deeply ethnicized corporate consociational framework of post-war Bosnia by adopting an approach marked by restricted political engagement. The mobilization's capacity to effect civic political change was strictly limited on the level of formal politics. Rather, its potential appeared to lie in longer term development of civil society (Murtagh 2016).

This case study demonstrates the opportunities and constraints faced by a civic social movement in Bosnia's consociational framework. Whilst the protests managed to seize discursive space by channelling public frustration with citizens' social and economic difficulties and the failure of political elites and the system to address these problems, they came up against severe constraints, in the form of ethnonational contestation and co-optation and ethnonational patronage. This opportunity structure shaped the movement's choices and saw it remain at the level of informal politics rather than engaging with or making the transition to formal politics. Whilst these choices appear wholly rational and perhaps most effective for the realization of the movement's goals, the case underlines a number of points central to civic politics. Its very emergence illustrates the blockage in the Bosnian political system to the advancement of non-ethnic issues. Its experience demonstrates the obstacles to any form of civic mobilization and limits to its progression to institutional politics. This illustrates, furthermore, the disjuncture between civic politics at the grassroots level and at the party-political level in Bosnia and the limited capacity for the former to feed into the latter.

Conclusion

The ethnonational rules of Bosnian politics make it extremely difficult for a party to play a different game. The naming and privileging of the three ethnonational groups through rules like ethnic quotas for political office and vetoes for each group work to 'other' civic actors and leave them peripheral. Meanwhile, division of the state into largely ethnically homogenous electoral units creates a near-impossible task for a party seeking to run across the state. Requirements for executive coalitions to include all three groups also marginalize civic parties and place them in awkward positions. Yet, the unwritten rules of that game are just as pernicious for civic parties, if not more. A dominant ethnonational discourse, a pervasive system of ethnonational clientelism and a deep disconnect between civil society and formal politics, all work to further marginalize, contest and frustrate civic politics. This chapter then demonstrates the power of institutions but also of informal institutions. What's more, these formal and informal effects exist in a mutually determining dynamic. Ethnonational discourses are reinforced by institutional structures that enshrine the principle of ethnic representation, such as quotas and vetoes. The practice of ethnonational patronage is enabled to an extent by territorial decentralization which grants parties considerable control over public resources. Formal and informal structures interplay in Bosnia to constrain civic parties' progressions. How then, against this backdrop, have civic parties managed to survive as a force in Bosnian politics? We next examine how civic parties have adapted to this environment and to what effect.

Chapter Seven

Navigating the System in Bosnia and Herzegovina

In the 2022 Bosnian general election, civic party leader Željko Komšić pulled off an impressive feat. In clinching the position of Croat member of the presidency, Komšić and his party had in many ways defied the logic of Bosnia's highly ethnicized and rigid power-sharing system. The tripartite state presidency comprising one Croat, one Bosniak and one Serb – to represent each one of the country's three 'constituent peoples' – is an institution seemingly designed with ethnonational parties in mind. Yet, the Croat seat was won, not by a candidate from one of the Croat parties, but by a self-identifying Croat from the explicitly civic party, Democratic Front (DF). More impressive still, this was Komšić's fourth time to secure the Croat member of the presidency under the banner of a civic party, having first done so in 2006 as an SDP member.[1] And this time he was not alone on the civic front. In the 2022 election, the Bosniak seat was won, for the first time not by the main Bosniak party but by the civic SDP. While this result might appear a triumph for civic politics in a severely divided state, however, in reality the story of Komšić's presidency is one of the complexity and contentiousness of civic politics in post-war Bosnia. Hailed by some as a symbol of civic Bosnia and resistance to ethnic politics, for others, Komšić's election as Croat member of the presidency, off the back of predominantly Bosniaks votes in the FBiH entity, represents an abuse of the system and attempt to deny Croats of their rightful representation under the post-war constitution.

On first glance, civic parties in Bosnia fare well, especially considering their conditions: a deeply ethnicized political system some thirty years removed from a brutal war. They make up a solid 20 per cent of the vote, take part in government, and play a prominent role in public consciousness and discourse. Yet, compelled to play an ethnic game, civic parties face steep hurdles and intense contestation in the Bosnian system. They experience many of the same issues as those in Northern Ireland: institutions that deny them space and legitimacy and informal political structures that make operating on a non-ethnonational basis exceedingly difficult. Yet, their journeys also speak to critical differences in the institutional environment of each place, both formal and informal. Formally, Bosnia's rigid corporate consociational power-sharing rules create even heftier barriers to civic actors, while informally, Bosnia's particular political culture, discourse, and ways in which politics is 'done' make their plight even more fraught.

How have civic parties survived in this heavily ethnicized environment? Effectively by finding cracks in the system and creatively navigating them – on formal and informal levels. These strategies come with risks, however. Having seen these barriers up close in chapter 6, let us now examine the strategies civic parties have used to navigate that environment – and the dilemmas those strategies evoke. We begin by examining party positioning,

Party Positioning

Civic parties in Bosnia position themselves in different ways with regard to the central ethnonational divide. For the SDP, 'multi-ethnicity' lies central to the party's self-image. In this sense, it can be classified as an *accommodationist civic party* under the typology set out in chapter 1. The assertion that the SDP is 'the only multi-ethnic party in Bosnia' was vocalized with pride at the outset of a number of interviews.[2] Some representatives, furthermore, linked this multi-ethnic image of the party to their vision for a harmonious, multi-ethnic Bosnia, and presented the party as a kind of microcosm of this ideal country.[3] This positioning is thus intrinsically connected to the SDP's construction of the nation of BiH. The party's association with the former Communist Party, socialist Yugoslavia and Bosnia's pre-war multi-ethnic past were also evident in representations. Indeed, a portrait of Josip Broz Tito, Yugoslav president 1953–80, still hangs in the Sarajevo SDP party office, as in other SPD offices.[4] Secularism formed a strong theme in the self-representations of SPD members. Many representatives interviewed identified with one of the three ethnic groups or religions on a personal level, but believed that such identity had no bearing on their politics.[5] Some stressed the multi-ethnicity of their own personal background, such as being the product of, or partner in, a 'mixed marriage'.[6]

On the question of what defines the party as multi-ethnic, the key factor articulated in interviews with SDP members was *representation* – descriptive representation, specifically. Members appeared to measure the multi-ethnic nature of the SDP primarily by the ethnic make-up of its representatives, rather than by that of its support.[7] Indeed, this definition fits with the party's strong culture of internal ethnic quotas, with every party council required to hold at least 20 per cent ethnic minority representation (Touquet 2012b, 214). Representation of all three ethnic groups and 'others' within the party stands central to the party's identity. This culture goes back to the socialist era (arguably even beyond) and the legacy of the 'national key' then used to fill positions within state institutions and the Communist Party. Pearson outlines how from the 1960s interethnic relations between Serbs, Muslims, and Croats became more important for the party as it established the goal of reaching proportional representation in party membership, elected bodies and in the administration – though this was not applied in a systematic way. Meanwhile the 'social key' – equal representation of groups such as workers, women, youth, and intellectuals – also mattered within the party, arguably just as much as the 'national key' (Pearson 2015, 216–17, 226).

DF, presents similarly to its predecessor, the SDP, in many ways, advocating a multi-ethnic Bosnia and taking up positions in the quota system for all three groups – most notably via its leader's occupancy of the position of Croat member of the presidency. DF members also celebrate the legacy of Yugoslavia, with leader Komšić notably hanging a portrait of Tito in his presidential office (Klix 2018). Interviews and party statements also demonstrate a somewhat more *integrationist* discourse, however. Representatives place more emphasis on human rights and the representation of 'others' and appear more forthright in their goal of achieving an integrated 'normal country', articulated as a 'civil Bosnia'.[8] Indeed, in 2023 three DF representatives from the FBiH House of Peoples (upper house), submitted an application to the European Court of Human Rights (ECHR) complaining that, as designated Others in the house, they are not permitted to run for the position of vice president of FBiH (Sarajevo Times 2023). This newest of the main civic parties is generally more difficult to place on any ideological spectrum, however, as noted. The party presents as based more on the personality of its leader, Komšić (referenced in the majority of interviews with DF members), who is depicted as something of a 'brand' symbolizing civic Bosnia, and on a broad, populist platform.

While SDP adopts a more accommodationist position and DF a more integrationist stance, Naša Stranka's stance aligns more closely with the *intersectional* model of a civic party. While acknowledging the multi-ethnic character of the party, in contrast to SDP which emphasized this trait as central, Naša Stranka representatives generally treated it as a given and not what the party stands for, nor what attracted them to it. Moreover, they depicted Naša Stranka, in line with its founding principles, as a modern, civic party based on the values of individual liberalism and equality. The model on which the party was based, according to some interviewees, was one of a 'normal' issue-based European party, such as the Greens in Germany.[9] Creating this new form of politics based on democratic accountability, civic engagement, and efficiency – in contrast to that practiced by all other parties in BiH – was uppermost in the reasons offered by interviewees for why they first became involved with the party. The multi-ethnic aspect of the party appeared secondary in their minds and, rather, a natural consequence of its civic ideology.[10] One senior leadership figure articulates: '[Multi-ethnicity] was a pre-given … it was a requirement that was self-understood due to the fact that we wanted to form a citizen-oriented movement; a movement of secular citizens who are aware that their individual rights are not being protected on the same level as the rights that they have protected as collectives.'[11]

Naša Stranka contrasts with SDP, not only in the importance to which it accords non-ethnic or multi-ethnic identity but in how it measures the concept. Rather than representation of the different ethnic groups within the party (the core criterion for SDP) Naša Stranka representatives rather stressed the *civic ethos* of its members. For a number of interviewees, it was not the ethnic designation of its representatives, its members, nor its territorial presence which made it a civic party but the values of its people and underpinning its policies.[12] The distinction could be characterized as substantive representation over descriptive representation.

In line with Naša Stranka's post-ethnic intersectional stance, and in contrast to the SDP's accommodationist strategy, the party does not operate a policy of internal ethnic quotas. As senior members of the party explained, when it comes to ethnic balance for positions within the party and on electoral lists, the party has moved since its foundation from a formal approach to a more 'relaxed' method whereby such standards are 'implied' rather than enforced.[13] Equal representation is an issue of which the party consistently 'takes care' and 'pays attention' and therefore does not require rules to uphold.[14]

In characterizing its strategy in responding to ethnonational party competition, Naša Stranka members stressed its focus on *positive campaigning* on the one hand and *avoidance* on the other. One senior official explained the party's strategy of 'ignoring' the issue of ethnicity in an attempt to move beyond it and focus on policies:

> I honestly don't know [the best way to move away from the focus on identity issues in Bosnian politics] because we ignore it. In some ways – this is perhaps not a good way to go – but we don't deal with issues of ethnicity.
>
> The moment you start discussing we're afraid [other parties] draw us into the war stories. They are very good at forcing you to do negative campaigning. We really, really try to avoid it. So, I honestly don't know. I think most people understand, looking at our party members, how we've dealt with certain issues, that we are multi-ethnic, and we just don't want to talk about it anymore.[15]

This underlines the careful navigation of issues relating to identity required by civic parties amidst the dominant discourse of ethnonationalism.

Engaging in the Power-Sharing System

How do parties founded on a civic agenda participate in a system so predicated on ethnic representation? Despite their ideological opposition to the system, all three parties participated fully in that system, taking up positions reserved for one of the ethnic groups and even taking part in governing coalitions with ethnic parties.

Ethnic Quotas

The SDP, in line with its 'multi-ethnic' principles, participates fully in the consociational ethnic quota regime, taking up positions reserved for Bosniaks, Croats, and Serbs at all levels of government. Elected SDP representatives accept ethnic quotas as the normal way of doing business and appear to have no issue with their party's participation in the system.[16] Indeed, some representatives interviewed owed their positions to such conventions, including one who held the role of deputy speaker of the House of Representatives of FBiH as a designated Serb delegate.[17] This strategy is facilitated by a policy of internal ethnic quotas, as the party effectively replicates the power-sharing structures within its own organization. Moreover, some depicted the party's ability to fill positions reserved for all three constituent peoples as a *measure* of its multi-ethnicity,[18] something of which they were 'proud',[19] and even a means to 'prove' its multi-ethnic credentials. DF representatives similarly voiced no reservations about engaging fully in the system and, if anything, used it even more explicitly to showcase its vision for a multi-ethnic, 'civil Bosnia' while maintaining a critical stance towards its exclusion of 'others'.[20]

Yet, beyond symbolism, participating in the ethnic quota system undoubtedly affords civic parties access to positions – and hence *power* – without which they would find themselves marginalized. In this way, the rules can be utilized creatively to civic parties' advantage. While ethnonational parties such as SDA and SNSD can and do manage to fill positions for other 'constituent peoples' beyond their core ethnic group, civic parties like SDP, supported by its policy of internal quotas, are particularly well positioned to assume positions reserved for all three groups.[21] This capacity proves particularly useful to these parties in areas where these groups form the minority, leaving them well placed, for example, to fill Serb positions in FBiH and Bosniak positions in the RS. Indeed, the parties have, on occasion, arguably navigated quota rules in this way to advance their multi-ethnic accommodationist agendas. A notable case in point was the abovementioned election to the position of Croat member of the state presidency (directly elected in FBiH) of Željko Komšić in 2006 and 2010 as an SDP representative and in 2018 and 2022 under the DF banner (see case study 7.1 below).

Naša Stranka's approach to Bosnia's power-sharing system demonstrates nuanced differences to that of SDP and DF. Members generally expressed ideological opposition to ethnic quotas, on the grounds of its discrimination against 'others' who do not identify as Serb, Croat, or Bosniak and its inefficiency and duplication of resources.[22] Some advocated a more limited system of ethnic quotas whereby minimum representation of each group were guaranteed.[23] On a practical level, however, representatives did not generally claim that ethnic quotas specifically disadvantaged the party. Indeed, some demonstrated how it had creatively used such quota rules to its own advantage. In 2010, for example, Naša Stranka gained a Serb seat in the upper House of Peoples of FBiH (elected by cantonal assemblies), after one of its then members of the canton of Sarajevo, Predrag Kojović, designated as Serb. Having identified as Yugoslav before the war and 'Bosnian and Herzegovinian' thereafter, Kojović describes the rationale behind his decision to designate as Serb and the 'strange' experience of doing so:

> I became a Serb only for elections in 2010 because when you apply to the Central Electoral Committee you have to determine the ethnic backgrounds of your candidates and since I come from a mixed marriage we decided that I'm going to be Serb because our chances of getting into the House of Peoples in the Federation [FBiH] would be best if we go that way. So it's completely opportunistic.
>
> And then when it came it was a strange thing, psychologically, to accept this party decision. It's not really easy being a Serb after the war here. If you could choose you'd probably choose something else – like, who wants to be a German right after the Second World War, living in Poland or France? But I thought, OK, maybe it's a challenge, maybe it's actually good to show that not all Serbs think like [Bosnian Serb war criminal, Radovan] Karadžić.[24]

While opposing the principle of ethnic quotas therefore, Naša Stranka retains the ability to pragmatically use the system to its own benefit. This chimes with Piacentini's observation that 'others' (voters and political representatives) in the corporate consociational systems of Bosnia and South Tyrol make the choice to 'opportunistically align' in order to participate fully in the institutions and reap the benefits of so doing (2021). SDP, DF, and Naša Stranka have thus adapted to the corporate consociational system by participating in the system, a strategy from which they have gained significant advantages.

However, this strategy also proves problematic for civic parties. The principle of ethnonational representation, embedded in the Dayton system and embodied most clearly in the quota regime, also creates a significant 'legitimacy problem' for civic actors. The institutionalization of a regime whereby certain positions are reserved for representatives of one ethnic group fosters a mindset and culture in which only individuals (and parties) of a certain ethnic group can adequately represent citizens of that group. Taken to its conclusion, this thinking deems ethnic representatives legitimate and authentic and their non-ethnic counterparts illegitimate and suspect – feeding into the strategic discourses outlined in chapter 6. The tensions are best captured by the elections to the state presidency, as the case study below unpacks.

Case Study 7.1: Civic Parties and the Presidency

The political career of Željko Komšić tells an illustrative tale about the struggle of civic politics in Bosnia's deeply ethnicized system. The reaction to his election as Croat member of the state presidency for SDP in 2006 and 2010 and for DF in 2018 and 2022 paints a clear picture of the legitimacy problem facing civic parties. Komšić is celebrated by many in the country as something of a symbol of 'multi-ethnic Bosnia'. A Bosnian Croat of mixed parentage (a Croat father and Serb mother) whose mother was killed during the war by a sniper from the Serb forces in Sarajevo, Komšić fought in the war for the Bosnian Army, rather than the Croatian HVO (Belloni 2007, 167), for which he earned the Order of the Golden Lily, the highest state order awarded for military service at the time. His election as Croat member of the presidency, first for SDP and later for DF, however, has stoked intense controversy. Elected under the system by voters in the Bosniak–Croat FBiH, he initially gained this seat for SDP, in part due to a split in the traditional vote for Croat ethnic parties between HDZ and HDZ-1990. Opponents, primarily from within these parties, questioned the legitimacy of his election as Croat member of the presidency on the basis that it was secured mainly by Bosniak votes in FBiH rather than those of Croats, as he failed to win a majority in any of the three Croat-majority cantons (Belloni 2007, 167; Basta 2016, 964). In this way, Komšić has been depicted as not being a true Croat representative and his election as a manipulation of the rules by these civic parties, in order to effectively gain two Bosniak representatives in the presidency.

'Especially after this second Komšić term, it's very clear – no one denies it – that he's elected by Bosniak votes ... He said that he's representative of all peoples, of all citizens ... He came to Mostar, to his party conventions and stuff like that, but he never came to Široki Brijeg or to where Croats are 100 per cent of the population,' said one member of the Croat party HDZ in the party's stronghold city of Mostar, exemplifying the 'illegitimacy' discourse.[25] He further cites Komšić's appointment of an official to a diplomatic post reserved for a Croat, who he alleges was in fact Bosniak and tactically declared as Croat.[26] In this sense Belloni argues that consociation condemns cross-ethnic voting and undermines the legitimacy of leaders who are not elected solely by and for one ethnic group (2007, 167).

Indeed, this legitimacy issue was evidenced in the focus groups conducted with voters in Bosnia. In two of these groups doubt was cast on the SDP's credibility as a non-ethnic or multi-ethnic party, due to its participation in the ethnic quota system and strategic use of that system to gain power and influence.[27] Participants in one group, conducted in Sarajevo, argued that it would be impossible for a true party of citizens to operate within this system.[28] Meanwhile, in a group conducted with university students in RS capital Banja Luka, highly suspicious attitudes were expressed towards both the SDP and Naša Stranka, as noted in chapter 6.[29] One participant referred in a derogatory manner to 'professional Serbs' who join the SDP as they can be effectively guaranteed a position through the quota system. Another shared the 'joke' that 'The only Croatian part of Željko Komšić's body is a bullet' – a reference to his membership of the Bosnian Army during the war, rather than the Croatian HVO.[30]

The legitimacy problem arises across the system for civic parties. A similar controversy erupted when the formation of the Council of Ministers was blocked following the 2010 elections when Croat party HDZ objected to the appointment of SDP representatives to Croat positions in government, challenging their credibility as authentic representatives of the Croat community.[31] One SDP member of the House of Representatives, herself an ethnic Croat, thus speaks to this contested legitimacy with which the party must contend:

> We basically ruined their [the ethnic parties'] system; we were destabilizing their system in which the Croat should be from the Croat party, the Bosniak from the nationalist Bosniak party, etc.
>
> For these parties we are not equivalent Croats because we are not from the Croat majority population areas. And then

we are not adequate Serbs because we are not from Republika Srpska. And we are not enough of Bosniaks because we do not go to the mosque.[32]

One SDP member of the House of Representation in FBiH cites the example of occasional instances where SDP representatives trigger the 'Vital National Interest' veto, for any constituent people but particularly Serb and Croat. Such interventions tend to be treated as illegitimate by their ethnic party colleagues, she explained, 'as if, "Who are you to raise this concern?"'[33] Yet, she describes how SDP members that assume Bosniak positions in government are likewise depicted as illegitimate representatives of the Bosniak community: 'It goes so far that when the SDP is required to take seats [anywhere], the Bosniak members are not perceived as the real Bosniaks.'[34]

This illegitimacy discourse presents strategic dilemmas for civic parties to which there are no obvious answers. One SDP representative criticized his own party's ethnic quota policy as ideologically problematic for a multi-ethnic party that seeks to move beyond such divisions, arguing that it should use every opportunity to highlight its opposition to these rules.[35]

The Komšić controversy, following his election in 2006 and 2010 for SDP also gave his then newly formed party, DF, strategic considerations in the 2014 general elections. The party faced something of a dilemma in whether to stand a Bosniak or Croat candidate for the three-member state presidency, according to a party strategist. If it solely ran a Croat candidate it could potentially be seen as a more multi-ethnic party, but, in doing so, it could also expose itself to attack from HDZ as undermining the representation of the Croat community. This, in turn could turn Croat voters against DF and thus make it less multi-ethnic in terms of its support.[36] In the event, the party stood candidates in both the Croat and Bosniak contest, neither of whom was elected.[37]

Civic parties therefore have a somewhat contradictory relationship with the ethnic representation measures in Bosnia's consociational system. While appearing to conflict with their principles, the parties utilize the system – even sometimes embracing it and attempting to use it to demonstrate their multi-ethnic credentials – and, in many ways, gain advantage from doing so. These rules prove something of a double-edged sword for civic parties: affording them access to power and positions and allowing them to vaunt their multi-ethnic nature, while at the same time calling those very credentials into question, opening them up to attack by ethnic parties, and raising a legitimacy issue with voters. Thus, the ethnic quota system presents civic parties in Bosnia with two options: participate by playing the system and experiencing ethnonational contestation or remain outside – hardly much of a choice for a party seeking to win elections and enact policies.

Governing Coalitions

Far from being completely marginalized, however, civic parties have at times found themselves at the centre of power in Bosnia – in governing coalitions at the state and entity level. Under the rules, civic parties are not excluded: they have the option of taking part in the Council of Ministers (state cabinet) as members of the three constituent peoples or as the one Other member. They have taken up these opportunities at various points, most notably from 2001–02 when SDP led the moderate coalition Alliance for Change (Bieber 2007, 86) and in the 2010–14 mandate when SDP played leading roles in governing coalitions at the state level and FBiH level, alongside ethnic parties. More recently, in the 2018–22 mandate, DF took part in the state-level coalition and following the 2022 election SDP and Naša Stranka joined the state cabinet (the latter taking up the position of Other).

Participating in coalitions can prove particularly tricky for civic parties, however. In chapter 6 we noted the disadvantage civic parties face within the 'grand coalition' style executive given the lack of civic partners. Forming and sustaining alliances with ethnic parties is an obvious challenge. When civic parties do manage to form a governing coalition, while affording them access to power and resources, taking part has not necessarily proven advantageous in the longer term. Working with ethnonational parties carries a risk for civic parties, threatening to taint their civic image and lead them to compromise their civic principles. The SDP's experience after emerging as the largest party in FBiH in the 2010 general election and subsequently at the helm of the governing coalition at state and FBiH level from 2010–14, is illustrative. This tenure was marked by instability, immobilism, and lack of cooperation between the governing parties. Its reign was notable for the severe delays, in government formation after the SDP failed in its attempt to form governments without the main Bosniak, Croat, and Serb parties and for disputes between the SDP and its coalition partners HDZ BiH, SNSD and – most notably – SDA, resulting in mid-term changes to the composition of government. During this term, the party pushed for a stronger focus on Bosniak interests. The term also witnessed ideological compromise on the part of the SDP, not least for its 'deal' with Serb and Croat nationalist parties, exposed in 2012, on reforms that would have seen the state weakened in favour of the entities, as well as agreeing, together with SNSD, to unpopular reforms in the media and justice sector (Hulsey and Keil 2019, 412; Freedom House 2013; Keil and Perry 2015, 85). The SDP then stood accused of seeking to retain power at the price of compromising its multi-ethnic principles (Stuebner 2012). A number of SDP representatives expressed regret and resentment at the legacy of their 2010–14 coalition experience and the damage it did to the party's image.[38] SDP suffered heavy losses in the 2002 and 2014 elections which directly followed its stints leading government (Bieber 2006, 102; Hulsey and Keil 2019, 412). The experience of DF following the 2014 general election, in which it emerged as the second largest party in FBiH, is also telling. The then fledgling party entered coalition at FBiH level with Bosniak nationalist party SDA and Croat nationalists HDZ BiH, yet the pact dissolved within months with the DF citing irreconcilable differences with the nationalist parties (Freedom House 2016). After this messy foray into government that lasted less than one hundred days, the party also took a hit in the 2018 election (Hulsey and Keil 2019, 412).

How can this negative impact be explained? On the one hand, while in coalition with ethnonational parties, civic parties find it particularly difficult to deliver on their campaign pledges and pursue their civic policies, as demonstrated in the frustration felt towards DF in 2018 (Hulsey and Keil 2019, 412). What's more, they can find themselves and their civic agendas tainted and compromised by the requirement to work with ethnic parties. This effect was clearly witnessed in the case of the SDP's 2010–14 tenure. The tumultuous term in office left the SDP widely accused of jeopardizing its ideals and engaging in corrupt and nepotistic practices on a par with its nationalist rivals. The party was punished harshly at the ballot box, losing nearly 70 per cent of its vote at central level in 2014 (Hulsey and Keil 2020, 347). All of this leads Hulsey and Keil to deduce, 'For civic parties, participation in government appears to be associated with electoral decline, owing to the mismatch between their party programmes and the practice of party patronage of parties in power' (2020,

355). The scholars surmise that civic parties have been unable to instigate major reforms, despite the fact that some (SDP and DF) have been part of several governing coalitions at entity and central state level. They blame the Bosnian power-sharing system in which non-nationalist parties can electorally compete and challenge ethnonational parties but 'they are unable to use their electoral support in order to push for substantial changes to the system, even when they are major players in the governing coalition.' (Hulsey and Keil 2019, 414). The difficulty for civic parties to achieve change from within government – and worse still their tendency to renege on their civic principles to do business with ethnonational partners – can lead to disillusion among voters, arguably fuelling the endemic distrust and apathy discussed in the last chapter. After voting for the civic alternative in the hope of change, voters are left disheartened, wondering if civic parties can make any difference, or, indeed, if there is any alternative to ethnonational politics.

Electoral Strategy

Amidst the relative closure of the three main party subsystems in BiH, Kapidžić and Komar find that the only partially open cleavage is between the Bosniak and 'nonethnic' blocs (2022, 549). Indeed, the dispute over civic parties' attempts to represent Croats in the presidency outlined above, contrasts with the general acceptance of these parties representing Bosniak interests, they argue: 'As they are not in direct competition for Serb or Croat votes, non-ethnic parties in BiH are accepted as having an electorate that overlaps with the Bosniak party subsystem, thus contributing to the stability of the segmented party system' (Kapidžić and Komar 2022, 549–50). This overlap presents something of a dilemma to civic parties when it comes to elections. Civic parties acknowledge that the concentration of their electoral support in Bosniak-majority areas creates an 'image problem'. SDP representatives generally characterized the issue as incidental, owing to ethnic cleansing and subsequent creation of homogenous political units,[39] some voicing a long-term constitutional goal of abolishing Bosnia's entities[40] and cantons.[41] Members invariably attested to the party's efforts to appeal to all three ethnic groups and to be a party of all of Bosnia and Herzegovina. Many expressed pride in the fact that the SDP persists in its attempts to maintain a presence across the state and to break into Serb and Croat dominated areas, despite limited electoral rewards.[42] The SDP's electoral strategy appears to include appealing to ethnic minorities and positioning itself as the 'party of minorities' in Bosnia.[43] Its 'multi-ethnic' accommodationist stance leaves it particularly well placed to attract votes from Bosniaks living in the RS and Croats and Serbs living in Bosniak-majority areas of FBiH. Indeed, one representative of an RS-based international democratization NGO, which works directly with parties in BiH, reported that the SDP was making little genuine effort to win votes beyond the Bosniak minority community in the Serb entity.[44]

Members of Naša Stranka interviewed likewise acknowledged the locus of the party's support to be in FBiH and its representation at that time exclusively within the Bosniak-majority city of Sarajevo.[45] Nevertheless, this was depicted as a practical issue concerning party finance and resources.[46] Naša Stranka opted not to stand candidates in the RS in the 2014 general elections and senior members confirmed that the Serb entity was not an electoral priority for the party at that time.[47] The then party general secretary reported a shift in party strategy since 2012, from attempting to mobilize and build support across BiH, to focusing on its areas of strength (the cities of Sarajevo, Tuzla, and Zenica in the 2014 elections) and consolidating its support in those centres. The official described this strategy in pragmatic terms as 'a practical thing, not a thing of ideas'. He recounted unapologetically how he had closed down at least twenty local party branches since 2012 (about half of which were in the RS), noting that in the 2012 municipal elections the party campaigned in twenty-three municipalities compared to fifty in the 2008 municipal polls, yet returned an almost identical number of local councillors. He and other members interpret the party's absence in RS at that time as a purely logistical issue and its Sarajevo-focus as natural for a relatively young party that originated in the capital.[48]

In outlining how Naša Stranka deals with the challenge of expansion in this ethnonational political framework, some resignation could also be detected. Breaking into certain areas and groups of voters in Bosnia was portrayed as beyond feasible for the civic party in the current climate. To do so, in some cases, would require the party to compromise its civic principles.[49] Similarly, on the issue of expanding its voter base, one senior representative suggested limits to how far Naša Stranka could advance. He relayed a story of when, soon after its founding in 2008, the party supported the first gay pride parade in BiH, in spite of warnings from actors, including the US embassy, that to do so would be politically damaging for the new party.

> We got warnings from everybody. And I thought, 'I'm going to compromise with gay people in Bosnia now, the next time it's not going to be popular to defend Bosniak people in Banja Luka?
>
> When we put the statement around at noon, our headquarters was full of people coming and burning their membership cards, tearing them up. We lost 30 per cent of our membership in a single day … And I said, I'm glad we did this because if we didn't do this these people who should not be in Naša Stranka would still be in Naša Stranka and then they would leave you at some other point down the road.[50]

When asked about the party's intentions to advance beyond its current urban base and break into rural areas, representatives expressed little ambition.[51] One senior official explained that the dominance of ethnic parties and their negative campaign tactics in these areas made it very difficult for Naša Stranka to gain any ground. Secondly, he believed attitudes in these areas were too conservative for the party to hope to win votes there.[52] This underlines Naša Stranka's move to occupy the narrow civic, liberal niche in Bosnian politics and own this terrain. Furthermore, it aligns with the party's electoral strategy of establishing a local presence in key cities – most notably Sarajevo – and building up from this base.

Civic parties' electoral strategies appear largely based on consolidation in Bosniak-majority areas of FBiH, with SDP making efforts to achieve greater spread and inroads to RS. This aligns with that party's multiethnic accommodationist ethos and also speaks to its legacy as the oldest civic party and successor of the Communist Party with the infrastructure that that affords.

Conclusion

Despite the inhospitable environment of post-Dayton Bosnia, civic parties have maintained a consistent space since the war. They have salvaged this space effectively by adapting to their environment. They have positioned themselves in various ways that allow them to participate in the system while offering a civic alternative to the ethnonational status quo, whether accommodationist, integrationist, or intersectional. They have engaged fully in the power-sharing institutions, including taking up positions for all three ethnic groups (and others) and participating in governing coalitions, alongside ethnic parties. They have adapted to the decentralized system by concentrating their electoral focus in Bosniak-majority areas of FBiH with limited presence in the Serb-majority RS. Yet, the space they have carved out in this way is deeply contested. Civic parties face continual challenge to their legitimacy, challenge that is often exacerbated by their strategies in navigating an ethnic system. Their participation in the quota system as ethnic representatives has left them subject to intense backlash from ethnonational actors. Their partnership with ethnonational parties in governing coalitions has, at times, seen their civic agenda diluted and compromised and frustrated their ability to make meaningful change, leaving voters disillusioned with civic politics and leaving civic parties, in turn, harshly punished at the polls. The 'success' of civic parties in the Bosnian system, then, is less solid than it first appears. It seems that surviving this system for civic parties in reality relies on capturing support from civic-minded Bosniaks, as well as the small population (some 4 per cent according to the 2013 census)[53] who do not identify with any of the ethnic groups, and tend to live in urban centres, rather than winning widespread cross-ethnic support. Forced to play an ethnonational game, they gain representation and, at times, positions of power but struggle to advance a civic agenda and achieve any moves towards changing the institutions that ultimately hold civic politics back.

Chapter Eight

Civic Parties in Northern Ireland, Bosnia, and Beyond

Contemporary Northern Ireland and Bosnia and Herzegovina might bear little resemblance at first glance. Yet, speak to the representatives of political parties and movements that mobilize across the divide in both places about their experiences and the echoes are striking: institutions devised on ethnonational lines that contradict their principles, frustrate their agenda, and thwart their form of politics; a political culture that continuously challenges their legitimacy and ability to pursue politics on their own terms. Nevertheless, creative ways to advance are found. Their stories reveal certain critical differences too, of both scale and substance. What do these parallels and differences tell us about civic parties in divided societies and their relationship to power-sharing institutions? And do they bear any resonance with civic parties in other divided societies?

This chapter draws together the experiences of civic parties in Northern Ireland and Bosnia, placing them in dialogue with other deeply divided and power-sharing cases. In so doing, it speaks to the systemic barriers in civic parties' structural environments: formally in the institutions and informally in the broader institutional culture. Zooming out, the chapter compares how civic parties in different divided places have dealt with these barriers and examines how their institutional structures inform their strategies.

Structural Barriers

Formal Institutions

In both Northern Ireland and Bosnia, civic parties find themselves 'othered' in a system based – to varying degrees – on ethnic rules. In both places, to guarantee proportional representation and protections for the main ethnic groups, political representatives are distinguished by their membership – or *not* – of those groups, and power and privilege is allotted (unequally) on that basis. In Northern Ireland, members entering the power-sharing legislature must designate as Nationalist, Unionist, or Other. That designation is used to ensure protection of unionist and nationalist interests – effectively granting them a veto on certain issues in the Assembly (and Executive) – with no such guarantees for 'others'. The rule also plays a role in guaranteeing representation of the groups, specifically for the co-premier positions. The positions of first and deputy first minister are theoretically open to Others but, in practice, with a high bar: even if an Other party becomes the second largest in the Assembly it would not be entitled to the deputy first minister post unless Others made up the second largest designation. In Bosnia, meanwhile, electoral candidates must declare their identity as Bosniak, Serb, Croat in order to access certain protections and positions reserved for these three 'constituent peoples'. They may also opt to declare as Other, but, in most cases, that would render them ineligible for the positions and protections in question. The three ethnic groups are granted vetoes at various levels in the multi-level governance system. Notably, in an elaborate system of 'ethnic quotas', they also have seats reserved for them, including in the tripartite state presidency and the state-level upper house – access to which is denied to Others. This situation has seen the state of Bosnia fall foul of the European Convention on Human Rights in five rulings and come under intense international pressure to reform the constitution, but, as yet, to no avail. In both Northern Ireland and Bosnia, the broad-based 'grand coalition' style of executive has also presented challenges for civic parties to participate and advance their policies, amidst a lack of civic partners and in a fractious, ethnicized climate.

Civic representatives in Northern Ireland and Bosnia share many similar experiences when it comes to their respective power-sharing institutions. They speak of feeling marginalized and disempowered by ethnic veto rules that exclude them. They describe struggling to advance their agenda in an ethnically divided government. Yet, critical differences also arise, relating to their distinct institutional environments. Patently, Bosnia's ethnic representation rules are more rigid and extensive. While both systems feature rules that distinguish and privilege ethnic actors, Northern Ireland's system at least allows civic parties to participate in the legislature and executive as Others, albeit on an unequal basis to their ethnonational partners. Bosnia on the other hand, while reserving seats for Others at entity level and allowing for one Other to be represented in the state-level executive, expressly denies them key reserved positions at state level. What's more, Bosnia's system features an ethno-territorial dimension that is absent in Northern Ireland. The internal decentralization of the Bosnian state into largely ethnically homogenous electoral units – most notably its two sub-state entities, one of which is further subdivided into ten cantons – presents a steep barrier to parties trying to operate across the state and across ethnonational lines, with which those in Northern Ireland do not have to contend. Finally, another key difference is the central role of external actors in Bosnia's system, most prominently in the shape of the Office of High Representative. While the US has played an important part in the Northern Ireland peace process, its role has been one primarily of facilitation and mediation, not active player in the governance system with executive and legislative powers as is wielded by the High Representative in Bosnia. If anything, the most comparable actors in Northern Ireland are the UK and Irish governments (particularly the former), as overseers or 'guarantors' of the GFA, albeit as 'kin states' to the conflict and, in the case of the UK, the sovereign state, so not an 'external actor' as such.

Informal Institutions

In both Northern Ireland and Bosnia, however, it is those rules 'hidden and embedded in the everyday practices' (Chappell 2014, 576) that appear most obstructive to civic solidarity. When it comes to discourse, the echoes are particularly strong. Civic parties in both places describe operating within a dominant discourse of ethnonationalism that directly contradicts their own and leaves their politics sidelined, devalued, and even invalidated. In a political debate where ethnonational conflict and fear of the 'other' retain currency, they find themselves and their messages drowned out and *marginalized*. What's more, with all politics filtered through a single (ethnonational) lens, their multiple lens (intersectional) approach is routinely misunderstood, resisted, misrepresented, and ultimately *contested*. Indeed, civic representatives relate strikingly similar discursive strategies used by ethnonational parties to contest civic politics: depicting it as variously weak, irrelevant, illegitimate, suspect, and even traitorous. This contestation was particularly obvious in the 2012–13 flag protest in Northern Ireland when Alliance was portrayed by its unionist rivals on different occasions as weak defenders of the Union, having suspect motivations, and, indeed, as traitors to unionists. In Bosnia such contestation has been keenly felt by civic parties who have taken up positions reserved for ethnic candidates. The illegitimate and traitor discourses have featured prominently in Croat parties' responses to Željko Komšić's election as Croat member of the presidency for the civic parties SDP in 2006 and 2010 and DF in 2018 and 2022.

Another informal institution that has presented a barrier in both cases is ethnonational clientelism. In Northern Ireland and Bosnia, as in other divided societies that are dominated by ethnonational parties, informal systems of clientelism and patronage have an ethnonational flavour, and work to entrench the power of ethnonational parties, placing civic parties at a competitive disadvantage. Furthermore, the relationship between civil society and the formal political sphere in both places is fraught in a way that presents challenges for civic parties. The post-conflict societies both feature high levels of apathy, distrust, and disillusion with politics. As such, a gap exists between civic politics at the grassroots level (in the shape of community associations, social movements and NGOs) and that at the institutional level (in the shape of civic parties). This disjuncture was particularly obvious during the movement for marriage equality in Northern Ireland in the years leading up to 2019 and in the 2014 Bosnian protests.

Of course, each of these informal institutions is inextricable from the formal structures. Ethnonational discourses that marginalize and contest civic parties are reinforced by power-sharing rules that legitimize ethnic representation. Ethnonational clientelism is facilitated by power-sharing mechanisms that grant ethnonational parties considerable autonomy over resources, territory, and policy for 'their' community. The civil–political disconnect is also exacerbated by a system that is heavily elite-centric and resistant to pressures from below.

Notwithstanding these parallels, however, we also see critical differences in the informal institutional obstacles that civic parties face in Northern Ireland and Bosnia. These differences speak to the distinct political cultures, economies, and historical legacies (particularly conflict legacies) of each place. Firstly, when it comes to discourse, the contestation civic parties face in the dominant discourse of Bosnian politics is of a different order to that experienced by civic parties in Northern Irish politics. While parties in Northern Ireland also encounter suspicion and challenge from ethnonational parties, there is a general level of acceptance of the legitimacy of the civic position. The same cannot be said for Bosnia. There, the very *existence* of civic parties is questioned by ethnonational parties, in a way that resonates with sections of the public, as illustrated by the focus groups in this research. This contestation can be traced to the conflation in Bosnian politics between the civic position and the majoritarian Bosniak position, discussed in chapters 6 and 7. It is underscored by the disproportionate representation of Bosniaks in civic parties (in terms of leadership, political representation and membership) and the relatively limited presence of these parties in majority Serb and Croat areas. Again, this also relates to the formal structures of post-Dayton politics, where mobilizing as a state-wide cross-ethnic party comes at a high cost. In working to have their voices heard, civic parties in Bosnia also come up against a more intense climate of fear and insecurity, which undoubtedly relates to the scale and severity of the 1992–95 war and the levels of trauma in society some thirty years on from that devastation. Furthermore, while civic parties in both cases experience marginalization and contestation in the dominant discourse, those in Northern Ireland have also faced the threat of cooptation in recent years, on issues such as LGBTQ+ rights. This threat is less pronounced in Bosnia, a difference that, somewhat ironically, points to further progress of these agendas in Northern Ireland and greater moderation of some of its ethnonational parties and the broader discourse.

Secondly, the challenge posed by ethnonational clientelism for civic parties in Bosnia is on a different scale that posed in Northern Ireland. While the problem certainly exists in the latter, it is by no means as pervasive as it is in Bosnia. This relates to major differences in the economic conditions of each state, with voters in Bosnia more vulnerable to resorting to patronage as a means of survival and to intimidation due to their greater economic insecurity (Piacentini 2021, 452). The difference also points to Bosnia's weaker state, democratic consolidation, and rule of law, holding its first multi-party elections only in 1990. And again, distinct conflict legacies arise, with Bosnia's clientelistic networks becoming particularly embedded during the war when the main parties acted as 'para states', able to seize control of state assets in their areas, such as utilities and transport networks (Cox 2003, 268; Grandits 2007, 110–11; Manning 2004, 68). But current institutions arguably also play a role: the heavily decentralized power-sharing system affords parties more autonomy than in Northern Ireland and thus leeway to operate clientelistic networks.

Third, the level of political apathy, disillusion, and disconnect evident in Northern Ireland is not as pronounced as that in Bosnia and the gap between civil society and formal politics not as wide. Formal politics is

Northern Ireland is certainly approached by civic grassroots actors with caution, as witnessed by gender and LGBTQ+ activists.[1] However, it is not considered to be as treacherous or dangerous as those in Bosnia perceive politics there, as witnessed in the 2014 protests (Milan 2020; Murtagh 2016). This difference speaks to a more ethnicized, polarized, and potentially violent political space for civic politics in Bosnia. Overall, a comparison of the informal barriers demonstrates a more clear and stable civic space that civic parties can inhabit in Northern Ireland with a more unstable, contested, and risky space available to them in Bosnia.

Navigating Barriers, Finding Openings

So, how do civic parties in Northern Ireland and Bosnia traverse these complex landscapes? The analysis in chapters 5 and 7 demonstrates innovative agency on their parts but also adaptation to their institutional structures to avail of opportunities that arise.

Positioning on the Divide

When it comes to the fundamental question of how they orient themselves with respect to the ethnonational divide, civic parties in both places show evolution over time. In Northern Ireland, the oldest and largest civic party Alliance began its life at the height of the Troubles as a largely accommodationist party, positioning itself as something of a bridge between nationalism and unionism. As time moved on, particularly following the GFA, the integrationist positioning became more prominent within the party and many members actively rejected the mediator image. By the early 2020s, while still championing integration, the party also appears increasingly intersectional – more open and at ease with a diversity of ethnonational and religious identities and constitutional positions within the party. Meanwhile, other civic parties that have broken through post-GFA – the Greens and PBP – adopt a distinctly more intersectional approach, presenting themselves as 'normal' issue-based parties and, in some ways, seeking to distance themselves from the entire post-conflict accommodation/integration framework. In this way, parties in Northern Ireland demonstrate adaptation in line with the movement of society from conflict towards peace and ultimately a more 'normal' future that is less preoccupied with issues of peace and reconciliation and more concerned with material security and broader equality and human rights. Some tensions are still apparent in this shift, however, particularly for Alliance, which is periodically called upon to play the role of intermediary during crises and, indeed, in the power-sharing system.

Civic parties in Bosnia also show adaptation over time, certainly between parties. The largest and oldest civic party, SDP, positions itself very clearly and proudly as an accommodationist party representing Bosniaks, Serbs, Croats, and Others. It measures its civic credentials in terms of descriptive representation and its ability to take up positions reserved for all three groups in the quota system. Newer parties DF and Naša Stranka, by contrast, adopt more integrationist and intersectional stances. DF demonstrates elements of all three positionings, yet adopts a bolder integrationist position with respect to Bosnia's constitution and appears less concerned with gaining representation across the state, including in the Serb-majority RS, than its predecessor, SDP. Naša Stranka, meanwhile, presents a more intersectional stance, acknowledging the ethnic diversity of its representatives and members but at the same time seeking to move beyond ethnicity. The party also takes up seats reserved for the three ethnic groups but does so in a more overtly and self-consciously strategic way than SDP.

In both Northern Ireland and Bosnia, then, we see a mix of approaches within and between parties at different times but a general shift over time from accommodationist to integrationist to intersectional as society moves further away from conflict.

Engagement with Power-Sharing

Another critical choice for civic parties is whether and how to engage in a power-sharing system, the ethnonational principles of which directly contradict their own. In both cases, civic parties demonstrate pragmatism and adaptation to the system. By Nagle's characterization of the choices available to civic movements in power-sharing systems – 'hegemonic compliance', 'constructive engagement', and 'active resistance' (Nagle 2018) – for the most part, they display the middle approach: constructively engaging with the system while seeking to reform it in a more civic direction. This strategy has provoked varying degrees of tension and challenge for the parties. Civic parties in Northern Ireland have participated fully in the power-sharing Assembly. Indeed, Alliance has even enjoyed inclusion in the Executive, alongside ethnonational parties, taking up ministerial positions awarded to it via the regular d'Hondt rules and, on an ad hoc basis, in the case of the Justice Ministry, owing to its nonaligned civic position. Civic parties in Bosnia have engaged fully in the system, going as far as to take up legislative and executive seats reserved for members of the three ethnic groups, including in the state-level presidency and the upper house of the state legislature, the House of Peoples. Different civic parties frame this strategy in different ways in line with their positionings on the accommodationist/integrationist/intersectional spectrum. The accommodationist SDP fully embraces the quota system as aligning with its multi-ethnic credentials – even evidence thereof – while the more intersectional Naša Stranka generally depicts it in more critical terms, as a strategic move. What's more, civic parties in Bosnia have also taken part in 'grand coalition' style executives at state and entity level, alongside ethnic parties of all three groups.

These strategies of engagement have had consequences for civic parties, both positive and negative. Alliance's participation in the power-sharing Northern Ireland Executive is credited with boosting its profile and, of course, increasing its influence with respect to policy. Yet, at times it has also forced the party back into the accommodationist role of mediator between nationalism and unionism, from which it seeks to move on, and exposed it to attack from both sides when difficult decisions need to be made. In Bosnia, civic parties' engagement with ethnic quota rules has opened them up to severe contestation and attack from their rivals in ethnic parties, as the case of Komšić's presidency so clearly illustrates. These attacks reinforce the narrative of suspicion and illegitimacy of civic politics. What of civic parties' participation in power-sharing executive coalitions together with ethnonational parties in Bosnia? While this strategy has afforded them visibility, power, and access to state resources, it has also come with serious image problems: association with polarized ethnonational politics, as well as civic parties' limited ability to advance their civic agendas or achieve any change to the system when sharing power with ethnonational parties. This has at times generated disillusion with civic politics and left civic parties harshly punished at the next election, as seen for SDP in 2014 and DF in 2018.

To claim that civic parties have been excluded from the power-sharing system in Northern Ireland and Bosnia would clearly be untrue. In both places, they have adapted to the system and creatively navigated its rules to seize positions at the very centre of government. This strategy has brought undoubted benefits in terms of image, power, and influence. Yet, it has also conflicted with party principles at times and left them vulnerable to contestation, potentially feeding into civil society apathy and contesting discourses. In this sense, Piacentini argues that 'the strategic alignment of "others"' even props up the very system they oppose (2021). A clear difference emerges in civic parties' engagement in each place too. In the Northern Ireland system, civic parties are forced into the lesser and problematic role of Other. In Bosnia, civic parties have little outlet in the Other role, at the state level at least: instead, they are forced into the role of ethnic representative – albeit, in a pluralistic way. The type and level of reaction these strategies provoke vary accordingly, with the contestation experienced in Bosnia on a higher level to that in Northern Ireland.

Negotiating Contentious Issues

Issues relating to the constitutional future of the state in a contested territory are potentially toxic for civic parties. Given that both Northern Ireland and Bosnia lie in varying states of constitutional crisis, how have civic parties experienced this issue? Civic parties' positions on constitutional issues have provoked contestation and this danger has prompted a general strategy of careful avoidance of such questions on their part. The constitutional position of the three main civic parties in Bosnia, towards greater integration and a stronger state, has been deeply contested, interpreted by some as part of a majoritarian Bosniak agenda for centralization and abolition of the RS. Achieving a safe and more neutral constitutional position has proven elusive, as Naša Stranka's experience suggests. In Northern Ireland, the question of whether the region should remain a part of the UK or reunify with the rest of Ireland has been similarly fraught for civic parties. Alliance's position post-GFA, even though an attempt at neutrality, was historically perceived as aligned to unionism. Yet, there is evidence that the toxicity of constitutional issues for civic parties in Northern Ireland has been somewhat tempered. Civic parties have actually expanded in the wake of the constitutional crisis reaped by Brexit. In terms of strategy, far from avoidance, Alliance has sought to get out in front and lead on the issue of Brexit, with pragmatic policy, rather than identity. Civic parties' fate in the developing debate about Irish unification remains to be seen. So far, however, their approaches appear to be driven less by avoidance and more by openness to engage than in the past. The similarities and differences in civic parties' navigation of constitutional crises in Bosnia and Northern Ireland speak to a growing space in the latter for civic discourse – for civic messages to be voiced and heard on their own terms.

Occupying the Civic Niche

In Northern Ireland and Bosnia, amidst ethnic polarization, space has been salvaged for civic politics, albeit fluctuating over time. In both cases, civic parties have sought to carve out a civic niche, separate to the ethnopolitical status quo. They have capitalized on an expansion of that space due to various demographic, social, and economic shifts – at domestic and global levels. Indeed, civic parties in both places have benefited from power-sharing crises, in which ethnonational parties are most implicated, and positioned themselves as the civic alternative to such polarization and dysfunction. In Northern Ireland, this civic space has expanded considerably over the last ten years and is increasingly more distinct and resilient. It has even grown to constitute a third bloc alongside unionism and nationalism, beginning to break the long-standing ethnonational binary. In Bosnia a civic alternative space has been consistently maintained, but, given the conflation with Bosniak politics, it is more difficult to distinguish and more contested.

Election Strategy

A civic party's strategy when it comes to contesting elections is important to its civic standing. When the ethnonational divide in society is territorially concentrated, critical choices arise for civic parties. They can adopt a more differentiated approach in different regions or a more uniform approach across the state. They can attempt to consolidate their position in certain geographic (perhaps ethnonationally homogenous) regions or seek to extend to achieve greater spread across regions (and ethnonational groups). In the case of Northern Ireland, civic parties have traditionally been more concentrated in the east, where the Protestant–unionist–loyalist community has been dominant. However, this pattern has shifted over the last fifteen years as Alliance's electoral support has grown and its electoral growth strategy has appeared to shift from one of consolidation towards one of spread, making inroads into the historically majority Catholic and nationalist west. In Bosnia, conversely, civic parties have been heavily concentrated in the Bosniak–Croat Federation of BiH (FBiH) and, therein, in Bosniak-majority areas. While SDP has mobilized in RS, its representation there has been scant and primarily reliant on Bosniak minority votes. This contrast is clearly underlain by structural and institutional differences between Northern Ireland and Bosnia. Ethnonational groups are nowhere near as geographically segregated in Northern Ireland as in Bosnia, a situation that is largely the product of ethnic cleansing in the latter. What's more, unlike Bosnia, Northern Ireland is not internally decentralized along ethnonational lines. The electoral strategies of civic parties in both places are clearly informed by their structural and institutional contexts and the opportunities presented in each.

A Broader View

What does the Northern Ireland–Bosnia comparison tell us about civic parties in divided societies and power-sharing systems that might travel beyond these two places?

Formal Institutions

Evidently, civic parties in both Northern Ireland and Bosnia are disadvantaged by the naming and privileging of ethnonational groups in the system. However, Bosnia's more 'corporate' form of power-sharing where ethnicity is more deeply embedded, puts up far steeper barriers than Northern Ireland's more 'hybrid' model where the groups are named, as per corporate power-sharing but with greater flexibility and openness to 'others', as per liberal power-sharing. Barriers to civic parties in corporate power-sharing institutions are undeniable and evident across different cases. The use of ethnic quotas or reserved seats to ensure proportional representation is an obvious barrier.

Quotas are a feature of 'corporate' consociational systems beyond Bosnia, including in Lebanon, Burundi, Belgium, and South Tyrol. In Lebanon the 1989 Ta'if Agreement created an 'allotment state' in which, by convention executive power has been separated between a troika whereby the president is a Maronite Christian, the prime minister a Sunni Muslim, and the Speaker of parliament a Shiite, while cabinet and legislative seats are allotted on a 50/50 Christian/Muslim basis, a system that is replicated throughout the public sector. This leads Nagle and Fakhoury to observe that 'Lebanon's consociational scaffold permits little encouragement for individuals to look outside of the ethnic communities to which they are institutionally categorized as belonging' (2018, 88–9). In this context, it is hardly surprising that civic parties have been few and far between in Lebanon (Fakhoury 2019). In Burundi, the 2005 constitution which followed the 2000 Arusha Peace and Reconciliation Agreement, had ethnic representation at its core (Vandeginste 2014, 268). Under the constitution, the lower house of the legislature (National Assembly) must be made up of 60 per cent Hutu and 40 per cent Tutsi (including a minimum of 30 per cent women), plus three deputies from the minority Twa ethnicity. A 50:50 Hutu:Tutsi ratio has been established for the upper house (senate), as well as for the army (Stojanović 2018). At executive level, a 60:40 ratio of Hutus to Tutsis is mandated for the cabinet. A president is directly elected with two vice-presidents appointed from different ethnic groups and different parties (Vandeginste 2014, 268). Aside from Twa, 'others' include members of the Ganwa (or Baganwa) ethnic group, 'foreign citizens' living in Burundi (including those with a Burundian mother), members of the Arab community, and citizens who cannot prove their identity because they do not know who their fathers are (Stojanović 2018, 19–21). Similarly, in the autonomous province of South Tyrol in northern Italy, under the 1972 Autonomy Statute ethno-linguistic quotas are used to protect the rights of German and Ladin linguistic minorities. Citizens over eighteen years must complete a linguistic declaration in order to be able to stand for public office, receive public subsidies, or get a job as a civil servant. Since 1991 citizens can declare themselves as Other, but those that do are left out of this system of representation and public goods. The discriminatory and 'ethnic caging' effect of these rules has been highlighted by the South Tyrol Green Party, the main civic party mobilizing in the province. Indeed, Green Party representative Alexander Langer was barred from running for mayor of Bolzano/Bozen because he refused to provide a linguistic declaration in the 1991 census (Piacentini 2021, 441–2; Alber 2021, 183). By contrast, more liberal cases like Northern Ireland and North Macedonia do not feature reserved seats. Voters vote on a common roll and neither voters nor election candidates need to declare their ethnonational identity prior to elections (although elected representatives in Northern Ireland are required to declare on entering the legislature) (McCulloch 2014a).

The impact of these 'corporate' rules is not just practical but ideational too. Scholars have pointed to the way such rules can work to legitimize ethnic representation in the minds of voters (Brubaker 2002; Howard 2012) – socializing them to the idea that Sunnis represent Sunnis, German speakers represent German speakers, etc. – and inadvertently delegitimizing other (civic) forms of representation in the process. Deets and Sulke Ouaiss describe how consociation can condition people to think in ethno-sectarian terms, creating a kind of 'cognitive lock' whereby they simply cannot imagine alternatives to ethnic party representation (2021, 160).

When it comes to 'group autonomy' in power sharing, this can manifest territorially via decentralization along ethnonational lines or culturally via devolution of certain policies to ethnonational groups. Territorial autonomy presents a clear impediment to civic parties seeking to reach across ethnonational groups – as the Northern Ireland–Bosnia contrast shows. Beyond Bosnia, this type of ethno-territorial decentralization can also be seen in ethnonationally diverse and divided societies including Nigeria, India, Nepal, Myanmar, and Belgium. In Belgium's corporate consociation, the extensive territorial decentralization along ethno-linguistic lines between the Flemish-majority Flanders, the French-speaking majority Wallonia, and the mixed Brussels region, obstructs state-wide civic parties from mobilizing across its three federal entities (Deschouwer 1999). Cultural autonomy for ethnic groups can also drag cultural issues into the realm of ethnic politics, limit space for the civic agenda, and ethnicize otherwise non-ethnic issues – all of which places civic parties in an awkward position. This feature is seen in both more liberal and more corporate power-sharing systems. In Northern Ireland, the protection of communal education has frustrated and contested Alliance's flagship policy of integrated education, as seen. Furthermore, the presumption of autonomy over cultural issues has led to divisive debates about issues like flags and Irish language, in which Alliance has at times found itself caught in the crossfire. In the case of Lebanon, Nagle and Fakhoury (2018; 2021) show how provisions for cultural autonomy for the different sects have seen morality issues, such as sexuality, devolved to religious leaders via fifteen personal status laws, where homosexuality and the gender expression of trans people are both criminalized. This kind of cultural autonomy clearly militates against the protection of universal human rights and the advancement of civic agendas such as gender and LGBTQ+ rights.

Vetoes are a core feature of power-sharing, in Northern Ireland, Bosnia and beyond. Under the Belgian Constitution, for example, Flemish and French-speaking groups can use the 'alarm bell' procedure to veto certain issues of 'vital' importance (Stojanović 2018). Veto rules like these clearly afford civic parties fewer protections in the system to their ethnonational counterparts, leaving them appearing weaker. Less directly, they also imbue politics with a zero-sum dynamic, creating an inhospitable environment for civic parties and making certain civic issues subject to ethno-politicization.

Coalition style executives facilitated by proportional representation seen in consociations, can allow for civic parties to take part, as in

Northern Ireland, Bosnia, and Burundi but it also means working with ethnonational partners which can prove tricky, as shown in Bosnia. Piacentini underlines the challenge for civic parties in Bosnia and North Macedonia in finding partners with whom to work, noting that Bosnia's Naša Stanka and Macedonia's Levica have tended to avoid cooperation and compromise with the major ethnonational parties (2019, 284).

Informal Institutions

The barriers to civic parties embedded in the political cultures of Northern Ireland and Bosnia find resonance in other divided societies. The dominant discourse in such places, largely controlled by ethnonational parties, leave civic parties marginalized, contested and coopted, as shown. Piacentini demonstrates the difficulty for civic parties in Macedonia advancing a message of hope while operating in a climate of fear, perpetuated by ethnic parties (2019, 284). Here she notes a '"clash of political cultures" – one grounded in the notion of citizenship and inclusive values, participation, and human rights, and another grounded in habits, distrust, passivity, and consolidated networks of trust and alliances' (2019, 283). In this way, civic party discourse buts up against the dominant ethnonational discourse.

Ethnonational clientelism has been identified by numerous scholars as among the most potent barriers to civic parties. In cases as diverse as Lebanon, North Macedonia, and Burundi patronage and clientelistic networks based on ethnicity have worked to keep civic parties out of the political game. In the cases of Bosnia and Macedonia, Piacentini deems 'ethno-clientelistic alliances, which prop up ethnicized masses' economic protection' to be a major obstacle to civic parties. Indeed, she judges this informal barrier to be even more determining than the formal barrier of ethnicized institutions in both places (2019, 273). In Lebanon, meanwhile, parties present themselves as 'protectors' of 'their' ethnic group, while simultaneously inhibiting citizens' abilities to independently access the full range of benefits to which they are entitled, such as education, healthcare, and social welfare (Deets 2015; 2018). As Lust argues, in systems where the rule of law is relatively weak and competition exists between ethnic identities, 'ruling elites can manage elections with relative ease' (2009, 130). Power-sharing in Burundi has also been deeply prone to clientelism and patronage, characterized by neo-patrimonialism (Vandeginste 2017, 184; Raffoul 2020). In these cases (largely corporate) power-sharing rules that grant ethnonational parties considerable autonomy combine with a weak state, fragile rule of law, economic insecurity and ethnonational division to create fertile conditions for ethnonational clientelism.

The fraught relationship between civil society and the political sphere seen in Northern Ireland and Bosnia can be witnessed in other divided, power-sharing societies, with similarly detrimental consequences for civic politics. The (ethnonational) elite-dominated nature of power-sharing in both places has been particularly closed and complex for movements for change, such as the 2014 protests in Bosnia or the marriage equality movement in Northern Ireland. This emerges as something of a blockage in the system, shutting off a potential pipeline between grassroots and institutional civic politics. Similarly, in the case of Lebanon, Fakhoury describes how power-sharing has inhibited mobilization from below (2019, 18). Against a backdrop of civil strife and protests against the sectarian system, a cross-ethnic, civil society electoral coalition Kollouna Watani, 'We Are All Lebanon', did mobilize for the first time in history in the 2018 election, yet in the end only secured one seat (Fakhoury 2019). Fakhoury notes the human rights implications of this disconnect, for example for women's and LGBTQ+ rights in Lebanon (2019, 18). That being said, in 2022, in the midst of a political and economic crisis following the mass uprising of ordinary citizens in 2019 and after the Beirut port explosion of 2020, opposition candidates aligned to that movement made significant gains, capturing thirteen out of 128 seats in parliament (Fakhoury 2019, 14; Nagle and Fakhoury 2022).

Getting Around the Barriers?

Yet, civic parties under all different forms of power-sharing – even the most rigidly corporate – have found ways around these barriers and even harnessed openings in the system. 'Others' may not be recognized in many power-sharing systems, but most of those systems that require ethnic declaration do not require 'proof' of ethnic membership. Therefore, 'strategic alignment' is a strategy open to 'others' and used effectively in systems including Bosnia, South Tyrol, and Burundi (Piacentini 2021; Stojanović 2018). Piacentini notes that citizens who identify as 'other' in these societies generally do not opt to self-exclude but participate as ethnic actors as a way to access positions of power, status, and material resources – thus, adapting to the system in a rational way. Comparing Bosnia with South Tyrol in this sense, she assesses that such strategic alignment is driven in South Tyrol by economic opportunism and in Bosnia by survival. This strategy allows 'others' to overcome the obstacles of the system and enjoy equal opportunities and benefits, while also keeping the consociational system in place (Piacentini 2021, 445).

Indeed, corporate rules like ethnic quotas can ironically be used, in combination with more centripetal rules, to incentivize and even mandate multi-ethnic parties. In Burundi, the 2003 Law on Political Parties mandates that parties cannot be made up of more than 75 per cent of one ethnic group. Meanwhile, under the proportional representation system, electoral lists must be 'zipped' so that one in three candidates must be from the other ethnic group (Raffoul 2020). Similarly, in Nepal parties are required to have proportional representation of women, minority ethnic groups, and regions (Breen 2022, 308). These kinds of rules resonate with the kind of centripetal measures advocated by Reilly to facilitate the formation of non-ethnic parties in divided societies, including rules surrounding party formation, electoral engineering (e.g. requiring party lists to be multi-ethnic), and targeting international resources and support to these parties (2006, 823).

Civic parties have also strategically navigated ethno-territorially decentralized states and some scholars have argued that that decentralized structure can facilitate such parties. Territories decentralized along ethnic lines are highly conducive to parties that present as multi-ethnic on the national/state level but ethnic at the regional level, as seen in Nigeria, Nepal, and Myanmar. Kendhammer (2010) presents the People's Democratic Party (PDP) of Nigeria as a multi-ethnic party that operates as a party with 'two faces' – as a multi-ethnic party on the national level where elites cooperate across the ethnic divide and as an ethnic party on the local level. Indeed, Breen highlights this trend as a strength of a new model of ethno-federalism emerging in Asia, that incentivizes such parties to form and participate in government alongside ethnic parties. This type of multi-ethnic party, as seen in Nepal and Myanmar, can facilitate dialogue between groups within their parties and exert a moderating effect on politics (Breen 2022).[2] Similarly, Bogaards highlights the 'congress type' of 'consociational party' that operates within a multi-party system and consists of factions and/or subnational party units, such as the Congress Party in India from 1947–67. In interaction with federal institutions, these parties play a role in *representation* of groups, and their *accommodation* within the system (Bogaards 2014).

Civic parties do have choices in power-sharing systems. Clearly, however, some of these choices are suboptimal and others place them in an invidious position. While civic parties can and do take up positions reserved for ethnic groups, Zuber finds that 'multi-ethnic' parties are not perceived as being as effective with respect to ethnic representation as their ethnic counterparts (Zuber, 2015). They will still find it difficult to compete with the ethnic tribunes on this score. What's more, some of these openings hold civic parties back in acting on their own terms – as civic parties with a civic agenda – and being seen in that way. While Piacentini highlights the way in which 'other' voters and political representatives in Bonsia and South Tyrol nevertheless engage with the system and reap benefits from doing so (2021), 'playing the ethnic game' so to speak does not allow them to participate on their own terms, nor really challenge the dominant ethnonational discourse nor advance an alternative civic policy agenda. What's more, corporate rules like ethnic quotas arguably make civic parties (however genuine in their 'multi-ethnic' principles) appear opportunistic and strategic for comprising members of different groups. As for rules that incentivize and mandate civic parties, these top-down measures have proven effective in relation to peacebuilding, as shown in places like Nepal. However, from a bottom-up and longer-term view, as societies seek to transition from peace towards a more 'normal' democracy, such rules reinforce the principle of ethnonational representation while leaving these parties open to accusations of opportunism and 'really' representing the majority ethnic group present within their party. They also lie in tension with their bid to be seen as an effective civic party in their own right, not simply a bridge between two sides in a conflict.

Conclusion

This chapter has depicted the clear parallels in the experiences of civic parties in power-sharing systems in Northern Ireland and Bosnia but also exposed some critical differences. Civic parties in both places are constrained by the formal institutions of power-sharing and the broader informal institutions, in complex and reinforcing ways. Yet those in Bosnia face steeper, more impenetrable barriers. In both places, civic parties have shown creative agency in navigating the system, finding openings wherever they can. At times, though, these openings have raised strategic dilemmas and threatened to compromise their civic principles and longer-term goals – again, with more obvious and damaging effect in Bosnia.

How might we explain these different outcomes? Broader structural differences make for distinct political cultures: disparate histories with democracy, vastly distinct experiences of war, economic conditions, rule of law, and state capacity, to name a few. While acknowledging this complexity and multiple causality, the findings also tell us something about the effects of the political institutions imposed as part of peace agreements in each place. They imply that, while power-sharing has been disadvantageous to civic parties in both places, Northern Ireland's more liberal framework has been more amenable to these parties than Bosnia's more rigid corporate model. Placing this comparison in a broader context, the chapter shows that power-sharing frustrates the goals of civic parties in power-sharing contexts across the world but most obviously and directly in more corporate systems. Civic parties retain the capacity to mobilize and participate, even in the most rigidly corporate system. However, while doing so can afford them access to representation and power in the short-term, it also compromises their ability to advance a civic policy agenda and achieve change (including towards a more civic model of governance) from within the system. Northern Ireland appears to be testing this limit. Civic parties there are threatening to break the longstanding binary of Northern Ireland politics and challenging the legitimacy of a power-sharing system based on ethnonational representation. This raises the question of whether flexible power-sharing rules, even while holding civic parties back in some respects, can allow them just enough space to advance to a point where they can change the system from within and serve as a vehicle to a more integrated, democratic future.

Conclusion

The struggles played out in these pages, in Northern Ireland, in Bosnia and Herzegovina, and beyond, make one thing about 'divided societies' clear: not all politics in these places are ethnonational politics. When we replace the traditional singular/binary lens with an intersectional one we see that civic politics – which eschews ethnonationalism and mobilizes on other issues and identity categories – far from being non-existent or even peripheral in such societies, is a site of lively contention. Civic solidarity, so often depicted as vulnerable and transient in the face of ethnonational forces, in fact displays vital agency and resilience. It has emerged and survived in even the most divided contexts – amidst polarizing violence, constitutional crises, and ethnonational protest. Indeed, it has made the transition to institutional politics in the form of political parties. It has even managed to survive institutions designed specifically to represent ethnonational groups. Confounding theories of ethnic politics (Horowitz 1985), conflict management (O'Leary 2004), and, to some extent, civic mobilization (Milan 2020), civic parties have broken through in deeply divided and power-sharing systems and played meaningful, critical roles.

In spite of the theoretical tensions between the two, civic solidarity can and does co-exist with consociational power-sharing – uneasily, yes, but with purpose. In both Northern Ireland and Bosnia, civic politics is a central battleground of politics. The dynamic is no longer purely bipolar or tripolar, between ethnonational players, with civic players obscured: civic politics is now mounting a real challenge to ethnonational politics and increasingly, politics in both places is being shaped by the struggle between the ethnic and civic paradigm. And this matters. Without actors that mobilize on issues and identities beyond ethnonational, and push open the discursive space for those agendas, progress on issues of broader human rights and equality, from gender to disability to migration, is easily pushed to the side or subsumed in the ethnonational vortex. The path for civic parties and their form of politics in divided power-sharing societies is not straightforward, however. They have survived by adapting to the system. And that entails risks and trade-offs.

Findings

Based on the analysis in the preceding chapters, a few clear conclusions can be drawn:

- Civic parties face *structural barriers in consociational power-sharing systems*, both directly in the formal institutions and less directly in the informal institutions.
  - As predicted in chapter 1, the *formal institutions* designed to ensure ethnonational representation and protections – grand coalition government, proportionality, group autonomy, and mutual veto – leave civic parties in both Northern Ireland and Bosnia constrained, marginalized and 'othered'.
  - Even more impactful for civic parties in both places though are the *informal institutions* or 'unwritten rules' of politics: the dominant ethnonational discourse, the system of ethnonational clientelism, and the strained relationship between civil society and politics.
  - Importantly, the formal and informal institutions do not exist in isolation but *interplay* with one another to obstruct civic parties, as rules to enshrine ethnonational representation reinforce discourses that question the legitimacy of civic representation, rules that grant ethnonational parties autonomy over state resources facilitate clientelism, and so forth.
- Civic parties possess *critical agency* to navigate barriers and seize openings in the power-sharing system.
  - These parties are not passive victims of the system. They creatively *navigate the rules and find openings* and opportunities within them. They are flexible and strategic in the way they

position themselves with respect to the divide in society, adapting to changing circumstances, institutional and societal. They engage constructively with power-sharing institutions, even while maintaining a critical stance towards those institutions and campaigning for their reform, taking up key legislative and executive positions, even those reserved for ethnonational groups, and taking part in governing coalitions. They carve out civic niches for themselves in politics that they seek to expand and occupy, capitalizing on political and societal shifts – even crises. They mindfully navigate contentious issues, including constitutional change. They develop electoral strategies that strike varying balances between growth and ethnonational spread.

- Opportunities that arise in the system can be double-edged, however, and strategies to navigate barriers and openings come with risk. 'Playing the ethnic system' can compromise their civic principles and their civic image among voters. Trade-offs can emerge between short-term expansion and access to power on the one hand and long-term advancement of the civic agenda and politics based on civic principles on the other: both institutionally and discursively, in the minds of politicians and voters.

- Comparatively, civic parties in Northern Ireland *face fewer and lesser barriers* in the power-sharing system and *fewer and lesser risks* in navigating the system than those in Bosnia.
  - Bosnia's more rigidly ethnic power-sharing rules, which comprise less legitimate space for 'others', afford civic parties less space to participate in the system as civic players. It almost compels them to align with ethnic groups and appeal to largely ethnically homogenous constituencies in order to grow and to access positions of power.
  - The strategies civic parties in Bosnia adopt to get around these impediments can secure electoral growth and influence but also leave them vulnerable to ethnonational contestation, challenge their legitimacy as civic actors and frustrate their ability to pursue politics on their own terms, and achieve their goals for a more civic politics and society.

- Northern Ireland's more flexible power-sharing rules allow more legitimate space for civic parties to participate as 'others', albeit not on equal terms with ethnonational representatives.
- As Northern Ireland has transitioned away from armed conflict, these institutions have granted civic parties space (albeit contested and unequal space) to grow, to a level where they are challenging the dominance of ethnonational politics.
- This suggests that under liberal, flexible conditions civic parties can emerge as contenders in power-sharing systems and effect change from within the institutions: at the discursive level, advancing civic discourse; at the level of policy advancing a civic agenda, and at the institutional level, advancing institutional reform.

Implications for Theory

What does all of this mean for how we think and theorize about the politics of 'divided societies'? It has something to say to a number of fields. For theories of conflict management, and power-sharing in particular, it demonstrates that not all politics in such places is ethnic politics: *civic politics exists, it matters, and it must be accounted for.* Both consociational and centripetal schools of thought, with their laser focus on the ethnonational divide in society, underestimate the agency of civic politics and the role it can play within power-sharing systems. Civic parties have been largely overlooked by consociational scholars as inconsequential to the bigger game of inter-ethnic accommodation. Meanwhile, centripetal scholars, in their critiques of consociation, are too deterministic, often stripping civic parties of agency, assuming their vulnerability in the ethnic system. The reality of politics in deeply divided places that feature consociational power-sharing is much more multi-dimensional and less binary. An intersectional lens reveals that civic solidarity exists amidst ethnonational dynamics and that the two intersect. Party systems in these transitional places – particularly those two or more decades removed from armed conflict – often feature a mix of ethnonational and civic parties, that compete within their own 'blocs' but also across those blocs (Zuber 2012). Ethnonational politics is not the only game in town. Indeed, in Northern Ireland and, to some extent in Bosnia, the contest between civic and ethnonational politics is centre stage of political debate.

The findings highlight the need for scholars of conflict resolution to take a more intersectional approach to the study of conflict and 'post-conflict' societies, to acknowledge the presence of civic parties as central players who can play key roles within power-sharing systems and, indeed, drive change from within. An intersectional understanding of society should also inform institutional models for conflict resolution, including innovations in the design of power-sharing.

The findings also make an intervention in the power-sharing debate about different forms that consociation can take, namely the more flexible self-determined 'liberal' form versus the more rigid, ethnic, imposed 'corporate' form. While by no means clear-cut nor definitive, the Northern Ireland–Bosnia comparison does suggest that liberal conditions are more conducive to the development and growth of civic parties over time and to the meaningful advancement of civic politics.

Yet, the effect of the institutional rules is complex and, in many ways, the informal institutions pertaining to political culture, political economy, conflict legacies, and beyond, are equally if not more determining for civic parties in Northern Ireland and Bosnia. But these formal and informal institutions cannot be separated out: they reinforce one another to constrain and enable civic politics. The link between provisions for territorial autonomy and clientelism in Bosnia and Lebanon is an obvious example. This research underlines the power of informal institutions and the need for power-sharing scholars to pay attention to them and to the way they interplay with formal rules, as feminist institutionalists advocate.

The findings also shed some light on the long-running debate about how societies might (if ever) transition out of power-sharing. While far too early to hail the end of power-sharing in Northern Ireland, the recent growth of civic politics, tentative realignment of the party system, and amplified calls for reform of the consociational system suggest that the expansion of civic parties could offer one potential route out of power-sharing over time, via incremental change. This possibility requires more attention.

Finally, beyond conflict resolution, the findings also have implications for theories of social movements in divided societies. While scholars have tended to be pessimistic about the prospects of civic mobilizations making the transition from grassroots to institutional politics in ethnonationally divided societies, particularly under power-sharing conditions, this book shows that this transition – while highly tricky – can be effected. The relationship between civic solidarity at the grassroots level and at the institutional level in divided societies is critical and demands better understanding to support that transition.

Implications for Practice

Some of these findings bear practical application too. Power-sharing may be problematic in democratic terms, but it remains one of few viable models at the disposal of international peace brokers. Indeed, with war ongoing in Gaza, Ukraine, Sudan, and beyond at the time of writing, power-sharing has continued relevance in conflict resolution debates in these and other future cases. The insights gleaned from this analysis have clear implications for institutional design. Where power-sharing is being implemented after conflict it should take as open, flexible, self-determined, and 'liberal' a form as possible, granting civic representatives and parties a role equal to their ethnic counterparts. Where possible, ethnic designations should be avoided and group protections extended to all significant groups, for example through designation-free veto rules based on super majorities. Thinking should move beyond provisions to represent and protect 'others'. While better than no such provisions for 'others', these rules still 'other' civic politics and do not allow for the reality of intersectionality or the potential for an individual to hold multiple, overlapping, and fluid identities. When politics is structured in this binary either/or way, it grants no outlet for recognition and representation of intersectional identities, for example a citizen of Bosnia who identifies as mixed Serb–Croat and LGBTQ+. The findings also support calls for institutional innovations that would facilitate greater civil society input into power-sharing systems, including deliberative democracy fora such as citizens' assemblies.[1]

After the design phase, the findings also bear lessons for external actors involved in overseeing and upholding peace in post-conflict societies. Top-down electoral engineering is a tool available to international actors, as noted by Reilly (2006), Breen (2022), Bogaards, Basedau, Hartmann (2013), and others, that has been used to promote moderation in places including in Bosnia. However, this book places more emphasis on international actors recognizing and appreciating the civic politics that already exists in divided societies and working to support the underlying conditions for its growth. International actors can use their positions to support the development of economic development, the rule of law and personal security, that can help over the longer term to nurture the development of civic community activism, social movements and parties, and alleviate some of the informal barriers they face. At the very least, the findings suggest that international actors should be mindful to avoid obstructing the bottom-up development of civic mobilizations or bolstering ethnonational parties in the name of stability over justice.

Beyond societies that are generally defined as 'post-conflict' or 'deeply divided', societies across the world are now contending with the struggle between civic and ethnonational politics, including in North America and Europe. Can these 'hard cases' of ethnicized institutional frameworks teach us something about the capacity of civic mobilization to prevail against the headwinds of ethnonational identity politics in societies across the world? The findings here may shed light on the dynamics of that struggle, and provide insights into the ethnonational strategies used to resist and subvert civic politics and, in turn, civic strategies used to withstand those pressures.

Civic Futures

Looking to the future, how might civic solidarity in divided societies fare amidst some of the major political and societal shifts taking place globally, including in relation to race, gender, climate change, migration, democracy, and borders? The rise of gender politics globally – including around reproductive rights, tackling sexual and gender-based violence, and LGBTQ+ rights – while politicizing these rights and opening them up to contestation in so-called 'culture wars', may also expand space for civic solidarity in divided societies. The existential crisis of climate change – a cross-cutting 'leveler' – is only set to become more salient in politics. Each of these issues has the potential to be polarizing, ethnicized, and coopted. Yet, as they become more urgent, they also bear the potential to expand civic space in divided societies. What's more, major global social movements of the last decade, like Black Lives Matter, Extinction Rebellion, and #metoo – and those like the Boycott, Divestment, Sanctions (BDS) movement in solidarity with Palestine – have taken increasingly intersectional approaches to identity, uniting on their core goal but prizing the diversity of other identities and causes they represent, relating to race, colonialism, peace, gender, class, religion, disability, and more. They each also bear generational elements that could feed into the expansion of civic issue space.

Meanwhile, mass migration, including as a result of war (notably to Europe from states including Ukraine, Syria, and Afghanistan) and climate change, are bringing greater diversity to post-conflict societies, greater numbers of 'others', and opening up new – albeit challenging – dimensions in political debate.

A sobering backdrop to all of this, of course, has been the global crisis of democracy, with one monitoring organization reporting the eighteenth consecutive decline in global democracy in 2023 (Freedom House 2024). Divided societies are not immune to this trend – indeed, they can be more susceptible. As seen, democratic backsliding and the rise of authoritarianism have emerged as critical challenges across the Western Balkans, including in Bosnia, over the last decade, while the UK and Ireland have witnessed the rise of right-wing populism and nativist anti-immigration movements more recently, including, notably, in Northern Ireland.[2]

At the same time, constitutional change and the redrawing of borders is an issue firmly on the agenda in both Northern Ireland and Bosnia, and other divided and polarized societies including Catalonia and Iraq. This polarizing issue undoubtedly presents challenges for non-aligned civic parties, as seen in Bosnia amidst secessionist threats by the RS. Yet, as shown in Northern Ireland by Alliance's handling of the Brexit debacle, they can also have the capacity in some cases to contribute a civic voice that can help inform the debate and move it in a more civic direction.

In the context of these shifts, civic parties can play a role in expanding the discursive space for such issues. In turn, these developments also have the potential to advance civic politics and, hence parties, in Northern Ireland, Bosnia, and beyond. Clearly, each one has the potential to be ethnicized. Yet, they also open up new cleavages and alternative solidarities, some with generational dimensions, that could further cross-cut ethnonational politics and present civic parties an opportunity to seize. These shifts warrant the attention of domestic and international actors and call for further research including on the role of civic parties in constitutional change, in combatting democratic backsliding and the implications of civic politics and parties for gender and LGBTQ+ rights.

However these struggles play out, civic politics look set to occupy a critical place in the futures of Northern Ireland, Bosnia, and other divided places.

Notes

Introduction

1 For further contemporary analysis of nationalism see Malešević (2019).

2 The Belfast Agreement of 1998 is also known as the Good Friday Agreement. The latter term, being the more common usage, is the one I generally use throughout this book, sometimes abbreviated to GFA. The Belfast Agreement, 1998. Northern Ireland Office, 10 April 1998.

3 In line with the 'most similar system' design in comparative political science, this comparison entails one key point of variation in the 'independent variable' (the potential explanatory driver of the phenomenon under examination) (Peters 1998, 38–40; Pennings et al. 2006, 34; Przeworski and Teune 1970, 39).

4 Each group was composed of mixed national identity, as disclosed in a participant questionnaire. Four groups were organized through 'gatekeepers' in the given organization with whom I secured contact. One was organized after a member responded to an advertisement I had placed in the Northern Ireland Council for Voluntary Action weekly newsletter. Three groups took place in Belfast (two with women's organizations and one with a students' association), one in the town of Enniskillen in County Fermanagh in the south west of the region (a community organization) and one in the city of Derry/Londonderry in the north west of the region (a community organization).

5 Each group was composed of a single national identity, two in the state and FBiH capital of Sarajevo (a university student-based group and a language school group, both exclusively Bosniak identifying) and one in the RS capital of Banja Luka (a university student-based group, exclusively Serb identifying). Each group was formed through a contact in the organization in question.

6 In the case of Northern Ireland, I carried out archival research at the Linen Hall Library in Belfast, as well as in the Alliance Party's own archive to which I was granted access on one occasion. I furthermore accessed a number of relevant documents online, including party manifestos and policy documents. In the case of BiH, I obtained a number of state and party documents online, as well as documents by request directly from the parties concerned.

7 This included a continuous stay of seven months in Bosnia in 2014 and of thirteen months in Northern Ireland in 2017–18. Fieldwork in Northern Ireland was primarily conducted during the following periods: March 2012, April–May 2013,

April 2015, November 2015, July 2017–June 2018, and October–November 2021. Fieldwork in Bosnia and Herzegovina was primarily conducted during the following periods: January–July 2014, June 2016, June 2019, and February–June 2023.

Chapter One

1 The 'deeply divided' frame of analysis has also been critiqued by scholars including Fakhoury and Aitken (2024) and Majed (2019).

2 Kymlicka's multicultural approach, for example, while ostensibly rooted in accommodation, is informed by a normative propensity towards integration and social unity for 'polyethnic' and 'multinational' states (1995, 176, 188). The crudeness of this integration–accommodation dichotomy has been noted by many, who underline the need in the real world to combine accommodative and integrative mechanisms (Swenden 2013; O'Flynn 2009; Choudhry 2008, 26).

3 A number of transversal scholars observe the unifying experience of violence for transversal coalitions, of women in particular (Mulholland and Patel 1999; Collins 1998; 2017).

4 In this way, transversalism speaks to tensions within feminism that came to the fore in the 1980s and '90s, about how to reconcile gender solidarity with other sources of community solidarity, be it ethnic, national, racial, religious, or other (Yuval-Davis 1997, 123; 2006, 278; Crenshaw 1989). On the global scale, this arose between feminists from the global north and south (Yuval-Dav is 1997, 123), while on national, regional, and local scales it has also been pronounced in societies marked by segregation and violence. This wholesale rejection of identity politics is challenged by other scholars in this school, however, who see it as a sometimes-necessary tool of empowerment and resistance, especially for marginalized groups (Byrne 2014; Collins and Bilge 2020).

5 Situating Hollinger's post-ethnicity theory within the cosmopolitan 'post-multiculturalist' school, Kymlicka is critical of its implicit hostility towards minority nationalism and assumption that all minority nationalisms are 'ethnic' in nature, i.e. relating to blood and descent (2004, 71, 81), whereas, in truth, both minority and majority nations can be 'post-ethnic' – such as Canada and Quebec, Britain and Scotland, the United States and Puerto Rico (2004, 74).

6 Hepburn also underlines the 'terminological confusion' in the relevant literature surrounding regionalist and nationalist parties (2009, 481).

7 Similarly, Gunther and Diamond define 'ethnicity-based parties' as those that promote the interests of a particular ethnic group or coalition of groups with the goal of securing material, cultural, and political benefits for that group or coalition (2003, 183–4).

8 Consociational power-sharing departs from centripetal power-sharing primarily in its approach to the nature and formation of government (Sisk 2002, 44–5). Consociational coalitions form after elections by elites who are mandated to do so by constitutional arrangements (including all the main parties, even 'extremes'), while centripetal coalitions form before the election on a voluntary basis. Centripetal power-sharing executives are formed voluntarily by either a coalition of parties from different ethnic groups in pre-election pacts or by parties with a multi-ethnic slate of candidates (Sisk 2002, 45; Jarstad 2009, 44).

9 Together with Richard Simeon, McGarry and O'Leary identify 'cross-community power-sharing' as the key conflict regulating mechanism in a consociation. Contrary to Lijphart's original 'grand coalition', they argue, not every community needs to be represented in the executive, nor must everybody within a particular community support all of its representatives in government – 'what matters is some element of jointness in executive government across the most significant communities'. They distinguish between 'complete consociations' ('grand coalitions'), 'concurrent consociations' in which representatives of the majority within each of the main groups is in government, and 'plurality consociations' in which at least a plurality of each of the main group's representatives are in government (McGarry et al 2008, 56–7).

10 None of this is to say that identity is unimportant. On the contrary, intersectional approaches appreciate the power of identity, and even identity politics, as a tool of resistance and empowerment, particularly for oppressed peoples (Byrne 2014; Collins and Bilge 2020, 78). However, such group solidarities are neither homogenous nor fixed. Flexible forms of solidarity are possible (Collins 2017).

11 For further discussion of the tensions between power-sharing and intersectional approaches see Byrne and McCulloch 2017; Nagle 2016a; Byrne 2020; McCulloch 2020; and Murtagh 2008.

12 In Lebanon, Nagle shows that even moderate reforms to the power-sharing system to support women's rights have been suppressed by ethnic elites and depicted as a threat to security (2020, 140). Bieber uses the term 'stabilitocracy' for semi-authoritarian regimes in the Western Balkans, including Bosnia, that receive external support and legitimacy – especially from the European Union – in return for the false promise of stability (Bieber 2018).

13 Feminist institutionalism is concerned with how institutions are formed and sustained and how gender is embedded within them (Lovenduski 2011, viii).

Chapter Two

1 For more on the US role in the Northern Ireland peace process see Guelke (2012b).

2 The Belfast Agreement, 1998. Northern Ireland Office, 10 April 1998.

3 The St Andrews Agreement, 2006. Northern Ireland Office, October 2006. Annex A.

4 The 2006 St Andrews Agreement, the 2010 Hillsborough Agreement, the 2014 Stormont House Agreement, the 2015 Fresh Start Agreement, the 2020 New Decade New Approach Agreement.

5 The St Andrews Agreement, 2006. Northern Ireland Office, October 2006.

6 The Stormont House Agreement, 2014. Northern Ireland Office and the Rt Hon Theresa Villiers MP, 23 December 2014.

7 A Fresh Start: The Stormont Agreement and Implementation Plan, 2015. Northern Ireland Executive. https://www.executiveoffice-ni.gov.uk/publications/fresh-start-stormont-agreement-and-implementation-plan.

8 Although the DUP emerged as the largest party in Northern Ireland in the 2019 UK general election, with eight seats to Sinn Féin's seven, unionist parties lost their majority of seats at Westminster: Out of eighteen seats, DUP won eight, Sinn Féin seven, SDLP two, Alliance one, and UUP none (*BBC News* 2019).

9 New Decade, New Approach, Northern Ireland Office, January 2020. assets.publishing.service.gov.uk/media/5e178b56ed915d3b06f2b795/2020-01-08_a_new_decade__a_new_approach.pdf.

10 Insecurity within unionism during this time was presumably heightened by the loss of the unionist majority at Westminster in 2019 and the results of the 2021 census in which Catholics outnumbered Protestants in Northern Ireland for the first time (46 per cent to 44 per cent).

11 Sinn Féin emerged as the largest party at Westminster with seven out of eight seats to DUP's five (*BBC News* 2024).

12 The reduction in the number of seats in the Northern Ireland Assembly from 108 to 90 followed the passing of the Assembly Members (Reduction of Numbers) Bill following provisions set out in the 2014 Stormont House Agreement. https://www.niassembly.gov.uk/assembly-business/legislation/2011-2016-mandate/primary-legislation-current-bills/assembly-members-reduction-of-numbers-bill/assembly-members-reduction-of-numbers-bill---efm/.

Chapter Three

1 Interview with Naomi Long, MP and deputy leader of Alliance Party of Northern Ireland. Interview by the author, 5 April 2012, Belfast.

2 Interview with Alliance Party MLA (a), Northern Ireland Assembly. Interview by the author, 18 April 2013, Belfast.

3 Interview with Alliance Party MLA (b), Northern Ireland Assembly. Interview by the author, 3 April 2012, Belfast.

4 Interview with Green Party Northern Ireland MLA (b), Northern Ireland Assembly. Interview by the author and Allison McCulloch, 21 February 2018, Belfast.

5 Interview with Green Party Northern Ireland MLA (a), Northern Ireland Assembly. Interview by the author, 9 April 2013, Belfast.

6 Interview with Alliance Party MLA (f), Northern Ireland Assembly. Interview by the author, 28 October 2021, Belfast.

7 Interview with Northern Ireland political journalist (a). Interview by the author, 16 April 2013, Belfast.

8 Interview with David Ford, MLA, Northern Ireland Assembly and party leader, Alliance Party of Northern Ireland. Interview by the author, 12 April 2013, Belfast.

9 Interview with Alliance Party MLA (f), Northern Ireland Assembly. Interview by the author, 28 October 2021, Belfast.

10 Interview with Naomi Long, MP and deputy leader of Alliance Party of Northern Ireland. Interview by the author, 5 April 2012, Belfast.

11 Interview with Alliance Party MLA (b), Northern Ireland Assembly. Interview by the author, 3 April 2012, Belfast; Interview with Alliance Party MLA (c), Northern Ireland Assembly. Interview by the author, 5 April 2012, Belfast; Interview with Alliance Party MLA (a), Northern Ireland Assembly. Interview by the author, 18 April 2013, Belfast; Interview with Alliance Party MLA (d), Northern Ireland Assembly. Interview by the author, 4 April 2013, Belfast; Interview with Green Party Northern Ireland MLA (a), Northern Ireland Assembly. Interview by the author, 9 April 2013, Belfast; Interview with Alliance Party MLA (f), Northern Ireland Assembly. Interview by the author, 28 October 2021, Belfast.

12 Interview with Alliance Party MLA (a), Northern Ireland Assembly. Interview by the author, 18 April 2013, Belfast; Interview with Alliance Party MLA (c), Northern Ireland Assembly. Interview by the author, 5 April 2012, Belfast; Interview with Alliance Party MLA (b), Northern Ireland Assembly. Interview by the author, 3 April 2012, Belfast; Interview with Naomi Long, MP and deputy leader of Alliance Party of Northern Ireland. Interview by the author, 5 April 2012, Belfast; Interview with Alliance Party MLA (d), Northern Ireland Assembly. Interview by the author, 4 April 2013, Belfast.

13 Interview with Alliance Party MLA (c), Northern Ireland Assembly. Interview by the author, 5 April 2012, Belfast.

14 Interview with Alliance Party MLA (f), Northern Ireland Assembly. Interview by the author, 28 October 2021, Belfast.

15 Remarks by Connie Egan Alliance Party MLA speaking at Galway International Arts Festival, July 2022; Interview with Green Party Northern Ireland MLA (b), Northern Ireland Assembly. Interview by the author and Allison McCulloch, 21 February 2018, Belfast; Interview with Monica McWilliams, former Northern Ireland Women's Coalition (NIWC) MLA and founder member of NIWC. Interview by the author, 4 April 2012, Belfast.

16 Interview with Monica McWilliams, former Northern Ireland Women's Coalition (NIWC) MLA and founder member of NIWC. Interview by the author, 4 April 2012, Belfast.

17 Indeed, the same argument could be made from the nationalist side about its historic links to the Catholic Church which remains doctrinally opposed to same-sex marriage.

18 Interview with David Ford, MLA, Northern Ireland Assembly and party leader, Alliance Party of Northern Ireland. Interview by the author, 12 April 2013, Belfast.

19 Interview with Naomi Long, MLA and leader of Alliance Party of Northern Ireland. Interview by the author, 4 May 2018, Belfast.

20 Interview with Naomi Long, MLA and leader of Alliance Party of Northern Ireland. Interview by the author, 4 May 2018, Belfast.

21 Bronagh Hinds speaking at 'Power-Sharing Pacts and The Women, Peace And Security Agenda: Constructive Engagements' workshop, Queen's University Belfast, 6–7 November 2015.

22 Interview with Naomi Long, MLA and leader of Alliance Party of Northern Ireland. Interview by the author, 4 May 2018, Belfast.

23 New Decade, New Approach, Northern Ireland Office, January 2020. assets.publishing.service.gov.uk/media/5e178b56ed915d3b06f2b795/2020-01-08_a_new_decade__a_new_approach.pdf.

24 Interview with Green Party Northern Ireland MLA (b), Northern Ireland Assembly. Interview by the author and Allison McCulloch, 21 February 2018, Belfast; Interview with Naomi Long, MLA and leader of Alliance Party of Northern Ireland. Interview by the author, 4 May 2018, Belfast.

25 Interview with LGBTQ+ rights organization representative (a). Interview by the author, 21 March 2018, Belfast.

26 Interview with LGBTQ+ rights organization representative (a). Interview by the author, 21 March 2018, Belfast; Interview with LGBTQ+ rights organization representative (b). Interview by the author, 4 May 2018, Belfast; Interview with LGBTQ+

rights organization representative (c). Interview by the author, 18 November 2021, Belfast.

27 Interview with LGBTQ+ rights organization representative (b). Interview by the author, 4 May 2018, Belfast.

28 Interview with LGBTQ+ rights organization representative (a). Interview by the author, 21 March 2018, Belfast.

29 Interview with LGBTQ+ rights organization representative (c). Interview by the author, 18 November 2021, Belfast.

30 Interview with LGBTQ+ rights organization representative (b). Interview by the author, 4 May 2018, Belfast.

31 Interview with LGBTQ+ rights organization representative (a). Interview by the author, 21 March 2018, Belfast; Interview with LGBTQ+ rights organization representative (b). Interview by the author, 4 May 2018, Belfast.

32 Interview with LGBTQ+ rights organization representative (a). Interview by the author, 21 March 2018, Belfast.

33 The Stormont House Agreement, 2014. Northern Ireland Office and the Rt Hon. Theresa Villiers MP, 23 December 2014.

34 The Stormont House Agreement, 2014. Northern Ireland Office and the Rt Hon. Theresa Villiers MP, 23 December 2014.

35 Interview with Irish language rights activist (a). Interview by the author, 26 April 2018, Belfast; Interview with Adrienne Peltz, President of National Union of Students – Union of Students of Ireland (NUS-USI). Interview by the author, 16 April 2013, Belfast.

36 Interview with LGBTQ+ rights organization representative (a). Interview by the author, 21 March 2018, Belfast.

37 Interview with LGBTQ+ rights organization representative (c). Interview by the author, 18 November 2021, Belfast.

38 Interview with LGBTQ+ rights organization representative (a). Interview by the author, 21 March 2018, Belfast; Interview with reproductive rights activist and campaign leader (b). Interview by the author and Timofey Agarin, 12 June 2018, Belfast; Interview with reproductive rights activist and campaign leader (a). Interview by the author, 10 April 2018, Belfast.

39 Interview with reproductive rights activist and campaign leader (b). Interview by the author and Timofey Agarin, 12 June 2018, Belfast.

40 Interview with LGBTQ+ rights organization representative (a). Interview by the author, 21 March 2018, Belfast; Interview with Green Party Northern Ireland MLA (b), Northern Ireland Assembly. Interview by the author and Allison McCulloch, 21 February 2018, Belfast.

41 Interview with LGBTQ+ rights organization representative (b). Interview by the author, 4 May 2018, Belfast.

42 Interview with Naomi Long, MP and deputy leader of Alliance Party of Northern Ireland. Interview by the author, 12 April 2013, Belfast.

43 Interview with LGBTQ+ rights organization representative (a). Interview by the author, 21 March 2018, Belfast; Interview with reproductive rights activist and campaign leader (b). Interview by the author and Timofey Agarin, 12 June 2018, Belfast; Interview with chair of the Community Relations Council. Interview by the author, 24 April 2018, Belfast.

44 Interview with civic politics and civil society activist and commentator, Northern Ireland. Interview by the author, 1 November 2021, Fermanagh.

45 Interview with civic politics and civil society activist and commentator, Northern Ireland. Interview by the author, 1 November 2021, Fermanagh; Interview with Alliance Party MLA (f), Northern Ireland Assembly. Interview by the author, 28 October 2021, Belfast.

Chapter Four

1 The Belfast Agreement, 1998. Northern Ireland Office, 10 April 1998. Annex A; emphasis added.

2 Interview with Alliance Party MLA (a), Northern Ireland Assembly. Interview by the author, 6 March 2018, Belfast; Interview with Green Party Northern Ireland MLA (b), Northern Ireland Assembly. Interview by the author and Allison McCulloch, 21 February 2018, Belfast; Interview with Green Party Northern Ireland senior member. Interview by the author, 25 April 2018, Belfast.

3 Interview with Irish language rights activist (b) and Irish language rights activist (c). Interview by the author, 8 May 2018, Belfast; Interview with Democratic Unionist Party (DUP) MLA (b), Northern Ireland Assembly. Interview by the author and Allison McCulloch, 13 February 2018.

4 Interview with Alliance Party MLA (a), Northern Ireland Assembly. Interview by the author, 6 March 2018, Belfast.

5 As noted, a nationalist party (Sinn Féin) emerged as the largest for the first time in Northern Ireland in the 2022 Assembly elections and following the 2024 local and Westminster elections became the largest at each level of government.

6 Interview with Alliance Party MLA (a), Northern Ireland Assembly. Interview by the author, 6 March 2018, Belfast.

7 Interview with Alliance Party MLA (a), Northern Ireland Assembly. Interview by the author, 6 March 2018, Belfast.

8 Interview with Alliance Party MLA (d), Northern Ireland Assembly. Interview by the author, 4 April 2013, Belfast.

9 Interview with Green Party Northern Ireland MLA (a), Northern Ireland Assembly. Interview by the author, 9 April 2013, Belfast; Interview with Alliance Party MLA (c), Northern Ireland Assembly. Interview by the author, 5 April 2012, Belfast.

10 Interview with Alliance Party MLA (c), Northern Ireland Assembly. Interview by the author, 5 April 2012, Belfast.

11 Interview with Green Party Northern Ireland MLA (b), Northern Ireland Assembly. Interview by the author and Allison McCulloch, 21 February 2018, Belfast.

12 Interview with civic politics and civil society activist and commentator, Northern Ireland. Interview by the author, 1 November 2021, Fermanagh.

13 Interview with Adrienne Peltz, President of National Union of Students – Union of Students of Ireland (NUS-USI). Interview by the author, 16 April 2013, Belfast.

14 Interview with Naomi Long, MP and deputy leader of Alliance Party of Northern Ireland. Interview by the author, 5 April 2012, Belfast; Interview with Alliance Party MLA (d), Northern Ireland Assembly. Interview by the author, 4 April 2013, Belfast.

15 Interview with Naomi Long, MP and deputy leader of Alliance Party of Northern Ireland. Interview by the author, 5 April 2012, Belfast.

16 Interview with Alliance Party MLA (d), Northern Ireland Assembly. Interview by the author, 4 April 2013, Belfast.

17 Interview with DUP MP and MLA (a), Northern Ireland Assembly. Interview by the author, 1 May 2013, Belfast.

18 Interview with Alliance Party MLA (a), Northern Ireland Assembly. Interview by the author, 18 April 2013, Belfast; Interview with Alliance Party councillor (a). Interview by the author, April 2013, Belfast.

19 Interview with Naomi Long, MP and deputy leader of Alliance Party of Northern Ireland. Interview by the author, 5 April 2012, Belfast.

20 Interview with Alliance Party councillor (a). Interview by the author, April 2013, Belfast.

21 Interview with Green Party Northern Ireland MLA (a), Northern Ireland Assembly. Interview by the author, 9 April 2013, Belfast.

22 Interview with Alliance Party MLA (f), Northern Ireland Assembly. Interview by the author, 28 October 2021, Belfast.

23 Interview with Sinn Féin MLA (b), Northern Ireland Assembly. Interview by the author, 30 April 2013, Belfast.

24 Interview with Ulster Unionist Party (UUP) MLA (a), Northern Ireland Assembly. Interview by the author, 15 April 2013, Belfast.

25 Interview with Alliance Party MLA (a), Northern Ireland Assembly. Interview by the author, 18 April 2013, Belfast; Interview with David Ford, MLA, Northern Ireland Assembly and Party Leader, Alliance Party of Northern Ireland. Interview by the author, 12 April 2013, Belfast.

26 Interview with Naomi Long, MP and deputy leader of Alliance Party of Northern Ireland. Interview by the author, 5 April 2012, Belfast. Furthermore, in focus groups with voters some participants referred to the common practice of 'tactical' or 'defensive' voting for the main ethnonational parties representing their community, in order 'to keep the other side out'. Focus group (f) conducted with members of a student association group, Belfast, 1 May 2013; Focus group (e) conducted with members of a women's rights organization, Belfast, 25 April 2013.

27 Interview with David Ford, MLA, Northern Ireland Assembly and party leader, Alliance Party of Northern Ireland. Interview by the author, 12 April 2013, Belfast; Interview with Alliance Party MLA (d), Northern Ireland Assembly. Interview by the author, 4 April 2013, Belfast.

28 Interview with Alliance Party MLA (a), Northern Ireland Assembly. Interview by the author, 18 April 2013, Belfast.

29 Interview with Alliance Party MLA (f), Northern Ireland Assembly. Interview by the author, 28 October 2021, Belfast.

30 Interview with Alliance Party MLA (f), Northern Ireland Assembly. Interview by the author, 28 October 2021, Belfast.

31 Interview with Alliance Party MLA (d), Northern Ireland Assembly. Interview by the author, 4 April 2013, Belfast; Interview with Alliance Party councillor (a). Interview by the author, April 2013, Belfast.

32 Interview with Naomi Long, MP and deputy leader of Alliance Party of Northern Ireland. Interview by the author, 12 April 2013, Belfast.
33 Interview with Alliance Party MLA (d), Northern Ireland Assembly. Interview by the author, 4 April 2013, Belfast.
34 Interview with Ulster Unionist Party (UUP) MLA (a), Northern Ireland Assembly. Interview by the author, 15 April 2013, Belfast; Interview with Democratic Unionist Party (DUP) MLA (a), Northern Ireland Assembly. Interview by the author, 1 May 2013, Belfast.
35 Interview with Ulster Unionist Party (UUP) MLA (a), Northern Ireland Assembly. Interview by the author, 15 April 2013, Belfast.
36 Bronagh Hinds speaking at Power-Sharing Pacts and The Women, Peace and Security Agenda: Constructive Engagements workshop, Queen's University Belfast, 6–7 November 2015.
37 Interview with LGBTQ+ rights organization representative (a). Interview by the author, 21 March 2018, Belfast; Interview with LGBTQ+ rights organization representative (c). Interview by the author, 18 November 2021, Belfast.
38 Interview with Alliance Party MLA (a), Northern Ireland Assembly. Interview by the author, 6 March 2018, Belfast.
39 Interview with Democratic Unionist Party (DUP) MLA (a), Northern Ireland Assembly. Interview by the author, 1 May 2013, Belfast.
40 Interview with Chair of the Community Relations Council. Interview by the author, 24 April 2018, Belfast.
41 Interview with Alliance Party MLA (a), Northern Ireland Assembly. Interview by the author, 6 March 2018, Belfast.
42 Interview with ethnic minority community organization representative (a). Interview by the author and Allison McCulloch, 21 February 2018, Belfast; Interview with environmental activist and NGO representative, Northern Ireland (a). Interview by the author, 2 November 2021, online via Zoom.; Interview with LGBTQ+ rights organization representative (c). Interview by the author, 18 November 2021, Belfast.

Chapter Five

1 Interview with Alliance Party MLA (a), Northern Ireland Assembly. Interview by the author, 18 April 2013, Belfast; Interview with Alliance Party MLA (c), Northern Ireland Assembly. Interview by the author, 5 April 2012, Belfast; Interview with David Ford, MLA, Northern Ireland Assembly and Party Leader, Alliance Party of Northern Ireland. Interview by the author, 12 April 2013, Belfast; Interview with Naomi Long, MP and deputy leader of Alliance Party of Northern Ireland. Interview by the author, 5 April 2012, Belfast.
2 Interview with Alliance Party MLA (c), Northern Ireland Assembly. Interview by the author, 5 April 2012, Belfast; Interview with Alliance Party MLA (d), Northern Ireland Assembly. Interview by the author, 4 April 2013, Belfast.
3 Interview with Alliance Party MLA (c), Northern Ireland Assembly. Interview by the author, 5 April 2012, Belfast.

4 Interview with Naomi Long, MP and deputy leader of Alliance Party of Northern Ireland. Interview by the author, 5 April 2012, Belfast.

5 Interview with Alliance Party MLA (c), Northern Ireland Assembly. Interview by the author, 5 April 2012, Belfast.

6 Interview with Alliance Party MLA (a), Northern Ireland Assembly. Interview by the author, 18 April 2013, Belfast; Interview with Naomi Long, MP and deputy leader of Alliance Party of Northern Ireland. Interview by the author, 5 April 2012, Belfast.; Interview with Alliance Party MLA (f), Northern Ireland Assembly. Interview by the author, 28 October 2021, Belfast.

7 Interview with Naomi Long, MP and deputy leader of Alliance Party of Northern Ireland. Interview by the author, 5 April 2012, Belfast.

8 Interview with David Ford, MLA, Northern Ireland Assembly and party leader, Alliance Party of Northern Ireland. Interview by the author, 12 April 2013, Belfast. In focus groups with voters, some participants expressed fatigue with civic parties' historic messaging of 'cross-community' and 'reconciliation'. Focus group (d) conducted with employees of a community organization, Enniskillen 23 April 2013; Focus group (e) conducted with members of a women's rights organization, Belfast, 25 April 2013.

9 Interview with Anna Lo, Alliance Party MLA, Northern Ireland Assembly. Interview by the author, 3 April 2012, Belfast.

10 Interview with Alliance Party MLA (d), Northern Ireland Assembly. Interview by the author, 4 April 2013, Belfast.

11 Interview with Monica McWilliams, former Northern Ireland Women's Coalition (NIWC) MLA and founder member of NIWC. Interview by the author, 4 April 2012, Belfast; Interview with Jane Morrice, former MLA, Northern Ireland Women's Coalition. Interview by the author, 5 April 2013, Hollywood, Co. Down,

12 Interview with Monica McWilliams, former Northern Ireland Women's Coalition (NIWC) MLA and founder member of NIWC. Interview by the author, 4 April 2012, Belfast.

13 Interview with Monica McWilliams, former Northern Ireland Women's Coalition (NIWC) MLA and founder member of NIWC. Interview by the author, 4 April 2012, Belfast.

14 Interview with Green Party Northern Ireland MLA (a), Northern Ireland Assembly. Interview by the author, 9 April 2013, Belfast; Interview with Green Party Northern Ireland councillor. Interview by the author, April 2013, Belfast.

15 Interview with Steven Agnew, Green Party MLA and party leader, Northern Ireland Assembly. Interview by the author, 9 April 2013, Belfast.

16 The position was occupied by an Independent Unionist MLA for a brief period from 2016–17 before the collapse of the Executive.

17 Interview with Sinn Féin MLA (b), Northern Ireland Assembly. Interview by the author, 30 April 2013, Belfast; Interview with Democratic Unionist Party (DUP) MLA (a), Northern Ireland Assembly. Interview by the author, 1 May 2013, Belfast.

18 Interview with Sinn Féin MLA (b), Northern Ireland Assembly. Interview by the author, 30 April 2013, Belfast; Interview with Alliance Party MLA (c), Northern Ireland Assembly. Interview by the author, 5 April 2012, Belfast; Interview with David Ford, MLA, Northern Ireland Assembly and party leader, Alliance Party of

Northern Ireland. Interview by the author, 12 April 2013, Belfast; Interview with Alliance Party MLA (b), Northern Ireland Assembly, Interview by the author, 3 April 2012, Belfast.

19 Interview with David Ford, MLA, Northern Ireland Assembly and Party Leader, Alliance Party of Northern Ireland. Interview by the author, 12 April 2013, Belfast.

20 Interview with Alliance Party MLA (a), Northern Ireland Assembly. Interview by the author, 18 April 2013, Belfast.

21 Interview with Alliance Party MLA (d), Northern Ireland Assembly. Interview by the author, 4 April 2013, Belfast.

22 Interview with Alliance Party MLA (a), Northern Ireland Assembly. Interview by the author, 18 April 2013, Belfast.

23 Interview with David Ford, MLA, Northern Ireland Assembly and party leader, Alliance Party of Northern Ireland. Interview by the author, 12 April 2013, Belfast.

24 Interview with David Ford, MLA, Northern Ireland Assembly and party leader, Alliance Party of Northern Ireland. Interview by the author, 12 April 2013, Belfast.

25 Interview with David Ford, MLA, Northern Ireland Assembly and party leader, Alliance Party of Northern Ireland. Interview by the author, 12 April 2013, Belfast; Interview with Alliance Party MLA (f), Northern Ireland Assembly. Interview by the author, 28 October 2021, Belfast.

26 Interview with Alliance Party MLA (f), Northern Ireland Assembly. Interview by the author, 28 October 2021, Belfast.

27 Interview with Alliance Party MLA (f), Northern Ireland Assembly. Interview by the author, 28 October 2021, Belfast.

28 65 per cent of people in the 2021 poll believe the GFA remains the best way for governing Northern Ireland, compared to 14 per cent who do not (ARK 2021b).

29 58 per cent of respondents agree that key votes in the Northern Ireland Assembly should be passed by weighted majority, regardless of nationalist/unionist/other designation, while 38 per cent objected to the current petition of concern rules with only 19 per cent supporting them (Hayward et al 2022).

30 See for example McClements 2022a.

31 Interview with Alliance Party MLA (c), Northern Ireland Assembly. Interview by the author, 5 April 2012, Belfast.

32 Interview with reproductive rights activist and campaign leader (a). Interview by the author, 10 April 2018, Belfast; Interview with reproductive rights activist and campaign leader (b). Interview by the author and Timofey Agarin, 12 June 2018, Belfast.

33 Interview with Naomi Long, MLA and leader of Alliance Party of Northern Ireland. Interview by the author, 4 May 2018, Belfast.

34 Remarks by Connie Egan, Alliance Party MLA speaking at Galway International Arts Festival, 16 July 2022.

35 Interview with Alliance Party MLA (a), Northern Ireland Assembly. Interview by the author, 6 March 2018, Belfast.

36 Interview with civic politics and civil society activist and commentator, Northern Ireland. Interview by the author, 1 November 2021, Fermanagh.

37 Most notably the Analysing and Researching Ireland North and South (ARINS) project. Accessed 15 August 2024. https://www.ria.ie/research-programmes/arins/.

38 Interview with Alliance Party MLA (f), Northern Ireland Assembly. Interview by the author, 28 October 2021, Belfast.

39 Remarks by Connie Egan, Alliance Party MLA, speaking at Galway International Arts Festival, 16 July 2022; Interview with Alliance Party MLA (a), Northern Ireland Assembly. Interview by the author, 18 April 2013, Belfast; Interview with Naomi Long, MLA and leader of Alliance Party of Northern Ireland. Interview by the author, 4 May 2018, Belfast; Interview with Alliance Party MLA (f), Northern Ireland Assembly. Interview by the author, 28 October 2021, Belfast; Interview with Naomi Long, MLA and leader of Alliance Party of Northern Ireland. Interview by the author, 4 May 2018, Belfast; Interview with Alliance Party MLA (f), Northern Ireland Assembly. Interview by the author, 28 October 2021, Belfast.

40 Interview with Naomi Long, MLA and leader of Alliance Party of Northern Ireland. Interview by the author, 4 May 2018, Belfast.

41 Interview with Naomi Long, MLA and leader of Alliance Party of Northern Ireland. Interview by the author, 4 May 2018, Belfast; Interview with Alliance Party MLA (f), Northern Ireland Assembly. Interview by the author, 28 October 2021, Belfast.

42 Interview with Alliance Party MLA (f), Northern Ireland Assembly. Interview by the author, 28 October 2021, Belfast.

43 Interview with Alliance Party MLA (f), Northern Ireland Assembly. Interview by the author, 28 October 2021, Belfast.

44 The party's 'united community' policy has come in for criticism in media commentary for ignoring the colonial roots of the Northern Ireland conflict (Feeney 2024).

45 One longstanding member observed that the party's strategy since the 1990s, after it lost much of its support in Catholic majority areas during the 1980s following the polarizing effect of the hunger strikes, had been to concentrate its resources in those areas in the east where it had established an electoral base. Interview with Alliance Party former official. Interview by the author, 28 April 2015, Belfast.

46 Interview with David Ford, MLA, Northern Ireland Assembly and party leader, Alliance Party of Northern Ireland. Interview by the author, 12 April 2013, Belfast.

47 Interview with Alliance Party MLA (a), Northern Ireland Assembly. Interview by the author, 18 April 2013, Belfast.

Chapter Six

1 Internal Displacement Monitoring Centre. Bosnia and Herzegovina: Displacement associated with Conflict and Violence, Figure Analysis – GRID 2020 https://api.internal-displacement.org/sites/default/files/2020-04/GRID%20 2020%20-%20Conflict%20Figure%20Analysis%20-%20BOSNIA%20AND%20 HERZEGOVINA.pdf.

2 The General Framework Agreement for Peace in Bosnia and Herzegovina is also known as the Dayton Peace Agreement (DPA) and Dayton Accords. It will generally be referred to in the book as the Dayton Peace Agreement and abbreviated to DPA in accordance with its popular usage.

3 The General Framework Agreement for Peace in Bosnia and Herzegovina, 1995, Annex 4 www.osce.org/files/f/documents/e/0/126173.pdf.
4 Veto rights in FBiH were limited by the High Representative in 2022 in a reform designed to make the entity more functional (OHR 2022).
5 See also 'Census 2013' http://www.statistika.ba/?lang=en.
6 The General Framework Agreement for Peace in Bosnia and Herzegovina, 1995, Annex 4 www.osce.org/files/f/documents/e/0/126173.pdf.
7 The General Framework Agreement for Peace in Bosnia and Herzegovina, 1995, Annex 3 www.osce.org/files/f/documents/e/0/126173.pdf. According to Kennedy and Riga, this reflects a tension for US policymakers during Dayton negotiations between practical acceptance of 'brutally achieved' ethnically homogenous territory and an aspiration to offset this reality through human rights provisions (Kennedy and Riga 2013, 164, 166; Riga and Kennedy 2013).
8 Keil also characterizes it as an 'internationally administered' multinational federation (2013, 4).
9 Sejdic and Finci v Bosnia and Herzegovina (GC), no. 2799/06 and 34836/06, 22 December 2009, ECLI:CE:ECHR:2009:1222JUD002799606; Pilav v Bosnia and Herzegovina, no. 41939/07, 9 June 2016, ECLI:CE:ECHR:2016:0609JUD004193907; Zornić v Bosnia and Herzegovina, no. 3681/06, 15 July 2014, ECLI:CE:ECHR:2014:0715JUD000368106; https://www.ohr.int/hr-urges-limited-constitutional-reform-and-changes-to-the-election-law-to-strengthen-the-fundamental-principles-and-transparency-of-elections/. Accessed 25 July 2023.
10 The international community has also stood accused at times of reinforcing ethnic rule through its actions, including High Representative Christian Schmidt's controversial electoral reforms in October 2022 which were seen to bolster the position of the Croat party HDZ (Euronews 2022)
11 For more on the potential of Russia's invasion of Ukraine to destabilize Bosnia see Bajrović (2022).
12 For more on civic parties SK-SDP and SRSJ BiH in Bosnia 1989–91 see Alfredo Sasso's PhD thesis (Sasso 2015).
13 Bochsler's analysis of post-communist party systems finds Bosnia's party system to have by far the least linkage of all twenty countries in the study. His findings underline ethno-territorial divisions as a key cause of poor party system linkage, particularly when combined with electoral rules that do not incentivize parties that compete across all districts (Bochsler 2010, 818).
14 Interview with Naša Stranka senior representative (a). Interview by the author, 6 May 2014. Sarajevo.
15 Alliance of Liberals and Democrats for Europe. aldeparty.eu. Accessed 15 August 2024.
16 Interview with DF member of the House of Peoples of the Federation of Bosnia and Herzegovina (FBiH) (a). Interview by the author and Runa Neely, 30 May 2023, online via Zoom.
17 Conversation with Bosnian political scientist (a), 29 May 2023; Conversation with Bosnian political scientist (b), 31 May 2023.
18 See also: Case of Šlaku v. Bosnia and Herzegovina, 2016 (European Court of Human Rights 2016a).

19 Interview with SDP member of House of Representatives, Federation of Bosnia and Herzegovina (FBiH) (a). Interview by the author, 14 May 2014, Sarajevo. Interpretation by Inga Kotlo; Interview with SDP member of House of Representatives, Federation of Bosnia and Herzegovina (FBiH) (b). Interview by the author, 20 May 2014, Sarajevo. Interpretation by Inga Kotlo; Interview with SDP member of the House of Representatives of Bosnia and Herzegovina (b). Interview by the author, 14 May 2014, Sarajevo. Interpretation by Inga Kotlo.

20 Interview with SDP member of the House of Representatives of Bosnia and Herzegovina (a). Interview by the author, 23 May 2014, Sarajevo. Interpretation by Inga Kotlo; Interview with SDP member of House of Representatives, Federation of Bosnia and Herzegovina (FBiH) (c). Interview by the author, May 2014, Sarajevo. Interpretation by Inga Kotlo.

21 Interview with SDP member of House of Representatives, Federation of Bosnia and Herzegovina (FBiH) (a). Interview by the author, 14 May 2014, Sarajevo. Interpretation by Inga Kotlo; Interview with SDP member of the House of Representatives of Bosnia and Herzegovina (a). Interview by the author, 23 May 2014, Sarajevo. Interpretation by Inga Kotlo.

22 Interview with SDP member of House of Representatives, Federation of Bosnia and Herzegovina (FBiH) (a). Interview by the author, 14 May 2014, Sarajevo. Interpretation by Inga Kotlo; Interview with SDP member of the House of Representatives of Bosnia and Herzegovina (a). Interview by the author, 23 May 2014, Sarajevo. Interpretation by Inga Kotlo; Interview with SDP member of the House of Representatives of Bosnia and Herzegovina (b). Interview by the author, 14 May 2014, Sarajevo. Interpretation by Inga Kotlo.

23 Interview with SDP member of House of Representatives, Federation of Bosnia and Herzegovina (FBiH) (a). Interview by the author, 14 May 2014, Sarajevo. Interpretation by Inga Kotlo; Interview with SDP member of the House of Representatives of Bosnia and Herzegovina (a). Interview by the author, 23 May 2014, Sarajevo. Interpretation by Inga Kotlo; Interview with SDP member and former city representative. Interview by the author, June 2014, Sarajevo.

24 Interview with SDP member of the House of Representatives of Bosnia and Herzegovina (b). Interview by the author, 14 May 2014, Sarajevo. Interpretation by Inga Kotlo.

25 Interview with Naša Stranka senior representative (c). Interview by the author, 27 May 2014, online via Skype.

26 Interview with Naša Stranka senior official. Interview by the author, 19 May 2014, Sarajevo.

27 Interview with Democratic Front member (b), Interview by the author, 16 June 2014, Sarajevo; Interview with DF member (c), member of the Party Presidency and 2014 General election candidate. Interview by the author, 23 May 2014, Sarajevo.

28 Interview with Naša Stranka senior representative (b). Interview by the author, 6 May 2014. Sarajevo.

29 Interview with SDP member of House of Representatives, Federation of Bosnia and Herzegovina (FBiH) (c). Interview by the author, May 2014, Sarajevo. Interpretation by Inga Kotlo.

30 Interview with SDP member of the House of Peoples of Bosnia and Herzegovina (a). Interview by the author, 19 June 2014, Sarajevo; Interview with SDP member of House of Representatives, Federation of Bosnia and Herzegovina (FBiH) (c). Interview by the author, May 2014, Sarajevo. Interpretation by Inga Kotlo.
31 Interview with SDP member of the House of Representatives of Bosnia and Herzegovina (b). Interview by the author, 14 May 2014, Sarajevo. Interpretation by Inga Kotlo; Interview with SDP member and former city representative. Interview by the author, June 2014, Sarajevo.
32 Interview with Naša Stranka senior representative (a). Interview by the author, 6 May 2014. Sarajevo.
33 Interview with Naša Stranka senior representative (a). Interview by the author, 6 May 2014. Sarajevo; Interview with Naša Stranka senior representative (b). Interview by the author, 6 May 2014. Sarajevo; Interview with Naša Stranka senior official. Interview by the author, 19 May 2014, Sarajevo.
34 Interview with Naša Stranka senior representative (b). Interview by the author, 6 May 2014. Sarajevo.
35 Interview with Naša Stranka senior representative (b). Interview by the author, 6 May 2014. Sarajevo.
36 Focus group (a) conducted with language school associates, Sarajevo, 20 May 2014; Focus group (b) conducted with postgraduate student group, University of Sarajevo, Sarajevo, 27 May 2014; Focus group (c) conducted with undergraduate student group, University of Banja Luka, Banja Luka, 28 May 2014.
37 Interview with SDP member of the House of Peoples of Bosnia and Herzegovina (a). Interview by the author, 19 June 2014, Sarajevo; Interview with SDP member of House of Representatives, Federation of Bosnia and Herzegovina (FBiH) (a). Interview by the author, 14 May 2014, Sarajevo. Interpretation by Inga Kotlo; Interview with SDP member of the House of Representatives of Bosnia and Herzegovina (a). Interview by the author, 23 May 2014, Sarajevo. Interpretation by Inga Kotlo.
38 Interview with SDP member of House of Representatives, Federation of Bosnia and Herzegovina (FBiH) (a). Interview by the author, 14 May 2014, Sarajevo. Interpretation by Inga Kotlo; Interview with SDP member of the House of Representatives of Bosnia and Herzegovina (a). Interview by the author, 23 May 2014, Sarajevo. Interpretation by Inga Kotlo; Interview with Naša Stranka senior representative (b). Interview by the author, 6 May 2014. Sarajevo.
39 Interview with HDZ BiH city council representative (a). Interview by the author, 26 June 2014, Mostar.
40 Interview with SNSD member of RS Assembly. Interview by the author, June 2014, Banja Luka.
41 Interview with SDP member of House of Representatives, Federation of Bosnia and Herzegovina (FBiH) (a). Interview by the author, 14 May 2014, Sarajevo. Interpretation by Inga Kotlo.
42 Interview with DF member (c), member of the party presidency and 2014 general election candidate. Interview by the author, 23 May 2014, Sarajevo.
43 Interview with Naša Stranka senior representative (b). Interview by the author, 6 May 2014. Sarajevo.

44 Interview with Naša Stranka senior representative (b). Interview by the author, 6 May 2014. Sarajevo.

45 Interview with SDP member of the House of Peoples of Bosnia and Herzegovina (a). Interview by the author, 19 June 2014, Sarajevo; Interview with SDP member of House of Representatives, Federation of Bosnia and Herzegovina (FBiH) (c). Interview by the author, May 2014, Sarajevo. Interpretation by Inga Kotlo.

46 Interview with SDP member of the House of Peoples of Bosnia and Herzegovina (a). Interview by the author, 19 June 2014, Sarajevo.

47 Interview with SDP member and former city representative. Interview by the author, June 2014, Sarajevo. See Cooley for analysis of ethnic and civic campaigns surrounding the 2013 census in Bosnia, and comparison of the politics of the census in the consociational systems of Bosnia and Northern Ireland (2020).

48 Interview with Naša Stranka senior representative (b). Interview by the author, 6 May 2014. Sarajevo.

49 Interview with SDP member of the House of Representatives of Bosnia and Herzegovina (a). Interview by the author, 23 May 2014, Sarajevo. Interpretation by Inga Kotlo.

50 Interview with Naša Stranka senior representative (b). Interview by the author, 6 May 2014. Sarajevo.

51 Interview with Naša Stranka senior representative (d). Interview by the author, 26 May 2014, Sarajevo.

52 Focus group (c) conducted with undergraduate student group, University of Banja Luka, Banja Luka, 28 May 2014.

53 Focus group (c) conducted with undergraduate student group, University of Banja Luka, Banja Luka, 28 May 2014.

54 Interview with Naša Stranka senior representative (a). Interview by the author, 6 May 2014. Sarajevo; Interview with Naša Stranka cantonal representative. Interview by the author, Sarajevo, 23 May 2014; Interview with Naša Stranka senior representative (c). Interview by the author, 27 May 2014, online via Skype; Interview with Naša Stranka senior official. Interview by the author, 19 May 2014, Sarajevo.

55 Interview with Naša Stranka senior representative (a). Interview by the author, 6 May 2014. Sarajevo.

56 Interview with Naša Stranka senior official. Interview by the author, 19 May 2014, Sarajevo.

57 Interview with Naša Stranka senior representative (c). Interview by the author, 27 May 2014, online via Skype.

58 Interview with SDP member of the House of Peoples of Bosnia and Herzegovina (a). Interview by the author, 19 June 2014, Sarajevo; Interview with SDP member of House of Representatives, Federation of Bosnia and Herzegovina (FBiH (b). Interview by the author, 20 May 2014, Sarajevo. Interpretation by Inga Kotlo; Interview with SDP member of the House of Representatives of Bosnia and Herzegovina (b). Interview by the author, 14 May 2014, Sarajevo. Interpretation by Inga Kotlo.

59 Interview with SDP member of the House of Peoples of Bosnia and Herzegovina (a). Interview by the author, 19 June 2014, Sarajevo.

60 Interview with SDP member of the House of Representatives of Bosnia and Herzegovina (a). Interview by the author, 23 May 2014, Sarajevo. Interpretation by Inga

Kotlo; Interview with SDP member and former city representative. Interview by the author, June 2014, Sarajevo.

61 Interview with Democratic Front member (a). Interview by the author, 1 April 2014, Sarajevo.

62 Focus group (a) conducted with language school associates, Sarajevo, 20 May 2014; Focus group (b) conducted with postgraduate student group, University of Sarajevo, Sarajevo, 27 May 2014; Focus group (c) conducted with undergraduate student group, University of Banja Luka, Banja Luka, 28 May 2014.

63 Focus group (a) conducted with language school associates, Sarajevo, 20 May 2014.

64 Focus group (c) conducted with undergraduate student group, University of Banja Luka, Banja Luka, 28 May 2014.

65 Focus group (a) conducted with language school associates, Sarajevo, 20 May 2014; Focus group (b) conducted with postgraduate student group, University of Sarajevo, Sarajevo, 27 May 2014.

66 Focus group (a) conducted with language school associates, Sarajevo, 20 May 2014.

67 Interview with NGO representative (a). Interview with the author, March 2014, online via Skype.

68 Interview with SDP member of the House of Representatives of Bosnia and Herzegovina (a). Interview by the author, 23 May 2014, Sarajevo. Interpretation by Inga Kotlo; Interview with SDP member of the House of Representatives of Bosnia and Herzegovina (b). Interview by the author, 14 May 2014, Sarajevo. Interpretation by Inga Kotlo.

69 Interview with SDP member of the House of Representatives of Bosnia and Herzegovina (b). Interview by the author, 14 May 2014, Sarajevo. Interpretation by Inga Kotlo.

70 Interview with SDP member and former city representative. Interview by the author, June 2014, Sarajevo.

71 Focus group (a) conducted with language school associates, Sarajevo, 20 May 2014.

72 Interview with SDP member of House of Representatives, Federation of Bosnia and Herzegovina (FBiH) (a). Interview by the author, 14 May 2014, Sarajevo. Interpretation by Inga Kotlo.

73 Interview with Naša Stranka senior representative (d). Interview by the author, 26 May 2014, Sarajevo.

74 Interview with Naša Stranka senior representative (a). Interview by the author, 6 May 2014. Sarajevo.

75 Arijana Memić, a leader of the movement and sister of Dženan, stood for and secured election to the Sarajevo Canton Assembly in 2018 (Repovac Nikšić et al 2022, 150).

76 Bosnia-Herzegovina Protest Files. http://bhprotestfiles.wordpress.com/.

77 Interview with NGO representative (a). Interview with the author, March 2014, online via Skype.

78 Interview with HDZ BiH city council representative (a). Interview by the author, 26 June 2014, Mostar.

79 Interview with activist and organizer, Sarajevo plenum and protests (b). Interview by the author, Sarajevo, 1 April 2014; Interview with activist and organiser, Tuzla plenum and protests (a). Interview by the author, Tuzla, 10 May 2014.

80 Interview with activist (a) and activist (c), Mostar plenum and protests. Interview by the author, Mostar, 10 April 2014.
81 Interview with activist and organiser, Mostar plenum and protests (b). Interview by the author, 2 July 2014, Sarajevo.
82 Interview with activist and organiser, Mostar plenum and protests (b). Interview by the author, 2 July 2014, Sarajevo.
83 Interview with activist (a) and activist (c), Mostar plenum and protests. Interview by the author, Mostar, 10 April 2014.
84 Interview with activist and organizer, Sarajevo plenum and protests (c). Interview by the author, Sarajevo, 2 April 2014.

Chapter Seven

1 In the 2006 and 2010 general elections Komšić stood as a candidate for the SDP before leaving the party in 2012 to establish DF. In 2018 and 2022 elections he stood as a DF candidate.
2 Interview with SDP member of House of Representatives, Federation of Bosnia and Herzegovina (FBiH) (a). Interview by the author, 14 May 2014, Sarajevo. Interpretation by Inga Kotlo; Interview with SDP member of the House of Peoples of Bosnia and Herzegovina (a). Interview by the author, 19 June 2014, Sarajevo; Interview with SDP member of the House of Representatives of Bosnia and Herzegovina (b). Interview by the author, 14 May 2014, Sarajevo. Interpretation by Inga Kotlo.
3 Interview with SDP member of House of Representatives, Federation of Bosnia and Herzegovina (FBiH) (a). Interview by the author, 14 May 2014, Sarajevo. Interpretation by Inga Kotlo; Interview with SDP member of House of Representatives, Federation of Bosnia and Herzegovina (FBiH) (b). Interview by the author, 20 May 2014, Sarajevo. Interpretation by Inga Kotlo; Interview with SDP municipal councillor, Sarajevo Centre Municipality. Interview by the author, Sarajevo, 5 May 2014.
4 Observed in interview with SDP municipal representative, Sarajevo Centre Municipality. Interview by the author, Sarajevo, 5 May 2014.
5 Interview with SDP member of the House of Peoples of Bosnia and Herzegovina (a). Interview by the author, 19 June 2014, Sarajevo.
6 Interview with SDP member of House of Representatives, Federation of Bosnia and Herzegovina (FBiH) (a). Interview by the author, 14 May 2014, Sarajevo. Interpretation by Inga Kotlo; Interview with SDP member of House of Representatives, Federation of Bosnia and Herzegovina (FBiH) (b). Interview by the author, 20 May 2014, Sarajevo. Interpretation by Inga Kotlo.
7 Interview with SDP member of House of Representatives, Federation of Bosnia and Herzegovina (FBiH) (a). Interview by the author, 14 May 2014, Sarajevo. Interpretation by Inga Kotlo; Interview with SDP member of the House of Representatives of Bosnia and Herzegovina (b). Interview by the author, 14 May 2014, Sarajevo. Interpretation by Inga Kotlo.
8 Interview with DF member of the House of Representatives of the Federation of Bosnia and Herzegovina (FBiH) (a). Interview by the author and Runa Neely, 31 May 2023, Sarajevo; Interview with DF member of the House of Peoples of the

Federation of Bosnia and Herzegovina (FBiH) (a). Interview by the author and Runa Neely, 30 May 2023, online via Zoom; Conversation with Bosnian political scientist (a), 29 May 2023.

9 Interview with Naša Stranka senior representative (a). Interview by the author, 6 May 2014. Sarajevo.

10 Interview with Naša Stranka senior representative (a). Interview by the author, 6 May 2014. Sarajevo; Interview with Naša Stranka cantonal representative. Interview by the author, Sarajevo, 23 May 2014; Interview with Naša Stranka senior representative (b). Interview by the author, 6 May 2014. Sarajevo; Interview with Naša Stranka senior official. Interview by the author, 19 May 2014, Sarajevo.

11 Interview with Naša Stranka senior representative (a). Interview by the author, 6 May 2014. Sarajevo.

12 Interview with Naša Stranka cantonal representative. Interview by the author, Sarajevo, 23 May 2014.

13 Interview with Naša Stranka senior representative (a). Interview by the author, 6 May 2014. Sarajevo; Interview with Naša Stranka senior representative (b). Interview by the author, 6 May 2014. Sarajevo.

14 Interview with Naša Stranka senior representative (a). Interview by the author, 6 May 2014. Sarajevo; Interview with Naša Stranka senior official. Interview by the author, 19 May 2014, Sarajevo.

15 Interview with Naša Stranka senior official. Interview by the author, 19 May 2014, Sarajevo.

16 Interview with SDP member of the House of Peoples of Bosnia and Herzegovina (a). Interview by the author, 19 June 2014, Sarajevo; Interview with SDP member of House of Representatives, Federation of Bosnia and Herzegovina (FBiH) (b). Interview by the author, 20 May 2014, Sarajevo. Interpretation by Inga Kotlo; Interview with SDP member of the House of Representatives of Bosnia and Herzegovina (a). Interview by the author, 23 May 2014, Sarajevo. Interpretation by Inga Kotlo; Interview with SDP member of the House of Representatives of Bosnia and Herzegovina (b). Interview by the author, 14 May 2014, Sarajevo. Interpretation by Inga Kotlo.

17 Interview with SDP member of House of Representatives, Federation of Bosnia and Herzegovina (FBiH) (b). Interview by the author, 20 May 2014, Sarajevo. Interpretation by Inga Kotlo; Interview with DF member of the House of Peoples of the Federation of Bosnia and Herzegovina (FBiH) (a). Interview by the author and Runa Neely, 30 May 2023, online via Zoom; Interview with DF member of the House of Representatives of the Federation of Bosnia and Herzegovina (FBiH) (a). Interview by the author and Runa Neely, 31 May 2023, Sarajevo.

18 Interview with SDP member of House of Representatives, Federation of Bosnia and Herzegovina (FBiH) (b). Interview by the author, 20 May 2014, Sarajevo. Interpretation by Inga Kotlo; Interview with SDP member of the House of Representatives of Bosnia and Herzegovina (b). Interview by the author, 14 May 2014, Sarajevo. Interpretation by Inga Kotlo.

19 Interview with SDP member of House of Representatives, Federation of Bosnia and Herzegovina (FBiH) (c). Interview by the author, May 2014, Sarajevo. Interpretation by Inga Kotlo.

20 Interview with DF member of the House of Representatives of the Federation of Bosnia and Herzegovina (FBiH) (a). Interview by the author and Runa Neely, 31 May 2023, Sarajevo; Interview with DF member of the House of Peoples of the Federation of Bosnia and Herzegovina (FBiH) (a). Interview by the author and Runa Neely, 30 May 2023, online via Zoom.

21 Interview with SDP member and political commentator (a). Interview by the author, 17 June 2014, Sarajevo.

22 Interview with Naša Stranka senior representative (a). Interview by the author, 6 May 2014. Sarajevo; Interview with Naša Stranka cantonal representative. Interview by the author, Sarajevo, 23 May 2014; Interview with Naša Stranka senior representative (d). Interview by the author, 26 May 2014, Sarajevo; Interview with Naša Stranka senior official. Interview by the author, 19 May 2014, Sarajevo.

23 Interview with Naša Stranka senior official. Interview by the author, 19 May 2014, Sarajevo; Interview with Naša Stranka senior representative (b). Interview by the author, 6 May 2014. Sarajevo.

24 Interview with Predrag Kojović, Naša Stranka member of Canton Sarajevo and the House of Peoples, Federation of Bosnia and Herzegovina. Interview by the author, Sarajevo, 6 May 2014.

25 Interview with HDZ BiH city council representative (a). Interview by the author, 26 June 2014, Mostar.

26 Interview with HDZ BiH city council representative (a). Interview by the author, 26 June 2014, Mostar.

27 Focus group (a) conducted with language school associates, Sarajevo, 20 May 2014; Focus group (c) conducted with undergraduate student group, University of Banja Luka, Banja Luka, 28 May 2014.

28 Focus group (a) conducted with language school associates, Sarajevo, 20 May 2014.

29 Focus group (c) conducted with undergraduate student group, University of Banja Luka, Banja Luka, 28 May 2014.

30 Focus group (c) conducted with undergraduate student group, University of Banja Luka, Banja Luka, 28 May 2014.

31 Interview with SDP member of House of Representatives, Federation of Bosnia and Herzegovina (FBiH) (a). Interview by the author, 14 May 2014, Sarajevo. Interpretation by Inga Kotlo; Interview with SDP member of the House of Representatives of Bosnia and Herzegovina (a). Interview by the author, 23 May 2014, Sarajevo. Interpretation by Inga Kotlo.

32 Interview with SDP member of the House of Representatives of Bosnia and Herzegovina (a). Interview by the author, 23 May 2014, Sarajevo. Interpretation by Inga Kotlo.

33 Interview with SDP member of House of Representatives, Federation of Bosnia and Herzegovina (FBiH) (a). Interview by the author, 14 May 2014, Sarajevo. Interpretation by Inga Kotlo.

34 Interview with SDP member of House of Representatives, Federation of Bosnia and Herzegovina (FBiH) (a). Interview by the author, 14 May 2014, Sarajevo. Interpretation by Inga Kotlo.

35 Interview with SDP member and former city representative. Interview by the author, June 2014, Sarajevo.

36 Interview with Democratic Front member (a). Interview by the author, 1 April 2014, Sarajevo.

37 This 'legitimacy problem' is also experienced by Naša Stranka at lower levels of government. One representative describes the animosity shown by the party's ethnic rivals towards its opposition to the ethnic representation system, as this position effectively threatens their interests. He recalls experiencing hostility from his Croat colleagues in the House of Peoples of the FBiH in 2011, surrounding a potential vote to remove then FBiH President Živko Budimir, a Croat representative from a small Croat party, in which it was implied he should not be involved as a non-Croat representative. Interview with Naša Stranka senior representative (b). Interview by the author, 6 May 2014. Sarajevo.

38 Interview with SDP member of the House of Representatives of Bosnia and Herzegovina (a). Interview by the author, 23 May 2014, Sarajevo. Interpretation by Inga Kotlo; Interview with SDP member of the House of Representatives of Bosnia and Herzegovina (b). Interview by the author, 14 May 2014, Sarajevo. Interpretation by Inga Kotlo.

39 Interview with SDP member of the House of Representatives of Bosnia and Herzegovina (b). Interview by the author, 14 May 2014, Sarajevo. Interpretation by Inga Kotlo.

40 Interview with SDP member of House of Representatives, Federation of Bosnia and Herzegovina (FBiH) (b). Interview by the author, 20 May 2014, Sarajevo. Interpretation by Inga Kotlo.

41 Interview with SDP member of House of Representatives, Federation of Bosnia and Herzegovina (FBiH) (a). Interview by the author, 14 May 2014, Sarajevo. Interpretation by Inga Kotlo.

42 Interview with SDP member of House of Representatives, Federation of Bosnia and Herzegovina (FBiH) (b). Interview by the author, 20 May 2014, Sarajevo. Interpretation by Inga Kotlo; Interview with SDP member of House of Representatives, Federation of Bosnia and Herzegovina (FBiH) (c). Interview by the author, May 2014, Sarajevo. Interpretation by Inga Kotlo.

43 Interview with SDP member of House of Representatives, Federation of Bosnia and Herzegovina (FBiH) (a). Interview by the author, 14 May 2014, Sarajevo. Interpretation by Inga Kotlo; Interview with SDP member of House of Representatives, Federation of Bosnia and Herzegovina (FBiH) (b). Interview by the author, 20 May 2014, Sarajevo. Interpretation by Inga Kotlo; Interview with SDP member of House of Representatives, Federation of Bosnia and Herzegovina (FBiH) (c). Interview by the author, May 2014, Sarajevo. Interpretation by Inga Kotlo; Interview with SDP member of the House of Representatives of Bosnia and Herzegovina (a). Interview by the author, 23 May 2014, Sarajevo. Interpretation by Inga Kotlo; Interview with SDP member of the House of Representatives of Bosnia and Herzegovina (b). Interview by the author, 14 May 2014, Sarajevo. Interpretation by Inga Kotlo.

44 Interview with NGO representative, International democratization NGO. Interview by the author, Banja Luka, 28 May 2014.

45 Interview with Naša Stranka senior representative (a). Interview by the author, 6 May 2014. Sarajevo; Interview with Naša Stranka senior official. Interview by the author, 19 May 2014, Sarajevo.

46 Interview with Naša Stranka senior official. Interview by the author, 19 May 2014, Sarajevo.

47 Interview with Naša Stranka senior representative (a). Interview by the author, 6 May 2014. Sarajevo; Interview with Naša Stranka senior official. Interview by the author, 19 May 2014, Sarajevo.

48 Interview with Naša Stranka senior representative (c). Interview by the author, 27 May 2014, online via Skype; Interview with Naša Stranka senior official. Interview by the author, 19 May 2014, Sarajevo.

49 Interview with Naša Stranka senior representative (a). Interview by the author, 6 May 2014. Sarajevo.

50 Interview with Naša Stranka senior representative (b). Interview by the author, 6 May 2014. Sarajevo.

51 Interview with Naša Stranka senior representative (b). Interview by the author, 6 May 2014. Sarajevo; Interview with Naša Stranka senior representative (a). Interview by the author, 6 May 2014. Sarajevo; Interview with Naša Stranka senior representative (d). Interview by the author, 26 May 2014, Sarajevo; Interview with Naša Stranka senior official. Interview by the author, 19 May 2014, Sarajevo.

52 Interview with Naša Stranka senior official. Interview by the author, 19 May 2014, Sarajevo.

53 'Census 2013,' http://www.statistika.ba/?lang=en.

Chapter Eight

1 Interview with LGBTQ+ rights organization representative (b). Interview by the author, 4 May 2018, Belfast; Interview with LGBTQ+ rights organization representative (c). Interview by the author, 18 November 2021, online via Zoom.

2 See also Breen 2018.

Conclusion

1 For recent and older debates about deliberative democracy in divided societies see: O'Flynn 2006; Pierson and Thomson 2018; Suitor 2021.

2 Indeed, racist and Islamophobic 'anti-immigration' protests in Belfast in August 2024 brought together an unlikely alliance between British loyalist protestors from the north and Irish republican protestors from the south (*BBC News* 2024b).

References

Abazović, D. 2007/08. 'Rethinking Ethnicity, Religion and Politics: The Case of Bosnia and Herzegovina'. *European Yearbook of Minority Issues* 7.

– 2014. 'Reconciliation, Ethnopolitics and Religion in Bosnia-Herzegovina'. In *Post-Yugoslavia: New Cultural and Political Perspectives*, edited by D. Abazović and M. Velikonja, 35–56. Hampshire and New York: Routledge.

Abu-Laban, Y., A.G. Gagnon, and A. Tremblay, eds. 2023. *Assessing Multiculturalism in Global Comparative Perspective: A New Politics of Diversity for the 21st Century?* New York: Routledge.

Agarin, T., and H. Jarrett. 2022. 'Cross-Segmental Parties in Consociational Systems: Downplaying Prowess to Access Power in Northern Ireland'. *The British Journal of Politics and International Relations* 24, no. 4: 723–40.

Agarin, T., A. McCulloch, and C. Murtagh. 2018. 'Others in Deeply Divided Societies: A Research Agenda'. *Nationalism and Ethnic Politics* 24, no. 3: 299–310.

Ahmetašević, N. 2024. *The Media as a Tool of International Intervention: House of Cards.* Oxon and New York: Routledge.

Aitken, R. 2007. 'Cementing Divisions? An Assessment of the Impact of International Interventions and Peace-Building Policies on Ethnic Identities and Divisions'. *Policy Studies* 28, no. 3: 247–67.

– 2010. 'Consociational Peace Processes and Ethnicity: The Implications of the Dayton and Good Friday Agreements for Ethnic Identities and Politics in Bosnia-Herzegovina and Northern Ireland'. In *The Challenges of Ethno-nationalism: Case Studies in Identity Politics*, edited by A. Guelke, 232–54. Basingstoke: Palgrave Macmillan.

Alber, E. 2021. 'South Tyrol's Model of Conflict Resolution: Territorial Autonomy and Power-Sharing'. In *Power-Sharing in Europe: Past Practice, Present Cases, and Future Directions*, edited by S. Keil and A. McCulloch, 171–200. Cham: Springer International Publishing.

Alliance Party of Northern Ireland. 1970a. 'Alliance Party of Northern Ireland: Declaration of Intent – a New Political Charter, 21 April 1970'. Belfast. Accessed at Linen Hall Library.

– 1970b. 'Guideline Statement for all news media on the formation of The Alliance Party of Northern Ireland'. Belfast. Accessed at Linen Hall Library.

- 1970c. 'Back to Work; An Open Letter to So Called Moderates: A Commentary Following the Westminster General Election in Northern Ireland'. Belfast. Accessed at Linen Hall Library.
- 1972a. 'The Policies of Alliance'. Belfast. Accessed at Linen Hall Library.
- 1972b. 'What is Alliance?' Belfast. Accessed at Linen Hall Library.
- 1973. 'The Manifesto of the Alliance Party of Northern Ireland – Regional Assembly Election, June 1973'. Belfast. Accessed at Linen Hall Library.
- 1988. 'Governing with Consent'. Belfast. Accessed at Linen Hall Library.
- 1997a. 'Multi-Party Talks: Alliance Analysis of the Problem (Relevant to all three Strands)'. 6 October 1997. Belfast. http://allianceparty.org/document/peace-process-papers/1997-multi-party-talks#document.
- 1997b. 'Multi-Party Talks: A New System of Government for Northern Ireland (Relevant to Strand One)'. 27 October 1997. Belfast. http://allianceparty.org/document/peace-process-papers/1997-multi-party-talks#document.
- 1997c. 'Multi-Party Talks: A New System of North-South Relations (Relevant to Strands Two and Three)'. 27 October 1997. Belfast. http://allianceparty.org/document/peace-process-papers/1997-multi-party-talks#document.
- 1998. 'Election Manifesto, Northern Ireland Assembly Election, 1998'. Belfast.
- 2003. 'Election Manifesto, Northern Ireland Assembly Election, 2003'. Belfast.
- 2004. 'Agenda for Democracy: Alliance Party Proposals for the Review of the Agreement'. 7 January 2004. Belfast. http://www.allianceparty.org/showpeacedoc.asp?id=4.
- 2007. 'Election Manifesto, Northern Ireland Assembly Election, 2007'. Belfast.
- 2011. 'Election Manifesto, Northern Ireland Assembly Election, 2011'. Belfast.
- 2013. 'For Everyone: The Alliance Party Blueprint for an Executive Strategy to Build a Shared and Better Future'. Belfast.
- 2015. 'Election Manifesto, UK General Election, 2015'. Belfast.
- 2016. 'Election Manifesto, Northern Ireland Assembly Election, 2016'. Belfast.
- 2017a. 'Election Manifesto, Northern Ireland Assembly Election, 2017'. Belfast.
- 2017b. 'The Case for Special Status: How to Mitigate the Impact of Brexit on Northern Ireland'. https://d3n8a8pro7vhmx.cloudfront.net/allianceparty/pages/3583/attachments/original/1537968484/how-to-mitigate-the-impact-of-brexit-on-northern-ireland.pdf?1537968484.
- 2019. 'Election Manifesto, General Election, 2019'. Belfast.
- 2022. 'Sharing Power to Build a Shared Future'. https://assets.nationbuilder.com/allianceparty/pages/7501/attachments/original/1656012825/Sharing_Power_to_Build_A_Shared_Future.pdf?1656012825.

Anderson, B. 1983. *Imagined Communities*. London: Verso.

Anderson, P. 2021. 'A Consociational Compromise? Constitutional Evolution in Spain and Catalonia'. In *Power-Sharing in Europe: Past Practice, Present Cases, and Future Directions*, edited by S. Keil and A. McCulloch, 201–26. Cham: Springer International Publishing.

Anthias, F., and N. Yuval-Davis. 1983. 'Contextualizing Feminism – Gender, Ethnic and Class Divisions'. *Feminist Review* 15 no. 1: 62–75.

ARK. 1998a. 'Do you regard yourself as belonging to any particular religion?'. *Northern Ireland Life & Times Survey*. https://www.ark.ac.uk/nilt/1998/Background/RELIGION.html.

– 1998b. 'The 1998 Referendums'. https://www.ark.ac.uk/elections/fref98.htm.
– 1999. 'Generally speaking, do you think of yourself as a unionist, a nationalist or neither?'. *Northern Ireland Life & Times Survey.* https://www.ark.ac.uk/nilt/1999/Political_Attitudes/UNINATID.html.
– 2015. 'Generally speaking, do you think of yourself as a unionist, a nationalist or neither?'. *Northern Ireland Life & Times Survey.* https://www.ark.ac.uk/nilt/2015/Political_Attitudes/UNINATID.html.
– 2018. 'Generally speaking, do you think of yourself as a unionist, a nationalist or neither?'. *Northern Ireland Life & Times Survey.* https://www.ark.ac.uk/nilt/2018/Political_Attitudes/UNINATID.html.
– 2019. 'The 2019 Local Government Elections in Northern Ireland'. https://www.ark.ac.uk/elections/flg19.htm.
– 2020. 'Generally speaking, do you think of yourself as a unionist, a nationalist or neither?'. *Northern Ireland Life & Times Survey.* https://www.ark.ac.uk/nilt/2020/Political_Attitudes/UNINATID.html.
– 2021a. 'Political Attitudes'. *Northern Ireland Life & Times Survey.* https://www.ark.ac.uk/nilt/2021/Political_Attitudes/.
– 2021b. 'There are a number of different opinions on the Good Friday or Belfast Agreement which was signed in 1998. Which one of these statements is closest to your view?'. *Northern Ireland Life & Times Survey.* https://www.ark.ac.uk/nilt/2021/Political_Attitudes/VIEWGFA3.html.
– 2022a. 'Do you regard yourself as belonging to any particular religion? If yes, which?'. *Northern Ireland Life & Times Survey.* https://www.ark.ac.uk/nilt/2022/Background/RELIGION.html.
– 2022b. Generally speaking, do you think of yourself as a unionist, a nationalist or neither?'. *Northern Ireland Life & Times Survey* https://www.ark.ac.uk/nilt/2022/Political_Attitudes/UNINATID.html
– 2022c. 'Northern Ireland Assembly Elections 2022'. https://www.ark.ac.uk/elections/fa22.htm.
– 2023a. 'And if you were deciding where to send your children to school, would you prefer a school with children of only your own religion, or a mixed-religion school?'. *Northern Ireland Life & Times Survey.* https://www.ark.ac.uk/nilt/2023/Community_Relations/OWNMXSCH.html.
– 2023b. 'Generally speaking, do you think of yourself as a unionist, a nationalist or neither?'. *Northern Ireland Life & Times Survey.* https://www.ark.ac.uk/nilt/2023/Political_Attitudes/UNINATID.html
– 2023c. 'Political Party Support'. *Northern Ireland Life & Times Survey.* https://www.ark.ac.uk/nilt/2023/Political_Attitudes/POLPART2.html.
Armakolas, I. 2011. 'The "Paradox" of Tuzla City: Explaining Non-Nationalist Local Politics during the Bosnian War'. *Europe–Asia Studies* 63 (2): 229–61.
Armakolas, I., and M. Maksimovic. 2013. '"Babylution": A Civic Awakening in Bosnia and Herzegovina?'. Hellenic Foundation for European and Foreign Policy, South East Europe Project, Working Paper 34. Athens: Hellenic Foundation for European and Foreign Policy.
Arsenijević, D. 2014. 'Introduction'. In *Unbribable Bosnia and Herzegovina: The Fight for the Commons*, edited by D. Arsenijević, 7–10. Baden: Nomos.

Bacchi, C., and M. Rönnblom. 2014. 'Feminist Discursive Institutionalism – A Post-structural Alternative'. *NORA – Nordic Journal of Feminist and Gender Research* 22, no. 3: 170–86.
Bahtić-Kunrath, B. 2011. 'Of Veto Players and Entity-Voting: Institutional Gridlock in the Bosnian Reform Process'. *Nationalities Papers* 39, no. 6: 899–923.
Bain, M. 2022. 'Integrated Education Bill Explained'. *The Belfast Telegraph*, 9 March 2022. https://www.belfasttelegraph.co.uk/news/education/integrated-education-bill-explained-41427556.html.
Bajrovic, R. 2022. 'Securing and Protecting Bosnia Amidst Russia's Invasion of Ukraine'. Foreign Policy Research Institute. United States of America. https://policycommons.net/artifacts/2293644/securing-and-protecting-bosnia-amidst-russias-invasion-of-ukraine/3053920/.
Bakan, A.B., and Y. Abu-Laban. 2017. 'Intersectionality and the United Nations World Conference Against Racism'. *Atlantis* 38, no. 1: 220–35.
Balkanist. 2014. 'Protests in Bosnia and Herzegovina: Live Blog and Updates', 9 February 2014. http://balkanist.net/protests-in-bosnia-and-herzegovina-live-blogs-and-updates/.
Bardi, L., and Mair, P. 2008. 'The Parameters of Party Systems'. *Party Politics* 14, no. 2: 147–66.
Bartle, J. 2003. 'Measuring Party Identification: An Exploratory Study with Focus Groups'. *Electoral Studies* 22: 217–37.
Bassuener, K. 'How Bosnia's Protest Movement Can Become Truly Transformative'. *Balkan Insight*, 25 February 2014. http://www.balkaninsight.com/en/blog/how-bosnia-s-protest-movement-can-become-truly-transformative.
Basta, K. 2016. 'The Symbolic Power of Formal Rules in Bosnia and Herzegovina'. *Slavic Review* 75, no. 4: 944–69.
– 2021. *The Symbolic State: Minority Recognition, Majority Backlash, and Secession in Multinational Countries*. Montreal and Kingston: McGill-Queen's University Press.
BBC News. 2019. 'Election 2019: Northern Ireland Results'. https://www.bbc.co.uk/news/election/2019/results/northern_ireland.
– 2020. 'Timeline: Renewable Heat Incentive Scandal', 23 October 2019. https://www.bbc.com/news/uk-northern-ireland-38301428.
– 2023. 'Northern Ireland Local Election Results 2023'. https://www.bbc.com/news/election/2023/northern-ireland/results.
– 2024. 'Northern Ireland Election 2024 Results'. https://www.bbc.com/news/election/2024/uk/regions/N92000002.
Belfast Interface Project. 2017. 'Interfaces Map and Database'. https://www.belfastinterf aceproject.org/interfaces-map.
Bell, C. 2015. *Unsettling Bargains? Power-sharing and the Inclusion of Women in Peace Negotiations*. Political Settlements Research Programme, University of Edinburgh.
Belloni, R. 2004. 'Peacebuilding and Consociational Electoral Engineering in Bosnia and Herzegovina'. *International Peacekeeping* 11: 334–53.
– 2007. *State Building and International Intervention in Bosnia*. Oxon and New York: Routledge.

– 2009. 'Bosnia: Dayton is Dead! Long Live Dayton!' *Nationalism and Ethnic Politics* 15: 355–75.

Benderly, J. 1997. 'Rape, Feminism and Nationalism in the War in Yugoslav Successor States'. In *Feminist Nationalism,* edited by L.A. West, 59–72. New York: Routledge.

Bew, P., P. Gibbon, and H. Patterson. 1995. *Northern Ireland 1921–1996: Political Forces and Social Classes.* London: Serif.

Bieber, F. 2006. *Post-War Bosnia: Ethnicity, Inequality and Public Sector Governance.* Basingstoke: Palgrave Macmillan.

– 2013. 'The Balkans: The Promotion of Power Sharing by Outsiders'. In *Power Sharing in Deeply Divided Places,* edited by J. McEvoy and B. O'Leary, 312–26. Philadelphia: University of Pennsylvania Press.

– 2018. 'The Rise (and Fall) of Balkan Stabilitocracies'. *Horizons: Journal of International Relations and Sustainable Development* 10: 176–85.

Bieber, F., and S. Keil. 2009. 'Power-sharing Revisited: Lessons Learned in the Balkans?' *Review of Central and Eastern European Law* 34: 337–60.

Bochsler, D. 2010. 'The Nationalization of Post-Communist Party Systems'. *Europe-Asia Studies* 62: 807–27.

Bogaards, M. 2013. 'Ethnic Party Bans and Institutional Engineering in Nigeria'. In *Ethnic Bans in Africa,* edited by M. Bogaards, M. Basedau, and C. Hartmann, 132–51. Abingdon and New York: Routledge.

– 2014. *Democracy and Social Peace in Divided Societies: Exploring Consociational Parties.* Basingstoke: Palgrave Macmillan.

– 2019. 'Formal and Informal Consociational Institutions: A Comparison of the National Pact and the Taif Agreement in Lebanon'. *Nationalism and Ethnic Politics* 25, no. 1: 27–42.

Bogaards, M., M. Basedau, and C. Hartmann. 2013. 'Ethnic Party Bans in Africa: An Introduction'. In *Ethnic Bans in Africa,* edited by M. Bogaards, M. Basedau, and C. Hartmann, 1–19. Abingdon and New York: Routledge.

Bose, S. 2002. *Bosnia after Dayton: Nationalist Partition and International Intervention.* London: Hurst & Company.

Bougarel, X., E. Helms, and G. Duijzings. 2007. 'Introduction'. In *The New Bosnian Mosaic: Identities, Memories and Moral Claims in a Post-War Society,* edited by X. Bougarel, E. Helms, and G. Duijzings, 1–37. Aldershot: Ashgate.

Breen, M.G. 2018. *The Road to Federalism in Nepal, Myanmar and Sri Lanka: Finding the Middle Ground.* Oxon: Routledge.

– 2022. 'Federal and Political Party Reforms in Asia: Is There a New Model of Federal Democracy Emerging in Ethnically Diverse Countries in Asia?'. *Government and Opposition* 57: 296–317.

Brubaker, R. 2002. 'Ethnicity Without Groups'. *European Journal of Sociology* 43, no. 2: 163–89.

– 2004. *Ethnicity Without Groups.* Cambridge: Harvard University Press.

Bryan, D. 2015. 'Parades, Flags, Carnivals, and Riots: Public Space, Contestation, and Transformation in Northern Ireland'. *Peace and Conflict: Journal of Peace Psychology* 21, no. 4: 565–73.

Bryan, D., and G. Gillespie. 2021. 'More Shared and More Divided: Northern Ireland'. In *Routledge Handbook of Irish Studies*, edited by R. Fox, M. Cronin, and B. Ó Conchubhair. Abingdon: Routledge.

Bryman, A. 2008. *Social Research Methods*. Oxford: Oxford University Press.

Busuladžić, E. 2014. 'Why?' In *Unbribable Bosnia and Herzegovina: The Fight for the Commons*, edited by D. Arsenijević, 11–26. Baden: Nomos.

Byrne, S. 2014. 'Troubled Engagement in Ethnicized Conflict: Negotiating Difference Among Feminist Activists in Israel/Palestine and Northern Ireland'. *International Feminist Journal of Politics* 16, no. 1: 106–26.

– 2020. 'Feminist Reflections on Discourses of (Power) + (Sharing) in Power-Sharing Theory'. *International Political Science Review* 41, no. 1: 58–72.

Byrne, S., and A. McCulloch. 2012. 'Gender, Representation and Power-Sharing in Post-Conflict Institutions'. *International Peacekeeping* 19, no. 5: 565–80.

– 2017. 'Gendering Power-Sharing'. In *Power-Sharing: Empirical and Normative Challenges*, edited by A. McCulloch and J. McGarry, 250–67. London and New York: Routledge.

CAIN. 2007. 'Fact Sheet on the Conflict in and about Northern Ireland'. 21 June 2007. https://cain.ulster.ac.uk/victims/docs/group/htr/day_of_reflection/htr_0607c.pdf.

Cammett, M., D. Kruszewska-Eduardo, C. Parreira, and S. Atallah. 2022. 'Coethnicity Beyond Clientelism: Insights from an Experimental Study of Political Behavior in Lebanon'. *Politics and Religion* 15: 417–38.

Central Election Commission Bosnia and Herzegovina. 2010. 'Confirmed Results – General Election 2010'. https://www.izbori.ba/Default.aspx?CategoryID=258&Lang=3.

– 2015. 'Verified Election Results'. Accessed 29 July 2015. http://www.izbori.ba/Default.aspx?CategoryID=48&Lang=3&Mod=0.

Chandra, K. 2004. *Why Ethnic Parties Succeed: Patronage and Ethnic Head Counts in India*. New York: Cambridge University Press.

– 2006. 'What is Ethnic Identity and Does it Matter?' *Annual Review of Political Science* 9: 397–424.

– 2011. 'What is an Ethnic Party?' *Party Politics* 17, no. 2: 151–69.

Chappell, L. 2014. '"New", "Old", and "Nested" Institutions and Gender Justice Outcomes: A View from the International Criminal Court'. *Politics & Gender* 10: 572–94.

Choudhry, S. 2008. 'Bridging Comparative Politics and Comparative Constitutional Law: Constitutional Design in Divided Societies'. In *Constitutional Design in Divided Societies: Integration or Accommodation?*, edited by S. Choudhry, 3–40. Oxford: Oxford University Press.

Clarke, V., and F. McClements. 2020. 'COVID-19: DUP veto of two-week extension to restrictions "was political perversion"'. *The Irish Times*, 13 November 2020. https://www.irishtimes.com/news/politics/covid-19-dup-veto-of-two-week-extension-to-restrictions-was-political-perversion-1.4408480.

Coakley, J. 2008. 'Ethnic Competition and the Logic of Party System Transformation'. *European Journal of Political Research* 47: 766–93.

– 2009a. *Ethnic Conflict Resolution: Routes Towards Settlement. Nationalism and Ethnic Politics* 15, no. 3: 462–83.
– 2009b. 'Implementing consociation in Northern Ireland'. In *Consociational Theory: McGarry and O'Leary and the Northern Ireland Conflict*, edited by R. Taylor. Oxon: Routledge.
– 2021. 'Is a Middle Force Emerging in Northern Ireland?'. *Irish Political Studies* 36, no. 3: 1–23.
Cochrane, F. 1999. 'The Past in the Present'. In *Politics in Northern Ireland*, edited by P. Mitchell and R. Wilford. Boulder: Westview Press.
Cockburn, C. 1998. *The Space Between Us: Negotiating Gender and National Identities in Conflict*. London: Zed Books.
Cohn, C. 2013. 'Women and Wars: Toward a Conceptual Framework'. In *Women and Wars*, edited by C. Cohn, 1–35. Cambridge: Polity Press.
Collins, P.H. 1998. 'The Tie that Binds: Race, Gender and US Violence'. *Ethnic and Racial Studies* 21, no. 5: 917–38.
– 2017. 'On Violence, Intersectionality and Transversal Politics'. *Ethnic and Racial Studies* 40, no. 9: 1460–73.
Collins, P.H., and S. Bilge. 2020. *Intersectionality*. 2nd ed. Cambridge: Polity.
Connolly, M. 2016. 'Gay blood donation: Lifetime ban in NI on gay men donating blood lifted'. *BBC News*, 1 September 2016. https://www.bbc.com/news/uk-northern-ireland-37235281.
Cooley, L. 2020. 'Consociationalism and the Politics of the Census in Bosnia and Herzegovina and Northern Ireland'. *Political Geography* 82, no. 2.
Council of Europe. 2006. 'Constitutional Reform in Bosnia and Herzegovina'. Parliamentary Assembly, Council of Europe, 27 June 2006. http://assembly.coe.int/ASP/Doc/XrefViewHTML.asp?FileId=11406&Language=en.
Cox, M. 2003. 'Building Democracy from the Outside: The Dayton Agreement in Bosnia and Herzegovina'. In *Can Democracy be Designed? The Politics of Institutional Choice in Conflict-Torn Societies*, edited by S. Bastian and R. Luckham, 253–76. New York: Zed Books.
Crenshaw, K. 1989. 'Demarginalizing the Intersection of Race and Sex: A Black Feminist Critique of Antidiscrimination Doctrine, Feminist Theory and Antiracist Politics'. *University of Chicago Legal Forum*, 139–68.
– 1991. 'Mapping the Margins: Intersectionality, Identity Politics, and Violence against Women of Color'. *Stanford Law Review* 43: 1241–99.
Cromie, C. 2015. 'Gay marriage now has overwhelming support in Northern Ireland – Poll'. *The Belfast Telegraph*, 6 July 2015. https://www.belfasttelegraph.co.uk/news/northern-ireland/gay-marriage-now-has-overwhelming-support-in-northern-ireland-poll-31355428.html.
Cushnahan, J. 1979. 'The History and Development of the Alliance Party: A Centre Party of Catholics and Protestants in Northern Ireland'. Text of a lecture given by Alliance Party General Secretary John Cushnahan at the John F. Kennedy School of Government, Harvard University, USA, April 1979. Belfast: Alliance Party of Northern Ireland. Accessed at Linen Hall Library.
Dabiri, E. 2021. *What White People Can Do Next: From Allyship to Coalition*. Dublin: Penguin.

Deets, S. 2015. 'Networks and Communal Autonomy as Practice: Health, Education, and Social Welfare in Lebanon'. *Ethnopolitics* 14, no. 4: 329–53.
– 2018. 'Consociationalism, Clientelism, and Local Politics in Beirut: Between Civic and Sectarian Identities'. *Nationalism and Ethnic Politics* 24, no. 2: 133–57.
Deets, S., and J. Skulte-Ouaiss. 2021. 'Breaking into a Consociational System: Civic Parties in Lebanon's 2018 Parliamentary Election'. *Ethnopolitics* 20, no. 2: 157–85.
Department of Education Northern Ireland. 'Integrated Schools'. 15 August 2024. https://www.education-ni.gov.uk/articles/integrated-schools#:~:text=About%20integrated%20schools,Post%20Primary%20and%202%20Nursery.
Deschouwer, K. 1999. 'From Consociation to Federation: How the Belgain Parties Won'. In *Party Elites in Divided Societies: Political Parties in Consociational Democracy*, edited by K.R. Luther and K. Deschouwer, 73–107. London: Routledge.
Dixon, P. 2001. *Northern Ireland: Politics of War and Peace*. London: Palgrave Macmillan.
– 2011. 'The Politics of Conflict: A Constructivist Critique of Consociational and Civil Society Theories'. *Nations and Nationalism* 18, no. 1: 1–24.
Dobrowolsky, A. 2003. 'Shifting States: Women's Constitutional Organising Across Time and Space'. In *Women's Movements Facing the Reconfigured State*, edited by L.A. Banaszak, K. Beckwith, and D. Rucht, 114–40. Cambridge: Cambridge University Press.
Drapeau-Bisson, M. 2020. 'Beyond Green and Orange: Alliance for Choice – Derry's Mobilisation for the Decriminalisation of Abortion'. *Irish Political Studies* 35, no. 1: 90–114.
Džankić, J. 2015. 'The Politics of Inclusion and Exclusion: Citizenship and Voting Rights in Bosnia and Herzegovina'. *International Peacekeeping* 22, no. 5: 526–44.
– 2018. 'Capturing Contested States: Structural Mechanisms of Power Reproduction in Bosnia and Herzegovina, Macedonia and Montenegro'. *Southeastern Europe* 42, no. 1: 83–106.
Eggins, B. 2015. *History & Hope: The Alliance Party of Northern Ireland*. Stroud: The History Press.
Elischer, S. 2013. *Political Parties in Africa: Ethnicity and Party Formation*. Cambridge: Cambridge University Press.
Emerson, N. 2022. 'Ground is shifting on integrated education in the North'. *The Irish Times*, 24 February 2022. https://www.irishtimes.com/opinion/newton-emerson-ground-is-shifting-on-integrated-education-in-the-north-1.4810241.
Enloe, C. 2014. *Bananas, Beaches and Bases: Making Feminist Sense of International Politics*. 2nd ed. Berkeley: University of California Press.
Erk, J., and L. Anderson. 2009. 'The Paradox of Federalism: Does Self Rule Accommodate or Exacerbate Ethnic Divisions?' *Regional & Federal Studies* 19, no. 2: 191–202.
Euronews. 2022. 'Bosnia's peace envoy changed laws mid-election. But what does it mean?', 7 October 2022. https://www.euronews.com/my-europe/2022/10/07/bosnias-peace-envoy-changed-laws-mid-election-but-what-does-it-mean.
European Commission. 2014. 'Bosnia and Herzegovina Progress Report, October 2014'. https://ec.europa.eu/neighbourhood-enlargement/sites/near/files/pdf/key_documents/2014/20141008-bosnia-and-herzegovina-progress-report_en.pdf.

– 2020. 'Bosnia and Herzegovina 2020 Report, Commission Staff Working Document'. Brussels, 6 October 2020, SWD (2020) 350 final.

European Council. 2015. 'Council Conclusions on Bosnia and Herzegovina'. 16 March 2015. http://www.consilium.europa.eu/en/press/press-releases/2015/03/16-council-conclusions-on-bosnia-and-herzegovina/.

European Court of Human Rights. 2014. 'Bosnia and Herzegovina must establish a political system for elections without discrimination'. Press Release ECHR 217 (2014), 15 July 2014. file:///Users/cmurtagh/Downloads/003-4820451-5878717%20(1).pdf.

– 2016a. 'Case of Šlaku v. Bosnia and Herzegovina: Judgement'. Strasbourg. 26 May 2016. file:///Users/cmurtagh/Downloads/CASE%20OF%20%C5%A0LAKU%20v.%20BOSNIA%20AND%20HERZEGOVINA%20(1).pdf.

– 2016b. 'Judgment Pilav v Bosnia and Herzegovina – exclusion of Bosnian politician residing in the Republika Srpska from election to the Presidency,' Press Release, 9 June 2016. https://hudoc.echr.coe.int/fre#{%22itemid%22:[%22003-5400827-6755339%22]}.

Evans, J.A., and J. Tonge. 2001. 'Northern Ireland's Third Tradition(s): That Alliance Party Surveyed'. *Journal of Elections, Public Opinion & Parties* 11, no. 1: 104–18.

– 2003. 'The Future of the "Radical Centre" in Northern Ireland after the Good Friday Agreement'. *Political Studies* 51: 26–50.

Fakhoury, T. 2019. 'Power-sharing after the Arab Spring? Insights from Lebanon's Political Transition'. *Nationalism and Ethnic Politics* 25, no. 1: 9–26.

Fakhoury, T., and M. Aitken. 2004. 'Rethinking Power-Sharing in Post-War Lebanon: The Case for a Pluralist and Multi-Level Research Agenda'. *Middle East Law and Governance* 16, no. 2: 216–29.

Farry, S. 2009. 'Consociationalism and the Creation of a Shared Future for Northern Ireland'. In *Consociational Theory: McGarry and O'Leary and the Northern Ireland Conflict*, edited by R. Taylor, 165–79. Oxon: Routledge.

Farry, S., and S. Neeson. 1999. 'Beyond the "Band-Aid" Approach: An Alliance Party Perspective Upon the Belfast Agreement'. *Fordham International Law Journal* 22: 1221–49.

Fearon, K. 1999. *Women's Work: The Story of the Northern Ireland Women's Coalition.* Belfast: Blackstaff.

Fearon, K., and M. McWilliams. 2000. 'Swimming Against the Mainstream'. In *Gender, Democracy and Inclusion in Northern Ireland,* edited by C. Roulston and C. Davies, 117–39. Basingstoke: Palgrave.

Feeney, B. 2024. '"Uniting the Community" is Alliance's Category Error'. *The Irish News,* 3 July 2024. https://www.irishnews.com/opinion/brian-feeney-uniting-the-community-is-alliances-category-error-3N5I4D4JKNHW7B3X2EFN7KVFGI/.

Finlay, A. 2010. *Governing Ethnic Conflict: Consociation, Identity and the Price of Peace.* Abingdon: Routledge.

Fontana, G. 2017. *Education Policy and Power-Sharing in Post-Conflict Societies: Lebanon, Northern Ireland and Macedonia.* Cham: Palgrave Macmillan.

Ford, D. 2001. 'Tough Decisions Leave Alliance with a Role'. *The Irish Times,* 5 November 2001.

Freedom House. 2013. 'Freedom in the World 2013: Bosnia and Herzegovina'. http://www.freedomhouse.org/report/freedom-world/2013/bosnia-and-herzegovina#.UxWTdfldUvF.
– 2016. 'Bosnia and Herzegovina: Freedom in the World 2016'. https://freedomhouse.org/report/freedom-world/2016/bosnia-and-herzegovina.
– 2024. 'Freedom in the World 2024: The Mounting Damage of Flawed Elections and Armed Conflict'. https://freedomhouse.org/report/freedom-world/2024/mounting-damage-flawed-elections-and-armed-conflict.
Gagnon, A.-G. 2000. 'Canada: Unity and Diversity'. *Parliamentary Affairs* 53, no. 1: 12–26.
– 2021. 'Multinational Federalism: Challenges, Shortcomings and Promises'. *Regional & Federal Studies* 31, no. 1: 99–114.
García Alcaraz, T. 2024. 'Embracing throwntogetherness: Unravelling the Relational Dynamics of Borderlands in Divided Cities'. *Cities* 150, Article 105048.
Garry, J. 2011. 'Northern Ireland 2011 Assembly Election and AV Referendum'. Report for the Electoral Reform Society. http://citeseerx.ist.psu.edu/viewdoc/download;jsessionid=F774241CB48BF8D7E72ED17E2C2DA5A6?doi=10.1.1.369.3748&rep=rep1&type=pdf.
– 2013. 'Holding Parties Accountable at Election Time: Multilevel, Multi-party Government and Electoral Accountability in Northern Ireland'. Paper presented at conference of the Electoral Commission, Belfast, 14 February 2013.
– 2014. 'Potentially Voting Across the Divide in Deeply Divided Places: Ethnic Catch-All Voting in Consociational Northern Ireland'. *Political Studies* 62, no. 1: 2–19.
Garry, J., B. O'Leary, P. Gillespie, and R. Gjoni. 2022. 'Public Attitudes to Irish Unification: Evidence on Models and Process from a Deliberative Forum in Ireland'. *Irish Studies in International Affairs* 33, no. 2: 247–87.
Garry, J., B. O'Leary, and J. Pow. 2022. 'Much More than Meh: The 2022 Northern Ireland Assembly Elections'. *LSE British Politics and Policy Blog*, 11 May 2022. https://blogs.lse.ac.uk/politicsandpolicy/2022-northern-ireland-assembly-elections/.
Gellner, E. 1983. *Nations and Nationalism*. Ithica: Cornell University Press.
Gidley, B. 2012. 'Doing Documentary Research'. In *Researching Society and Culture*. 3rd ed. Edited by C. Seale. Los Angeles: Sage.
Gilmartin, N. 2019. 'Gendering the "Post-Conflict" Narrative in Northern Ireland's Peace Process'. *Capital & Class* 43, no. 1: 89–104.
Gordon, G. 2024. 'Alliance leader pulls out of Ireland's Future event'. *BBC News*, 7 June 2024. https://www.bbc.com/news/articles/c4nnpo75kyno.
Gordy, E. 'From Antipolitics to Alterpolitics: Subverting Ethnokleptocracy in Bosnia and Herzegovina'. In *Unbribable Bosnia and Herzegovina: The Fight for the Commons*, edited by D. Arsenijević. Baden: Nomos.
Grandits, H. 2007. 'The Power of "Armchair Politicians": Ethnic Loyalty and Political Factionalism among Herzegovinian Croats'. In *The New Bosnian Mosaic: Identities, Memories and Moral Claims in a Post-War Society*, edited by X. Bougarel, E. Helms, and G. Duijzings. Aldershot: Ashgate.

Green Party Northern Ireland. 2011. 'The Green Party Manifesto for the Northern Ireland Assembly Election 2011'.
– 2016. 'The Green Party Manifesto for the Northern Ireland Assembly Election 2016'.
– 2017. 'The Green Party Manifesto for the Northern Ireland Assembly Election 2017'.
– 2022. 'The Green Party Manifesto for the Northern Ireland Assembly Election 2022'.
Guelke, A. 2012a. *The Politics of Deeply Divided Societies*. Cambridge: Polity Press.
– 2012b. 'The USA and the Northern Ireland Peace Process'. *Ethnopolitics* 11, no. 4: 424–38.
– 2017. 'Britain After Brexit: The Risk to Northern Ireland'. *Journal of Democracy* 29, no. 1: 42–52.
– 2019. 'Northern Ireland, Brexit, and the Interpretation of Self-Determination'. *Nationalism and Ethnic Politics* 25, no. 4: 383–99.
Gunther, R., and L.J. Diamond. 2003. 'Species of Political Parties: A New Typology'. *Party Politics* 9, no. 2: 167–99.
Hall, J.A. 2003. 'Conditions for National Homogenizers'. In *Nationalism and its Futures*, edited by U. Ozhurmh. London: Palgrave Macmillan.
Hall, P.A., and R.C.R. Taylor. 1996. 'Political Science and the Three New Institutionalisms'. *Political Studies* 44: 936–57.
Hall, S. 1990. 'Cultural Identity and Diaspora'. In *Identity: Community, Culture, Difference*, edited by J. Rutherford. London: Lawrence and Wishart.
Halliday, D., and N. Ferguson. 2016. 'When Peace is Not Enough: The Flag Protests, the Politics of Identity and Belonging in East Belfast'. *Irish Political Studies* 31, no. 4: 525–40.
Hartzell, C., and M. Hoddie. 2003. 'Institutionalizing Peace: Power Sharing and Post-Civil War Conflict Management'. *American Journal of Political Science* 47, no. 2: 318–32.
Haughey, S. 2019. 'Worth Restoring? Taking Stock of the Northern Ireland Assembly'. *The Political Quarterly* 90, no. 4: 705–12.
– 2020. 'Back to Stormont: The *New Decade, New Approach* Agreement and What it Means for Northern Ireland'. *The Political Quarterly* 91, no. 1: 134–40.
Hayes, B., and J. Nagle. 2016. 'Ethnonationalism and Attitudes Towards Gay and Lesbian Rights in Northern Ireland'. *Nations and Nationalism* 22, no. 1: 20–41.
Hayward, K. 2018. 'The Pivotal Position of the Irish Border in the UK's Withdrawal from the European Union'. *Space and Polity* 22, no. 2: 238–54.
– 2020. 'The 2019 General Election in Northern Ireland: The Rise of the Centre Ground?' *The Political Quarterly* 91, no. 1: 49–55.
Hayward, K., M. Komarova, and B. Rosher. 2022. 'Political Attitudes in Northern Ireland after Brexit and Under the Protocol'. Research Update Number 147. ARK. May 2022.
Hayward, K., and C. McManus. 2019. 'Neither/Nor: The Rejection of Unionist and Nationalist Identities in Post-Agreement Northern Ireland'. *Capital and Class* 43, no. 1: 139–55.

Hayward, K., and M.C. Murphy. 2018. 'The EU's Influence on the Peace Process and Agreement in Northern Ireland in Light of Brexit'. *Ethnopolitics* 17, no. 3: 276–91.

Hearty, K. 2015. 'The Great Awakening? The Belfast Flag Protests and Protestant/Unionist/Loyalist Counter-memory in Northern Ireland'. *Irish Political Studies* 30, no. 2: 157–77.

Helmke, G., and S. Levitsky. 2004. 'Informal Institutions and Comparative Politics: A Research Agenda'. *Perspectives on Politics* 2, no. 4: 725–40.

Helms, E. 2007. '"Politics is a Whore": Women, Morality and Victimhood in Post-War Bosnia-Herzegovina'. In *The New Bosnian Mosaic: Identities, Memories and Moral Claims in a Post-War Society*, edited by X. Bougarel, E. Helms and G. Duijzings. Aldershot: Ashgate.

Hepburn, E. 2009. 'Introduction: Re-Conceptualizing Sub-State Mobilization'. *Regional and Federal Studies* 19, no. 4–5: 477–99.

Hodžić, E. 2014. 'Jer me se Tiče'. In *Unbribable Bosnia and Herzegovina: The Fight for the Commons*, edited by D. Arsenijević. Baden: Nomos.

Hodžić, E., and N. Stojanović. 2011. 'New/Old Constitutional Engineering? Challenges and Implications of the European Court of Human Rights Decision in the Case of Sejdić and Finci v. BiH'. Sarajevo: Analika Center for Social Research.

Hollinger, D.A. 2005. *Postethnic America: Beyond Multiculturalism*. New York City: Basic Books.

Horowitz, D.L. 1985. *Ethnic Groups in Conflict*. Berkeley: University of California Press.

– 1991. *A Democratic South Africa? Constitutional Engineering in a Divided Society*. Berkeley: University of California Press.

– 2001. 'The Northern Ireland Agreement: Clear, Consociational and Risky'. In *Northern Ireland and the Divided World: The Northern Ireland Conflict and the Good Friday Agreement in Comparative Perspective*, edited by J. McGarry. Oxford: Oxford University Press.

– 2002a. 'Explaining the Northern Ireland Agreement: The Sources of an Unlikely Constitutional Consensus'. *British Journal of Political Science* 32, no. 2: 193–5.

– 2002b. 'Constitutional Design: Proposals Versus Processes'. In *The Architecture of Democracy: Constitutional Design, Conflict Management, and Democracy*, edited by A. Reynolds, 37–54. Oxford: Oxford University Press.

– 2014. 'Ethnic Power Sharing: Three Big Problems'. *Journal of Democracy* 25, no. 2: 5–20.

Howard, L.M. 2012. 'The Ethnocracy Trap'. *Journal of Democracy* 23, no. 4: 155–69.

Hulsey, J. 2015a. 'Electoral Accountability in Bosnia and Herzegovina under the Dayton Framework Agreement'. *International Peacekeeping* 22, no. 5: 511–25.

– 2015b. 'Party Politics in Bosnia and Herzegovina'. In *State-Building and Democratization in Bosnia and Herzegovina*, edited by S. Keil and V. Perry. Oxon: Ashgate.

Hulsey, J., and S. Keil. 2019. 'Ideology and Party System Change in Consociational Systems: The Case of Non-Nationalist Parties in Bosnia and Herzegovina'. *Nationalism and Ethnic Politics* 25, no. 4: 400–19.

– 2020. 'Change amidst Continuity? Assessing the 2018 Regional Elections in Bosnia and Herzegovina'. *Regional & Federal Studies* 30, no. 3: 343–61.

– 2021. 'Power-Sharing and Party Politics in the Western Balkans'. In *Power-Sharing in Europe: Past Practice, Present Cases, and Future Directions*, edited by S. Keil and A. McCulloch, 115–40. Cham: Springer International Publishing.

Hulsey, J., and D. Stjepanović. 2017. 'Bosnia and Herzegovina: An Archetypical Example of an Ethnocracy'. In *Regional and National Elections in Eastern Europe*, edited by A. Schakel, 35–58. London: Palgrave Macmillan.

Husarić, H. 2014. 'February Awakening: Breaking with the Political Legacy of the Last 20 Years'. In *Unbribable Bosnia and Herzegovina: The Fight for the Commons*, edited by D. Arsenijević. Baden: Nomos.

Ibrišimović, M. 2014. 'My Union Fight'. In *Unbribable Bosnia and Herzegovina: The Fight for the Commons*, edited by D. Arsenijević. Baden: Nomos.

ITV. 2016. 'DUP "will keep blocking same-sex marriage in NI"', 26 October 2016. https://www.itv.com/news/utv/2016-10-27/dup-will-keep-blocking-same-sex-marriage-in-ni.

Jarrett, H. 2016. 'The Single Transferable Vote and the Alliance Party of Northern Ireland'. *Representation* 52, no. 4: 311–23.

Jarstad, A.K. 2009. 'The Prevalance of Power-Sharing: Exploring the Patterns of Post-Election Peace'. *Africa Spectrum* 3: 41–62.

Jarstad, A.K., and D. Nilsson. 2008. 'From Words to Deeds: The Implementation of Power-Sharing Pacts in Peace Accords'. *Conflict Management and Peace Science* 25: 206–23.

Jenne, E.K. 2009. 'The Paradox of Ethnic Partition: Lessons from de facto Partition in Bosnia and Kosovo'. *Regional & Federal Studies* 19, no. 2: 273–89.

Jukic, E.M. 2014. 'Dodik Accused of Manipulating Referendum Issue'. *Balkan Insight*, 2 April 2014. http://www.balkaninsight.com/en/article/opposition-accused-dodik-of-manipulating-with-referendum.

Kane, A. 2019. 'Why Demonising the Alliance Party as Sinn Fein Fellow Travellers Backfired on DUP'. *The Belfast Telegraph*, 16 December 2019. https://www.belfasttelegraph.co.uk/opinion/news-analysis/alex-kane-why-demonising-the-alliance-party-as-sinn-fein-fellow-travellers-backfired-on-dup/38789601.html.

Kapidžić. D. 2015. 'Democratic Transition and Electoral Design in Plural Societies: The Case of Bosnia and Herzegovina's 1990 Elections'. *Ethnopolitics* 14, no. 3: 311–27.

– 2018. 'The Dominance of Ethnic Parties in Bosnia and Herzegovina Will Continue,' *Perspectives Southeastern Europe* 6.

– 2020a. 'Subnational Competitive Authoritarianism and Powersharing in Bosnia and Herzegovina'. *Southeast European and Black Sea Studies* 20, no. 1: 81–101.

– 2020b. 'The Rise of Illiberal Politics in Southeast Europe'. *Southeast European and Black Sea Studies* 20, no. 1: 1–17.

Kapidžić, D., and O. Komar. 2022. 'Segmental Volatility in Ethnically Divided Societies: (Re)assessing Party System Stability in Southeast Europe'. *Nationalities Papers* 50, no. 3: 535–53.

Karčić, H. 2022. 'What Bosnia's EU Candidate Status Really Means'. *Balkan Insight*, 20 December 2022. https://balkaninsight.com/2022/12/20/what-bosnias-eu-candidate-status-really-means/.

Kaufman, E. 2015. 'Partition: It's Time to Recognise Reality in Syria'. *LSE Blogs*, 1 October 2015. https://blogs.lse.ac.uk/politicsandpolicy/partition-its-time-to-recognise-reality-in-syria/.

Keating, M. 2022. 'Taking Back Control? Brexit and the Territorial Constitution of the United Kingdom'. *Journal of European Public Policy* 29, no. 4: 491–509.

Keil, S. 2013. *Multinational Federalism in Bosnia and Herzegovina*. Farnham: Ashgate.

– 2014. 'Whatever Happened to the Plenums in Bosnia?' *Balkan Insight*, 16 June 2014. http://www.balkaninsight.com/en/article/whatever-happened-to-the-plenums-in-bosnia.

Keil, S., and A. McCulloch. 2021. 'Conclusion: The Past, Present and Future of Power-Sharing in Europe'. In *Power-Sharing in Europe: Past Practice, Present Cases, and Future Directions*, edited by S. Keil and A. McCulloch, 257–74. Cham: Springer International Publishing.

Keil, S., and V. Perry. 2015. "Back to Square One?: An Analysis of the 2014 General Elections in Bosnia and Herzegovina'. *Electoral Studies* 38: 82–136.

Kendhammer, B. 2010. 'Talking Ethnic but Hearing Multi-Ethnic: The Peoples' Democratic Party (PDP) in Nigeria and Durable Multi-Ethnic Parties in the Midst of Violence'. *Commonwealth & Comparative Politics* 48, no. 1: 48–71.

Kennedy, J., and L. Riga. 2013. 'A Liberal Route from Homogeneity?: US Policymakers and the Liberalization of Ethnic Nationalists in Bosnia's Dayton Accords'. *Nationalism and Ethnic Politics* 19, no. 2: 163–86.

Kennedy, R., C. Pierson, and J. Thomson. 2016. 'Challenging Identity Hierarchies: Gender and Consociational Power-Sharing'. *The British Journal of Politics and International Relations* 18, no. 3: 618–33.

Kilmurray, A., and M. McWilliams. 2011. 'Struggling for Peace: How Women in Northern Ireland Challenged the Status Quo'. *Solutions* 2, no. 2.

King, G., R.O. Keohane, and S. Verba. 1994. *Designing Social Inquiry: Scientific Inference in Qualitative Research*. Princeton: Princeton University Press.

Klix. 2018. 'Željko Komšić returned the picture of Josip Broz Tito to his cabinet in the BiH presidency'. Klix.ba, 6 December 2018 https://www.klix.ba/vijesti/bih/zeljko-komsic-vratio-sliku-josipa-broza-tita-u-svoj-kabinet-u-predsjednistvu-bih/181206089.

Kymlicka, W. 1995. *Multicultural Citizenship: A Liberal Theory of Minority Rights*. Oxford: Oxford University Press.

– 2004. 'Nationalism, Transnationalism and Postnationalism'. In *From Liberal Values to Democratic Transition: Essays in Honor of Janos Kis*, edited by R. Dworkin, 227–68. Budapest: Central European University Press.

– 2010. 'The Rise and Fall of Multiculturalism? New Debates on Inclusion and Accommodation in Diverse Societies'. *International Social Science Journal* 61: 97–112.

Leonard, A. 1999. 'The Alliance Party and the Third Tradition in Northern Ireland'. MSc thesis, University College Dublin.

Lijphart, A. 1969. 'Consociational Democracy'. In *Thinking About Democracy: Power-Sharing and Majority Rule in Theory and Practice*, edited by A. Lijphart, 2008. London: Routledge.

– 1971. 'Comparative Politics and the Comparative Method'. *The American Political Science Review* 65, no. 3: 682–93.

– 1977. *Democracy in Plural Societies: A Comparative Exploration.* New Haven and London: Yale University Press.
– 1984. *Democracies: Patterns of Majoritarian and Consensus Government in Twenty-One Countries.* New Haven: Yale University Press.
– 1991. 'Self-Determination Versus Pre-Determination of Ethnic Minorities in Power Sharing Systems'. In *Thinking About Democracy: Power-Sharing and Majority Rule in Theory and Practice,* edited by A. Lijphart, 66–74. London: Routledge.
– 1995. 'Multiethnic Democracy'. In *The Encyclopedia of Democracy,* edited by S.M. Lipset. Washington, DC: Congressional Quarterly.
– 2002. 'The Wave of Power-Sharing Democracy'. In *The Architecture of Democracy: Constitutional Design, Conflict management, and Democracy,* edited by A. Reynolds, 37–54. Oxford: Oxford University Press.
Lovenduski, J. 2011. 'Foreword'. In *Gender, Politics and Institutions: Towards a Feminist Institutionalism,* edited by M.L. Krook and F. Mackay, vii–xi. New York: Palgrave Macmillan.
Lowndes, V., and M. Roberts. 2013. *Why Institutions Matter: The New Institutionalism in Political Science.* Basingstoke: Palgrave Macmillan.
Lust, E. 2009. 'Democratization by Elections? Competitive Clientelism in the Middle East'. *Journal of Democracy* 20, no. 3: 122–35.
Luther, K.R. 1999. 'A Framework for the Comparative Analysis of Political Parties and Party Systems in Consociational Democracy'. In *Party Elites in Divided Societies: Political Parties in Consociational Democracy,* edited by K.R. Luther and K. Deschouwer. London: Routledge.
Lynch, G. 2014. 'Anna Lo, and the Myth that Northern Ireland Politics is about the Border'. *Slugger O'Toole,* 23 March 2014. https://sluggerotoole.com/2014/03/23/anna-lo-and-the-myth-that-northern-ireland-politics-is-about-the-border/.
Mackay, F. 2014. 'Nested Newness, Institutional Innovation, and the Gendered Limits of Change'. *Politics & Gender* 10: 549–71.
Mackay, F., M. Kenny, and L. Chappell. 2010. 'New Institutionalism through a Gender Lens: Towards a Feminist Institutionalism?' *International Political Science Review* 31, no. 5: 573–88.
Mackay, F., and C. Murtagh. 2019. 'New Institutions, New Gender Rules? A Feminist Institutionalist Lens on Women and Power-Sharing'. *feminists@law* 9, no. 1.
Madden, A. 2019. 'Alliance Leader Naomi Long defends stance on "divisive and sectarian" electoral pacts'. *The Belfast Telegraph,* 8 November 2019. https://www.belfasttelegraph.co.uk/news/politics/general-election-2019/alliance-leader-naomilong-defends-stance-on-divisive-and-sectarian-electoral-pacts-38673118.html.
Majed, R. 2019. 'What is So Deep About "Deeply Divided Societies"?'. *Centre for Lebanese Studies.* https://www.lebanesestudies.com/wp-content/uploads/2019/11/What-is-So-Deep-About-%E2%80%98Deeply-Divided-Societies%E2%80%99.pdf.
Mako, S. 2023. 'Divided Opposition, Fragmented Statebuilding: Elite Bargaining in Pre- and Post-2003 Iraq'. *International Peacekeeping* 30, no. 5: 585–610.
Makul, A. 2022. 'The Enlargement Process on Hold? Comparison of The French and German Positions Towards the Widening of the EU. *Društveni Ogledi* 4, no. 2: 7–30.

Makul, A., and Z. Kalamujić. 2024. 'Revitalising EU Enlargement? A New Dawn in EU Accession Post-Ukraine Invasion'. MAP *Social Sciences* 5: 27–39.
Malcolm, N. 1996. *Bosnia: A Short History*. London: Pan Books.
Malešević, S. 2011. 'Ethnicity in Time and Space: A Conceptual Analysis'. *Critical Sociology* 37, no. 1: 67–82.
– 2019. *Grounded Nationalisms: A Sociological Analysis*. Cambridge: Cambridge University Press.
Manley, J. 2013. 'End Catholic Education'. *The Irish News*, 29 January 2013.
– 2020. 'Naomi Long ready to engage with any conversation about Irish unity'. *The Irish News*, 6 March 2020. https://www.irishnews.com/news/northernirelandnews/2020/03/06/news/naomi-long-is-ready-to-engage-with-any-conversation-about-irish-unity-1860279/.
Manning, C. 2004. 'Elections and Political Change in Post-War Bosnia and Herzegovina'. *Democratization* 11, no. 2: 60–86.
Mason, J. 2002. *Qualitative Researching*. 2nd ed. London: Sage.
McAllister, I. 1977. *The Northern Ireland Social Democratic Labour Party: Political Opposition in a Divided Society*. London: Macmillan Press.
McAllister, I., and B. Wilson. 1978. 'Bi-Confessionalism in a Confessional Party System: The Northern Ireland Alliance Party'. *Economic and Social Review* 9, no. 3: 207–25.
McCaffery, S. 2012. 'Alliance: A decade of escalating abuse'. *The Detail*, 6 December 2012. https://www.thedetail.tv/articles/alliance-a-decade-of-escalating-abuse.
McCann, E. 2015. 'Assembly "safeguard" blocks decisions on abortion'. *The Irish Times*. 4 June 2015. https://www.irishtimes.com/opinion/eamonn-mccann-assembly-safeguard-blocks-decisions-on-abortion-1.2236269.
McClements, F. 2022a. 'Naomi Long: I said I've done something a bit mad. I've joined the Alliance Party'. *The Irish Times*, 28 May 2022. https://www.irishtimes.com/life-style/people/2022/05/28/who-is-naomi-long-the-woman-leading-the-successful-northern-party-that-is-neither-unionist-nor-nationalist/.
– 2022b. 'Stormont Assembly could sink into history as Other options may break stalemate,' *The Irish Times*, 29 October 2022. https://www.irishtimes.com/politics/2022/10/29/stormont-assembly-could-sink-into-history-as-other-options-may-break-stalemate/.
McCormack, J. 2018. 'Social Investment Fund: Audit Reveals 'Significant Failings.' *BBC News*, 8 November 2018. https://www.bbc.com/news/uk-northern-ireland-46109733.
McCormick, C., and T. Stewart. 2020. 'The Legalisation of Same-Sex Marriage in Northern Ireland'. *The Northern Ireland Legal Quarterly* 71, no. 4.
McCrudden, C., J. McGarry, B. O'Leary, and A. Schwartz. 2013. 'Memorandum for the Northern Ireland Assembly and Executive Review Committee'. *Review of D'Hondt, Community Designation and Provisions for Opposition*, Northern Ireland Assembly, June 2013.
McCrudden, C., and B. O'Leary. 2013. 'Courts and Consociations, or How Human Rights Courts May Destabilize Power-Sharing Settlements'. *The European Journal of International Law* 24, no. 2: 477–501.

McCulloch, A. 2014a. 'Consociational Settlements in Deeply Divided Societies: The Liberal-Corporate Distinction'. *Democratization* 21, no. 3: 501–18.

– 2014b. *Power-Sharing and Political Stability in Deeply Divided Societies*. London and New York: Routledge.

– 2018. 'The Use and Abuse of Veto Rights in Power-Sharing Systems: Northern Ireland's Petition of Concern in Comparative Perspective'. *Government and Opposition* 53, no. 4: 735–56.

– 2020. 'Power-sharing: A Gender Intervention', *International Political Science Review* 41, no. 1: 44–57. doi:10.1177/0192512119861021.

– 2021. 'Introduction'. In *Power-Sharing in Europe: Past Practice, Present Cases, and Future Directions*, edited by S. Keil and A. McCulloch, 1–18. Cham: Springer International Publishing.

McCulloch, A., and J. McEvoy. 2018a. '"Bumps in the Road Ahead": How External Actors Defuse Power-Sharing Crises'. *Journal of Intervention and Statebuilding* 13, no. 2: 216–35.

– 2018b. 'The International Mediation of Power-Sharing Settlements'. *Cooperation and Conflict* 53, no. 4: 467–85.

McDonald, H. 2015. 'Northern Ireland Assembly votes to legalise same sex marriage'. *The Guardian*, 2 November 2015. https://www.theguardian.com/uk-news/2015/nov/02/northern-ireland-assembly-votes-to-legalise-same-sex-marriage.

– 2015. 'Northern Ireland coalition close to collapse in row over welfare cuts'. *The Guardian*, 26 May 2015. https://www.theguardian.com/politics/2015/may/26/northern-ireland-coalition-collapse-row-welfare-cuts.

McEvoy, J. 2015. *Power-Sharing Executives: Governing in Bosnia, Macedonia and Northern Ireland*. Philadelphia: University of Pennsylvania Press.

– 2013. 'We Forbid! The Mutual Veto and Power-Sharing Democracy'. In *National and Ethnic Conflict in the 21st Century: Power-Sharing in Deeply Divided Places*, edited by J. McEvoy and B. O'Leary. Philadelphia: University of Pennsylvania Press.

McEvoy, J., J. Todd, and D. Walsh. 2022. 'Participatory Constitutionalism and the Agenda for Change: Socio-Economic Issues in Irish Constitutional Debates'. *Irish Studies in International Affairs* 33, no. 2: 140–66.

McGarry, J. 2004. 'The Nature of the Agreement'. In *The Northern Ireland Conflict: Consociational Engagements*, edited by J. McGarry and B. O'Leary. Oxford: Oxford University Press.

– 2017a. 'Centripetalism, Consociationalism and Cyprus: The Adoptability Question'. In *Power-Sharing: Empirical and Normative Challenges*, edited by A. McCulloch and J. McGarry. London: Routledge.

– 2017b. 'Conclusion: What Explains the Performance of Power-Sharing Settlements?' In *Power-Sharing: Empirical and Normative Challenges*, edited by A. McCulloch and J. McGarry. London: Routledge.

– 2019. 'Classical Consociational Theory and Recent Consociational Performance'. *Swiss Political Science Review* 25, no. 4: 538–55.

– 2021. 'Why Has Cyprus Been a Consociational Cemetery?' In *Power-Sharing in Europe: Past Practice, Present Cases, and Future Directions*, edited by S. Keil and A. McCulloch, 227–56. Cham: Springer International Publishing.

McGarry, J., and N. Loizides. 2015. 'Power-Sharing in Re-United Cyprus: Centripetal Coalitions vs. Proportional Sequential Coalitions'. *International Journal of Constitutional Law* 13, no. 4: 847–72.
McGarry, J., and B. O'Leary. 1990. 'Northern Ireland's Options: A Framework and Analysis'. In *The Future of Northern Ireland*, 1st ed., edited by J. McGarry and B. O'Leary. Oxford: Oxford University Press.
– 1995. *Explaining Northern Ireland: Broken Images*. Oxford: Blackwell.
– 2006a. 'Consociational Theory, Northern Ireland's Conflict and its Agreement. Part 1. What Consociationalists can Learn from Northern Ireland'. *Government and Opposition* 41, no. 1: 43–63.
– 2006b. 'Consociational Theory, Northern Ireland's Conflict, and its Agreement. Part 2. What Critics of Consociation Can Learn from Northern Ireland'. *Government and Opposition* 41, no. 2: 249–77.
– 2007. 'Iraq's Constitution of 2005: Liberal Consociation as Political Prescription'. *International Journal of Constitutional Law* 5, no. 4: 670–98.
– 2009. 'Power Shared After the Deaths of Thousands'. In *Consociational Theory: McGarry and O'Leary and the Northern Ireland Conflict*, edited by R. Taylor. Oxon: Routledge.
McGarry, J., B. O'Leary, and R. Simeon. 2008. 'Integration or Accommodation? The Enduring Debate in Conflict Regulation'. In *Constitutional Design for Divided Societies: Integration or Accommodation?*, edited by S. Choudhry. Oxford: Oxford University Press.
McGuinness, M. 2017. 'In Full: Martin McGuinness' Resignation Letter'. *News Letter*. 9 January 2017. https://www.newsletter.co.uk/news/in-full-martin-mcguinness-resignation-letter-750757.
McKay, S. 2021. *Northern Protestants on Shifting Ground*. Newtownards: Blackstaff Press.
McLeod, L. 2011. 'Configurations of Post-Conflict: Impacts of Representations of Conflict and Post-Conflict Upon the (Political) Translations of Gender Security within UNSCR 1325'. *International Feminist Journal of Politics* 13, no. 4: 594–611.
McLoughlin, P.J. 2008. 'Horowitz's Theory of Ethnic Party Competition and the Case of the Northern Ireland Social Democratic and Labour Party, 1970–79'. *Nationalism and Ethnic Politics* 14: 549–78.
– 2012. *John Hume and the Revision of Irish Nationalism*. Manchester: Manchester University Press.
McManus, C. 2022. 'Rise of Alliance reveals surprising facets of North's shifting politics'. *The Irish Times*, 17 May 2022. https://www.irishtimes.com/opinion/rise-of-alliance-reveals-surprising-facets-of-north-s-shifting-politics-1.4880004.
McNicholl, K. 2018. 'Political Constructions of a Cross-Community Identity in a Divided Society: How Politicians Articulate Northern Irishness'. *National Identities* 20, no. 5: 495–513.
– 2019. 'The Northern Irish Identity: Attitudes Towards Moderate Political Parties and Outgroup Leaders'. *Irish Political Studies* 34, no. 1: 25–47.
Merdzanovic, A. 2015. *Democracy by Decree: Prospects and Limits of Imposed Consociational Democracy in Bosnia and Herzegovina*. Hannover: Ibidem.

– 2017. "Imposed Consociationalism': External Intervention and Power Sharing in Bosnia and Herzegovina'. *Peacebuilding* 5, no. 1: 22–35.
Meredith, R. 2021. 'NI Education: No religious mix in 'nearly a third of schools'. *BBC News*, 11 November 2021. https://www.bbc.com/news/uk-northern-ireland-59242226.
Meyer, D.S. 2004. 'Protest and Political Opportunities'. *Annual Review of Sociology* 30: 125–45.
Meyer McAleese, M.K. 2009. 'Assessing the Impact of the Northern Ireland Women's Coalition on Politics in Northern Ireland: Marginalization, Co-optation, or Transformation for Women?' Paper Presented to the First European Conference on Politics and Gender.
Milan, C. 2020. *Social Mobilization Beyond Ethnicity: Civic Activism and Grassroots Movements in Bosnia and Herzegovina*. Oxon: Routledge.
– 2022. 'Navigating Ethnicity. Collective Identities and Movement Framing in Deeply Divided Societies'. *Nationalities Papers* 50, no. 6: 1057–70.
Mitchell, D. 2015. *Politics and Peace in Northern Ireland: Political Parties and the Implementation of the 1998 Agreement*. Manchester: Manchester University Press.
– 2018. 'Non-Nationalist Politics in a Bi-National Consociation: The Case of the Alliance Party of Northern Ireland'. *Nationalism and Ethnic Politics* 24: 336–47.
Mitchell, D., and M. Miller. 2017. 'Reconciliation through Language Learning? A Case Study of the Turas Irish Language Project in East Belfast'. *Ethnic and Racial Studies* 42, no. 2: 235–53.
Mitchell, P., G. Evans, and B. O'Leary, B. 2009. 'Extremist Outbidding in Ethnic Party Systems is Not Inevitable: Tribunes in Northern Ireland'. *Political Studies* 57: 397–421.
Mitchell, T.G. 2002. *Indispensable Traitors: Liberal Parties in Settler Conflicts*. Westport: Greenwood Press.
Moroff, A. 2013. 'Comparing Ethnic Party Regulation in East Africa'. In *Ethnic Bans in Africa*, edited by M. Bogaards, M. Basedau, and C. Hartmann, 152–70. Abingdon and New York: Routledge.
Morris, A. 2017. 'Stormont Speaker Robin Newton accused of misleading Assembly over ties to UDA-linked Charter NI.' *The Irish News*, 11 October 2017. https://www.irishnews.com/news/2017/10/11/news/pressure-grows-on-stormont-speaker-robin-newton-over-links-to-charter-ni-1158990/.
Mujanović, J. 2017. *Hunger and Fury: The Crisis of Democracy in The Balkans*. New York: Oxford University Press.
Mujkic, A. 2008. *We, the Citizens of the Ethnopolis*. Sarajevo: University Human Rights Centre.
– 2014. 'The Evolution of Bosnia and Herzegovina's Protests in Five Theses'. In *Unbribable Bosnia and Herzegovina: The Fight for the Commons*, edited by D. Arsenijević. Baden: Nomos.
– 2016. 'Bosnian Days of Reckoning: Review of the Sequence of Protests in Bosnia and Herzegovina 2013–14'. *Southeastern Europe* 40, no. 2: 217–42.
Mujkić, A., and J. Hulsey. 2010. 'Explaining the Success of Nationalist Parties in Bosnia and Herzegovina'. *Politička Misao* 47, no. 2: 143–58.

Mulholland, M., and P. Patel. 1999. 'Inclusive Movements/Movements for Inclusion'. *Soundings* 12: 127–43.

Murphy, M.C. 2023. 'The Rise of the Middle Ground in Northern Ireland: What does it Mean?' *The Political Quarterly* 94, no. 1: 95–103.

Murphy, M.C., and J. Evershed. 2022. *A Troubled Constitutional Future: Northern Ireland after Brexit*. Newcastle-upon-Tyne: Agenda Publishing.

Murtagh, C. 2008. 'A Transient Transition: The Cultural and Institutional Obstacles Impeding the Northern Ireland Women's Coalition in its Progression from Informal to Formal Politics'. *Irish Political Studies* 23, no. 1: 21–40.

– 2015. 'Reaching Across: Institutional Barriers to Cross-Ethnic Parties in Post-Conflict Societies and the Case of Northern Ireland'. *Nations and Nationalism* 21, no. 3: 544–65.

– 2016. 'Civic Mobilization in Divided Societies and the Perils of Political Engagement: Bosnia and Herzegovina's Protest and Plenum Movement'. *Nationalism and Ethnic Politics* 22, no. 2: 149–71.

– 2020. 'The Plight of Civic Parties in Divided Societies'. *International Political Science Review* 41, no. 1: 73–88.

– 2021. 'Towards Inclusive Power-Sharing in Northern Ireland: Two Steps Forward, One Step Back'. In *Power-Sharing in Europe: Past Practice, Present Cases, and Future Directions*, edited by S. Keil and A. McCulloch. Cham: Springer International Publishing.

– 2022. 'Northern Ireland is politically divided. Maybe that's changing'. *The Monkey Cage, The Washington Post*, 14 June 2022. https://www.washingtonpost.com/politics/2022/06/14/northern-ireland-alliance-party-union-republican/.

Murtagh, C., and A. McCulloch. 2021. '"Beyond the Core": Do Ethnic Parties "Reach Out" in Power-Sharing Systems?' *The British Journal of Politics and International Relations* 23, no. 3: 533–51.

Murtagh, C., and M.C. Murphy. 2025. 'Civic Politics and Constitutional Change in Ireland'. In *Political Change across Britain and Ireland: Identities, Institutions and Futures*, edited by P. Gillespie, M. Keating, and N. McEwen, 50–74. Edinburgh: Edinburgh University Press.

Nagle, J. 2011. 'Plying Nostrums or Exporting Peace Models? An Examination of the Contradictions between the Northern Irish Peace Process and International Peacebuilding'. *Democracy and Security* 7: 160–83.

– 2013. '"Unity in Diversity": Non-Sectarian Social Movement Challenges to the Politics of Ethnic Antagonism in Violently Divided Cities'. *International Journal for Urban and Regional Research* 37, no. 1: 78–92.

– 2016a. *Social Movements in Violently Divided Societies: Constructing Conflict and Peacebuilding*. Oxon: Routledge.

– 2016b. 'What are the Consequences of Consociationalism for Sexual Minorities?: An Analysis of Liberal and Corporate Consociationalism and Sexual Minorities in Northern Ireland and Lebanon'. *Political Studies* 64, no. 4: 854–71.

– 2018. 'Beyond Ethnic Entrenchment and Amelioration: An Analysis of Non-Sectarian Social Movements and Lebanon's Consociationalism'. *Ethnic and Racial Studies* 41, no. 7: 1370–89.

– 2020. 'Consociationalism is Dead! Long Live Zombie Power-Sharing!' *Studies in Ethnicity and Nationalism* 20, no. 2: 137–44.

Nagle, J., and T. Fakhoury. 2018. 'Between Co-Option and Radical Opposition: A Comparative Analysis of Power-Sharing on Gender Equality and LGBTQ Rights in Northern Ireland and Lebanon'. *Nationalism and Ethnic Politics* 24, no. 1: 82–99.

– 2021. *Resisting Sectarianism: Queer Activism in Postwar Lebanon*. London: Zed Books.

– 2022. 'Lebanese election sees significant gains for independent non-sectarian politicians'. *The Conversation*, 4 May 2022. https://theconversation.com/lebanese-election-sees-significant-gains-for-independent-non-sectarian-politicians-183238.

Naša Stranka. 2008a. 'General Programme Principles'. Sarajevo.

– 2008b. 'General Programme Objectives'. Sarajevo.

– 2008c. 'Getting Started'. Sarajevo.

– 2010. 'Election Programme, General Election Bosnia and Herzegovina 2014'. Sarajevo.

– 2014. 'Election Programme: Constitutional Policy, General Election Bosnia and Herzegovina 2014'. Sarajevo.

National Democratic Institute. 2022. 'Bosnia and Herzegovina's October 2022 Elections', 27 October 2022. https://www.ndi.org/publications/bosnia-and-herzegovina-s-october-2022-elections.

Noel, S. 2005. 'Introduction'. In *From Power Sharing to Democracy: Post-conflict Institutions in Ethnically Divided Societies*, edited by S. Noel, ix–xiii. Montreal and Kingston: McGill-Queen's University Press.

Nolan, P. 2013. *Northern Ireland Peace Monitoring Report: Number Two*. Belfast: Community Relations Council.

Nolan, P., D. Bryan, C. Dwyer, K. Hayward, K. Radford, and P. Shirlow. 2014. *The Flag Dispute: Anatomy of a Protest*. Queen's University Belfast. pureadmin.qub.ac.uk/ws/files/13748797/The_Flag_Dispute_report_PRINTED.pdf.

Northern Ireland Assembly. 2013. 'Review of D'Hondt, Community Designation and Provisions for Opposition'. Assembly and Executive Review Committee.

– 2024. 'Standing Orders of the Northern Ireland Assembly as amended 26 November 2024.' http://www.niassembly.gov.uk/assembly-business/standing-orders/.

Northern Ireland Statistics Research Agency. 2011. '2011 Census'. https://www.nisra.gov.uk/statistics/census/2011-census.

– 2021. 'Long-Term International Migration Statistics for Northern Ireland (2020)'. 26 August 2021. https://www.nisra.gov.uk/publications/long-term-international-migration-statistics-northern-ireland-2020.

– 2022a. 'Census 2021: Main Statistics for Northern Ireland Statistical Bulletin: Country of Birth'. 22 September 2022. https://www.nisra.gov.uk/system/files/statistics/census-2021-main-statistics-for-northern-ireland-phase-1-statistical-bulletin-country-of-birth.pdf.

– 2022b. 'Main Statistics for Northern Ireland; Statistical Bulletin: Religion'. 22 September 2022. https://www.nisra.gov.uk/system/files/statistics/census-

2021-main-statistics-for-northern-ireland-phase-1-statistical-bulletin-religion.pdf.
– 2022c. 'Main Statistics for Northern Ireland; Statistical Bulletin: National Identity'. 22 September 2022. https://www.nisra.gov.uk/system/files/statistics/census-2021-main-statistics-for-northern-ireland-phase-1-statistical-bulletin-national-identity.pdf.
Northern Ireland Women's Coalition. 1998. 'Election Manifesto, Northern Ireland Assembly Election, 1998'. Belfast.
– 2003. 'Change the Face of Politics: Election Manifesto, Northern Ireland Assembly Election, 2003'. Belfast.
Ó Dochartaigh, N. 2021. 'Beyond the Dominant Party System: The Transformation of Party Politics in Northern Ireland'. *Irish Political Studies* 36, no. 1: 7–28.
OECD. 2020. Government at a Glance: Western Balkans. Paris: OECD Publishing. https://doi.org/10.1787/a8c72f1b-en.
Office of the High Representative. 2022. 'Decision Enacting Amendments to the Constitution of the Federation of Bosnia and Herzegovina'. 10 February 2022. https://www.ohr.int/decision-enacting-amendments-to-the-constitution-of-the-federation-of-bosnia-and-herzegovina-3/.
O'Flynn, I. 2006. *Deliberative Democracy and Divided Societies*. Edinburgh: Edinburgh University Press.
– 2009. 'Progressive Integration (and Accommodation Too)'. In *Consociational Theory: McGarry and O'Leary and the Northern Ireland Conflict*, edited by R. Taylor. Oxon: Routledge.
O'Keefe, T. 2021. 'Bridge-Builder Feminism: The Feminist Movement and Conflict in Northern Ireland'. *Irish Political Studies* 36, no. 1: 52–71.
O'Leary, B. 2004. 'The Nature of the Agreement'. In *The Northern Ireland Conflict: Consociational Engagements*, edited by J. McGarry and B. O'Leary. Oxford: Oxford University Press.
– 2012. 'The Federalization of Iraq and the Break-up of Sudan'. *Government and Opposition* 47: 481–516.
– 2017. 'Power-Sharing and Partition amid Israel–Palestine'. In *The Israeli-Palestinian Conflict: The Politics of Stalemate*, edited by K. Cordell, B. O'Leary, and S. Wolff. Oxon: Routledge.
– 2018. 'The Twilight of The United Kingdom and *Tiocfaidh* Ár Lá: Twenty Years After the Good Friday Agreement'. *Ethnopolitics* 17, no. 3: 223–42.
– 2019. *A Treatise on Northern Ireland*. Vol. 3. Oxford: Oxford University Press.
– 2021. 'A referendum on Irish unity is coming, whether we like it or not'. *The Irish Times*, 11 January 2021. https://www.irishtimes.com/opinion/a-referendum-on-irish-unity-is-coming-whether-we-like-it-or-not-1.4454681.
– 2022. *Making Sense of a United Ireland: Should it Happen? How Might it Happen?* Penguin.
O'Neill, E. *Wave Goodbye to Dinosaurs* (2017. UK: Fine Point Films).
Oppenheim, M. 2022. '"Critical step": UK Government to commission abortion services in Northern Ireland amid gridlock'. *The Independent*, 25 October 2022. https://www.independent.co.uk/news/uk/home-news/abortion-northern-ireland-uk-government-announces-b2210195.html.

Parodi, F., and B. Cegar. 2019. 'State-Owned Enterprises in Bosnia and Herzegovina: Assessing Performance and Oversight'. IMF Working Paper No. 19/201.
Parr, C. 2017. *Inventing the Myth: Political Passions and the Ulster Protestant Imagination*. Oxford: Oxford University Press.
Pearson, S. 2015. 'The "National Key" in Bosnia and Herzegovina: A Historical Perspective'. *Nationalities Papers* 43, no. 2: 213–32.
Pennings, P., H. Keman, and J. Kleinnijenhuis. 2006. *Doing Research in Political Science: An Introduction to Comparative Methods and Statistics*. 2nd ed. London: Sage.
People Before Profit. 2017. 'Manifesto 2017'. https://cain.ulster.ac.uk/issues/politics/docs/pbp/pbp_2017-02-21_nia-man.pdf.
– 2022. 'Manifesto 2022: Brexit and Partition'. https://www.pbp.ie/ae2022-manifesto/brexit-and-partition/.
Peters, B.G. 1998. *Comparative Politics: Theory and Methods*. Basingstoke: Palgrave Macmillan.
Phinnemore, D., K. Hayward, and L.C. Whitten. 2023. 'Taking the Temperature VII: What do Voters in Northern Ireland Think about The Protocol on Ireland/Northern Ireland?', February 2023. Belfast: Queen's University Belfast.
Piacentini, A. 2019. '"Trying to Fit In": Multiethnic Parties, Ethno-Clientelism, and Power-Sharing in Bosnia and Herzegovina and Macedonia'. *Nationalism and Ethnic Politics* 25, no. 3: 273–91.
– 2021. 'Making an Identity Choice: "Opportunistic Alignment" In and Beyond Consociational Systems: Evidence from South Tyrol and Bosnia Herzegovina'. *Nationalism and Ethnic Politics* 27, no. 4: 439–55.
Pickering, P.M. 2009. 'Explaining Support for Non-Nationalist Parties in Post-conflict Societies in the Balkans'. *Europe-Asia Studies* 61, no. 4: 565–91.
Pierson, C. 2018. '"One Step Forwards, Two Steps Back": Women's Rights 20 Years after the Good Friday Agreement'. *Parliamentary Affairs* 71, no. 2: 461–81.
Pierson, C., and J. Thomson. 2018. 'Allies or Opponents? Power-Sharing, Civil Society, and Gender'. *Nationalism and Ethnic Politics* 24, no. 1: 100–15.
Pilav v Bosnia and Herzegovina, no. 41939/07, 9 June 2016, ECLI:CE:ECHR:2016:0609JUD004193907.
Przeworski, A., and H. Teune. 1970. *The Logic of Comparative Social Inquiry*. New York: Wiley-Interscience.
Rabushka, A., and K.A. Shepsle. 1972. *Politics in Plural Societies: A Theory of Democratic Instability*. Columbus: Charles E. Merrill Publishing.
Raffoul, A.W. 2020. 'The Politics of Association: Power-Sharing and the Depoliticization of Ethnicity in Post-War Burundi'. *Ethnopolitics* 19, no. 1: 1–18.
Rebouché, R., and K. Fearon. 2005. 'Overlapping Identities: Power Sharing and Women's Rights'. In *Power Sharing: New Challenges for Divided Societies*, edited by I. O'Flynn and D. Russell. London: Pluto.
Reilly, B. 2001. *Democracy in Divided Societies: Electoral Engineering for Conflict Management*. Cambridge: Cambridge University Press.
– 2006. 'Political Engineering and Party Politics in Conflict-Prone Societies'. *Democratization* 13, no. 5: 811–27.
– 2018. 'Centripetalism and Electoral Moderation in Established Democracies'. *Nationalism and Ethnic Politics* 24, no. 2: 201–21.

Repovac Nikšić, V., J. Hasanović, E. Adilović, and D. Kapidžić. 2022. 'The Social Movement for Truth and Justice – Pragmatic Alliance-building with Political Parties in Bosnia and Herzegovina'. *Philosophy and Society* 33, no. 1: 143–61.

Riga, L., and J. Kennedy. 2013. 'To Build a Notion: US State Department Nation Building Expertise and Postwar Settlements in 20th Century East Central Europe'. *Sociological Research Online* 18, no. 2.

Rose, R. 1971. *Governing Without Consensus: An Irish Perspective.* London: Faber and Faber.

Roulston, C. 1999. 'Feminism, Politics, and Postmodernism'. In *Contesting Politics: Women in Ireland, North and South*, edited by Y. Galligan, E. Ward, E. and R. Wilford, 1–17. Boulder, CO: Westview Press.

– 2000. 'Democracy and the Challenge of Gender: New Visions, New Processes'. In *Gender, Democracy and Inclusion in Northern Ireland*, edited by C. Roulston and C. Davies. Basingstoke: Palgrave Macmillan.

Rouse, M. 2016. '"In Need of a Fresh Start": Gender Equality in Post-GFA Northern Ireland'. *Northern Ireland Legal Quarterly* 67, no. 2: 233–40.

RTE News. 2022. 'Does the growth of Alliance represent a new era for Northern Ireland?' 9 May 2022. https://www.rte.ie/radio/radio1/clips/22094215/.

Salamey, I., and T. Katoul Rahbani. 2023. 'Power-Sharing Models for Postwar Syria: Consociational vs. Centripetal Options'. *Nationalism and Ethnic Politics* 29, no. 2: 179–203.

Sarajevo Times. 2020. 'Edin Forto has resigned from his post as Prime Minister of Sarajevo Canton'. 5 February 2020. https://sarajevotimes.com/edin-forto-has-resigned-from-his-post-as-prime-minister-of-sarajevo-canton/.

– 2023. 'Delegates from BiH submitted an application to the European Court of Human Rights'. 14 April 2023. https://sarajevotimes.com/delegates-from-bih-submitted-an-application-to-the-european-court-of-human-rights/.

Sarčević, E. 2012. 'Projection of the Constitution of Bosnia and Herzegovina'. Public Law Centre. Commissioned by Naša Stranka, Sarajevo, 1 June 2012.

Sasso, A. 2015. '"Just a Few Years Left for Us" Non-Nationalist Political Actors in Bosnia-Herzegovina (1989–1991)'. Doctoral thesis, Universitat Autònoma de Barcelona.

Schmidt, V. 2008. 'Discursive Institutionalism: The Explanatory Power of Ideas and Discourse'. *Annual Review of Political Science* 11: 303–26.

Schwartz, A. 2011. 'How Unfair is Cross-Community Consent? Voting Power in the Northern Ireland Assembly'. *Northern Ireland Legal Quarterly* 61, no. 4: 349–62.

Sedo, J. 2010. 'The Party System of Bosnia and Herzegovina'. In *Party Politics in the Western Balkans*, edited by V. Stojarova and P. Emerson. London and New York: Routledge.

Sejdic and Finci v Bosnia and Herzegovina (GC), no. 2799/06 and 34836/06, 22 December 2009. ECLI:CE:ECHR:2009:1222JUD002799606.

Simpson, C. 2022. 'Anti-Protocol voices given "open mike" on BBC, Naomi Long says'. *The Irish News*, 30 March 2022. https://www.irishnews.com/news/northernirelandnews/2022/03/30/news/anti-protocol-voices-given-open-mike-on-bbc-naomi-long-says-2628342/.

Sisk, D. 2002. *Power Sharing and International Mediation in Ethnic Conflicts.* Washington: Carnegie Commission on Preventing Deadly Conflict and the United States Institute of Peace Press.
Social Democratic Party of Bosnia and Herzegovina. 2010a. 'Economic Policy Programme, General Election, Bosnia and Herzegovina 2010'.
– 2010b. 'Education Policy Programme, General Election, Bosnia and Herzegovina 2010'.
– 2010c. 'Health Policy Programme, General Election, Bosnia and Herzegovina 2010'.
– 2010d. 'Justice Policy Programme, General Election, Bosnia and Herzegovina 2010'.
– 2010e. 'Social Policy Programme, General Election, Bosnia and Herzegovina 2010'.
– 2014. 'Election Programme, General Election, Bosnia and Herzegovina 2014'.
– 2015. 'Program. October 2015'.
Social Overview Service. 2016. 'Bosnia and Herzegovina Reaches Tipping Point in 2016'. Report 3:16, Social Overview Service, Sarajevo. http://www.sos.ba/PDF/BiH%20Reaches%20a%20Tipping%20Point%20in%202016.pdf.bel.
Spedding, G. 2012. 'Northern Ireland's Greens lead push for marriage equality'. *HuffPost*, 10 September 2012. https://www.huffingtonpost.co.uk/gary-spedding/northern-ireland-greens-marriage-equality_b_1864197.html.
Statistical Agency Bosnia and Herzegovina. 2013. 'Census of Population, Households and Dwellings in Bosnia and Herzegovina'. https://www.popis.gov.ba/popis2013/doc/RezultatiPopisa_BS.pdf.
Štiks, I., and S. Horvat. 2014. 'The New Balkan Revolts: From Protests to Plenums and Beyond'. In *Unbribable Bosnia and Herzegovina: The Fight for the Commons*, edited by D. Arsenijević. Baden: Nomos.
Stjepanović, D. 2014. 'Post-Conflict Territories and Citizenship: The Case of Bosnia's Brčko District'. SSRN: http://ssrn.com/abstract=2421477 or http://dx.doi.org/10.2139/ssrn.2421477.
Stojanović, N. 2018. 'Political Marginalization of Others in Consociational Regimes'. *Zeitschrift für Vergleichende Politikwissenschaft* 12, no. 2: 1–24.
Stojarova, V. 2010a. 'Introduction'. In *Party Politics in the Western Balkans*, edited by V. Stojarova and P. Emerson. London and New York: Routledge.
– 2010b. 'Legacy of Communist and Socialist Parties in the Western Balkans'. In *Party Politics in the Western Balkans*, edited by V. Stojarova and P. Emerson. London and New York: Routledge.
– 2010c. 'Nationalist Parties and the Party Systems of the Western Balkans'. In *Party Politics in the Western Balkans*, edited by V. Stojarova and P. Emerson. London and New York: Routledge.
Stuebner, W.A. 2012. 'Bosnia's SDP sold out to forces of darkness'. *Balkan Insight*, 13 September 2012. http://www.balkaninsight.com/en/article/bosnia-s-sdp-sold-out-to-forces-of-darkness.
Suitor, J. 2021. 'A Modest Proposal: Building a Deliberative System in Northern Ireland'. *Irish Studies in International Affairs* 32, no. 2: 247–70.

Swenden, W. 2012. 'The Territorial and Non-Territorial Management of Ethnic Diversity in South Asia'. *Regional & Federal Studies* 22, no. 5: 613–31.
– 2013. 'Territorial Strategies for Managing Plurinational States'. In *Routledge Handbook of Federalism & Regionalism*, edited by J. Loughlin, J. Kincaid, and W. Swenden. London: Routledge.
Tarrow, S., and D.S. Meyer. 2018. 'Challenges of the Anti-Trump Movement', *Partecipazione e Conflitto* 11, no. 3: 614–45.
Taylor, R. 2009. 'The Injustice of a Consociational Solution to the Northern Ireland Problem'. In *Consociational Theory: McGarry and O'Leary and the Northern Ireland Conflict*, edited by R. Taylor. Oxon: Routledge.
The Guardian. 2020. 'First same-sex marriage takes place in Northern Ireland'. 11 February 2020. https://www.theguardian.com/uk-news/2020/feb/11/first-same-sex-marriage-northern-ireland-belfast-robyn-peoples-sharni-edwards.
Thomson, J. 2016. 'Abortion and Same-Sex Marriage: How are Non-Sectarian Controversial Issues Discussed in Northern Irish Politics?'. *Irish Political Studies* 31, no. 4: 483–501.
Todd, J. 2018. *Identity Change After Conflict: Ethnicity, Boundaries and Belonging in the Two Irelands*. Switzerland: Palgrave.
Toe, R. 2014. 'Bosnia-Herzegovina and the Failed Revolution of the SDP (2010–2014) – Part 1'. *Transconflict*, 14 November 2014. http://www.transconflict.com/2014/11/bosnia-herzegovina-and-the-failed-revolution-of-the-sdp-2010-2014-part-1-241/.
Tonge, J. 1998. *Northern Ireland: Conflict and Change*. London: Prentice Hall Europe.
– 2005. *The New Northern Irish Politics?* Basingstoke: Palgrave Macmillan.
– 2020. 'Beyond Unionism versus Nationalism: The Rise of the Alliance Party of Northern Ireland'. *The Political Quarterly* 91, no. 2: 461–6.
Tonge, J., and J. Evans. 2015. 'Another Communal Headcount: The Election in Northern Ireland'. *Parliamentary Affairs* 68: 117–32.
Touquet, H. 2011. 'Multi-Ethnic Parties in Bosnia-Herzegovina: Naša Stranka and the Paradoxes of Postethnic Politics'. *Studies in Ethnicity and Nationalism* 11, no. 3: 451–67.
– 2012a. 'Escaping Ethnopolis: Postethnic Mobilization in Bosnia-Herzegovina'. PhD thesis, KE Leuven.
– 2012b. 'The Republika Srpska as a Strong Nationalizing State and the Consequences for Postethnic Activism'. *Nationalities Papers* 40, no. 2: 203–20.
– 2015. 'Non-Ethnic Mobilisation in Deeply Divided Societies, the Case of the Sarajevo Protests'. *Europe-Asia Studies* 67, no. 3: 388–408.
Tripp, A.M. 2015. *Women and Power in Post-Conflict Africa*. Cambridge: Cambridge University Press.
United Nations Development Programme. 2009. 'The Ties that Bind: Social Capital in Bosnia and Herzegovina'. *National Human Development Report 2009*, Sarajevo.
Vandeginste, S. 2014. 'Governing Ethnicity After Genocide: Ethnic Amnesia in Rwanda Versus Ethnic Power-Sharing in Burundi'. *Journal of Eastern African Studies* 8, no. 2: 263–77.

– 2017. 'Power-Sharing in Burundi: An Enduring Miracle?' In *Power-Sharing: Empirical and Normative Challenges*, edited by A. McCulloch and J. McGarry. London: Routledge.

Varshney, A. 2002. *Ethnic Conflict and Civic Life: Hindus and Muslims in India.* New Haven and London: Yale University Press.

Vrgova, R. 2012. 'Intra-Party Democracy in Consociational Democracies: The Cases of Bosnia and Herzegovina and Macedonia'. Master's thesis, University of Sarajevo – University of Bologna.

Vuletić, D. 2007. 'Internal Party Democracy in Bosnia-Herzegovina – An Interaction between Crises and Development'. In *Reshaping the Broken Image of Political Parties: Internal Party Democracy in South Eastern Europe*, edited by K. Georgi. Sofia: Gorexpress.

Wade, R.H. 2022. 'A Diplomatic Solution to the War in Ukraine'. *LSE Blogs*, 2 March 2022. https://blogs.lse.ac.uk/europpblog/2022/03/02/a-diplomatic-solution-to-the-war-in-ukraine/.

Walsh, D. 2017. *Independent Commissions and Contentious Issues in Post-Good Friday Agreement Northern Ireland.* Cham: Palgrave Macmillan.

– 2024. 'The British and Irish Governments' Role in Restoring the Assembly in Northern Ireland: October 2002 to May 2007 and January 2017 to January 2020'. *Nationalism and Ethnic Politics* 30, no. 40: 1–20.

Walsh, D., and J. Doyle. 2018. 'External Actors in Consociational Settlements: A Re-examination of Lijphart's Negative Assumptions'. *Ethnopolitics* 17, no. 1: 21–36.

Whiting, M., and S. Bauchowitz. 2022. 'The Myth of Power-Sharing and Polarisation: Evidence from Northern Ireland'. *Political Studies* 70, no. 1: 81–109.

Whitten, L.C. 2020. 'Breaking Walls & Norms: A Report on the UK general election in Northern Ireland, 2019'. *Irish Political Studies* 35, no. 2: 313–30.

Wilford, R. 2009. 'Consociational Government: Inside the Northern Ireland Executive'. In *Consociational Theory: McGarry and O'Leary and the Northern Ireland Conflict*, edited by R. Taylor. Oxon: Routledge.

– 2010. 'Northern Ireland: The Politics of Constraint'. *Parliamentary Affairs* 63, no. 1: 134–55.

Wilson, R. 2009. 'From Consociationalism to Interculturalism'. In *Consociational Theory: McGarry and O'Leary and the Northern Ireland Conflict*, edited by R. Taylor. Oxon: Routledge.

– 2010. *The Northern Ireland Experience of Conflict and Agreement: A Model for Export?* Manchester and New York: Manchester University Press.

Wolff, S. 2009. 'Peace by Design? Towards "Complex Power-Sharing"'. In *Consociational Theory: McGarry and O'Leary and the Northern Ireland Conflict*, edited by R. Taylor. Oxon: Routledge.

– 2010. 'Building Democratic States after Conflict: Institutional Design Revisited'. *International Studies Review* 12: 128–41.

Yehuda, L. 2023. *Collective Equality: Human Rights and Democracy in Ethno-National Conflicts.* Cambridge: Cambridge University Press.

Yin, R.K. 1994. *Case Study Research: Design and Methods.* 2nd ed. Thousand Oaks: Sage.

Young, C. 2021. 'Kate Hoey says she would take part in a Dublin anti-protocol rally'. *The Irish News*, 21 June 2021. https://www.irishnews.com/news/northernirelandnews/2021/06/21/news/kate-hoey-says-she-would-take-part-in-a-dublin-anti-protocol-rally-2361715/.

Young, D. 2016. 'Alliance sets its price for taking Justice Ministry'. *Belfast Telegraph*, 18 May 2016. http://www.belfasttelegraph.co.uk/news/politics/alliance-sets-its-price-for-taking-justice-ministry-34724435.html.

– 2022. 'Alliance proposes Stormont reforms to end veto on Executive formation'. *The Examiner*, 10 June 2022. https://www.irishexaminer.com/news/politics/arid-40892945.html.

Yuval-Davis, N. 1997. *Gender and Nation*. London: Sage.

– 1999. 'What is 'Transversal Politics'?'. *Soundings* 12: 127–43.

– 2006a. 'Human/Women's Rights and Feminist Transversal Politics'. In *Global Feminism: Transnational Women's Activism, Organizing and Women's Rights*, edited by M. Marx Ferree and A. Mari Tripp. New York: New York University Press.

– 2006b. 'Intersectionality and Feminist Politics'. *European Journal of Women's Studies* 13, no. 3: 193–209.

Zdeb, A. 2016. 'The Need to Have Something "Of Their Own": Croat Parallel Institutions in Bosnia and Herzegovina'. *Swiss Political Science Review* 22, no. 4: 545–64.

Zornić v Bosnia and Herzegovina, no. 3681/06, 15 July 2014. ECLI:CE:ECHR:2014:0715JUD000368106; https://www.ohr.int/hr-urges-limited-constitutional-reform-and-changes-to-the-election-law-to-strengthen-the-fundamental-principles-and-transparency-of-elections/.

Zuber, C.I. 2012. 'Ethnic Party Competition Beyond the Segmented Market'. *Nationalities Papers* 40, no. 6: 927–44.

– 2015. 'Reserved Seats, Political Parties, and Minority Representation'. *Ethnopolitics* 14, no. 4: 390–403.

Index

abortion, 56, 59, 74, 80, 83, 104, 108, 122, 124–5, 217
accommodationist approaches, 19–20, 30
Alliance for Change coalition BiH 2001–02, 159, 187–8
Alliance Party of Northern Ireland, 3, 43, 46, 50, 111–14; formation, 46, 111, 198
Anglo-Irish Agreement, The, 47, 95
authoritarianism. *See* democracy: democratic backsliding

Belfast: Belfast City Council, 3, 56, 85, 94, 98–103
Belfast Agreement, The. *See* Good Friday Agreement, The
Belgium, 205
Bosnian Uprising 2014. *See* plenum protests
Brčko, 141
Brexit, 3, 58–60, 63, 96–8, 109, 126–30, 132, 137, 201, 218; Northern Ireland Protocol, 59–60, 81, 96–8, 128; protocol protests, 3, 13, 60, 91, 96–8, 125
Burundi, 203–4, 206, 208

Canada, 7, 217
cantons, Bosnia and Herzegovina, 141–2, 145, 155–6, 158, 174, 189, 195, 189, 195
census: Northern Ireland census, 135; Bosnia and Herzegovina census, 142–3, 234n47
Central Bank of Bosnia and Herzegovina, 143
centripetalism, 19, 33, 118, 208–9, 214
citizenship, 52
Civic Forum, 48, 83–4
civic parties: conceptualization, 6, 9, 24–8, literature, 27, 29–30, typology, 38–40
civic politics. *See* civic solidarity
civic solidarity, 4–6, 9, 17, 21–5, 33–5, 211
civil society, 82–4, 168–70, 175, 196–8, 200, 207, 212, 216–17
clientelism. *See* patronage
climate change. *See* environmental politics
coalition formation, 159–60, 185, 187–9, 192, 194, 200, 205–6, 213
Communist Party, 145, 146, 178–9, 191
Communists, League of. *See* Communist Party
'confidence and supply' arrangement, 59
consociational democracy. *See* consociational power-sharing
consociational power-sharing, 3–4, 10, 17, 19–20, 30–5, 36, 42, 212–14, 220n8, 221n9–12; corporate versus liberal, 11–12, 32–3, 40, 42, 53, 68–9, 72, 119, 140, 143, 178, 183, 194–5, 203–6,

207–10, 213–16; power-sharing reform, 213; power-sharing reform in Northern Ireland, 69, 117–20, 123, 215; power-sharing reform in Bosnia and Herzegovina, 144–5, 145–6, 147, 162–3
constitutional change, 213, 218; constitutional change, Northern Ireland, 122, 126–9, 130–5, 136–7, 201, 218 (*see also* Irish unity); constitutional change, Bosnia and Herzegovina, 144–5, 145–6, 147, 162–3, 164, 172, 174, 189, 201, 218
Constitutional Court of Bosnia and Herzegovina, 143, 157
constitutional reform. *See* consociational power-sharing: power-sharing reform; constitutional change
Council of Ministers, Bosnia and Herzegovina, 142, 148, 155, 158, 200. *See also* coalition formation
culture, 87–8, 205

Dayton Peace Agreement, The, 11, 138, 140–5; constituent peoples, 140, 141, 144, 155, 177, 182, 186, 194; federalism in Bosnia and Herzegovina, 140–2, 143, 154, 156, 189, 195, 197, 203
decommissioning of weapons, 51, 54
democracy, 210; deliberative democracy, 48, 171, 240n1; democratization, 144, 151, 197; democratic backsliding, 154, 170, 218; direct democracy, 171
Democratic Unionist Party (DUP), 49, 53–5, 76, 99
designation, Northern Ireland Assembly, 52, 54, 68–73, 105–6, 117–18, 120–1, 194, 204
devolution, 51, 130
DF (Demokratska fronta; Democratic Front), 146, 148, 151, 177, 179–80, 199
D'Hondt, 47, 52, 55, 57, 61, 69, 79–80, 118–20, 199
discourse, 37; ethnonational discourse, 37, 89, 90, 92–6, 101–3, 160–4, 173–4, 175, 184–6, 193, 195–7, 206, 209, 212; civic discourse, 214
divided societies, definition, 8, 20–1, 220n1
Dodik, Milorad, 143, 154, 160, 174

East Belfast, 57, 92–3, 96, 99–101, 134, 135
economy: political economy, 125–6
education: educational autonomy, 53, 88; integrated education, 56, 75, 88–90, 111, 116, 123, 205
environmental politics, 55, 115, 126, 217–18
Equality Commission for Northern Ireland, 51, 87
ethnic cleansing, 140, 189, 203
ethnicity 7–8, 18; ethnic politics, 8
ethnic parties, 8, 25–7, 29–30, 92, 220n6–7
ethnonationalism, 8, 18
ethnonational parties, 25–7, 29–30, 92, 220n6–7
European Convention on Human Rights, 144, 155, 194
European Court of Human Rights, 144, 155, 179, 194
European integration, 144–5
European Union (EU), 14, 58, 109, 127–9, 132, 144–5, 148

federalism. *See* territorial decentralization
federalism in Bosnia and Herzegovina. *See* Dayton Peace Agreement, The
Federation of Bosnia and Herzegovina, 140–1, 144, 147–8, 154, 155–7, 179, 190–2, 202
feminist approaches, 22–3, 24, 33, 35. *See also* transversal politics
first and deputy first minister of Northern Ireland, 52, 54, 60, 70, 72, 80–2, 106, 118–19, 194
flag protest, the, 3, 13, 56, 85–6, 87, 94, 96, 98–103, 108, 125, 130, 137, 195, 205
Ford, David, 71, 74, 119

Forum for Political Dialogue and Multi-Party Peace Talks, 47
Fresh Start, A, 56

Gaza. *See* Palestine
gender: gender identity 34–5; gender rights, 46, 48, 55, 56, 59, 103, 124, 198, 205, 207, 217–18; gender politics, 48, 83, 151
General Framework Agreement for Peace in Bosnia and Herzegovina. *See* Dayton Peace Agreement, The
generational change, 217–18
Good Friday Agreement, The, 51–2, 58, 69, 86–7, 117, 219n2; consent principle, 52, 58, 109, 127, 131–2, 195; parity of esteem, 87, 101
Gratz, Dennis, 162
Green Party Northern Ireland, 49, 55, 72, 115–16, 118, 126, 198

HDZ (Hrvatska Demokratska Zajednica Bosne i Hercegovine, Croat Democratic Union of Bosnia and Herzegovina), 145, 184, 186; HDZ 1990, 184
healthcare, 4, 108, 125–6
High Representative, Office of (OHR), 143, 144, 195
Hillsborough Agreement, 55, 119
House of Peoples, Bosnia and Herzegovina, 142, 144, 155, 157, 179, 194, 200
House of Representatives, Bosnia and Herzegovina, 142, 156, 157
Human Rights Commission, Northern Ireland, 51
hunger strike, Republican prisoners', 95

identity politics, 22–3
India, 24, 25–6, 39, 208
institutionalism, 35–8; feminist institutionalism, 35–6, 215, 221n13; informal institutions, 14, 35–6, 36–8, 195–6, 206, 212, 215; new institutionalism, 32
integrationist approaches, 19
International Court of Justice (ICJ), 140
International Criminal Tribunal for the former Yugoslavia (ICTY), 140
international intervention, 29, 30, 31–2; in Bosnia and Herzegovina, 140, 143–5, 169, 190–1, 195, 216–17, 231n10
international peacebuilding. *See* international intervention
intersectionality, 10, 18, 20–1, 22, 34–5, 113, 195, 214–17, 221n10–11
Irish language, 59, 60–1, 63, 87–8, 104, 205
Irish unity, 58–9, 95, 109, 116, 126, 128–9, 130–5, 136–7, 201, 218, 229n37, 230n44
Israel, 22, 31

JMBG protests, 170
Justice for David movement, 170, 196
Justice for Dženan movement, 196, 235n75
Justice Ministry, Northern Ireland, 55, 57, 60, 61, 79, 110, 118–21, 199

Komšić, Željko, 148, 162, 179–80, 182, 184–7, 196, 200, 236n1

Lebanon, 203, 205–7
LGBTQ+ rights, 56, 59, 67, 76–9, 80, 82, 103–4, 105, 107, 108, 116, 124–5, 190–1, 197, 198, 205, 207, 217–18
liberal/conservative cleavage, 124, 191
Lo, Anna, 113, 133
Long, Naomi, 57, 94, 99–102, 119, 121, 128, 132, 133, 134, 135

Macedonia. *See* North Macedonia
marriage equality, 4, 56, 59, 67, 73–5, 75–9, 103–4, 105, 122, 124–5, 196, 207, 223n17
McWilliams, Monica, 72, 114
media, 90–2, 93, 166
methodology, 10–14, 219n4–7
migration, 122, 240n2; migrant rights, 116

Mostar, 171, 174, 184–5; Mostar City Council, 162
multiculturalism, 22–3, 220n2
multi-ethnic parties, 25–6. *See also* civic parties
Myanmar, 208

Naša Stranka (Our Party), 146, 148, 180–1, 199
nationalism, 9–10. *See also* ethnonationalism
Nepal, 208–9
nepotism. *See* patronage
New Decade New Approach Agreement, 54, 60, 75, 82, 84, 88, 121
Nigeria, 39, 208
non-ethnic parties, 25–6. *See also* civic parties
Northern Ireland Assembly, 51, 52–3, suspension/collapse, 53–4, 57–61, 76–9, 80, 81–2, 106, 127, 199
Northern Ireland Executive, 51, 52–3, 79–80, 106–7, 118–20, 194, 199–200
Northern Ireland Labour Party, 46
Northern Ireland Women's Coalition, 47–8, 50, 71–2, 83, 114–15
North Macedonia, 32, 204, 206

Palestine, 22, 31, 216, 217
parity of esteem. *See* Good Friday Agreement, The
party system: Bosnia and Herzegovina party system, 145–6, 149–54; Northern Ireland party system, 46–7, 49, 53–4
past, dealing with the, 59
patronage, 37–8, 106–7, 144, 151, 164–8, 174–5, 196–7, 206, 212, 215
peace process Northern Ireland, 47–50, 59, 111, 117
People Before Profit, 49, 57, 72, 116, 126, 198
Petition of Concern, 53, 56, 60, 68, 73–5, 76, 90
plenum protests: Bosnia and Herzegovina, 2014, The, 13, 138, 169–70, 171–6, 196, 198, 207
policing, 51, 54, 55
postethnicity, 23–4, 220n5
power-sharing. *See* consociational power-sharing; centripetalism
presidency, Bosnia and Herzegovina, 141–2, 144, 147, 155–7, 177, 179, 182, 184–7, 189, 194, 196, 200
proportional representation, 53, 142, 158, 179, 193–4, 205; list pr electoral system, 156, 208; Single Transferrable Vote (STV) pr electoral system, 53
public opinion, 57, 83, 108, 113–14, 122–4, 130, 168, 229n29–30

quotas: ethnic quotas, 112, 142, 147, 155–6, 179–84, 184–7, 192, 194–6, 199–201, 203, 208–9, 213, 239n37; gender quotas, 104, 114. 147, 151, 179, 208; religious quotas, 114

race, 20, 22, racial and ethnic minorities, 107, 122, 134
refugees: Bosnian War returnees, 142–3, 157, 163, 231n7
renewable heat initiative, 59, 106
Republika Srpska (RS; Serb Republic), 140–1, 143, 144, 145, 147–8, 154, 155–7, 163, 190–2, 201–2, 218

same-sex marriage. *See* marriage equality
Sarajevo, 139, 147–8, 171, 190–1; Canton of Sarajevo, 159, 164
SDA (Stranka Dekratske Akcije; Party for Democratic Action), 145
SDP, Bosnia and Herzegovina (Socijaldemokratska Partija Bosne i Hercegovine; Social Democratic Party), 146–8, 151, 177, 178–9, 199
SDS (Srpska Demokratska Stranka; Serb Democratic Party), 145
sectarianism, 55

Sejdić-Finci, 144, 155
shared future agenda, 85, 89, 123–4
shared Island initiative, 131, 132
Single Transferrable Vote. *See* proportional representation
Sinn Féin, 49, 53–5
SNSD (Savez Nezavisnih Socijal-demokrata; Alliance of Independent Social Democrats), 143, 145
Social Democratic and Labour Party (SDLP), 46, 49, 53–5
social movements, 24, 34–5, 169–76, 196, 207, 215–17
socio-cultural polarization. *See* liberal/conservative cleavage
South Tyrol, 203–4, 207–9
Srebrenica, 140
St Andrew's Agreement, 53, 54, 55, 80, 87, 119
Stormont House Agreement, 56, 79–80
Sunningdale Agreement, The, 1973, 47, 51, 54, 111, 117

territorial decentralization, 19, 208, 215
territorial pluralism. *See* territorial decentralization
third entity, Bosnia and Herzegovina, 145
transversal politics, 22–3, 24, 48, 220n3–4
Troubles, The, 10, 44–5
Tuzla, 147–8, 171–2, 190

Ukraine, war in, 160, 218, 231n11
Ulster Unionist Party (UUP), 49, 53–5, 99
United States of America (USA), 7, 22, 195, 217, 220n5, 221n1
uprising, The Bosnian. *See* plenum protests
urban/rural divide, 135, 147–8, 191–2

veto, 53, 56, 60, 68, 73–5, 90, 117–18, 157–8, 186, 194, 205, 231n4. *See also* Petition of Concern

War, Bosnian, 1992–95, 11, 137, 139–40, 183, 184, 197
West Belfast, 95, 116
Windsor Framework, The, 60
Women's Coalition. *See* Northern Ireland Women's Coalition
women's rights. *See* gender: gender rights

Yugoslavia, Socialist Federal Republic of, 145, 178–9